Withdraw

D0192902

Items should be returned on or before the last date shown below. Items not already requested by other borrowers may be renewed in person, in writing or by telephone. To renew, please quote the number on the barcode label. To renew online a PIN is required. This can be requested at your local library.
Renew online @ **www.dublincitypubliclibraries.ie**
Fines charged for overdue items will include postage incurred in recovery. Damage to or loss of items will be charged to the borrower.

Leabharlanna Poiblí Chathair Bhaile Átha Cliath
Dublin City Public Libraries

Dublin City
Baile Átha Cliath

Ballymun Library Tel: 8421890

Date Due	Date Due	Date Due
16. MAR 12		
11. MAR 15		
3 1 JUL 2015		
08 /07/16		

Morrissey

Morrissey

The Pageant of His Bleeding Heart

GAVIN HOPPS

continuum

NEW YORK • LONDON

2009

The Continuum International Publishing Group Inc
80 Maiden Lane, New York, NY 10038

The Continuum International Publishing Group Ltd
The Tower Building, 11 York Road, London SE1 7NX

www.continuumbooks.com

A catalog record for this book is available from the Library or Congress.

Printed in the United States of America

9780826418661

For Liane—for what it's worth

CONTENTS

If life be, as it surely is, a problem to me, I am no less a problem to life.

—Oscar Wilde, *De Profundis*

PREFACE

There were all sorts of reasons for *not* writing this book: the perennial accusation of dancing to architecture; the parlous results of previous attempts to write about Morrissey's lyrics; the blokeish piety that furtively polices discussions of popular music; and the peculiar elusiveness of its object of study.[1] There were two reasons for persisting: firstly, love; and secondly, agreement with the counterobjection in defence of criticism articulated by Friedrich Schlegel: 'If some mystical art lovers who think of every criticism as a dissection and every dissection as a destruction of pleasure were to think logically, then "wow" would be the best criticism of the greatest work of art.'[2] I believe it is both possible and worthwhile to say more than 'wow.'

The aim of the book is, quite simply, to argue that Morrissey is a significant artist, working in a medium that still tends to be thought of as trivial. In doing so, I compare his work to that of a number of canonical writers—principally Larkin, Beckett, Betjeman, Wilde, Hardy and Christina Rossetti—who are invoked alongside a range of more familiar influences, such as punk, glam rock, the New York Dolls, Patti Smith, George Formby and the *Carry On* films. I also consider his work in the light of larger cultural traditions and critical theories—such as aestheticism, romanticism, camp, the carnivalesque and deconstruction. This is unusual for a book on popular music, but then Morrissey is an unusual artist.[3] A word of explanation is therefore in order.

Morrissey is undoubtedly the most literary singer in the history of British popular music, and he has always conspicuously related his

---

1. Whilst I have found the existing studies of Morrissey's work disappointing, to put it soberly, there are numerous articles and shorter discussions to which I am indebted. Most prominent amongst these is the work of Michael Bracewell, Simon Reynolds, Armond White, Nadine Hubbs, Nabeel Zuberi and John Harris.

2. Schlegel, *Philosophical Fragments*, p. 7.

3. According to Pat Reid, Morrissey is 'the greatest lyricist in the English language since the Second World War,' and has 'probably had a more profound effect on British minds than any novelist, poet, playwright or film-maker of his generation. . . . By this I mean Morrissey is a serious artist, worthy of the kind of critical scrutiny usually reserved for poets like Ted Hughes or Philip Larkin, novelists such as Martin Amis, playwrights like Noël Coward and Joe Orton' (Reid, *Morrissey*, p. 8).

work to other artistic traditions (he has referred to himself as a 'poet' and frequently speaks about pop songs as literature;[4] he cites Oscar Wilde as his greatest influence, and when asked in 2006, 'who do you admire lyrically?' he replied: 'Nobody in pop or rock. Elsewhere, the poet John Betjeman';[5] he alludes in his lyrics to Virginia Woolf, George Eliot, Shelagh Delaney, Herman Melville, Graham Greene, Elizabeth Smart, Keats, Yeats and Pier Paolo Pasolini, to name but a few; his sleeve designs pay homage amongst others to Andy Warhol, Truman Capote, Jean Cocteau and Alain Delon; he has begun concerts with excerpts from Prokofiev as well as readings from John Betjeman and Maya Angelou; he has read out Proust at the start of a Luxuria concert; and has sung in front of a forty-foot portrait of Edith Sitwell). To restrict the consideration of his significance as an artist to what went before and came after him in the world of popular music is therefore to efface the continuities he self-consciously establishes and neglect a range of interpretative contexts which help us to appreciate his cultural importance.

In tandem with this widening of the customary focus, the book involves a countervailing emphasis upon close reading. This is also unusual for a book on popular music. However, if Morrissey is 'a serious artist,' and if a major element of that art is linguistic, we might reasonably expect his lyrics to repay this kind of attention. The underlying purpose of such close reading has been helpfully explained by one of its greatest practitioners. Speaking of what prompted his exquisite linguistic analyses of poetry in the preface to *Seven Types of Ambiguity*, William Empson comments as follows:

> I felt sure that the example was beautiful and that I had, broadly speaking, reacted to it correctly. But I did not at all know what had happened during this 'reaction'; I did not know why the example was beautiful. And it seemed to me that I was in some cases partly able to explain my feelings to myself by teasing out the meanings of the text.[6]

The close readings of Morrissey's lyrics that follow are likewise rooted in a reaction to something 'beautiful' or aesthetically significant, which is accompanied by a kind of itch—a reflexive inquisitiveness

---

4. In his foreword to Toni Visconti's autobiography, he speaks of Marc Bolan's 'poetry,' the 'musical literacy' of David Bowie and the 'versifying' of Ron Mael of Sparks, who he claims 'introduced a new style of pop poetry' (*Bowie, Bolan and the Brooklyn Boy*, pp. 9 and 10).
5. True-To-You website, Questions and Answers, January 4, 2006.
6. Empson, *Seven Types of Ambiguity*, p. x.

about this reaction—which prompts an attempt 'to explain my feelings to myself by teasing out the meanings of the text.' In Morrissey's case, the 'text' obviously includes a range of extraverbal elements—such as his voice, his appearance, his persona and the music (indeed, there is nothing outside the text)—but the basic principle still holds. These are the ways in which I attempt to exhibit his significance as an artist.

ACKNOWLEDGEMENTS

My first debt is to the Research Councils UK and Trevor Hart at the University of St. Andrews for the Academic Fellowship which made the writing of this book possible. I am also greatly indebted to David Barker at Continuum for his advice, patience and faith in the project. I would like to thank Angela Chnapko for her expert copyediting of the final manuscript and Max Novick for overseeing the book's production. Thanks as well to Paul Slattery for permission to use the cover image, and Gabriella Page-Fort for her work on this. Mark Elliott and Paul Curtis read and commented helpfully on early drafts of certain chapters, for which I am very grateful. For advice on more particular matters, I wish to express my gratitude to Paul Baker, Paul Bishop, Philip Davis, Steve Holmes, Mark Nixon and Marina Warner. I also owe thanks to the students with whom I have discussed such subjects—at the University of Aachen, Lady Margaret Hall and the University of St. Andrews. For their encouragement and support during the long evolution of the book, I wish to thank Helen Barr, David Brown, Geoffrey Davis, Niall Fox, Peter Hawkins, Chris Jones, Marie-Chantal Killeen, Pete Marsden, Andrew Palmer, Dirk Prinz, Alan Rawes, Kathrin Schödel, Jane Stabler, Dale Townshend and Cornelia Wächter. I am indebted more than I can say to Bernard Beatty, who cares little for pop music, but who taught me to think. Above all, I want to thank Michael Campbell for twenty-five years of conversation which have informed the writing of this book.

St. Mary's College
February 2008

INTRODUCTION

_____◦◦◦◦_____

Saving Eccentricity

There is no such thing in life as normal.

—*The Youngest Was The Most Loved*

A Taste of Honey—the film to which Morrissey's lyrics most frequently allude—begins with a game of netball in which a harried and inept Rita Tushingham struggles to join in, followed by a sympathetically hectic camera and ironized by a cartoon musical score. The opening dialogue, afterwards in the girls' changing room, runs as follows:

— You're not much good at netball, are you, Jo? [Tushingham's character]
— No—I'm bad on purpose.
— Are you going dancing tonight?
— I can't.
— You never go anywhere, do you?
— I haven't got any clothes to wear, for one thing. And for another . . .
— What?
— We might be moving home again.
— Like a couple of gypsies, you and your mother.
— So what!

It's remarkable how many features of Morrissey's art are prefigured in this short exchange. The notion of being 'bad on purpose'—of turning an ineptitude into a virtue—lies at the centre of the singer's early persona. The series of negations—'No,' 'can't,' 'never,' 'haven't got'—calls to mind the singer's incorrigible no-saying, whilst the pause after 'I can't' bespeaks of a paralysing force invisibly in play and puts one in mind of the unnameable, 'excessive' and ingenious darkness

1

that makes itself felt throughout his work. And finally—leaving aside the more explicit allusions—the notion of being a 'gypsy,' a wanderer, of 'moving home again,' which strangely coexists with a sense of 'never going anywhere,' is one of the most recurrent themes in Morrissey's lyrics.

Let us consider another exchange, this time involving Morrissey himself. On *Later . . . with Jools Holland*, in May 2004, in a last-ditch attempt to get the profoundly embarrassed and awkward Morrissey to play the game and take part in the interview, Holland falls back on the apparently foolproof conventions of the participatory joke:

> *Holland*: Knock, knock!
>
> *Morrissey*: I'm not joining in.
>
> *Holland*: Oh go on, please!
>
> *Morrissey*: [to laughing audience] You can join in. [laughter] No, Jools, I refuse to open the door.
>
> *Holland*: That's very good, that's very clever. You don't even know who it is!
>
> *Morrissey*: I'm not curious.

This short exchange reveals a lot about Morrissey. It reveals, for instance, that he's witty and slippery and remains in character even when he's offstage. It also suggests that central to this 'character' is a not-joining-in or a refusal to make friends with everyday experience—a being 'bad on purpose,' one is tempted to say. Perhaps most interestingly of all, though, what it reveals is that his not-joining-in is a double gesture which subverts and paradoxically *takes part in* the game. That is to say, in making a joke *of* the joke—which lays bare but nonetheless relies upon its conventions—his refusal is itself a sort of 'knock, knock' joke and a continuation of its tradition. These two snippets of awkward dialogue illustrate some of the central subjects considered in this book.

Awkwardness, refusal and not-joining-in are hardly a promising basis for an artist. However, it was by standing in its midst and yet refusing to take part that Morrissey thrust a wedge into the spokes of the complacently turning wheel of popular music, and out of this disturbance fashioned his art. It is likewise his awkwardness—his not-fitting-in—that paradoxically resuscitates the very tradition it subverts. This is partly because his refusal of the escapist morphine of 1980s New Pop was based upon a conviction that popular music could be a space where one might reflect upon the most urgent realities, irrespective of whether they were messy, embarrassing or unwieldy—as of course most urgent realities are. (The space doesn't need to be large—think of the Psalms—but it needs to be open.) And it was partly because in speaking 'eccentrically'—from a decentred space of nonbelonging—Morrissey's art of awkwardness reclaimed popular music as a genuinely countercultural force and the voice of dysfunction and alienation.

The underlying claim of this study, then, is that Morrissey is a superlatively 'disturbing' artist, whose greatest virtue is his awkwardness. This appears to be consonant with the singer's view of himself as 'ringleader of the tormentors.' When asked, for instance, how he would like to be remembered, he replied: as 'Manchester's answer to the H-bomb.'[1] When the subject of his career came up in another interview, he interjected: 'Is that what I've had? A career? You make it sound like I went down to the Job Centre and asked if they had any vacancies for "dire troublemaker."'[2] And when asked if he had thought about life after fame, he said: 'One way or another, I will always be somewhere just skating about the edges of global fame, pestering people and throwing glasses.'[3]

This 'disturbance' is obviously an aesthetic matter, and the study examines the variegated ways in which Morrissey's work has had a seismic effect within the world of popular music. But it is also, importantly, an ideological matter, for these tremors affect and are reciprocally informed by a much wider disturbance that isn't limited to the aesthetic sphere. His work, for instance, intersects with contemporary debates about gender and sexuality, 'essentialism' and the discursive constitution of identity; his propensity towards irony, camp and linguistic play bespeaks an affinity with 'poststructuralist' thought on the nature of the sign; the recent turn towards the religious in his work ties in with a wider tendency to contest the sovereignty of an unreflective and complacent secularism; and his radical antipathy towards notions of 'normality'—as explicitly stated ('There is no such

---

1. *Uncut*, August 1988.
2. *NME*, May 18, 1991.
3. Reynolds, *Bring the Noise*, p. 83. Two recent prose pieces in which Morrissey reflects on his life before The Smiths confirm this impression. In 'We Are Your Thoughts,' his contribution to Linder Sterling's *Works 1976–2006*, he writes: '[Linder and I] both somehow knew that our presence on earth was trouble enough for those around us' (p. 101); and in the foreword to Toni Visconti's autobiography, he remarks: 'Many of the early records bearing Toni Visconti's name made me eager to get out into the world—if only to agitate' (*Bowie, Bolan and the Brooklyn Boy*, p. 9)

thing in life as normal') and as evinced in the persistent 'eccentricity' of his art—is the corollary of contemporary philosophies of difference. All of which makes his work thoroughly postmodern.

Writing about Morrissey feels a little like Monty Python's 'Spanish Inquisition' sketch, as one is forever having to back up and begin again to take in some additional, often contradictory perspective. For this reason, the study begins in a sense *before* the beginning, as Morrissey puts it in 'Maladjusted,' by addressing various general issues which affect what things mean and how they mean. In other words, it's necessary to say something about 'the pageant' before we can speak about 'his bleeding heart.'

Broadly speaking, the first three chapters are concerned with the former, and focus on such things as the singer's persona, extra-lyrical aspects of his work (his voice, his appearance, the performance of meaning and the meaning of performance) and a range of destabilizing elements, which contribute to the radical elusiveness of his work. (In particular, attention is focused on such things as the songs' advertisement of their own artifice, their playing with signifiers, their self-reflexive gestures, their cartoon ontology and their deployment of mobile or equivocal voices.) Chapters 4 and 5 then take up the subject of 'his bleeding heart' and focus on darkness and light, respectively.

More specifically, chapter 1 is concerned with the formation, function and peculiar status of the singer's persona, which is born of his lyrics and everything he does,[4] but which also *reflexively affects* his work. Crucially, his persona is something which doesn't stand still and is continually evolving. Nevertheless, it was decisively shaped by the musical and ideological context of the 1980s, in which it emerged (implicitly but resonantly at the centre of which is what I refer to as the negative inspiration of Thatcherism). Walter Benjamin once famously remarked that revolution is not a runaway train but the application of an emergency brake. And the appearance in the midst of 1980s New Pop of Morrissey's iconic 'destitute' persona—frail, pale, damaged and inept, looking as if he'd been raifed in a cupboard on a diet of crisps—was a revolution in precisely this sense.

---

4. 'I don't have another life,' Morrissey has insisted. 'I don't exist as another person, somewhere else doing something else with other people. There is no other me. There is no clocking off' (*The Times* magazine November 6, 1999).

Essential to his early revolutionary persona is embarrassment. (This too is prefigured in the opening scene of *A Taste of Honey*, whose netball match is a miniature allegory of embarrassment, the filming of which encourages our imaginative participation in the experience, even as its whimsical accompaniment makes fun of it.) According to the social psychologist Erving Goffman, our lives are shaped by the desire to avoid embarrassment—a condition he refers to as 'wearing the leper's bell.'[5] The artist, however, runs in the opposite direction—*towards* the things that others flee, towards the epicentre of the disturbance. In his fine study *Keats and Embarrassment*, Christopher Ricks shows how the romantic poet was 'especially sensitive to, and morally intelligent about, embarrassment,'[6] and argues that it was one of the poet's unpraised virtues that he did not flinch or flee from what Darwin describes as this 'most human' of emotions, and instead turned awkwardness into 'a human victory.'[7] Morrissey, likewise, this study suggests, is acutely sensitive to embarrassment, and it is this sensitivity—which is at once social, moral and aesthetic—that is central to his significance as an artist. Like Keats—whose 'To a Nightingale' is read out and made fun of in *A Taste of Honey*—he frequently writes about embarrassment ('Ask,' 'Girl Afraid,' 'The Youngest Was The Most Loved,' etc.), documenting others' and lamenting or ironizing his own awkwardness and ineptitude. Although instead of 'exploiting misfortune,' as Armond White perceptively points out, 'Morrissey accepts it and extracts an empathic metaphor about human difference.'[8] What makes his work so extraordinary, though, is the way he seeks out *and heroically holds himself in* embarrassing situations—suffering as it were sacrificially in front of us on behalf of humanity. 'Ecce Homo,' his characteristic posture suggests. If this sounds embarrassingly melodramatic, well, that's because it is. Yet to say so is in no way to diminish his achievement; on the contrary, it is in braving the embarrassing grandeur of his own gestures that his greatness significantly consists.

Of course, for anyone seeing him for the first time now or unfamiliar with the work of The Smiths, nothing of this early persona is apparent. And yet, in some strange way, it persists and haunts everything he does, as a kind of ghostly effect, which may reinforce,

5. Goffman, 'Embarrassment and Social Organization,' p. 269.
6. Ricks, *Keats and Embarrassment*, p. 1.
7. Ibid., p. 77.
8. White, *The Resistance*, p. 222.

complicate or exist in ironic tension with any given gesture. An analogy may be helpful here.

At the start of 'The Queen Is Dead,' after the sample from *The L-Shaped Room* but before the drumming begins, we hear what Simon Goddard refers to as 'Marr's ghostly, controlled-feedback whistle,'[9] which is at times exposed and at times unapparent but which persists—in a sense 'unperformed' by anyone—throughout the song.[10] Like all good ghosts it has a particular form, and the feedback whistles the song's keynote B. This means that Morrissey's voice—and the bass too, which frequently moves between B and A—has something to coincide with or pull away from, as he does, for example, in singing 'life is very long when you're lonely,' holding a subtly dissonant A in the second syllable of 'lone-ly' against the ghostly keynote B. In doing so he introduces an 'unresolved' cadence into the melody which imitates the suspended condition of which he sings. Morrissey's spectral persona is a similarly self-begetting effect or 'unheard melody' that floats throughout his work, which may underwrite or ironize any particular performance.

Chapter 2 is concerned with different kinds of 'doubling' and focuses on the conjunction of apparently contradictory traits which constitute the singer's persona (hence the 'oxymoronic' self). He is, for example, typically described as 'an ordinary, working-class "anti-star" who nevertheless loves to hog the spotlight, a nice man who says the nastiest things about other people, a shy man who is also an out-rageous narcissist,' etc.[11] Similarly, when asked if there was any sex in Morrissey, he replied, 'None whatsoever,' but added, 'which in itself is quite sexy.'[12] And likewise, in terms of how he communicates, the singer is viewed as someone who 'advocates, simultaneously and with equal vigour, relevance and accessibility, indeterminacy and ambiguity.'[13] These 'oxymoronic' characteristics have been frequently noted of course. However, the ways in which such 'doubling' constitutes a

---

9. Goddard, *The Smiths*, p. 176.
10. The genesis of the ghostly whistle is explained by Marr as follows: 'I'd done the rhythm track and left the guitar on the stand. . . . The wah-wah pedal just happened to be half open, and putting the guitar down made it suddenly hit off this harmonic. We were back at the desk playing back the rhythm track and I could still hear this harmonic wailing away, so we put the tape back on to record while I crept back into the booth and started opening up the wah-wah, thinking "don't die, don't die!"' (Ibid).
11. Stringer, 'The Smiths,' p. 16.
12. *Blitz*, April 1988.
13. Hubbs, 'Music of the "Fourth Gender,"' p. 270.

kind of irony—since so often he is as well something *other than* what he is—have been insufficiently appreciated.

The chapter proposes two ways of characterizing the singer's elusiveness: firstly, as a matter of 'mobility,' by which I mean the ways in which the singer manages to be neither this *nor* that; and secondly, as a matter of 'multiplicity,' which refers, by contrast, to the ways he manages to be this *as well as* that. Obviously, this is odd and interesting in itself. But it also has crucial implications for any interpretation of his work. For, in the same way that his multiplicity has an ironizing function—since being any one thing is haunted by the sense of being its opposite as well—his corollary mobility effects a linear subversion of meaning, since it dissociates the singer from what appears to be his own utterance. (This 'equivocal' voice is considered in more detail in chapter 4.) In parallel ways, then, his mobility and multiplicity engender something akin to irony, which radically effects where the singer stands in relation to his utterance, which is to say it fundamentally affects what things mean.

The second half of chapter 2, which deals with multiplicity, focuses in particular on the tension between artifice and sincerity, on the one hand, and seriousness and humour or 'gravity' and 'levity,' on the other. But the majority of its attention is devoted to a discussion of those aspects of Morrissey's work which have been most neglected or misunderstood in commentary on the singer—namely play, artifice, lightness and camp. Recognizing the significance of these 'lighter' elements of his work is necessary to counter the abiding impression that Morrissey's work is univocally earnest (and that 'lightness' is a deficiency of seriousness). Yet it is just as important to point up the significance of things such as genre, irony, textuality and reflexivity, as well as the prevalence of nonrealist modes, as a corrective to the kind of Scooby-Doo paraphrase that passes for commentary on the singer's lyrics.

The underlying focus of chapter 3 is Morrissey's sexuality. However, the discussion is as much concerned with *how* things mean as with *what* they mean, and proposes as an organizing principle the singer's notorious coyness. Here too, we find an 'oxymoronic' tension on the one hand between secrecy and exposure, and on the other between 'excess' and 'lack.' One thing in particular that makes Morrissey's lyrics so peculiarly coy is that they frequently flaunt and are *about* their own secrecy—which is brought into being by the very gesture that purports to disclose it. In between the discussion of exposure and secrecy is a section on the extraordinary staging of presence in Morrissey's lyrics. This staging of presence is vital to all sorts of effects in his work, such as the dramatization of the moment of suffering—which takes place in the timeless present of the song and opens into the present of the listening experience—but also the benevolent quasi-religious offering of relation in the moment of the song, which means so much to so many listeners.

The second part of the chapter, on lack and excess, examines the singer's correlative habits of innuendo and interruption. These obviously relate Morrissey to the familiar world of the *Carry On* film, yet they also connect him to the larger sociocultural tradition of the carnivalesque, whose logic is that of the back-to-front or the upside-down—which underlies so much of the singer's art. His habit of interruption is additionally involved in the dramatization of extreme states—the interior flooding of excess joy and the bottomless descent of negative ecstasy—the 'light' and 'dark' examples of which considered in this chapter are 'Now My Heart Is Full' and 'Sweet And Tender Hooligan.'

The first three chapters, then, serve to introduce some of the singer's central concerns—melancholy, eccentricity, nonbelonging, sexuality, subjugation, comedy, the everyday and the aesthetic. All of which have something to do with his overriding subject, love. But as importantly, they also highlight a range of epistemological issues whose significance has been neglected. Most discussions of Morrissey's lyrics, for example, consider his allusions to other songs, films and novels, etc. Yet such inquiries invariably have a 'trainspotterly' character and tend only to be concerned with the question: where is it from? (Rogan's works offer us a nice line in displacement when it comes to such matters, seeking out the most tenuous of circumstantial connections for the benefit of 'source hunters.') The kinds of questions that don't get asked are: What is the effect of bringing one text into another? What kind of status does the 'imported' text have? What happens to its voice? To whom does it 'belong'? What of its original context does it bring with it and what does it leave behind? Similarly, with respect to the singer's use of personae and his speaking with a voice which is other than his own, what are the implications of this kind ventriloquism? How does the 'spacing' between the singer and speaker affect the utterance's meaning? And, finally, to take but a few examples, what are we to make of the multiplicity of sites of meaning (the lyrics, the cover images, the song's performance, the 'matrix messages,' the commentary offered in interviews, etc.), which are frequently at variance with one another? Where, if anywhere, does authority lie? The almost wholesale failure to take account of these and other ways in which the singer destabilizes his own meanings is a serious shortcoming shared by the commentaries of Rogan, Simpson, Goddard and Bret. Seemingly oblivious to 'the death of the author,' the 'heresy of paraphrase' and all the songs' internal signs that insist 'This Is Art and That Is Life,' such commentators read the lyrics literally, as transparent disclosures of the singer's biography, which is to say they have a tendency to look *through* his writing, rather than *at* it.[14]

The title of this book is borrowed from Matthew Arnold's description of Byron in 'Stanzas from the Grande Chartreuse,' in which he speaks of how the romantic poet bore,

> With haughty scorn which mocked the smart,
> Through Europe to the Aetolian shore
> The pageant of his bleeding heart.
>
> (133–6)

The bleeding of the poet's heart, according to Arnold, is an elaborately staged spectacle, and it is thus conspicuously communicated by means of art. It is additionally something which is complicated by the self-reflexive mocking gaze of the poet himself, who bore its bleeding 'With haughty scorn which mocked the smart.' We are therefore looking at the poet looking at a representation of his bleeding heart. Nevertheless, in spite of the complexities of its mediation, at the centre of everything is a bleeding heart. Having considered in the first three chapters a range of issues to do with 'the pageant' and the folds of the singer's reflexive irony, the study turns in chapters 4 and 5 to Morrissey's 'bleeding heart.'

In a certain sense, chapters 4 and 5 are opposed to one another, for the former is about darkness whilst the latter is about light. More

---

14. There is a kind of bad faith underlying the enterprise of such 'psychobiography,' since it privileges the artist to the detriment to the art that we care or come to know about the artist.

precisely, chapter 4 focuses on melancholy, despair, the unravelling of self, alienation, destitution, the torment of desire, the self-fuelling and self-*haunting* character of depression, as well as racism, violence, evil and death. (The issue of racism, which has drearily been blown out of all proportion, is first addressed in chapter 2, in relation to a larger discussion of the singer's staging of character perspectives, and then in more detail in chapter 4, where a whole range of disturbing subjects confronted by Morrissey is considered.) Chapter 5, on the other hand, focuses on the religious, which has recently come to the fore in his work, but has always been a resonant and shadowy presence—intriguingly, both as a source of animosity and yet also as a privileged system of values, by means of which he articulates his most urgent concerns. In another sense, however, chapters 4 and 5 are two parts of a continuous inquiry, with the same fundamental questions in view, which repeatedly open into each other's territories. In the midst of darkness, for example, in chapter 4, we find the singer's greatest affirmation of love, and at the heart of the religious in chapter 5, we come upon an all-encompassing and windowless darkness. Chapter 5 additionally returns to a number of recurrent subjects—such as eccentricity, not-fitting-in, the sense of being 'a stranger on the earth,' the tormenting insatiability of desire, as well as the singer's no-saying, the difficulties he seems to have with the word 'love,' his imaginative sympathy for the outsider, and his peculiar ability to provoke a disturbance—and brings to light an underlying and hitherto unnoticed coherence in his work.

The argument of the book and the key to this coherence may be summed up with reference to the two senses of 'Saving Eccentricity.' On the one hand, the study claims that what 'saves' Morrissey as an artist is his 'eccentricity,' which literally means being 'out of the centre.' It is this participation from a position of nonbelonging that allows him to ironize or 'deconstruct' his own gestures in the very moment of their performance—and makes him a bone in the throat of popular music. Such non-belonging, however, also plays a vital role in his ability to speak for and extend our sympathies towards the outcast, the marginalized, the 'unlovable' and the other. It is in view of this radical charity—which has nothing genteel or squeamish about it—that the study claims on the other hand that Morrissey's art is essentially concerned with 'saving eccentricity.'

CHAPTER 1

—ⴲ—

Celibacy, Abstinence and Rock 'n' Roll

I am a ghost
and as far as I know
I haven't even died.

—*I'll Never Be Anbody's Hero Now*

ON BEING A LIVING SIGN

In the last song on *Ringleader Of The Tormentors*, with a gift for the upside-down, Morrissey sings:

At last I am born
historians note
I am finally born.[1]

Speaking of the birth of Morrissey—an obvious and apparently straightforward way of beginning—is a peculiarly difficult thing to do. This is not simply because over the years Morrissey has repeatedly insisted that in some fundamental sense his life has never quite come into being (he speaks, for example, of being a ghost, of 'a half-life,' of being 'scarcely born,' of 'not actually living' and of a life 'not even begun').[2] It is additionally difficult because, on the one hand, what 'Morrissey' refers to isn't simply the person who was born on May 22, 1959, to Elizabeth (née Dwyer) and Peter Morrissey, and christened Steven Patrick, but is a spectral entity or mythic personality which

---

1. 'At Last I Am Born,' in which he sings it is his 'final hour' and 'soon I will be dead.'
2. The singer also articulates this curious sense of not quite belonging to being by conversely insisting that his life has in some sense passed out of existence before coming to an end (he speaks of half-dying; of being 'a was'; and on *Ringleader Of The Tormentors*, maintains 'I walk around—somehow / But you have killed me').

11

paradoxically exceeds its creator; and, on the other hand, it is difficult because this spectral and fugitive subject *continues* to be born, since the story which constitutes this dramatic projection continues to unfold.[3]

'Morrissey' was born or began coming into being in the summer of 1983, when, according to Johnny Marr's version of events, a directive was issued by Rough Trade Records forbidding the use of Steven Patrick Morrissey's forenames.[4] From this moment on, rather like the portrait in Dorian Gray's attic, Morrissey's eponymous creation began acquiring a quasi-life of its own—a dramatically constituted life, to which every lyric and public act would contribute—which effectively subsumed its creator. This sublimation of self seems to have been consciously willed by the singer. When asked in an interview, 'Is Steven Morrissey dead?' he replied, 'Yes. When The Smiths began it was very important that I wouldn't be that horrible, stupid, sloppy Steven. He would have to be locked in a box and put on top of the wardrobe. I needed to feel differently and rather than adopt some glamorous pop star name, I eradicated Steven, which seemed to make perfect sense. Suddenly I was a totally different person.'[5]

The existence of Morrissey as a mythic personality projected by his lyrics and other public performances was not perhaps immediately apparent. It was only following the 'glamorous turn' in his solo career that a contrapuntal tension seemed to emerge, which revealed the existence of this spectral persona and a 'something more' invisibly in play. The remainder of this chapter will attempt to explain more precisely what this means, how it came about, and why it is important to an understanding of Morrissey's work. As this is all a little abstract, I shall offer an illustration of what is at stake.

When at the end of 'Dear God Please Help Me,' Morrissey sings:

---

3. The perpetual genesis of Morrissey's persona is not a matter of serial reinvention and so differs, for instance, from the 'chameleon aesthetics' of David Bowie or the 'plastic' flux of Madonna's subjectivity. The difference may be clarified with reference to Isaiah Berlin's heuristic distinction between the fox and the hedgehog, which he claims represents 'one of the deepest differences which divide writers and thinkers.' According to Berlin, 'the fox knows many things but the hedgehog knows one big thing'; hence the former 'pursue many ends, often unrelated and even contradictory, connected, if at all, only in some de facto way,' whilst the latter 'relate everything to a single central vision' (Berlin, 'The Hedgehog and the Fox,' p. 71). In terms of this model, then, Bowie and Madonna would be foxes whereas Morrissey would be a hedgehog.
4. Marr's account of the event is given in Goddard, *The Smiths*, p. 20. Morrissey's pre-Smiths publications—*New York Dolls* (1981) and *James Dean Is Not Dead* (1983)—have 'Steven Morrissey' on their title pages, though this was altered to 'Morrissey' in post-Smiths reprints.
5. *The Face*, July 1984.

And now I'm walking through Rome
and there's no room to move
but the heart feels free

—repeatedly insisting 'the heart feels free,' it is hard to explain why the utterance is so moving. The melody, to be sure, conveys a restrained pathos that is difficult to resist, and Morrissey's singing reaches out towards us with a plaintive urgency. Yet there are plenty of other songs that do this without the same effect. However, the narrative in itself seems to offer little that would account for it either (it is, after all, an apparently positive assertion!). How might we explain the effect then? The utterance is so moving, I suggest, because it represents the latest stage in a long and elaborate drama—which is the life and work of Morrissey—and is therefore densely resonant with what has preceded it. Such resonances routinely inform and complicate Morrissey's songs, but they are especially operative here, as the utterance occupies the space of and recalls Morrissey's other great fade-out refrains ('I Know It's Over,' 'That Joke Isn't Funny Anymore,' 'Last Night I Dreamt That Somebody Loved Me,' etc.). Almost in spite of itself, it thus implicitly speaks of a longing that hasn't been cancelled out—as other songs on the album attest—but which isn't entirely present either. This ghostly 'excess' or 'something more' invisibly in play is attributable to the shadow of Morrissey's persona, which informs and is informed by everything he does, and which helps to explain why his lyrics seem to mean more than they say and why this meaning lies in a sense 'elsewhere.'

The story is old; but to understand this 'elsewhere' and why Morrissey is, quite literally, 'a living sign,' we need to go back to the beginning and trace the trajectory of the singer's career.

I

THE ART OF WEEKNESS

STANDING ON ONE'S HEAD

When Morrissey started appearing in public as the backward frontman of The Smiths in 1983, he was spectacularly gauche. The most popular bands at the time were the likes of Wham!, Duran Duran, Spandau Ballet, Frankie Goes To Hollywood and Kajagoogoo, whose names, like their public appearances, were extravagant and courted a highly stylised and exotic glamour. The songs of such bands tended to be subsumed within a kind of operatic spectacle or kitsch *Gesamt-kunstwerk*, involving lavish videos and technicolor stage appearances, whose performers became associated with shiny surfaces, the synthetic and hedonistic fun.[6] It is of course easy to patronize this and overlook the ways in which New Pop was itself responsible for a revolution of sorts—rejecting the antiaesthetic tendencies of punk and challeng-ing the pseudo 'authenticity' of guitar-based pop.[7] We should also not ignore the wealth of 'alternative' bands—such as The Jam, The Specials and Dexy's Midnight Runners—and chivalrous exceptions to both of these rules, such as David Bowie and Elvis Costello. Neverthe-less, it remains fair to say that British pop music in the early 1980s was dominated by a range of bands who cared little about lyrics and a lot about glossy surfaces, and whose aerated and cosmetic charm perpetu-ated the dream of 'sex and drugs and rock 'n' roll.'[8]

The most shocking and paradoxically rebellious thing it was possible to be in such a world, as Morrissey with singular prescience intuited, was ordinary.[9] Of course, now that we live in a more thor-oughly postmodern time of flattened hierarchies and collapsed oppo-sitions—in which the antitheses of fashion coexist without interval, priority or fixed value—it is hard to imagine the significance and perhaps even the *possibility* of such dialectical cultural shifts. Similarly, now that the market is flooded with anaemic imitations, it's becom-ing increasingly difficult to see that the things Morrissey was doing were once shockingly new and a desirable corrective. Yet the shift that was inaugurated by The Smiths in the early 1980s was arguably more

6. Such characteristics had important ideological connotations. As Simon Reynolds notes, 'New Pop, far from being a bright new beginning, turned out to be merely an inauguration of global designer-soul, the soundtrack of the new yuppie culture of health and efficiency' (Reynolds, *Bring the Noise*, p. 44).

7. Matthew Bannister goes even further: 'New Pop discourses were mainly concerned to demon-strate how postmodernism, poststructuralism and postfeminism as manifested in MTV, Madonna, Prince and digital sampling celebrated a shiny new androgynous semiotic wonderland, where continuous self-invention through artifice and intertextual pastiche erased sexual difference, prob-lematized authorship and created polysemic and polysexual possibilities' (Bannister, *White Boys, White Noise*, p. xxii).

8. For a good, nuanced account of pop music in the early 1980s, which keeps its heterogeneity in view and deals justly with the aesthetics of synthpop, see Simon Reynolds, *Rip It Up and Start Again*.

9. In a tour programme in 1985, his 'likes' were listed as: 'Films, books, moderation, conversation, civility' (cited in Harris, *The Last Party*, p. 5).

profound than anything in popular music, with the possible exception of punk. As Michael Bracewell points out, this shift involved a 'return' to something that hadn't existed before in the medium:

> In its return to the cat's cradle of English ordinariness, the impact on English pop of Morrissey's writing and performance could be likened to the revolution caused in English theatre in 1956 by John Osborne's *Look Back in Anger*. The sophisticated tragedy and the ironic comedy of manners had been usurped. And a return to the glamour of the ordinary, in the face of honed sophistication, could be achieved only by a writer who knew how to lift poetic truths out of the mass of common experience; a novelistic skill which had never been applied with such constancy and literary use of language within the English pop song.[10]

The Smiths were extravagantly, revolutionarily ordinary. The band's name, which quietly carries connotations of craftsmanship and Englishness—qualities of manifest importance to Morrissey—is an obvious metonymy of this ordinariness. However, as with so many things about the band, its significance lies to a large extent in what it is not as well as what it is; that is to say, it is importantly also a *refusal*—in this case of the fashion for ostentatious names.[11] The point is obvious enough, though the implications are worth teasing out a little.

Morrissey's art, in all sorts of ways, is an art of refusal.[12] There are, for example, the explicit refusals to make videos or use certain instruments, which from a thoroughly altered cultural perspective may well seem a little pointless or naive but were evidently part of a coherent and carefully thought-out stance, which had an important aesthetic and ideological rationale.[13] There are additionally the

---

10. Bracewell, *England Is Mine*, p. 222. There were of course foreshadowings of this shift. Perhaps the most significant was the aesthetic stance of Orange Juice (1979–84), whose name betokened an anti–rock 'n' roll temperance, who sang about male vulnerability ('I Guess I'm Just A Little Too Sensitive'), who musically aimed for 'a sophisticated amateurism' that didn't 'place slickness as the ultimate virtue,' and whose singer-songwriter Edwyn Collins once declared 'worldliness must be kept apart from me' (Reynolds, *Rip It Up and Start Again*, p. 409).
11. 'When we started, inflated and elongated names were the order of the day. I wanted to explain to people that it wasn't necessary to have long names, dress in black and be po-faced. Our task was to choose the most ordinary of names and yet produce something of artistic merit' (Robertson, ed., *Morrissey: In His Own Words*, p. 58).
12. When the singer was asked, 'Which words or phrases do you most overuse?' he replied: ' "No, I won't," "Why should I?" "What's the point?" and "I'd like to terminate our agreement" ' (*Kill Uncle* tourbook, 1991).
13. There is an interesting parallel between the aesthetic 'chastity' of the early Smiths and the agenda of the Dogme 95 movement—a collective of avant-garde Danish filmmakers, who were radically opposed to what they perceived as 'the use of cosmetics' in film, which they sought to counter by adhering to a cinematic 'vow of chastity.'

explicit *lyrical* refusals—the singer's no-saying that compulsively erupts in so many of his ad libs.[14] Undoubtedly, the most dramatic and 'disturbing' refusal, though, was embodied in Morrissey's notorious asceticism—a 'monastic' combination of celibacy, abstinence and hermitic nonparticipation ('I would never ever do anything as vulgar as having fun,' he claimed[15])—which was a scandal to the hedonistic world of popular music. Yet these are but the visible signs of a more pervasive implicit refusal of the dominant cultural norms of the period; for, rather than being a protest against consumer culture, pop music had come to be a hyperbolic instance of it.[16]

Morrissey's subversive refusal of glamour—which he cunningly retrieved at the back door, as it were—crucially went beyond 'an ideology of ordinariness'[17] and involved the foregrounding of ineptitude and frailty. As Matthew Bannister observes, 'Failure and incompetence became precious because they reversed the normative emphasis on technique and mastery.'[18] To be radically in disarray or mutilated, as a result of self-inflicted violence, was obviously punk's way of synecdochically objecting to a system whose own representative signs were order, comfort, civility and so on. By comparison, Morrissey's protest was much more subtle, and had less visible targets, but it was more carefully aimed and arguably just as profound. Moreover, to present oneself as damaged and weak by nature—and in spite of one's efforts, as a failure or loser—not as the proud protagonist of

---

14. At a musical level, too, there was a self-conscious avoidance of conventional structures and a refusal of guitar solos—the signature gesture of rock. (The exception that reveals the rule is 'Shoplifters Of The World Unite,' which features a guitar solo in quotation marks.)

15. *NME*, June 7, 1986.

16. John Harris has written lucidly on the underlying ideological significance of the opposition to New Pop: 'Within the universe of pop music, the battle-lines were as clearly drawn as anywhere else. On the one side, led by Duran Duran, stood the denizens of the "New Pop," whose delight in their new-found wealth was fully in keeping with the Thatcher ethos. . . . For most of the Thatcher years, a loose coalition of musicians stood on the opposing side. . . . In the scratchy, shambolic guitar music that defined the 80s left field, there was a clear sense of the rejection of all kinds of dominant cultural norms: the slick commerciality of the 80s mainstream, ambition as defined by sales figures and chart positions, and the swaggering masculinity that united the likes of Simon Le Bon, Spandau Ballet's Tony Hadley. . . . No-one, however, embodied the anti-Thatcher current as well as Steven Patrick Morrissey, the singer of The Smiths. Between 1983 and 1987, The Smiths' run of peerless albums and singles—just about all of them innovative, poetic and steeped in a profound sense of Englishness—gave rise to a huge and passionate cult. No matter that Morrissey's three colleagues . . . were as fond of rock 'n' roll excess as any other group of young male musicians; it was Morrissey's ascetic lifestyle, every aspect of which seemed imbued with ideological power, that captured the imagination of the group's most hard-bitten fans' (Harris, *The Last Party*, pp. 4–5).

17. Bannister, *White Boys, White Noise*, p. 80.

18. Ibid., p. 114.

one's own impairment, is a far braver and almost 'Christ-like' way of protesting.[19] And whilst the details, outside their context, seem rather theatrical, are easily parodied, and are retroactively robbed of much of their significance by subsequent approximations, Morrissey's ailing and inept appearance, wearing National Health glasses, an unconcealed hearing aid, and maiden-auntly charity-shop clothes—which lacked the choreographed carelessness of punk but more daringly meant running the risk of being laughed at—was just such a brave and radical protest. The subversive nature of Morrissey's advertisement of dysfunction has been summed up well by Simon Reynolds:

> In the face of the benign totalitarianism of leisure capitalism and its off-the-peg self-improvement, The Smiths glamorized debility and illness, advocated absenteeism, withdrawal, the failure to meet quotas of enjoyment. The profound embarrassment of Morrissey's dancing turned the lack of oneness with one's body into glamour. All the self-squandering and deficiency of lifeskills that animated The Birthday Party and The Fall, The Smiths turned into brilliant, glamorous, consumable pop, two-minute bursts of otherness in the heart of the charts.[20]

It's easy enough in all of this to see what the singer was protesting against. But what, if anything, was he defending or protesting *for*? In foregrounding his frailties, his ordinariness and his eccentricity, Morrissey was heroically standing up for humanness—in all its damaged, marginalized, forsaken and stigmatized manifestations. And like the monastics, to whom he is often rather flippantly compared, he was attempting to show that the world as it was was standing on its head by doing what in *its* eyes was standing on *his* head.

THE STRENGTH OF A FLOWER

Undoubtedly, one of the oddest things about Morrissey's appearance in the early 1980s—and one of the wittiest ways in which he turned prevailing pop-star behaviour on its head—was his use of flowers, bunches of which he used to swing with abandon whilst singing on stage or have sprouting out of the back pocket of his trousers, as

---

19. Mark Simpson's *Saint Morrissey*—which is a book about Mark Simpson that occasionally digresses to say something about Morrissey—is repeatedly drawn to religious language and reference points, and on several occasions compares Morrissey to Christ.
20. Reynolds, *Bring the Noise* , pp. 44–5.

if it were the most natural thing in the world. (Usually, these were gladioli, daffodils or tulips; however, when The Smiths performed 'Heaven Knows I'm Miserable Now' on *Top of the Pops* in May 1984, he wore—if that's the correct verb—a shrub the size of a chandelier.)

Over the years, various explanations of Morrissey's unorthodox floral practices have been ventured. According to the singer, the extravagant 'injection' of flowers—which he claimed were 'virtually more important than the PA system'[21]—relates to his defence of the human:

> When we first began there was a horrendous sterile cloud over the whole music scene in Manchester. Everybody was anti-human and it was so very cold. The flowers were a very human gesture. They integrated harmony with nature—something people seemed so terribly afraid of. It had got to the point in music where people were really afraid to show how they felt—to show their emotions. I thought that was a shame and very boring. The flowers offered hope.[22]

This 'romantic' aspect of the singer's gesture is only part of the story though, because whilst his floral exuberance is obviously in some sense set over against the privileging of the synthetic in New Pop—as well as its underlying ideological corollary—it does not, as many commentators assume, unproblematically align him with the 'natural.'[23] For, as the singer *also* claimed, he used flowers 'because Oscar Wilde always used flowers.'[24] And here is what Wilde has to say about nature, in what he considered his best critical dialogue and Morrissey's favourite text:[25]

> Enjoy Nature! I am glad to say that I have entirely lost that faculty. People tell us that Art makes us love Nature more than we loved her before. . . . My own experience is that the more we study Art, the less we care for Nature. What Art really reveals to us is Nature's lack of design, her curious crudities, her extraordinary monotony, her absolutely unfinished condition. Nature has good intentions, of course, but, as Aristotle once said, she cannot carry them out. When I look

21. Robertson, *Morrissey: In His Own Words*, p. 29.
22. *Melody Maker*, September 3, 1983.
23. During the romantic period, as Philip Knight points out, the flower took on unprecedented importance and became 'an indispensible emblem of [a] new sensibility,' which idealized nature and human sentiment (Knight, *Flower Poetry in Nineteenth-Century France*, p. 61).
24. Robertson, *Morrissey: In His Own Words*, p. 77.
25. Interview with Robert Chalmers, *The Observer*, December 6, 1992.

at a landscape I cannot help seeing all its defects. It is fortunate for us, however, that Nature is so imperfect, as otherwise we should have no art at all. Art is our spirited protest, our gallant attempt to teach Nature her proper place.[26]

Of course, Wilde is rightly associated with flowers. However, he was an aesthete, and the kind of flowers that appealed to him owed more to Keats and Huysmans than they did to nature.[27] Morrissey also is a kind of dandy, and his use of flowers likewise owes as much to aestheticism as it does to the romantics.[28] (Notice his remark that the flowers 'integrated harmony with nature,' which seems to parallel Wilde's aphorism that 'a really well-made buttonhole is the only link between Art and Nature.'[29]) Indeed, in Morrissey's case, the aesthetic character of his floral extravagance is even more pronounced, since—as a kind of gauche variant of the buttonhole—it announces an awareness of itself as a sign speaking of other signs, which is to say it has a parodic quality (and, as the 'inflation' from flowers to shrubs suggests, almost immediately became a *self*-parody).

To call the singer's use of flowers parodic is to recognize that it is no longer innocent. And how could it be? For it doesn't only come after Wilde, it is also comes after the *parody* of Wilde (one thinks of *The Green Carnation* by Robert Hichens, George Du Maurier's sketches in *Punch* or the famous lines from Gilbert and Sullivan's *Patience*: 'Though the philistines may jostle, you will rank as an apostle in the high aesthetic band, / If you walk down Piccadilly with a poppy or a lily in your mediaeval hand'). His back-pocket buttonhole additionally follows on from Baudelaire's famous association of flowers with 'le Mal'—which the singer seems comically to reperform, in having flowers appear to sprout out of his backside.[30]

---

26. Wilde, *The Decay of Lying*, p. 163. There are thus problems with both parts of Simon Goddard's assertion that the singer's use of flowers symbolized his 'professed love of nature (the direct influence of Oscar Wilde)' (Goddard, *The Smiths*, p. 32).

27. For Wilde, the greatest flower was the green carnation—not because, like the blue flower of Novalis, it represented an ideal that was preserved by its very unattainability, but precisely because it is *un*natural and an artificial 'improvement' upon nature.

28. *Iain Webb*: Although your general appearance is quite casual, there are those who would see your look as highly pretentious (the beads and the flowers and whatever)?

   Morrissey: Yes.

   Webb: Would they be right making such an assumption?

   Morrissey: Yes. I think they are right, but it's not necessarily a bad thing. So many pretentious people are really treasurable. In a way it's like Oscar Wilde's dandyism . . . (*Undress*, 1984).

29. Wilde, 'Phrases and Philosophies for the Use of the Young,' p. 572.

30. Morrissey's ironic posture may also owe something to Dame Edna Everage, who used to encourage interaction with the gladiolus.

Yet the irony of the 'latecomer'—apparent in the allusiveness of Morrissey's practice—does not obtain at the expense of the gesture itself, which remains a protest against the aesthetics of New Pop. On the contrary, the singer's self-consciously allusive gesture continues even as it makes fun of the tradition, and illustrates Morrissey's ability simultaneously to perform a gesture *as well as* its parody.

How else might Morrissey's use of flowers be explained? We must of course be careful to avoid naively supposing there is any fixed scheme of symbolism involved. Morrissey is too playful, too multiple, and is incorrigibly given to delight in the coyness that conjoins with the promiscuity of signs. Nevertheless, there are certain connotations that resonate with other aspects of his art, which are thereby brought to the fore. The most prominent of these is vulnerability or weakness.

In Sonnet 65, Shakespeare speaks of a beauty 'whose action is no stronger than a flower,' a line which Wilde admired and approvingly quotes in 'The Portrait of Mr W.H.'[31] In the same dialogue, Wilde refers to the tender 'flower-like' grace of the sonnets' mysterious addressee, a phrase he returns to in 'The Soul of Man under Socialism' and repeatedly in *De Profundis*, where he speaks of Christ as the first to say that people should live 'flower-like lives.'[32] Morrissey, as we know, picks up the phrase in 'Miserable Lie'; though we should notice that the speaker applies it to *himself*, and subtly alters its connotations in the process ('you have destroyed my flower-like life').[33] This statement is typical of Morrissey's early lyrics and contributes to a pervasive impression of vulnerability, which is on the one hand obviously to do with the kind of claims being made ('she's too rough / and I'm too delicate'; 'I'm not the man you think I am'; 'under the iron bridge we kissed / and although I ended up with sore lips'). Yet it is on the other hand also something that is more subtly established in recurrently speaking from the perspective of a rhetorically figured passivity—as a suffering object, acted upon rather than acting, or 'done to' rather than doing, in the idiom of 'Billy Budd' ('you took a child / and you made him old'; 'you have corrupt my innocent mind'; 'you took me behind a dis-used railway line'; 'you

---

31. Wilde, 'The Portrait of Mr W.H.,' p. 54.
32. Wilde, 'The Soul of Man under Socialism,' p. 26; *De Profundis and Other Writings*, pp. 124 and 176.
33. The singer's habit of wearing flowers—which he claimed were 'an extension of [his] body' (*The Face*, July 1984)—manifestly reinforces the epithet.

tug my arm and say "Give in to lust, / give up to lust"').[34] Morrissey's garlanding himself with flowers is thus linked to the adoption in his lyrics of a position that is conventionally gendered feminine, which—along with his staging of the damaged body and his radically fallible voice—helped to turn him into an icon of vulnerability.

What, it may be asked, is the value of this? Wasn't Morrissey wantonly foregoing a space of power in advertising his vulnerability and popularizing an art of weakness? He was; but this is the key to its subversiveness. Of course, now that such battles have in a sense been won, the singer's anatomy of his vulnerability is apt to look like an apolitical retreat into self-pity—or worse, like the cynically cultivated vulnerability of Coldplay ('Is there anybody out there who / Is lost and hurt and lonely too?'[35]). However, if the exercise of power is *itself* part of the problem—and it was the swaggering assurance of politicians and pop stars in the early 1980s that Morrissey found so distasteful—how else without colluding with what one wishes to depose is it possible to protest? In other words, Morrissey's 'art of weakness' was *in its very manner* a critique of the brash aspirational ideology of the 1980s. To invoke a notion popular in the study of subculture, we could say that there was a 'homological' relationship between the weakness of Morrissey's protest and the values he was protesting for.[36] Indeed, the singer's habit of delicately throwing daffodils, gladioli and tulips into the audience may be seen as a brilliant camp parody of the spitting and beer-can throwing interactions of punk bands and a characteristic turning of conventional pop-star transgression on its head. (It's perhaps not too fanciful to see his attachment to the 'weakness' of flowers as an antithesis also to the 'handbagging' authoritarianism of Margaret Thatcher.[37]) To answer our question, then, concerning the value of Morrissey's advertisement of vulnerability—in which his use of flowers played a crucial

---

34. 'Pretty Girls Make Graves,' 'Still Ill,' 'Reel Around The Fountain,' 'Miserable Lie,' 'These Things Take Time,' 'Pretty Girls Make Graves.'

35. 'Square One.'

36. In his discussion of style as signifying practice, Dick Hebdige defines the notion of homology as 'the symbolic fit between the values and life-styles of a group.' Thus, in punk, for example, he argues that there was 'a homological relation between the trashy cut-up clothes and spiky hair, the pogo and the amphetamines, the spitting, the vomiting, the format of the fanzines, the insurrectionary poses, and the "soul-less," frantically driven music' (Hebdige, 'Style as Homology and Signifying Practice,' pp. 56–7).

37. The verb 'to handbag' is recorded in the *OED* and glossed as follows: 'To batter with a handbag. Only *fig.*, to subject to a forthright verbal assault or to strident criticism; to coerce in this way. Orig. and predominantly with reference to Margaret Thatcher.'

role—he was, as Milton phrases it in *Paradise Lost*, 'by things deemed weak / Subverting worldly strong.'[38]

All the 'explanations' entertained here have fragile foundations, for though the rose may speak 'all languages,'[39] the speech of flowers is infinitely *suggestive*, and there is a 'weakness' in their significations too, which are never categorical, never secure. Theirs, we might say, is 'a language without force.'[40] Yet once again, paradoxically, there is a strength in this weakness, which has a peculiar relevance for Morrissey's art.

Flowers appear to be wholly exposed—to hold nothing of themselves back, and to be *unequivocally* themselves. And yet they always exceed explanation and remain somehow mysterious. ('Rose is a rose is a rose is a rose,' wrote Gertrude Stein in *Sacred Emily*,[41] which suggests that tautology is the only adequate predication.) Indeed, hyperbole is, as it were, of their essence and the flower has become a symbol of symbolism itself. As we shall see, this mystery that paradoxically coincides with exposure is something that applies to Morrissey as well. Furthermore, the *suggestiveness* of a flower's speech—along with the 'infinity' of its suggestions—is an essential element of his 'art of coyness.' In waving around his gladioli, therefore, Morrissey was in a sense flaunting his processes.

The green carnation—worn by Aesthetes and 'invented' by Wilde[42]—is once again an obvious precedent. For it came to be suggestive of homosexuality, even though, according to Wilde, it had no symbolic meaning. (When asked what it meant, he replied: 'Nothing whatever, but that's just what nobody will guess.'[43]) Morrissey's flowers were manifestly less of a badge, with a more diffused significance. But they too were a kind of visual innuendo, which bore connotations of transgressive effeminacy—and insofar as they recalled the floral practice of Wilde, they carried a suggestion of a

---

38. Book XII, 567–8. Milton's lines allude to 1 Corinthians, the significance of which for Morrissey's art of weakness is considered in chapter 5, p. 246–250.
39. The epigraph to Ralph Waldo Emerson's famous essay *Nature* includes the lines 'The eye reads omens where it goes, / And speaks all languages the rose.'
40. Michel de Certeau, 'The Weakness of Believing,' p. 234.
41. Gertrude Stein, *Writings*, p. 395.
42. Letter to *The Pall Mall Gazette*, October 2, 1894, in *Complete Writings of Oscar Wilde: Miscellanies*, p. 276.
43. Cited in Ellmann, *Oscar Wilde*, p. 345. Arguably, the flower's meaning became fixed retrospectively by Wilde's trial—only *after* which, as Talia Schaffer points out, 'effeminacy became reduced to a sign of homosexuality' ('Fashioning Aestheticism by Aestheticizing Fashion,' p. 52)—and Noël Coward's *Bitter Sweet*: 'Pretty boys, witty boys, / You may sneer / At our disintegration. / Haughty boys, naughty boys, / Dear, dear, dear! / Swooning with affectation . . . / And as we are the reason / For the Nineties being gay, / We all wear a green carnation.'

suggestion of homosexuality. (These implications were reinforced by Morrissey's inverted buttonhole, which drew attention to the singer's backside whilst simultaneously making fun of such gestures.) Crucially, though, the suggestions remain just that—suggestions—and never cross the line into more explicit or definite assertiveness. As Schaffer notes, Wilde's use of sunflowers, lilies and peacock feathers 'invited yet repudiated feminine associations, teasing the viewer's impetus towards gender categorization.'[44] Morrissey, likewise, clearly enjoys and takes advantage of the way in which flowers 'invite and yet repudiate' transgressive associations. He is also, however, more generally drawn to the peculiar anarchic liberty with which such teasing significations play—sporting like sylphs in *The Rape of the Lock* with a lightness beyond our control.

RADICAL NOISES

In common with his appearance, Morrissey's onstage and studio performances were a subversive celebration of ineptitude ordinariness and a camp eccentricity. His singing—which is crucially inseparable from and complicates what he says—is one of the most conspicuous ways in which Morrissey set himself against the dominant conventions of popular music. As this is an important but slippery matter, it will be helpful to divide the subject into a number of subcategories.

Against the grain

In 'The Smiths: Repressed (But Remarkably Dressed),' John Stringer describes Morrissey's image as that of a 'traditional, eccentric, English gent,' who uses 'very clipped, precise enunciation' and in singing 'strains for "correct," clear English diction.'[45] This impression is reinforced by Stan Hawkins, in 'Anti-rebel, Lonesome Boy: Morrissey in Crisis?,' who speaks of the singer's 'distinctly English mannerism,' which he suggests 'has its origins in British music hall, whose traditions are found in artists such as Gracie Fields, Marie Lloyd and Nöel Coward.'[46] To paraphrase Wilde, there is something in this but not everything in this. As we have seen, it's certainly the case, especially whilst he was with The Smiths, that Morrissey was something of a

44. Schaffer, 'Fashioning Aestheticism by Aestheticizing Fashion,' p. 44.
45. Stringer, 'The Smiths,' p. 19.
46. Hawkins, *Settling the Pop Score*, pp. 85; 101 n 25.

dandy. This is apparent in his flamboyant ennui, his 'drawing-room' wit, in turning himself into a work of art, in his *culte de soi-même*, his hostility towards bourgeois utilitarianism, his 'aristocratic' aversion to work and his fastidious devotion to style.[47] But it leaves out the 'carnivalesque' side of Morrissey, which exists in tension with his dandyism and is equally essential to his vocal style.[48]

This 'carnivalesque' spirit is most apparent in his penchant for performed noises: groaning, sneezing, stage belching, spoof vomiting, etc.[49] Such noises render the apparently absent body visible and assert the importunate claims of the flesh. Hence, in contrast to the 'health and efficiency' of New Pop, where the body is a source of pleasure and pride, in Morrissey's songs it becomes a source of trouble and embarrassment. Such noises are also a sign of the pleasure the singer takes in bringing the 'unpoetic' into an aesthetic medium and widening its sphere to include all aspects of human life, however 'light' or 'low.' Yet there is perhaps too a reflexive protest involved in his carnivalesque noises; that is, an irreverence towards the aesthetic as such and the world of popular music in particular. (Morrissey's splendid machine-gun dance during 'How Soon Is Now?' on *Top of the Pops*—in which he blithely sprays the audience with imaginary bullets—suggests a less coded animosity towards the business he's in.)

The singer's carnivalesque tendencies are further manifest in his 'manhandling' of language. What I mean by this is his bold stretching out of words, far beyond their customary length or shape, and, conversely, his squashing of words or complicated syntax into the conventional spaces of popular music (consider the cramming in of 'the pain was enough to make / a shy bald Buddhist reflect and plan a mass-murder' and the languid protraction of 'nothing / appears / to be

---

47. The artwork for The Smiths' albums and singles' covers—all of which was designed by Morrissey—was itself strikingly innovative and revealed that here too was an underused space for beauty, communication and the play of meaning. The record sleeves—which tended to feature a film still or iconic photograph, washed in colour—were peculiarly resonant works in their own right, which enigmatically contributed in another medium to Morrissey's narratively constituted persona by suggesting stories and associations which they didn't quite disclose. For whilst they carried something of their original context with *them*, they were of interest because of—and in a sense transformed by—Morrissey's interest in them, and thus functioned as signs within another 'spectral' metanarrative of Morrissey's creating (which helped create 'Morrissey').
48. Like Byron and Wilde, Morrissey is too many other things as well to give himself up to dandyism completely. He is too fiercely working-class, too down-to-earth, demotic and *awkward* for the aesthete in him wholly to prevail. As Bracewell notes, 'Morrissey, like Genet, combines the temperament of an aesthete with a yearning to identify with the passionate failure of society's criminal outsiders' (Bracewell, *England Is Mine*, p. 223).
49. 'Never Had No One Ever,' 'Interesting Drug,' 'Death At One's Elbow,' 'Paint A Vulgar Picture.'

/ between the ears of / the lazy sunbathers'). Pat Reid has observed that 'many early Smiths songs have an oddly cumbersome feel to them— lines containing too many or too few lyrics, necessitating peculiar vocal quirks in order to make them scan.'[50] I agree with his observation of the phenomenon but not with the negative character of his assessment. Rather than being some kind of deficiency or imperfection—as if Morrissey were making the best of a bad job—such 'quirkiness' and the lyrics' 'oddly cumbersome feel' are, I think, *positive* deviations from the norm and evidence of different priorities.[51] They are a sign, that is, of his refusal to confine himself to a conventional pop vocabulary of easily rhyming words or normative syntax, and concomitantly of his determination at whatever cosmetic cost to say exactly what he wants to say, however little or much this may be.

Such 'manhandling' of language is characteristic of Morrissey. Even so, in this, as in most things, he is importantly capricious. At times he plays with words for no discernable reason—such as 'money' in 'The Headmaster Ritual,' 'clothesline' in 'Late Night, Maudlin Street' or 'were' in 'The Queen Is Dead.'[52] In live performances too he delights in travestying his own lyrics, with bizarre noises, acts of phonetic violence, and outright alterations, which fundamentally destabilize not only the song's meaning (for what status do such alterations have?—Is it parody? Is it whimsy? Is it a revelation?) but also meaningfulness *as such*, since they suggest a playing with signifiers without commitment to meaning. Indeed, what we can see in Morrissey's habit of altering his lyrics in live performances is a perpetual usurptation of textual authority and something of a return to the radical instability of oral literature, which is reconstituted with each performance and has no definitive 'original' text. In other cases, though, he seems to have it in for certain words (or certain words

---

50. Reid, *Morrissey*, p. 72.
51. Morrissey has himself spoken about testing the 'elasticity' of language: 'Because I come from a penniless background—a shack upon a hill—people find it fake that I come bounding down the hill clutching a copy of *De Profundis*. By rights I should be sitting here talking about Sheffield Wednesday or the length of Jimmy Hill's beard. But I was locked away for years, reading volume after volume. I don't want to talk like Henry VIII, but it's nice to test how elastic vocabulary can be' (Robertson, *Morrissey: In His Own Words*, p. 21).
52. In the case of the latter—'I never even knew what drugs *were*'—in which he seems to throw himself at the final word, there is perhaps an attempt to perform whilst simultaneously making fun of his ingenuousness. His pronunciation of 'delicate'—to rhyme with 'wait'—in 'Pretty Girls Make Graves' ('but she's too rough / and I'm too delicate') likewise appears to involve a homological performance of what it describes, since there is a kind of camp delicacy in his quaint mispronunciation of 'delicate.'

seem to have it in for him), and one word in particular: 'love'—which so often collapses, tickles or turns to ashes in his mouth.[53] Such carnivalesque tendencies qualify—without cancelling out—his 'English gent' image, but they also illustrate how the way in which he sings complicates and can communicate as much as what he sings.

The homeless voice

There are two further features of Morrissey's singing that marked him out as conspicuously 'other': his use of melisma (the singing of multiple notes to a single syllable of text) and his trademark falsetto. One might additionally include his marvellous occasional flirtations with yodelling, which evince a daring and comical appropriation of the kitsch. In all three cases, though in different ways, his voice may be said to lack a site or figure a kind of vagrancy, in that it inhabits a 'borrowed space' and is constituted by its mobility.

Morrissey's use of melisma—as, for example, in 'What Difference Does It Make?' and perhaps most extravagantly in 'This Charming Man'—represents an abandoning of the 'horizontal' narrative line in favour of an ornamental 'verticality.' Such treading of water, as it were, midutterance has a variety of effects. In the first place, the singer's putting of phonetic kinks into words may be seen as a thing of skill and unusual beauty, and an obvious illustration of the way in which Morrissey plays with words as *sounds*, adding phonetic convolutions for the sake of decoration, like the florid undulations in art nouveau.[54] Alternatively, it may be seen as another example of his 'manhandling' of language, and hence as an *anti*aesthetic gesture or a kind of thorn in the side of its own euphony, which advertises a

---

53. See, for example, 'A Rush And A Push And The Land Is Ours,' in which he sings 'Urrgh, I think I'm in lerv'; 'November Spawned A Monster,' where, as he sings about the deferral of love's arrival, the word itself eludes him and dissipates without closure: 'Sleep on and dream of love / because it's the closest you will get to lo-oh-ooh-oh.'; 'Sheila Take A Bow,' in which the word floats off at the end like a helium balloon as he sings 'The one that you love and who loves-a-you-oh-hoo-ho'; or 'How Soon Is Now,' where every word in the repeated first section is delivered in 'clipped, precise enunciation'—except for 'love,' in which there is a sudden buckling, as though the ground gives way in the middle of the word: 'I am human and I need to be lo-oh-oved.'

54. The analogy with the 'gratuitous' ornamentation of art nouveau brings into view the camp quality of Morrissey's melisma. In the words of Susan Sontag: 'Camp is a vision of the world in terms of style—but a particular kind of style. It is a love of the exaggerated, the "off," of things-being-what-they-are-not. The best example is Art Nouveau, the most typical and fully developed Camp style. Art Nouveau objects, typically, convert one thing into something else: the lighting fixtures in the form of flowering plants, the living room which is really a grotto' (Sontag, 'Notes on Camp,' p. 108). The 'superfluity' of Morrissey's melisma likewise converts the components of what purports to serve a communicative purpose—namely, words—into discrete *objets d'art*.

yawning disdain for his profession ('sometimes I'd feel more fulfilled / making Christmas cards with the mentally ill'[55]). Either way, his use of melisma has a disruptive character, which hampers easy identification by not allowing us to forget we're confronting a world that is made of words, and which signals its 'otherness' from everyday speech.

Not all such semantic suspensions are purely ornamental. In some cases, Morrissey's use of melisma has a teasing quality—as in 'This Charming Man'—and paradoxically plays a part by *impeding* the narrative (though arguably it has an expressive dimension too; as Nadine Hubbs observes, 'Morrissey's prolongation and inflection of the melisma on "seat" tells us more [than the lyrics themselves]: it seems a marked indulgence, and tantalizingly connotes (while the text denotes) a surrender to sensual pleasure'[56]). On other occasions, the melismatic extension of words—such as 'I' and 'now' in 'Heaven Knows I'm Miserable Now'—appears to be a sort of 'spillage' or overflow, as though the words were not big enough to contain all that the singer wanted to put into them. In this sense, the proliferation of florid involutions may be seen as the stigmata of ineffability—the telltale signs of a heart whose fullness is beyond expression—which are invisible on the page and yet crucially complicate what the words 'say.'

Bizarre as Morrissey's 'carnivalesque' noises are and quirkily original as his use of melisma is, of all the strange things he did with his voice, there was nothing so wonderfully odd as his falsetto. This was not the effortless flight of George Michael or the 'shamelessly synthetic' distension of the Bee Gees.[57] It was a voice *on stilts*—comically and distressingly reaching beyond its 'natural' limits,—and sounded like the exposure of something that's normally encased in a shell.

'Falsetto' is the Italian diminutive of 'false,' and as the adult male's approximation of the female voice, choir-boy or castrati alto, has blatantly transgressive connotations. Yet its transgression is paradoxically revealed more by failure than it is by success (a perfect imitation is not apparent as such). Morrissey's falsetto was therefore especially transgressive *because of* its 'deficiency.'[58] Indeed, it was so

---

55. 'Frankly, Mr Shankly.'
56. Hubbs, 'Music of the "Fourth Gender," ' p. 282.
57. François, 'Fakin' It/'Makin' It,' p. 442.
58. Speaking of the clamorous oppositional stance of bands such as Jesus and Mary Chain or New Model Army, Simon Reynolds has remarked: 'For me there's more disruption in a single trail of Morrissey's falsetto' (Reynolds, *Bring the Noise*, p. 2).

gauche it had a pantomime quality, and seemed in its openly over-stretched weediness to advertise its own incompetence. The amateurish falsetto doodling in 'Pretty Girls Make Graves,' for instance, sounds as if he's in the bathroom singing over someone else's song.

This ineptitude—which was expertly staged and ironized by the singer—was of course part of the point. He was, as Jo puts it in *A Taste of Honey*, being 'bad on purpose.'[59] It was a defiant sign of human frailty and a refusal of the slickness and synthetic perfection fetishized in the 1980s—which, as Harris, Reynolds and others have argued, was an aesthetic corollary of the 'new conservatism'—both of which to Morrissey seemed culpably to belie the most urgent human realities and to be proudly devoid of feeling.[60] In fact, whilst punk, glam rock, kitchen-sink cinema and the aestheticism of Wilde all helped to form the singer's early persona, arguably one of the most crucial shaping influences was Thatcherism—which was itself more of a style than a set of policies or a coherent ideology—and was to some extent the 'constitutive outside' of his art of weakness.[61] It is therefore possible to discern in the advertised ineptitude of Morrissey's falsetto—which is homologous with other aspects of his early persona—not only a general 'ideological' dimension, but more specifically what we might refer to as the negative inspiration of Thatcherism.

The 'ineptitude' of Morrissey's vocal performance manifestly enhances its expressive effects, and it is in this sense also a nonpejorative

---

59. Morrissey makes fun of his own voice in 'The Queen Is Dead': 'so, I broke into the Palace / with a sponge and a rusty spanner / she said: "Eh, I know you, and you cannot sing" / I said: "that's nothing—you should hear me play piano." Like his falsetto, the joke is an oversized impersonation of itself and is successful because it is *worse* than bad.

60. Typically, Morrissey's foregrounding of his fallibility was thrown into relief by the immaculate many-angled beauty of Johnny Marr's melodies. However, we find a musical parallel of Morrissey's foregrounding of his fallibility in 'Stop Me If You Think You've Heard This One Before,' which Marr felt sounded *too* accomplished and therefore added what Simon Goddard aptly refers to as 'some contrived inexperience in its closing guitar line' (Goddard, *The Smiths*, p. 237).

61. According to Simon Jenkins, by the mid-1980s 'Thatcher as prime minister had acquired a specific public persona' (*Thatcher and Sons*, p. 102), which in many respects was the mirror-image of Morrissey's. In the words of John Campbell, she was 'devoid of either irony or humour, intolerant of ambiguity and equivocation' (*Margaret Thatcher*, p. 64); for David Marquard, 'Victorian values, and the rhetoric of Victorian values' were central to her persona ('The Paradoxes of Thatcherism,' p. 164); and according to Juliet S. Thompson and Wayne C. Thompson, her public image as an aggressive ruthless and domineering woman, who was seen as insensitive and lacking in empathy, involved a 'reversal of gender stereotypes' (*Margaret Thatcher: Prime Minister Indominable*, pp. 10 and 43). This obviously caricatured opposition between the leadership style of the 'Iron Lady' and Morrissey's 'art of weakness' is intriguingly complicated by a number of parallels. As the singer's friend James Maker points out, 'In terms of having a clear, concise agenda, implementing it with total prejudice to compromise and executing it, [Morrissey's] style was Thatcherite' (cited in Brown, *Meetings with Morrissey*, p. 82). See also Simpson, 'The Man Who Murdered Pop,' *The Guardian* magazine, November 5, 1999 and *Saint Morrissey*, pp. 167–8.

imperfection.[62] Falsetto, for Anne-Lise François, is the voice of crisis and a form of 'exceptional' speech.[63] Even so, this is less apparent in its more accomplished users. Michael Jackson, for instance, sings so fluently in this register, it seldom bespeaks crisis. In Morrissey's case, the effort and 'exceptionality' of its reaching is vividly exposed; indeed, his falsetto voice has a distressing rawness—which often communicates as much as or more than the words themselves—and as such is expressive of vulnerability. (Just as amateurism and ineptitude came to be positively connoted in indie music as a counterpose to the slickness and cosmetic perfection of New Pop, so vulnerability—in the form of frailty, 'infantilism' or male 'femininity'—was foregrounded as a protest against its brashness and 'brazenly aspirational' gestures.[64]) Sometimes this vulnerability performatively underwrites what is being said—as in 'Miserable Lie,' where he sings 'I need advice' in a way that sounds like someone who is indeed in need of advice. But on other occasions it adds to or *alters* the words. In 'Heaven Knows I'm Miserable Now,' for example, when he sings 'In my life, / why do I give valuable time / to people who don't care if I . . .' and then in falsetto, with exposed vulnerability, '. . . *live or die,*' it has a sacrificial quality, as though he were challenging such insensitivity by making himself even more vulnerable.

There is also, conversely, an otherworldly and 'immaterial' quality to falsetto. To cite François again: 'Denaturalized, denied access to manhood and maturity, the castrati were said to have access to the heavens; theirs were the voices of angels.'[65] In its evocation of an 'angelic' disembodiment, the falsetto voice may therefore be linked to Morrissey's asceticism, which was in part a polemical opposition to the 'greed is good' hedonism of the 1980s and the cult of the body that characterized New Pop. In the words of Simon Reynolds:

---

62. Christopher Ricks makes a similar point about Bob Dylan's unconventional voice: 'Dylan when young did what only great artists do: define anew the art he practiced. Marlon Brando made people understand something different by *acting*. He couldn't act? Very well, but he did something very well, and what else are you going to call it. Dylan can't sing?' (Ricks, *Dylan's Visions of Sin*, p. 15). Whilst the element of strategic ineptitude in Morrissey's early vocal performance was a vital feature of his art of weakness, it should be borne in mind that once the point had been made he proved himself capable of singing with the assurance of a blindfolded trapeze artist.
63. François, 'Fakin' It/Makin' It,' p. 445.
64. Reynolds, *Rip It Up and Start Again*, p. 410. In *James Dean Is Not Dead*, Morrissey contrasts its subject with the conventional masculine 'rebel-hero' (such as Cagney, Brando and John Wayne), just as the singer would himself be contrasted with the conventional rock star, and celebrates Dean as the 'new alternative male hero,' who 'could make good tea, grow geraniums, and keep his house spotless without losing any of his obvious masculinity.'
65. François, 'Fakin' It/Makin' It,' p. 445.

'Pop has always been bodymusic, but the body is now [in the 1980s] the prime locus of power's operation, where power solicits us. Being a *success in life* involves a maximisation of your body's potential for health and pleasure (aerobics, sexology, nutrition, massage, touch therapy, TM, etc.). . . . The alternative scene, home of oppositional meanings, has always defined itself as pop's other. So in today's independent label music, diverse as it is, we can find a common impulse to rise above the body.'[66]

At this point we can see a characteristic tension emerging in Morrissey's art between his 'carnivalesque' noises and the claims of the body on the one hand, and a 'stepping out of' or escape from the body in falsetto on the other.[67] In fact, it's possible to see in these divergent vocal tendencies an extratextual staging of the question he asks in 'Still Ill' (and which haunts his work): 'does the body rule the mind or does the mind rule the body?' An articulate answer— even an articulate acknowledgement of an *inability* to answer—runs the risk of siding with 'the mind' and hence prejudicially terminating the inquiry under the very appearance of objectivity. The bathos of Morrissey's response—'I dunno'—which foregrounds its inarticulacy, is therefore more of an answer—and a better joke—than it might at first appear.

There is one other way in which Morrissey's falsetto was a synecdoche of his central concerns. Speaking of the voice of castrati, Goethe remarked: 'In their representations, the concept of imitation and of art was invariably more strongly felt, and through their able performance a sort of conscious illusion was produced . . . in that these persons are not women, but only represent women. . . . They represent not themselves, but a nature absolutely foreign to them.'[68] François similarly speaks of falsetto as a 'borrowed voice,' but highlights the double alienation involved in such 'borrowing,' since it announces a 'homelessness with respect to either gender.'[69] Falsetto in this sense is revealed as a refusal of the given categories and a

---

66. Reynolds, 'Against Health and Efficiency,' p. 246.
67. These two poles are conjoined in the 'oxymoronic' voice of yodelling, which consists in an abrupt modulation between what's known as 'chest voice' and 'head voice.'
68. Cited in Heriot, *The Castrati in Opera*, p. 26.
69. François, 'Fakin' It/Makin' It,' p. 443. In her discussion of early nineteenth-century Italian opera, Naomi André speaks illuminatingly of a 'third' option for gendering the singing voice, which is 'made up of codes that are both masculine and feminine': 'This third category could be neither masculine nor feminine, but something new that results from the combination (a + b = c). Or, it could be both simultaneously (a + b = ab), invoking something new, yet a synthesis of both older elements' (André, *Voicing Gender*, p. 48).

volitional assignation of identity, which corresponds to the singer's persistent refusal of heterosexual and homosexual classifications. Moreover, in openly putting identities on and off at will, it lays bare the constructedness of the categories themselves and the performative constitution of gender.[70] We can therefore see in Morrissey's falsetto, alongside its staging of vulnerability, and the ideological refusals of its ineptitude, a 'deconstructive' tendency which crucially affects, but isn't apparent in, the lyrics themselves.

Androgynous spaces

The final aspect of Morrissey's vocal performance that sets itself against the norms of popular music is what we might refer to as his 'wandering' voice. To explain what I mean and the significance of this, it will be necessary to say a word or two about certain features of The Smiths' music. One of the most conspicuous and influential aspects of their music, harmonically speaking, is its ubiquitous use of certain types of chords; namely, major and minor sevenths and suspended seconds and fourths.[71] Needless to say, The Smiths are by no means the first band to favour such dissonant or occluded structures, and interestingly it seems to be precisely this sort of 'jingly-jangly' tendency from which Johnny Marr was trying to distance the band on later albums, tiring of its all-too successful influence and fearing a slide into repetition or self-parody.[72] Nevertheless, the distinctive sound of the early Smiths may be characterized harmonically by a prominence of such chords.[73] Why is this of significance?

70. In *The Queen's Throat*, Wayne Koestenbaum discusses the 'break' in the operatic voice or the crossing between registers as 'the place within one voice where the split between male and female occurs.' The singer schooled in *bel canto*, he explains, 'will avoid eruptions by disguising the register breaks and passing smoothly over them. The register line, like the colour line, the gender line, or the hetero/homo line, can be crossed only if the transgressor pretends that no journey has taken place. . . . By revealing the register break, a singer exposes the fault lines inside a body that pretends to be only masculine or only feminine' (Koestenbaum, *The Queen's Throat*, p. 167). Morrissey's early hoarse falsetto wittingly exposes this crossing of the register line by inhabiting the space of the 'break' and carrying something of this 'brokenness' with it. In doing so, his voice dispels the bel canto illusion—perfectly mastered by George Michael, for example—of a seamless continuity between 'masculine' and 'feminine' oral registers. As with so many of Morrissey's gestures, his falsetto is thus in a sense 'about' what it's doing, which it reveals in being slightly awry.

71. Johnny Marr has spoken about being 'chordally oriented,' which he attributes to his early habit of trying 'to cover the strings, piano and everything with [his] right hand, trying to play the whole record on six strings' (Carman, *Johnny Marr*, p. 32).

72. See Marr's comments cited in Goddard, *The Smiths*, p. 227.

73. Speaking of 'Reel Around The Fountain,' the opening song on their first album, Richard Carman observes that Johnny Marr 'adds a series of major seventh and sixth notes into the phrasing—accents which were to become a trademark of his playing' (Carman, *Johnny Marr*, p. 75). Julian Stringer similarly notes that 'Marr's influential personal technique is to mix major rock chords with minor, jazzy-sounding embellishments' (Stringer, 'The Smiths,' p. 19).

Apart from a return that it helped to inaugurate—along with such bands as Prefab Sprout and Aztec Camera—to more complex and finely shaded melodic structures, which was itself a sea change in British popular music (witness the difference between The Jam and The Style Council), the prominence of such harmonic structures offers an unusual degree of openness, on account of their radical ambiguity. To explain: the central and fundamental distinction in tonal music is between major and minor, which is a distinction of intervallic construction.[74] Now, in different ways and to different degrees, major and minor sevenths, on the one hand, and suspended seconds and fourths, on the other, cloud or evade this central distinction between major and minor. In the first case, this is because the addition of the extra note to the triad (so that, for example, A minor becomes A minor seventh with the addition of a G, and A major becomes A major seventh with the addition of a G♯) carries the chord away from the undiluted clarity of its root and leaves it poised more or less *in between* two chords. Thus, A minor seven hovers in a space between A minor and C major[75] and A major seven is poised between A major and C♯ minor.[76] In the second case—with suspended fourths and seconds—the chord is left in an even more equivocal space. This is because the note which determines whether a chord is major or minor (the third) is replaced by another note (either a second or a fourth) and hence 'suspended.'

This digression helps me to make two simple but important points. Firstly, we can see that the sort of ambiguity for which Morrissey is notorious—which, as we shall see, is typically a matter of multiplicity or mobility—obtains at a musical level as well. That is to say, we can see in Marr's pervasive use of major and minor seventh chords as well as suspended seconds and fourths the opening up of musical spaces which are, in the first case, both this *and* that, and, in the second case, neither this *nor* that—spaces, we might say, which are 'androgynous' or 'neuter.'[77] Secondly, this means that the addition

74. The former triad consists of a major third (an interval of four semitones) and a perfect fifth above its root, whereas the latter consists of a minor third (an interval of three semitones) and a perfect fifth above its root. This would mean, for example, in the key of A, a triad formed of A-C♯-E as opposed to A-C-E.
75. Between the triads of A-C-E and C-G-E.
76. Between the triads A-C♯-E and C♯-G♯-E.
77. The nineteenth-century musicologist Karl Mayrberger famously described the 'Tristan chord'—the radically ambiguous combination of F-B-D♯ and G♯ with which *Tristan und Isolde* opens—as a 'Zwitterakkord,' that is, an 'androgynous' or 'bisexual' chord (see Nattiez, *Music and Discourse*, pp. 219–29).

of a vocal line over such chords—which may of course avoid, hold or move between the key notes—is potentially much more decisive, since it can, for example, in the first case tilt the 'in between' chord in one direction or another (by reinforcing its A-minor-ness or C-major-ness, as it were) and in the second case it could even more decisively determine the mode of the chord (by singing a C or C♯ over a suspended A chord, in this way turning it into a major or a minor chord). One of the things that is therefore significant about Morrissey's 'wandering' voice is that it has what we might refer to as a performative function; which is to say that it is radically *constitutive* and has a sort of reverse chameleon effect, in that it can force things to conform to its musical colouring, determining the character of what it touches.[78] Good examples of this kind of constitutive wandering are to be found in 'This Charming Man' and 'Reel Around The Fountain.'[79]

Several points of general importance may be extracted from this discussion. In the first place, it was found that the singer's voice—as well as sound more generally—is not 'a mere accompaniment of the message delivered in speech' but rather something that '[contains or transmits] a message of its own.'[80] This is especially true of Morrissey's falsetto, which performatively speaks of an acute vulnerability and whose very timbre is a distress call; though the same may be said of the melodic and metrical 'wandering' of his voice, which figures a radical 'nonbelonging.' In the second place, it is possible to discern an 'oxymoronic' conjunction of antitheses in the singer's vocal habits: in his tendency towards a dandyish refinement as well as the carnivalesque; in the conflicting claims of the mind and the body that are figured in his falsetto; in the opening up of a 'third' space that conjoins both masculine and feminine codes; and in the often inseparable fusion of seriousness and play that is apparent in his more 'eccentric' gestures (on the one hand, his straining and 'breaking' voice has a serious ideological dimension,

---

78. This tendency is encouraged by Johnny Marr's preference for picking as opposed to strumming, since in the former the chord is in a sense dispersed and emerges 'horizontally,' rather than all at once, which allows the voice more scope in determining the song's melodies.

79. For a fine later example, see 'Hold Onto Your Friends,' in which Morrissey sings a B over a C major chord ('. . . fighting the people you like . . . defending your name . . .'), pulling it passingly into a major seventh and evoking the emotive cajoling the lines describe.

80. Žižek, *The Parallax View*, p. 229.

whose advertisement of ineptitude and vulnerability is implicitly but crucially a flag of the human, whilst on the other hand the 'doodling' of his melisma and yodelling is an example of the singer's wonderful light-heartedness, which springs up all over the place like flowers through marble). And finally, a 'deconstructive' tendency has come into view, both in Morrissey's adoption of a 'borrowed voice,' which in its performative constitution of identity within 'a stolen space' points towards 'the imitative structure of gender itself,'[81] and also in his travestying of his own lyrics, which opens up a space between the speaking subject and what is said, and in doing so fundamentally destabilizes its meaning.

EMBARRASSMENT

Let us pause for a moment to consider the significance of what we have looked at so far. At every level, there was something slightly 'off,' askew or out of step about Morrissey—something literally eccentric. His ailing and frail appearance, for example, was clearly opposed to the sun-tanned vitality of Wham! and the supernatural beauty of David Sylvian, John Taylor and the like.[82] This infirmity was foregrounded by antifashion accessories—NHS glasses and his old-fashioned hearing aid—which he facetiously referred to as 'disability chic.'[83] Likewise, his incongruous, ill-fitting clothes, which were a 'hotchpotch' of masculine and feminine, contrasted both with the stereotypical 'ruggedness' of the rock star and the fancy-dress cosmetic effeminacy of the New Romantics.[84] The singer's extravagant floral practices—which were ticklishly poised between seriousness and comedy—should of course also be mentioned in this connection. His vocals, similarly, set him apart—in particular his superlatively eccentric

---

81. François, 'Fakin It/Makin' It,' p. 447; Butler, *Gender Trouble*, p. 138.

82. 'I look ill, don't I?' the singer pointed out, glorying in his countercultural frailty (*Smash Hits*, January 31, 1985).

83. This is a good example of Morrissey's habit of making fun of the fun that had been made of him: 'Disability chic will reign rampant in 1985. The hearing aid is replaced by the neck brace. No serious musicologist will be spotted in an audience minus a neck brace' (cited in Middles, *The Smiths*, p. 66).

84. Just as Morrissey's falsetto voice opens up a 'third' space that conjoins masculine and feminine registers, his clothing—which typically included flowery blouses from D.H. Evans outsize shop—constitutes a 'third' category, which as Marjorie Garber has argued, writing on the subject of cross-dressing more generally, calls into question the stability of the other two: 'transvestitism is a space of possibility structuring and confounding culture: the disruptive element that intervenes, not just a category crisis of male and female, but the crisis of category itself' (Garber, *Vested Interests*, p. 17).

falsetto, which sounded distressingly like a voice with its clothes off. And the same could be said of his dancing too, which was a kind of choreographed awkwardness that included a pantomime pelvic gyration and looked as though it was made up of bits others had left *out* of their dance routines. As Mick Middles observed, commenting on the band's early live performances, Morrissey

> acted out the totally ridiculous spectacle which, somehow, absurdly fitted into the field of pop music. Never was it more obvious just what an unlikely figure Morrissey cut as a pop star. This ungainly fellow, dressed in dishevelled robes and dancing with a curiously lopsided but fetching clumsiness, somehow managed to touch thousands. It was truly the most absurd of happenings.[85]

In all of these ways, we can see Morrissey carrying himself out of conventional categories, collapsing their boundaries, inhabiting their edges, or carrying that which is other than them *into* them. At every level, in other words, there was something *embarrassing* about Morrissey.[86] Pat Reid's way of putting it is rather uncharitable, but it gives us some idea of the radical oddity of Morrissey's appearance: 'In his early pictures, before he became an icon, I always thought he looked a bit simple, like a doltish, idiot savant farmhand who carries a chicken everywhere.'[87] Paul Morley, who knew the singer before he was famous, confirms this view: 'I remember who and what you used to be. You were like the village idiot, the odd one out, the backward boy.'[88] In Morrissey's own words, he was 'the strangest living oddity.'[89]

One of the most embarrassing things is embarrassment itself, which is a peculiarly contagious sensation, as well as one that feeds on itself. Morrissey is deeply embarrassing in this way too. Indeed, surely no one has ever been so sublimely uncomfortable about being a pop star as Morrissey. (One need only witness the turbulent squirming of his face in televised interviews, which vividly bespeaks a ferment of interiority.) This was certainly the view of Ken Friedman,

---

85. Middles, *The Smiths*, p. 79.
86. The homological relationship I am trying to highlight between Morrissey's singing, dancing and appearance, etc., obviously extends to his lyrics as well, in which he foregrounds his awkwardness and speaks of 'a bungling desire,' 'a fumbling politeness' and evinces an affection for 'loafing oafs.' The singer's celibacy, abstinence and 'monastic' seclusion, which even more conspicuously set him apart as a pop star, are considered in the section on Holy folly (pp. 24–50).
87. Reid, *Morrissey*, p. 48.
88. *Blitz*, April, 1988.
89. *The Times*, February 1995.

one of The Smiths' many managers: 'He's afraid of success, like a lot of English people. I don't know what it is. To us, in America, it's what you achieve—everybody wants to be a millionaire or president or whatever. What I found baffling in England was that people didn't really want to make it; they were so embarrassed about it. Morrissey had that attitude more than anybody I'd ever known.'[90]

Whilst it's easy enough to see something endearing and even virtuous in Morrissey's inability to make friends with everyday experience—however much it may contagiously discompose us—to describe the singer as slightly off or askew will certainly seem to detract from his significance as an artist, which is naturally seen as a matter of achievement rather than 'just missing.' Nevertheless, I wish on the contrary to argue that being embarrassing in the sense of missing the mark was an essential and *positive* feature of Morrissey's art. He was, in other words, *aiming* to just miss. How can we explain this?

In the first place, as ever, it is a matter of comedy, like Les Dawson's piano playing or Frank Spencer's mishaps; though his blending of slapstick and pathos aligns him, beyond this, with the 'Chaplinesque' tradition of lovable fumblers, such as George Formby and Norman Wisdom.[91] Such tonal heterogeneity is in a sense 'embarrassing,' in that the listener is caught between seriousness and laughter, and 'can be neither of two people' or must be both at once.[92] This is evidently the desired effect: 'The Smiths tease people,' Morrissey explained, 'making them laugh, then making them cry—operating at opposite ends of the emotional scale. What we're ultimately hoping to do is to make them laugh and cry at the same time.'[93] (Recently,

---

90. Cited in Rogan, *Morrissey and Marr*, p. 268. Tony Parsons similarly relates Morrissey's embarrassment to his Englishness: 'One of his great themes is what it means to be English. Nobody else cares as much as he does about the shyness . . . , the humour, the pride and the capacity for embarrassment that are your birthright when you are English. And nobody else—*nobody else*—has written and sung about it as brilliantly as Morrissey' (*Vox*, April 1993).
91. Morrissey has frequently spoken about his fondness for George Formby, whose comic songs of terminal lucklessness are clearly part of his artistic heritage. Here is a representative snippet:

> Now I know I'm not handsome, no good looks or wealth
> But the girls I chase say my plain face will compromise their health.
> Now I know fellows worse than me, bow-legged and boss-eyed
> Walking out with lovely women clinging to their side.
> Now if women like them like men like those, why don't women like me?
> (Why Don't Women Like Me?)

92. The phrase in quotation marks is taken from the social psychologist Erving Goffman, who speaks of an individual 'showing embarrassment when he can be neither of two people' (Goffman, 'Embarrassment and Social Organisation,' p. 270).
93. Robertson, ed., *Morrissey in His Own Words*, p. 62.

we've been made much more familiar with this 'ticklish' simultaneity of pain and pleasure by the TV series *The Office*, which brilliantly succeeds in alienating us even as it elicits our sympathy.) In this sense, the embarrassment that embarrassment causes ceases to be an impediment or baffled form of speech and is revealed instead as the insignia of a complex mode of appreciation.

The embarrassing in Morrissey might, in the second place, be seen as a metasemiotic gesture—that is, as a sign that self-consciously reflects upon signs. If we take, for example, his gauche falsetto, which is as openly in drag as the 'fine ladies' in *Little Britain*, it announces itself as an impersonation in being wonderfully off the mark. In doing so, it draws attention to itself as a staged gesture and shows us its knowledge of what it is doing in the act of doing it. In this way, it offers a sort of commentary on itself and its intertextual 'panto' ancestry.

The singer's pelvic gyration dance, aired on *Top of the Pops*, performing 'The Boy With The Thorn In His Side,' provides an even clearer example of a gesture that raises a conspiratorial eyebrow at its own practice. The 'pelvic thrust' is perhaps the *ur*-rock gesture, and carries a whole miniature history in itself. Its origins are of course associated with Elvis—who was nicknamed 'the pelvis' and scandalized audiences in the 1950s with his suggestive gyrations. Since then, it has been endlessly recycled, almost to the point of invisibility, but it is continually rediscovered as a more or less explicit sign of sex. If, however, with Elvis, Salt-N-Pepa or Murdoc Faust Niccals, for instance, the pelvic commotion is a sign of sex, with Morrissey it becomes a sign of *a sign* (of sex). It is, so to speak, a portrait or textbook illustration of the pelvic gyration, which is flooded with a sense of doing what has been done before and seems to be saying 'This is what pop stars do, isn't it?' In this way, like his use of flowers, it speaks of itself *as* a sign or quotation and opens up an interval between the gesture and what it 'means.' (This liberation of the signifier—which is held up as something that is produced by and points towards other signifiers—was reinforced when Steve Wright, the presenter on *Top of the Pops*, imitated Morrissey's pelvic gyrations at the end of the song, parodying what was itself a parody, increasing the sense that signs are things that can be performed and passed around without commitment or expressing anything other than themselves.) There is of course a sort of coyness in this, in that Morrissey is performing an action, as it were, behind the towel of his irony, which leaves us wondering whether he means it or not (and what 'meaning it' means). But it is also a way of dealing with the burden of belatedness. Umberto Eco has explained this postmodern predicament and the escape strategy of quotation in the following memorable way:

> The past, since it cannot really be destroyed, because its destruction leads to silence, must be revisited: but with irony, not innocently. I think of the postmodern attitude as that of a man who loves a very cultivated woman and knows he cannot say to her, 'I love you madly,' because he knows that she knows (and that she knows that he knows) that these words have already been written by Barbara Cartland. Still, there is a solution. He can say, 'As Barbara Cartland would put it, I love you madly.'[94]

Similarly, in being slightly askew, too carefully performed or suspended in the amber of self-consciousness, Morrissey's gestures subtly dissociate themselves from what they are doing and speak 'with sideways glance' of their quotational character—which undermines, even as it enables, the act of signification.[95]

There is something even more subversive about embarrassment—something subtly but radically disturbing—which lies at the centre of Morrissey's art. Doubtless, this will itself seem somewhat topsyturvy, for we are used to seeing embarrassment as a form of censure, which re-enshrines the norm and stigmatises that which is embarrassing. Indeed, embarrassment tends to function as the scarecrow of normality—serving its interests in discreetly policing its borders. But it may work the other way round as well. In revealing that there *are* boundaries, that 'the normal' is a proscribed territory, it may prompt us to ask why the line has been drawn here, by whom it has been drawn, and whose interests it serves. In this sense, embarrassment may be seen as the first ripples of deconstruction—bringing to light the lack of any secure ground upon which such judgements are based, and laying bare the contingency, the constructedness, the *fabrication* of the 'normal,' along with the power relations that

---

94. Eco, *Reflections on* The Name of the Rose, p. 67.

95. It is possible to discern the pressure of such postmodern belatedness in the elaborate difficulties Morrissey has saying the word 'love,' whose gnarled, sarcastic and stammering pronunciations may be seen as an equivalent of the ironic framing gesture 'as Barbara Cartland would put it.' Perhaps the clearest illustration of this in Morrissey's lyrics is the wonderful swerving away from the word in 'I Like You,' where the singer's lingering pronunciation of 'I' ('could it be I . . . like you / it's so shameful of me / I . . . like you') teasingly conjures up whilst simultaneously figuring a resistance to the conventionally expected word 'love.'

inform or produce it. Morrissey of course doesn't speak in these terms. Nevertheless, he clearly believes 'there is no such thing in life as normal' and seeks to unmask it as an arbitrary and oppressive construction. When asked in interview in 1987 'What are you driven by?' he replied:

> This will sound almost unpleasant but *distaste for normality*. . . . I don't like normal situations. I get palpitations. I don't know what to do. So this obsessive drive against normality—which I know sounds unprintable and unfathomable—that's what it is.[96]

Compared to the hyperbolic gestures of punk and the flag-waving transgressions of the so-called 'gender benders,' Morrissey's 'embarrassing' subversion of the normal will appear decidedly tame. Yet, as with a 'bum' note, the greatest disturbance is sometimes caused by being *slightly* out.[97] And such is the case, I would argue, with Morrissey. In being embarrassing—and in being embarrassed—we see something of him spilling slightly outside the mould, like a coat trapped in a closing door, which renders apparent the structures he is inhabiting, more effectively than simply inverting or abandoning them. It is this dissonant aura of embarrassed self-consciousness—this not quite being identical with what he is doing—that is peculiar to Morrissey and furtively so subversive.[98]

There is one other, related way of explaining why embarrassment is an essential and positive feature of Morrissey's art. In considering the causes and purposes of blushing, Charles Darwin notes that, from one point of view, 'it makes the blusher to suffer and the beholder uncomfortable, without being of the least service to either of them.'[99] If, however, as I am suggesting, embarrassment in

---

96. *Q*, August 1987.

97. As Julian Stringer perceptively remarks, 'Unlike strong female singers like Madonna or gay male singers like Boy George and Culture Club, The Smiths never proudly transgress the boundaries of normality, because their music refuses to define what constitutes "normality" in the first place' (Stringer, 'The Smiths,' p. 24).

98. Simon Reynolds has commented on the subversiveness of the singer's embarrassment: 'Morrissey on *Top of the Pops* is deeply embarrassing. Only Ian McCulloch has visited an equivalent outrage—both bared their nipples, acted drunk or spastic, swooned. Were "prats." Which means only that they've tried to puncture for a few minutes the glacial cool of pop, make a sort of divine grace of awkwardness, get through. . . . The performance side of The Smiths is crucial. The standard scripted pop moves let us know where we are—in the presence of "charisma," "sexiness," "stardom." It is the "naturalness" and inevitability of these gestures, this unreflecting, incommunicative showbiz language, that Morrissey tries to disrupt—an eloquent incoherence' (Reynolds, *Bring the Noise*, p. 6).

99. Darwin, *The Expression of the Emotions in Man and Animals*, p. 336.

Morrissey exposes the arbitrary and oppressive fabrication of 'normality,' it will turn out to be a vantage point as much as a lapse or loss of composure and have an ideological function. This is because in not quite being the same shape as the role he is inhabiting—in advertising his eccentricity, that is—Morrissey once again appears to be showing solidarity with the marginalized. (The singer claimed that he wore the celebrated hearing aid as 'a symbol that spoke for downtrodden and lonely people'[100] and to show a deaf fan who had written to him of her misery 'that deafness shouldn't be some sort of stigma that you try to hide.'[101]) This is how he explained more generally what The Smiths are 'supposed to *do* to people':

> We want to release people from their shackles—let them be themselves!
> . . . We are really making an embarrassingly fundamental request to accept yourself and for people to display their weaknesses.[102]

Morrissey's not quite fitting in, which separates, as it were, the dancer from the dance, is a performative way of making this request and an undoing of the shackles by demonstration. His refusal to edit out his weaknesses and tidy up his oddity is thus clearly related to his defence of the human, in that its exposure of the 'normal' as a cultural construct concomitantly calls into question our categorization of the excluded, the marginalized, the 'queer' and the other.[103]

WHERE MEMBERSHIP'S A SMILING FACE

So far, we have considered the band's name, Morrissey's appearance, and certain aspects of his vocal performance. At the centre, however, of the revolution brought about by The Smiths—and underwriting the multivalent semiotics of their appearance, performance and even their 'packaging'—are Morrissey's lyrics. I have deliberately approached the matter in this topsy-turvy fashion in order to emphasize the importance of extralyrical elements—the significance of which all too easily evaporates in the analysis of particular lyrics and even more surely with the passage of time. In Morrissey's case, losing sight of

---

100. Haupfuhrer, 'Roll Over Beethoven, and Tell Madonna the News,' p. 106.
101. Robertson, *Morrissey: In His Own Words*, p. 23.
102. *The Face*, February 1984.
103. This is, I suppose, what Morrissey meant when in response to a question about whether his songwriting was political he said, 'I think it's all political. I think my very being is political' (*Musician*, June 1991).

the various nonlinguistic ways of communicating or 'performing' meaning would be especially damaging, since his work is an ongoing dramatization of self, and his appearance, performances and public pronouncements all have an essential part in that drama. So, whilst his lyrics are manifestly the primary means of projecting that self, and although it may be necessary in another context to emphasize their *poetic* character, they should be treated as a transcript of dramatic utterances rather than as self-sufficient texts.

What, then, was so revolutionary about Morrissey's lyrics? When The Smiths released their first record, 'Hand In Glove,' in May 1983, the number one single was 'True' by Spandau Ballet, and when they released their first LP, *The Smiths*, in March, 1984, the number one album in the UK was the Thompson Twins' *Into The Gap*. Probably the most successful band and icon of the time, though, was Wham!. In order to remind ourselves of the *Zeitgeist* of those rather *geistlosen* times and of the lyrical conventions that were dominant then, so as better to appreciate the otherness of The Smiths, I propose briefly to consider by way of exemplar the song 'Club Tropicana' by Wham!, which is taken from the number one album *Fantastic*, released in July 1983.

The song begins with the faded-in sound effects of a tropical location and the arrival out of a revving car of someone in what sounds like high heels, walking across a gravel driveway to a party at which the song proper is playing, which seems to have been awaiting this arrival in order to begin. In this way, the song draws us into a world of its imagining, partly by means of the frame's focalization—which presents us with the 'event' of the song from the point of view of an arriving guest—but also, importantly, by presenting itself as part of the experience it describes. As a result, it fosters a sense of unmediated participation, for the audience is in fact listening to the very music which is being played at the club. This sense of participation and of being welcomed into another world is explicitly encouraged in the opening lines of the song. Here is the first verse and chorus:

> Let me take you to the place
> Where membership's a smiling face,
> Brush shoulders with the stars.
> Where strangers take you by the hand,
> And welcome you to wonderland—
> From beneath their panamas . . .

> Club Tropicana, drinks are free,
> Fun and sunshine—there's enough for everyone.
> All that's missing is the sea,
> But don't worry, you can suntan!

The listener is directly and individually addressed by the polite imperative of one of the song's 'stars' ('Let me take you') in a way that immediately engages our attention and appears to authenticate its promise about brushing shoulders with the stars. (This impression is reinforced by the greeting 'Hi, George,' which is faintly audible amidst the general welcome of the song's frame and creates the illusion that there is in fact no illusion.) The world into which we are welcomed is presented as available to everyone ('Where membership's a smiling face'), a place of immediate intimacy ('Where strangers take you by the hand') and a land of plenty ('there's enough for everyone'). The illusion it creates is, to be sure, a light and self-conscious construction—with its fairytale opening ('Let me take you to a place . . .') and its unsqueamish hyperbole ('And welcome you to wonderland')—so it is hard to imagine anyone actually turning up expectantly at Sony with their bags packed. Nonetheless, it seductively draws us into its escapist fantasy—and this is of course the measure of its skill and success.

It would be absurd to suggest that pop music in the 1980s was a monolithic thing, conforming to conventions as alien to the contemporary mind as those of courtly love. Indeed, compared to the staggeringly formulaic character of reality-TV influenced pop, the daring and eccentricities of the 1980s immediately obtrude. Even so, considering the hit singles of Wham!—as straws which reveal the prevailing wind—it would be reasonable to identify certain dominant tendencies within the period, which are brought into view by and reciprocally reveal the counter-reaction of The Smiths. Essentially, these tell a story of a kind of airbrushed hedonism, whose lineaments may be crudely summarized as follows.

---

104. The only exception out of the four singles is 'Bad Boys,' which is *about* but doesn't use the word 'fun.' According to Lawrence Grossberg, this is the essential value of rock (which he catchily defines as 'the entire range of post-war, "youth"-oriented, technologically and economically mediated, musical practices and styles'): 'rock defines a politics of fun. . . . Youth itself is transformed from a matter of age into an ambiguous matter of attitude, defined by its rejection of boredom and its celebration of movement, change, energy; that is, fun. And this celebration is lived out in and inscribed upon the body—in dance, sex, drugs, fashion, style and even the music itself' (Grossberg, 'Is Anybody Listening? Does Anybody Care?' p. 51).

The key word that recurs in Wham!'s early singles, all taken from the album *Fantastic*, is 'fun.'[104] However, if 'Club Tropicana' presents this as a readily and universally available commodity, the others focus on its purported enemies (the traditional work ethic ['Wham Rap! (Enjoy What You Do?)']; marriage ['Young Guns (Go For It!)']; and parents ['Bad Boys']). The kind of fun they espouse is sensual and social, and it is primarily a matter of going out. It thereby conspicuously privileges and promotes a cult of the physical, which entails a corollary neglect of the mind, and (less visibly) valorizes consumerism. All of these values, it was noted earlier, are reinforced and ideally embodied in the band members.[105] The music, too, reinforces these values, and in several ways. In the first place, it is essentially danceable—which marks it out as what Simon Reynolds refers to as 'bodymusic'[106]—and provides a soundtrack for the sorts of experiences its performers endorsed. It is also, importantly, highly polished—the increasing significance and prominence of the record's 'production,' which became almost a thing in its own right, serving as an extra layer of gloss—and proudly synthesized. 'Proudly,' because whilst it's hard from our contemporary perspective to see anything polemical about the choice of instruments, at the time there was a fierce polarization between guitar bands and synthesizer bands, such that the use of synthesized instruments (drums, handclaps and other effects, or as a primary instrument in place of the guitar) was tantamount to taking an ideological stance.[107]

Plainly, the image such music fostered was a fantasy. Britain in the 1980s was riven with mass unemployment (reaching over three

---

105. Wham! originally consisted of George Michael, Andrew Ridgeley, Dee C. Lee—who was soon replaced by Pepsi DeMacque—and Shirlie Holliman.

106. Reynolds draws a broad distinction between the 'body culture' of chartpop, which was 'based around the primacy of the dance beat,' and the 'head culture' of indie-pop, with its attendant 'undanceability': 'Of course, people will dance to indie-pop, even when it's as fiercely anti-dance as Jesus and Mary Chain's "Never Understand," but, strictly, indie-pop really demands physical responses that contravene the norms of dance-as-sexual-flaunting, that involve a sacrifice of cool. Jangly-pop ought to be danced with Morrisseyesque feyness, above-it-all gestures that echo the "free dancing" of the counter-culture.' (Reynolds, *Bring the Noise*, p. 14).

107. This was an opposition which The Smiths—for a time and to a certain extent—upheld, refusing to use synthesizers, and preferring to see, as Morrissey put it, 'real people on stage, playing real instruments' (Bret, *Morrissey*, p. 155). This stance was manifestly something that was promoted by Morrissey and about which Johnny Marr had mixed feelings (after The Smiths split up, Marr of course went on to form the tellingly named 'Electronic,' but as early as 1984 he was involved in 'electro' dance music outside The Smiths, playing guitar with Quando Quango on 'Atom Rock' and 'Triangle'). However, as we have seen in his use of flowers, Morrissey's attitude towards 'artifice' is much more complicated than his early strategic championing of the 'natural' suggests.

million or 13 percent of the work force between 1983 and 1986),[108] recession and industrial decline, coupled with a stock market boom, and profound class and racial tensions (riots attributed to poverty, unemployment and racial discrimination took place in Brixton, Toxteth and Handsworth in 1981 and 1985).[109] It would be a mistake, however, to pat ourselves on the back for being so percipient and smile at the delusion of those who enjoyed such music. Escapism negatively evokes what it flees; and that it was a fantasy, it seems safe to assume, was as obvious then as it is now.[110] The problem, though, as the cultural critic Slavoj Žižek has shown, is that fantasy can somehow survive its own exposure and is not necessarily inimical to cynicism.[111] To the contrary, he argues, today's cynical variant of such fantasy is a 'paradox of an enlightened false consciousness,' according to which 'we know very well what we are doing, but still do it.' The illusion, therefore, 'is not on the side of knowledge, it is already on the side of reality itself, of what people are doing,' such that it in fact structures their reality.[112] Hence, we might know very well that the world of plenty of which Wham! sing is a fantasy, which our 'enlightened' reason does not believe, and yet—in buying or enjoying their records—behave as if we do. In this way, cynicism turns out to be a feature of naiveté and may paradoxically support the fantasy it is supposed to 'see through.'

It is important for us to bear this in mind, not only to keep us from a sort of historical condescension, but also because it helps us to see why such a dramatic overturning was necessary—the danger being that with hindsight the illusion is so obvious it makes the reaction seem unnecessary, and in doing so robs it of its revolutionary character. Whereas the truth of the matter, as Žižek has argued, is that cynicism turns out to be a way in which fantasy paradoxically inoculates itself against exposure—which helps us to understand how the 1980s could be a time of such disillusionment and illusion as well. It therefore at the same time helps us to see why an even more radical

---

108. This reached 15 to 20 percent in the north of England, Scotland, Wales and Northern Ireland.

109. The underlying tensions of the period were dramatically brought to light in 1984 with the miners' strike, which became a symbolic struggle between the socialist principles of the trade unions and the free market policies of the Conservative government.

110. In point of fact, it was part of the avowed intent of 'synthpop'—whose avant-garde agenda tends to be forgotten—to call into question the very notion of authenticity in art, by way of its 'one hand behind its back' performance and by flaunting its artifice.

111. Žižek, *The Sublime Object of Ideology*.

112. Ibid., pp. 29 and 32.

reaction was required. And this is what I am arguing The Smiths represented. For it was in the midst of this fantasy world of hedonism, glamour, flamboyance and plenty, which was covertly shored up by the cynicism that unmasked it, that The Smiths emitted what Morrissey described as 'a complete cry in every direction.'[113]

GLORYING IN INFIRMITY

Like the boy in the story 'The Emperor's New Clothes,' with a mutinous candour, Morrissey wrote about failure, lack, frailty and 'the bleak realities of ordinariness.'[114] Stan Hawkins recalls the dazzling oddity of his appearance in 1985 alongside the likes of Madonna and Prince—whose aggrandizing names reflect their Hollywood glamour and sexual self-confidence:

> In the same year, dressed in a large, pink blouse with crystal necklace, singing 'Heaven Knows I'm Miserable Now' on BBC's *Top of the Pops,* the misery of the decade—the underside of the consumer boom—was captured by Manchester's favourite son, Steven Morrissey.[115]

In articulating 'the misery of the decade,' Morrissey was at the same time voicing a comprehensive complaint about the state of popular music. Indeed, like Luther nailing his itemized protest to the door of the castle church at Wittenberg, it was as though he was going through a list of the values central to pop music in the 1980s and was turning each of them on its head. What is even more remarkable is that, in a way that parallels Wilde's critique of Victorian culture—whose epigrammatic wit miraculously inverted the most conventional and apparently reasonable values in the manner of a somersault to reveal the perfect sense of their antitheses—some of the most subversive things that Morrissey stood for were in fact some of the most traditional values and ordinary things. This point has been well made by Michael Bracewell:

> Arriving in a pop medium that had been dominated by synthesizers, metropolitan stylishness as pop's ultimate ambition, chic or robotic internationalism and a predominance of narcissistic glamour . . . , Morrissey's first strategic triumph was to reverse all of the current

---

113. This is how he characterized their first single, 'Hand In Glove' (*Jamming!*, May 6, 1984).
114. Morrissey, *New York Dolls.*
115. Hawkins, *Settling the Pop Score*, p. xi.

values of fashionable pop, thus reclaiming realism and the undisguised sincerity of awkward emotions as the province of the three-minute pop song—itself an archaic form. . . . With formidable literary brilliance, Morrissey chose to make a creative virtue of his semi-suburban northern upbringing; this was recast, in his writing, by an epicurean selection of minutely studied and darkly romantic fables from English mythology . . . , whose presence informed the comedy or violence of his language as the socially and emotionally imprisoned aesthete. This was a revolutionary reworking of English pop, strip-mining the half-forgotten icons of Englishness in the face of post-punk alienation as a stylism mask, and re-routeing, though their resonance, the power of the romantic imagination back to the undefended self—gauche, ordinary, lonely, misunderstood or frustrated.[116]

The 'undefended self' is a fine phrase, which suggestively gestures towards the bravery, daring and strength involved in Morrissey's 'art of weakness.' We can get a sense of how revolutionary this was, if we compare some of Morrissey's recurrent concerns with those of our earlier exemplar, Wham!.

At a time when fun was supposed to be what pop stars had—and in having it, provided it—Morrissey sang instead about misery and flaunted his ennui ('I was bored before I even began'). Whilst other pop stars presented fun as readily available—as well as the ultimate value—and a matter of socializing, Morrissey sang about sustained loneliness, a shyness 'that is criminally vulgar' and a congenital sense of not fitting in. (The club that Morrissey sings about in 'How Soon Is Now'—where 'you go, and stand on your own / and you leave on your own / and you go home / and you cry and you want to die'—is the antithesis of Wham!'s 'Club Tropicana.') At a time when hedonism was virtually synonymous with 'rock 'n' roll,' Morrissey—like Bartleby—said he would prefer not to, and contrarily sang about the appeals of chastity ('the hills are alive with celibate cries'). Whilst pop stars in general were boldly asserting themselves and their sexuality, Morrissey wrote about his inadequacies ('I look at yours, you laugh at mine') and his debilitating anxieties ('others conquered love—but I ran'). And at a time when glamour was the dominant feature of the music industry—which fostered a cult of 'health and efficiency'— Morrissey made a song and dance of his ineptitude and gloried in his

---

116. Bracewell, *England Is Mine*, pp. 218–9.

infirmity ('I'm the most inept that ever stepped'; 'I am sick and I am dull and I am plain').[117]

As a lyricist, there were two principal things that Morrissey was doing that were at once 'ordinary' and subversive. The first was that, in the small spaces of popular music, he dared to think about the big things—life, desire, art, God, evil, suffering, the abyss. He refused, that is, to treat popular music as a second-class art form or a kind of aesthetic paddling pool 'designed for crashing bores.'[118] In this way, he revealed the unbounded possibilities it hadn't been using, and reminded us it is a *poetic* space, in which there is room for almost anything.[119] The second, related thing was that at a time when popular music openly filled its lyrical spaces with disposable fantasies of 'fun and sunshine' that one wasn't supposed to take seriously, Morrissey risked embarrassment and spoke candidly about his most urgent and intimate concerns. And in presenting us with 'the pageant of his bleeding heart,' he brought about a revolution.[120]

II

THE GLAMOROUS TURN

However it happened and whatever the continuities between his persona as frontman of The Smiths and as a solo artist, by the time *Your Arsenal* was released in July 1992, Morrissey was 'not a thin swirling creature anymore.'[121] On the front of the album, in a picture taken by Linder Sterling at the Nassau Veterans Memorial Coliseum, Morrissey is depicted live onstage—as the slightly grainy and blurred sepia indicates—with a bulbous-headed microphone suggestively tilted and held at crotch height, with his other hand apparently curled, as if it were holding a similar object, and raised

---

117. Quotations taken from: 'Shoplifters Of The World Unite,' 'How Soon Is Now,' 'These Things Take Time,' 'Miserable Lie,' 'Accept Yourself,' 'These Things Take Time,' 'Accept Yourself.'
118. As Morrissey himself remarked: 'I have to make records that transcend the assumed importance of pop' (*Blitz*, April 1988).
119. This at least is Morrissey's contention. Asked in interview if there were 'certain subject matters where you might belittle it by putting it in a three-minute lyric,' he replied: 'No' (Greater London Radio, 1999; cited in Simpson, *Saint Morrissey*, p. 214).
120. Morrissey evidently thought as much himself: 'Language consists almost entirely of fashionable slang these days, therefore when somebody says something very blunt lyrically it's the height of modern revolution' (*Melody Maker*, November 3, 1984).
121. *Morrissey, interviewed by James Brown*, February 11, 1989.

to his mouth and protruding tongue, as though he were about to lick the lid of a yoghurt carton. His stomach is exposed by his open shirt—its muscularity emphasized by the shadowy light— and occupies the centre of the picture, which draws the eyes to the singer's navel.[122] His face is only visible in profile, but he appears to be on the verge of smiling. Indeed, one might say he seems to be having fun. On the back of the album is a parallel picture, featuring the singer again with his tongue out (though this time he looks as though he were trying to touch his nose) and again with a revealingly open shirt and brandishing the microphone towards an unseen audience. It is instructive to imagine such a figure singing 'I am sick and I am ill and I am plain.'[123]

It may of course be argued that there was something glamorous about Morrissey from the start. He was the dandy of ordinariness, who danced 'stained-glass' postures, and there was a sort of connoisseurship in his very awkwardness. He also had an extraordinary boldness—as a young man doing some of the strangest things, in a business that for all its vaunted permissiveness is in fact deeply conservative and turns an intense and merciless gaze upon its subjects— which was undoubtedly alluring.[124] Additionally, the thin, pale and overwrought Morrissey of the early 1980s had an androgynous Pre-Raphaelite languor and an epicene beauty that was born of his exorbitant fragility. (It is worth noting as well that he is pictured posturing somewhat suggestively with a microphone on the back of The Smiths' debut album, and has *always* had a habit of losing his shirt and putting out his tongue.) It is furthermore true, to anticipate an objection coming in the opposite direction, that Morrissey continued—and continues—to sing about his loneliness, unattractiveness and dysfunction. In 'Seasick, Yet Still Docked,' on *Your Arsenal*, for example, he sings:

> I am a poor freezingly cold soul
> so far from where I intended to go

122. In recognition of its being the centre of attention—and the only *conspicuous* sign of irony— there is a credit on the inner sleeve for the 'stomach scar courtesy of Davyhulme Hospital.'

123. Around this time, Morrissey was also becoming increasingly tough and masculine both in his appearance (during the 'Boxers' tour of 1995, he sported mock scars and slash marks—as if to reverse the signals sent out previously by his National Health glasses and hearing aid) and in his lyrics (which deal with skinheads, hooligans, gang violence and so on).

124. Interviewing the singer in 1983, David Dorrell remarked: 'He is imbued with the same sense of enormity that marks the great men of religion' (*NME*, September 24, 1983).

scavenging through life's very constant lulls
so far from where I'm determined to go.

I wish I knew the way to reach the one I love
there is no way.
I wish I had the charm to attract the one I love
but you see, I've got no charm . . .

and you can tell I have never really loved.

It is therefore apparent, from the intimations of glamour in his early persona and the persistence of a self-image of alienation and ineptitude throughout his solo work, that the difference we are talking about is by no means absolute and is sundered by all sorts of continuities.[125] Nevertheless, whatever qualifications are inserted, there is an unignorable divergence in Morrissey's solo career from the 'gauche' persona he established with The Smiths. Paul Morley alludes to this change as follows in an interview with the singer: 'How did you move from being the village idiot to being the gangleader?'[126] Richard Smith puts the matter rather differently, but confirms the underlying point: 'Morrissey's changed . . . and is now more interested in thuggery than buggery. His stylings are increasingly masculinist, both in terms of his recent band's harder guitar edges . . . and his scrapping of his fey ways in avour of professing a predilection for boxing, skinheads, the Krays, tattoos and Herman Melville.'[127] Another assessment is offered by Cathy Dillon, who described him around this time as: 'Woody Allen's mind in Montgomery Clift's body.'[128] And whilst Morrissey himself sometimes played down the change—insisting that there had always been something tough and physical about The Smiths—and invariably speaks in a flippant way that destabilizes the significance of what he says, his comments could be nonetheless revealing: 'I don't like it when people think of me as a wimpy, poetic, easily-crushed softie. I'm quite the opposite. I'm a

---

125. Recently, things took a further, curiously appropriate turn, when it was reported that a number of fans 'now actually feel rather embarrassed' when Morrissey, at the age of forty-eight, removes his shirt onstage (*Daily Express*, May 30, 2007). Whilst the singer has spoken disparagingly about aged rockers ('The Rolling Stones are an after death experience') and has made fun of his own 'overstaying' ahead of its occurrence in the self-reflexive 'Get Off The Stage,' it would confer a certain symmetry on the dramatized narrative which constitutes his persona, if he were to continue exposing himself *in spite of* any embarrassment it may cause.
126. Morrissey's reply was: 'I started to make records' (*Blitz*, April, 1988).
127. Bret, *Morrissey*, p. 214.
128. Ibid., p. 150.

construction worker!'[129] Whichever way one wants to formulate the matter, it is at this point in Morrissey's career that things start to get rather strange.

HAUNTED BY IRONY

To help explain this 'strangeness,' I want to refer to a somewhat bizarre work of art that made the headlines a few years ago in Britain. The winner of the Turner Prize in 2005 was an artwork called 'Shedboatshed (Mobile Architecture No 2),' by Simon Starling. To all appearances, the work looked exactly like a large common or garden shed. And in fact it had indeed begun its life as such, before being transformed into a boat, and then transformed back into a shed.[130] Not surprisingly, perhaps, the work gained a certain amount of notoriety and excited not a little laughter. Yet it is precisely the apparent lack of significance which caused such amusement that is the central point of the work. That is to say, it is *about* the discrepancy between what appears and what a thing 'means' or signifies (which invisibly exceeds and spectrally inhabits its appearance). Hence the extremely long 'narrative' subtitles that Starling's works frequently have, which provide us with a kind of condensed physical, historical and cultural 'biography' of the artefact.[131] In this way, the title at once reveals something essential about the object and that something's lack of signification. As Paul Shepheard has remarked, 'The thing we're looking at isn't the whole work.'[132] Its 'meaning'—or the history of what it is—lies in a sense elsewhere, and yet it is at the same time essential to it. The central point of interest, then, in 'Shedboatshed'—and what makes it genuinely funny—is that, once we know its history, something of the object's 'having-been-a-boat-ness' survives without material evidence and complicates the

129. Bret, *Morrissey*, p. 191. On other occasions, his sense of the change was much more categorical. When asked in 2001 how he would feel if he met the Morrissey of 1983, he replied: 'I've no wish to meet that person. I'd be down the fire-escape before you could sound the alarm bells' (*Mojo*, April 2001).

130. The construction was found in Schweizerhalle, on the banks of the Rhine, taken to pieces, and part of it used—as a 'Weidling' (a local type of boat)—to carry the rest of itself ten kilometres down the river to Basel, where it was reconstructed and exhibited as a shed in the Museum für Gegenwartskunst.

131. The wooden chair entitled 'H.C./H.G.W., 1999,' for example, exhibited in Leipzig at the Galarie für zeitgenossische Kunst, carries the snappy subtitle: 'A replica of a "Swan Chair" designed in England in 1885 by Charles Francis Ainsley Voysey, built using the wood from an oak tree from the grounds of the Villa at 11 Karl-Tauchintz-Strasse, Leipzig, designed in 1892 by Bruno Eelbo and Karl Wichardt for the geologist Herman Credner.'

132. Tate Britain, Simon Starling audio transcript.

meaning of its subsequent 'shed-ness.' In other words, here we have an object that somehow exceeds or differs from itself—without any apparent manifestation of that difference or excess.[133] There is plainly something quite mad about this. It 'is,' evidently, simply a shed. And yet the kind of claim that the work is making is something that in an everyday context we take for granted and seems even banal; namely, that the actions of people whose histories we know have more significance for us—in the sense of 'having' or communicating more meaning (I use quotation marks around 'have,' since the location or 'possession' of meaning is precisely what is at issue). Knowing things about a person—what they have done and been, how they came to be what they are and so on—reveals something about that person which isn't 'added' to them after we know, but which previous to knowing wasn't exactly present either. This meaning (or history of what they are) has a ghostly status—which is to say, it can produce effects without having any apparent existence.

It should be obvious by now that the ghostly effects of Starling's 'Shedboatshed' correspond to what was said earlier about 'Morrissey' being a spectral entity or dramatized projection, which his lyrics and public performances engender, and from which they reciprocally take their meaning. It should also be emerging to view how a consideration of this spectral persona is crucial to an understanding of his art and can help us understand why, for example, the climactic refrain of 'Dear God Please Help Me' is so compelling in spite of its relative diegetic thinness and so moving in spite of its apparently positive cast. This is because the song carries with it a Starlingesque subtitle—which is the career-long dramatized narrative of Morrissey's personality—to whose story it adds another twist and another note, which recalls and resonates with all that preceded it, and causes the whole emerging symphony to be altered and replayed in the light of its alteration.

The invisible narrative personality that haunts Morrissey's work can function in a more antagonistic way. This is because its 'doubling' of what is signified has the structure of irony.[134] It can therefore signal a detachment from—as well as reinforce—a gesture. If we

---

133. In this respect, 'Shedboatshed' is an aesthetic staging of the Ship of Theseus paradox.

134. Romantic irony—which is an attitude towards existence rather than a rhetorical device—refers to the act of a thing signalling that it is other than it is. This is thought's way, according to Schlegel et al., of attempting to hold onto becoming or the vitality of creative emergence and thereby outwit the falsifying inertia of objectification. In signalling a lack of integrity, it is therefore paradoxically trying to be true to itself and its creative character or 'essential' transience, revealing itself as a process rather than a product (see Claire Colebrook, *Irony*, pp. 47–71).

recall the cover of *Your Arsenal*, for example, it is on the one hand ludicrously suggestive (dogs that pass on the street are less overt); and yet, on the other hand, it crucially differs from the fruity microphone posturing of, say, Mick Jagger. Why is this? I would suggest it is because Morrissey's gesture has within it a surplus fold of irony or self-consciousness—equivalent to a wink or the raising of an eyebrow—which means that without any manifestation of this excess, he is able to signal a detachment from or critical attitude towards an action he is simultaneously performing.[135] This fold of all but invisible irony results from the haunting interplay of the singer's persona (which is why he so often looks arch or wry or on the verge of smiling when doing 'pop-star' things). This is partly an indelible memory of his dramatized history and his 'having-been-otherwise'—which inheres as 'a living sign' within his subsequent self—and partly something which persists in a stronger sense, since what he 'was' hasn't been left behind.[136] As he sings in 'Life Is A Pigsty' (after he has publicly—if rather enigmatically—revealed he has had sexual relations):

> It's the same old SOS
> But with brand new broken fortunes
> I'm the same underneath
> But this you . . . *you surely knew?*

So, to refer back to Paul Morley's comment, it is not simply a matter of moving from 'village idiot' to 'gang leader,' which would certainly be remarkable enough. What we see in Morrissey's persona in his later solo work is a strange persistence of what he 'was' *alongside of his divergence from it*. And each of these aspects of his later persona is capable of placing quotation marks around the other. In this way, Morrissey is able, without visible sign, to be more than he 'is,' to do more than he's doing, and say more than he's saying. This similarly explains why his individual lyrics are in a sense crucially 'self-transcending,' in that they participate in and contribute to something outside themselves—namely, the ghostly narrative personality of 'Morrissey.'

---

135. In the following chapter, such ironic self-alienation is considered in relation to camp.
136. When asked in interview about his suggestive posturing, Morrissey responded as follows:

> *David Keeps*: You've got your tongue out all over the cover of your new album. Any reason?
> *Morrissey*: If you're asking me if I'm trying to pass in a darkened room as a sex symbol, the answer is definitely no. I'm not trying to excite anybody in Illinois, if that's your question.
> *Keeps*: But you do. What about those people who jump onstage and kiss you?
> *Morrissey*: That's more romantic than sexual. I think it is love, not rock stardom.

(*Details*, December 1992).

THE ASHES OF POP MUSIC

Morrissey's iconic gauche persona had a much wider and 'unsettling' significance within popular music more generally. Indeed, at a stroke, it made the excesses of 1980s pop seem like the punchline to a joke that had been told whilst its back was turned. And as Nietzsche points out, 'He who wants to kill most thoroughly—*laughs*.'[137] There were of course all kinds of 'alternative' bands in post punk pop that had it in for mainstream music. However, as Michael Bracewell observes, 'It would require a Samson—in the shape of Morrissey—to bring down the pillars of pop complacency.'[138] It is no wonder, then, it has become something of a commonplace to refer to Morrissey as 'the last pop star' and to speak about the 'death' of popular music.[139] The singer has himself commented on the latter: 'Popular music is slowly being laid to rest in every conceivable way. . . . The ashes are already about us, if we could but notice them.'[140] But what does it mean to describe Morrissey as 'the last pop star'? And what comes after the 'death' of popular music, since in characteristic postmodern fashion it continues to arrive?

Simon Napier-Bell has written an entertaining book about British popular music, which traces its history from the emergence of rock 'n' roll in the 1950s to the vogue for 'ready-made' bands in the 1990s. Its irresistible, anecdotally woven thesis—as the title *Black Vinyl White Powder* suggests—is that 'drugs and drug culture [have] been absolutely central to the development of the British music business.'[141] Thus, the music of the 1960s was inspired by LSD, glam rock was in some sense the product of cocaine, and punk the product of speed, etc.[142] Having managed, amongst others, The Yardbirds, Marc Bolan, Japan and Wham!, Napier-Bell is very well qualified to comment on such things and, given his decision 'to focus on the most visible trends in each decade,'[143] it's hard to quarrel

---

137. Nietzsche, *Thus Spoke Zarathustra*, p. 324.
138. Bracewell, *England Is Mine*, p. 129.
139. See Rogan, *Morrissey and Marr*, p. 18; Bracewell, *England Is Mine*, p. 226; and Mark Simpson 'The Man Who Murdered Pop' (*The Guardian*, November 5, 1999).
140. *Spin*, June 1988.
141. Napier-Bell, *Black Vinyl White Powder*, p. x.
142. Pop music is of course conventionally associated with transgression and excess (whence the hedonistic trinity of sex and drugs and rock 'n' roll). However, most commentators prefer to characterize it more generally as a countercultural phenomenon. As Nabeel Zuberi, for example, recounts the story, rock music—the progenitor of pop—was a 'generational rebellion' that was born in the 1950s and became in the 1960s 'a constellation of sociopolitical values in opposition to a perceived mainstream or dominant society.' And whilst its oppositional character waned in the decades after punk, its essence for Zuberi remains 'the negation of the everyday' (Zuberi, *Sounds English*, p. 69).
143. Napier-Bell, *Black Vinyl White Powder*, p. ix.

with the story he tells. Until we get to the 1980s, that is—and the juncture between 'Dollars and Decadence,' at the end of part two, and 'Renaissance,' at the start of part three. At this point, he claims:

> If the early sixties were ancient Greece—the first great flowering of rock culture, then the early seventies were like the Roman Empire—initially confident and brash but descending into total degeneracy as rock's superstars left for America to exchange their talent for dollars and decadence. . . .
>
> In December 1980, exactly ten years after the Beatles had dissolved their partnership, a degenerate decade of rock was brought to an end with the assassination of John Lennon. . . .
>
> The age of rock was over.
> It was time for the Renaissance.[144]

For Napier-Bell, the 'Renaissance' came in the form of the New Romantics—and most especially Wham!—who ushered in an era he characterizes as 'glamorous and hedonistic.'[145]

From the point of view of record company executives (and their artists' managers), this was undoubtedly a kind of 'Renaissance.' What Napier-Bell sweeps under the carpet, however, is the counternarrative that emerged at the same time in the early 1980s, which *also* saw rock as a degenerate, unwitting parody of itself, but which was opposed to the New Romantics *too*, as the same dog with different fleas, and which represented an even more radical rejection of the cliché that popular music had become (and in doing so offered hope of a *real* renaissance in popular music). This counternarrative was most clearly embodied in Morrissey's 'anti-pop-star' persona, and more widely reflected in the 'indie' movement.[146]

---

144. Napier-Bell, *Black Vinyl White Powder*, pp. 246–7.
145. Ibid., p. 255. Napier-Bell celebrates an escapism based on consumerism, which he suggests links the politics of Thatcherism and the aesthetics of New Pop: 'When Margaret Thatcher had become Prime Minister, she'd promised we would "escape from the drab seventies and enter a vibrant new decade." Prince Charles and Diana were the first to set the escapist tone with a Hollywood-style romance and a royal wedding. Then the walkman came on the market, allowing people to escape their surroundings even while remaining within them. But the greatest escapism was the music of the New Romantics. All of a sudden, almost out of nowhere, there were young, colourful, fashion-conscious pop groups, promoted with videos as glossy as TV commercials—Visage, Ultravox, the Human League, ABC, Soft Cell, the Thompson Twins, the Eurythmics, Culture Club, Tears For Fears, Kajagoogoo, Heaven 17, Spandau Ballet, and Duran Duran' (ibid., pp. 255–6).
146. Aside from a short chapter on 'Pop and Politics,' which touches briefly on postpunk 'alternative' music, the indie revolution of the 1980s is written out of Napier-Bell's history of pop. Unfortunately, this isn't quite covered by his disclaimer about focussing on 'the most visible trends in each decade,' since he acknowledges that 'the charts were filled with dull groups like Fairground

Morrissey's early gauche persona—which as we have seen involved an unlikely combination of ordinariness, ineptitude and an extravagant asceticism—was thus manifestly a mirror-image of the conventional pop star (and Napier-Bell's history of popular music reveals just how far-reaching and well-targeted Morrissey's critique was, even as it leaves his work out of account). What was so extraordinary, then, about Morrissey's emergence as a pop star in the 1980s was that it at once represented a continuation and a radical *subversion* of the traditional values of popular music. For with a wit that sees around corners, he revealed that the conventional spectacle of 'sex and drugs and rock 'n' roll' had become a kind of pantomime horse, and that in such a situation ordinariness, ineptitude and monastic virtues were paradoxically transgressive.[147] Morrissey has emphasized this point himself:

> When I started to make records, I thought, well, rather than adopt the usual poses I should just be as natural as I possibly could, which of course wasn't very natural at all. For me to be making records at all was entirely unnatural, so really that was the only way I could be. Unnatural. Which in a sense was my form of rebellion, because rebellion in itself had become quite traditional, certainly after punk.[148]

What we can see in Morrissey's early persona is not only the inversion and parody of the conventional pop star but also, in its antithetical realization, its deconstruction; for a caricature of that against which popular celebrity had been relationally defined became a *source* of popular celebrity. Hence, in his renunciation of transgression (which was singularly transgressive) and in carrying ordinariness over into a glamorous realm (which made the ordinary seem glamorous and the glamorous seem ordinary), he effected a transvaluation of the very terms. And suddenly transgression looked like a kind of conformity. (It's no surprise that The Smiths and *This Is Spinal Tap* emerged

---

Attraction, Aztec Camera, The Christians, Everything But The Girl,' etc. (ibid., p. 326). For an alternative assessment of what came after the 'Dollars and Decadence' of the 1970s,' see Joe S. Harrington's *Sonic Cool: The Life and Death of Rock 'n' Roll,* in which he argues that 'rock had reached the crossroads where popularity and creativity would separate' and that 'anyone doing *anything* creative in the name of Rock 'n' Roll existed within . . . the underground, because mainstream Rock had become just another wing of the entertainment industry' (Harrington, *Sonic Cool,* pp. 322 and 333).

147. As Simon Reynolds observes, 'Faced with the infinite accommodation of consumer capitalism, the radical response is to abstain, to cling stubbornly to the will to misfit' (*Bring the Noise,* p. 18).

148. *Blitz,* April 1988.

around the same time in the early 1980s.) In this way, the apparently stable opposition between deviance and normality, the glamorous and the ordinary—which had been furtively upheld by the ostensibly subversive practices of pop stardom—was audaciously dismantled. Morrissey, in this sense, is a 'deconstructive' pop star.[149]

Deconstruction, we should note, is not destruction—which is why things 'live on,' in a spectral fashion, in spite of the unhinging of their foundational logic—but a seismic disturbance which reveals an instability or 'anarchy' that was always already in play. In this particular case, it reveals that the values and concepts that structure the discourse of popular music are differentially constituted and have no stable foundation or essential meaning (transgression is defined against that which is 'normal,' the glamorous is opposed to the 'ordinary,' etc.). Deconstruction therefore renders apparent the invisible quotation marks around its pivotal evaluative terms and thereby disturbs the meaningfulness of the system as such. This doesn't mean that transgression is no longer possible, but that it's etiolated into 'transgression'—which is to say, a karaoke quotation of itself (witness the corniness of the antics of Oasis—whose music was an openly 'doing it again'—or the Widow Twankey transgressions of Donny Tourette). In this sense, Morrissey's deconstruction of the pop-star persona marks the completion of its coherent trajectory, and condemns—or liberates—those that follow to a world of parody or unwitting pastiche. *Après lui le deluge . . .*

THE GAIETY OF LANGUAGE

What makes things even odder—odder than the continuation of something after its 'death'—is that Morrissey himself emerges and continues his pop-star career on the other side of his deconstruction of popular celebrity. He is therefore 'the last pop star' but also (and because) he is the paradigmatic *postmodern* pop star. Looking at things in this light helps us to make sense of the singer's subsequent

---

149. Morrissey only receives a passing mention in Napier-Bell's history of British popular music (which is largely confined to the singer's views on Margaret Thatcher, his comments on Live Aid and Henry Rollins' dislike of him). In one sense of course, this isn't an oversight, given the book's focus on the relationship between drug culture and popular music. But in another more important sense it is, for what Napier-Bell fails to see is that Morrissey's refusal of the pantomime excesses of the pop-star world was one of the most well-timed and well-told jokes in popular music—at the expense of the very mores with which Napier-Bell is concerned—and is *itself* a move within that tradition.

'pop star' behaviour and its curious 'yes' and 'no' character. For what is opened up by deconstruction's prising apart of signifier and signified is a realm of spectrality, pastiche and play. This is because if words (signs, gestures, etc.) are seen as ciphers with no *intrinsic* meaning—as their ability to mean differently in different contexts makes clear—they gain a certain lightness and engender a new freedom.[150] We have seen something of this gay—that is, *fröhlich*— playing with signifiers in Morrissey's quotational gestures (such as his pelvic gyration), which speak of themselves as a sign of a sign; in his putting on and off of identities in the adoption of a 'borrowed voice' (his camp falsetto); and at a textual level in his habit of travestying his own lyrics, which calls into question any commitment to meaning. Perhaps the clearest illustration, though, of such playing with signifiers occurs in 'Sheila Take A Bow,' where Morrissey sings:

> Take my hand and off we stride
> La la la la la la la la
> You're a girl and I'm a boy
> La la la la la la la la
> Take my hand and off we stride
> La la la la la la la la
> I'm a girl and you're a boy
> La la la la la la la la.

There is of course a coyly transgressive identification with feminine subjectivity in these lines, which gives the switch from 'boy' to 'girl' its lovely gentle *frisson*. Yet the lines even more subversively advertise a levity with respect to meaning—as though the singer interrupted the narrative in order to show us his juggling of words. There is likewise a sort of capricious 'etc.' in Morrissey's 'la la la,' which with a wonderfully playful defiance underlines the subversive teasing away of words, even as apparently fixed in their reference as 'girl' and 'boy,' from any stable meaning. (The song's playing with signifiers is additionally foregrounded by the music, which is a conspicuous generic glam-rock pastiche, and by the cover, which featured an image of the transsexual Candy Darling.[151])

---

150. The title of this section is taken from Wallace Stevens' 'Esthétique du Mal': 'Natives of poverty, children of malheur, / The gaiety of language is our seigneur' XI, 10–11 (Stevens, *Collected Poems*, p. 322).

151. 'To be able to inflict Candy Darling on the record buying public was a perfect example of my very dangerous sense of humour' (Morrissey, *NME*, February 25, 1989).

We have arrived, then, it seems, at the far side of Morrissey's art—which is ironic, self-conscious and radically unstable; which ventriloquizes its meaning, delights in the play of signification, and opens the curtains to reveal its own workings—all of which seems to be a long way away from the melancholy, candour and heartfelt urgency for which he became famous. This is useful, in that it guards against a lingering tendency to caricature the singer after the manner of his early persona. But the drawback is that it gives the impression we have arrived at some sort of endpoint and implies a development of successive stages, which is not the case. For whilst this chapter has told a linear story—tracing the trajectory from Morrissey's early gauche persona to the 'glamorous turn' of his solo career—which corresponds to something that holds in reality, it is also true, and important to bear in mind, that there was *always* something playful and arch about Morrissey, and he *still* reaches towards us with heartfelt urgency and 'out-stretched voice.'[152] This is because there is something essentially multiple and mobile about Morrissey; something teasingly elusive; something that is intimately present, disclosed and disturbing, and yet at the same time fugitive, withheld and calling from afar—qualities of course one expects from a ghost.

---

152. Behn, 'A Paraphrase on Oenone to Paris,' 1. 217, *The Works of Aphra Behn*, p.17.

CHAPTER 2

The Oxymoronic Self

Irish blood, English heart
this I'm made of.

—*Irish Blood, English Heart*

TEN PARTS CRUMLIN, TEN PARTS OLD TRAFFORD

'Ireland,' according to George Bernard Shaw, 'is of all countries the most foreign to England.'[1] One feature of this 'foreignness' in particular stands out for Shaw: 'To the Irishman,' he tells us, 'there is nothing in the world quite so exquisitely comic as an Englishman's seriousness.' Shaw's comments occur in his review of the first production of Wilde's *An Ideal Husband* (1895), whose most distinctive and subversive quality is its 'subtle and pervasive levity.' Wilde 'plays with everything,' he explains, 'with wit, with philosophy, with drama, with actors and audience, with the whole theatre. Such a feat scandalizes the Englishman.'[2] What happens, however, if this foreignness constitutes part of the self?

Wilde, like Shaw, was Anglo-Irish, and thus 'a kind of internal exile in one's homeland'[3] or, in Shaw's terms, a foreigner to himself. Jerusha McCormack speaks of Wilde's self-estrangement as follows: 'Born into an oxymoron, and doomed to live out his life as paradox, Wilde became adept at living on both sides of the hyphen.'[4] For Terry Eagleton, this 'doubleness' or 'oxymoronic' self-differing was a defining feature of Wilde's life, which informs his paradoxical and subversive art:

1. Shaw, *Our Theatres in the Nineties*, pp. 9–10.
2. Ibid.
3. Eagleton, introduction, *Oscar Wilde*, p. viii.
4. McCormack, *Wilde the Irishman*, p. 1.

He [Wilde] was deeply contradictory. If he was the flamboyantly decadent dandy who took fashionable London by storm, he was also the bankrupt, reviled, ulcerated inmate of Reading gaol. . . . Wilde hailed from the city which his literary compatriot James Joyce spelt as 'Doublin,' and everything about him was doubled, hybrid, ambivalent. He was socialite and sodomite, upper-class and underdog, a Victorian *paterfamilias* who consorted with rent boys, a shameless *bon viveur* who laid claim to the title of socialist. . . . As a celebrity who was secretly homosexual, Wilde lived out a conflict between his public identity and his private self; and the fissure between the two is interestingly typical of his age. . . . For him, however, there were reasons rather closer to home for this disturbingly dual selfhood. If he was 'doubled' in his sexuality, as both husband and homosexual lover, he was equally Janus-faced in his nationality. Wilde was born into an Anglo-Irish family in mid-Victorian Dublin, and the tension between England and Ireland is there in his very name.[5]

Throughout his career, Morrissey has advertised his devotion to Wilde, and in recent years he has foregrounded his own Anglo-Irish descent, singing of his 'Irish blood' and 'English heart' and describing himself as 'ten parts Crumlin, ten parts Old Trafford'[6] (though whereas in Wilde's case, to be Anglo-Irish is to be a descendent of English Protestant immigrants in Ireland, in Morrissey's case, it is to be a descendent of Irish Catholic immigrants in England).[7] It is therefore perhaps no surprise to discover that a sense of exile or nonbelonging is a recurrent subject in Morrissey's lyrics, and that the singer's persona is similarly composed of an 'oxymoronic' conjunction of antitheses.

As we have seen, Morrissey is glamorous and gauche, a pop star and an anti–pop star, an outspoken celebrity and a reclusive introvert, an aesthete and an icon of ordinariness. We have also noted the flamboyant androgyny of his early appearance and the 'third space' of his camp falsetto as well as his notorious eroticized celibacy—which dissolves the boundaries between homo- and heterosexuality and opens a space which is at once asexual and flooded with sexuality. His lyrics are likewise distinguished on the one hand by their irony and artifice,

5. Eagleton, *Oscar Wilde*, pp. vii–viii.
6. *Who Put the 'M' in Manchester*, DVD (Sanctuary Records, 2005).
7. Wilde was in fact baptized twice, first as a Protestant and then as a Catholic (see Ellman, *Oscar Wilde*, pp.18–19).

and on the other by their melancholy and candour (an antithesis which, as we shall see, is further compounded by the coincidence of intimacy and distance). And, finally, at a musical level, it was observed that the singer seems to have a predilection for 'hermaphroditic' harmonic structures, which conjoin major and minor modes.[8] In this chapter, I want to focus on two versions of the 'oxymoronic' logic that is emerging to view: one is 'mobility' or an oscillation between what are customarily seen as alternatives, and the other is 'multiplicity' or a simultaneity of contraries—the foremost manifestation of which is the 'Anglo-Irish' conjunction of seriousness and levity.

I

MOBILITY

Morrissey's career has been marked by an overarching vagrancy, whose principal coordinates are Manchester, London, Los Angeles and Rome. His lyrics, too, are full of departures, desertions and valedictions and continually recur to a sense of being an alien at home and 'a traveller to the grave.'[9] This pattern is also discernible in his 'homeless voice,' which figures a metrical and melodic 'wandering.' There is another kind of mobility though, which is less apparent but just as pervasive. Consider, for example, the following comment made by Morrissey in an interview with Stuart Maconie in response to an innocuous question about football:

> In a sense I am delicate but in another sense I'm not and I've never been anxious to be seen as Kenneth Williams' apprentice. Although that was daubed on my back door in heavy paint, which I didn't like at all. . . . So, yes, I played football a few weeks ago on Sunday morning and I scored four goals. I should add the game was against Brondesbury Park ladies.[10]

---

8. According to Richard Carman, there is a further tonal 'androgyny' to which the music contributes and which was an essential characteristic of The Smiths; he writes: 'The dichotomy between the mournfulness of Morrissey's vocal and the optimism of the electric guitar, between the jolly strumming and the minor key is perfect Smiths, the ability to maintain two or more concepts at one moment within the same song' (Carman, *Johnny Marr*, p. 76). Whilst the fullness of Marr's extraordinary textural and melodic complexity isn't quite brought out in 'jolly strumming,' there is nevertheless something in Carmen's point.

9. 'How Can Anybody Possibly Know How I Feel.'

10. *Q*, April 1994.

Here, in the space of a few lines on a chance topic of conversation, we have a yes 'I am,' a no 'I'm not' and a playful piece of evidence for the latter which turns into an argument in favour of the former. This kind of 'oxymoronic' mobility—a light-footed tendency to turn on himself, and then turn on this turning, and in doing so inhabit without being exclusively identified with a variety of divergent positions—is typical of Morrissey and a salient feature of his brilliant conversational acrobatics, which leave so many of his questioners' attempts to pin him down looking like a series of cartoon missed catches. This mobility is a characteristic feature of his lyrics as well.

NEITHER HERE NOR THERE

Take, for example, 'You're Gonna Need Someone On Your Side,' the opening song on *Your Arsenal*—an album that conspicuously renounces the lightness of *Kill Uncle*, with lyrics about hooligans and the National Front, and Mick Ronson's dirty glam-rock production. The song begins in a rather menacing way, with clouds of distorted feedback and prominent bass (whose bending of notes into in-between spaces constitutes a kind of tonal mobility) and with Morrissey seeming to threaten violence, singing 'Someone kindly told me you'd wasted / eight of your nine lives,' and repeating 'You're gonna need someone on your side.' Yet, after a couple of verses, this apparent threat turns into an offer of support ('And here I am'), which is then overthrown by a music-hall rejoinder to the addressee's implied response ('well, you don't need to look so pleased') that comically recasts the singer in the more familiar role of the fumbler or maladroit. We find an even more disturbing and destabilizing mobility, to take a second example, in 'Certain People I Know,' on the same album. In this case, the song appears to begin innocently enough with the singer asserting 'I take the cue from certain people I know,' accompanied by a sparse 'Ride A White Swan' pastiche,[11] which has a boy scout cheeriness and holds its smile for the duration of the song. There is a sinister turn in the second line, however, which reveals what sort of 'cue' is meant and, given the character of these people he knows, implies an unexpected act of violence, of which the rest of the song seems unaware ('I use the cue and then I hand it

---

11. In a note to Boz Boorer, reproduced in *Peepholism*, Morrissey refers to the song as 'Certain White Swans I Know' (Slee, *Peepholism*).

on to you'). At this point, the song evinces an oxymoronic tonality, engendered by the dissonance between what is described and the manner of its description, comparable in its light-hearted treatment of extreme brutality to the balletic assault in *A Clockwork Orange*.[12] This sinister turn, which is enabled by a play on words, is then itself undermined by a further play on words ('And when I swing it / So it catches his eye'), which bizarrely holds together the image of a camp sexual swinging and a slapstick snooker accident, involving a highly ambiguous 'it.' (In the midst of its capricious twists and turns, the song appears to comment obliquely on its own frivolity—asking, ostensibly of its subjects' dress-sense, 'don't you find this absurd?') The song has a further turn up its sleeve, though, as the singer's pride in the company he keeps evolves into detachment and disapproval ('they'd sacrifice all their principles / for anything cashable / I do believe that's terrible'). The song then pulls a comic face and concludes with the delightful singing of plumy chortling—like an impersonation of an impersonation of Groucho Marx—which with a shrug of whimsy turns its back on all the song's prior turnings.

In both of these examples we can see the singer inhabiting and relinquishing a range of often conflicting positions—sometimes abruptly revealing himself in a place other than where you think he is, and on other occasions sidling incrementally between positions by playing with words.[13] This mobility—which in the second case gives rise to a generic heterogeneity, fusing cartoon brutality and whimsy with more conventionally realist modes—is of course simply entertaining. But it also crucially complicates by fundamentally destabilizing the songs' meaning. Why is this so crucial?

COMPOSITE VOICES

In between 'You're Gonna Need Someone On Your Side' and 'Certain People I Know' are two songs which got Morrissey into a

---

12. In its fusion of the nightmarish and the everyday, and its collapsing the conventional distinction between 'what is serious or trivial, horrible or ludicrous, tragic or comic,' the song may be seen as a miniature instance of magic realism (Abrams, *A Glossary of Literary Terms*, p. 122).

13. Morrissey has a related habit of using the conjunction 'or' as a way of introducing an alternative possibility which undermines the antecedent statement with which it is coordinated. In 'He Knows I'd Love To See Him,' for example, he sings: 'He knows (he knows) / or, I *think* he does' (and ends the song asserting 'he really doesn't know'); and in 'Friday Mourning' he claims, 'I will never stand naked / in front of you / or if I do / it won't be for a long time.' The ironic 'urr' in 'Sweet And Tender Hooligan' serves a similar purpose: 'he'll never, never do it again / urr—not until the next time.'

lot of trouble: 'We'll Let You Know' and 'The National Front Disco.' The former is 'about' football hooliganism and its particular brand of nationalism; the latter, as its title suggests, is 'about' a member of the National Front. I say 'about' because in both cases the singer adopts the viewpoint of his subject, without entirely letting go of an external perspective, and so seems to speak from within as well as reflect from without upon his disturbing subjects. The nature of this disturbance is the apparently racist views they espouse (the culminating refrain of the former is 'we are the last truly British people you will ever know'; the troublesome burden of the latter is 'England for the English'), which the singer was accused of endorsing. Now it should be said at the outset that there is no question that Morrissey is interested—to the point of fascination—in violence, crime and, to use an old-fashioned word, evil (witness his songs about the Moors murders, the Krays, gang violence and parricide), so it is no surprise that the violence of racism and football hooliganism attracted his attention as well. We might even go a little further, and accept that the singer *intends* to disturb us and, even more riskily, describes from within the *appeal* of such things.[14] Nevertheless, this is not the same as endorsing them. The first important thing to note, which would seem plain enough, is that the singer speaks in both songs as a *character*. (This has been reinforced by Morrissey in interview: 'The phrase "England for the English" is in quotes, so those who call the song racist are not listening.'[15]) Now, whilst this manifestly distances the singer from the views he is singing, it might be countered that even if he is other than the character whose position he adopts for the duration of the song, he is nonetheless presenting their views in such a way as to make them seem appealing—which, it might be argued, is tantamount to endorsement. It is at this juncture that we can see why it is crucial to take into account the kind of mobility with which I am concerned. In both songs—'We'll Let You Know' and 'National Front Disco'—the singer does not adopt his subject's perspective without remainder. Crucially, he also steps outside and introduces an exterior perspective *into* his character's position, which ironizes—in signalling an alternative stance towards—the views he is ostensibly

---

14. As Armond White notes, Morrissey 'risks the anger of people who want to pretend that the kids are always all right or that fascism has no attraction' ('Anglocentric: Morrissey' in *Village Voice*, September 1, 1992, p. 70).
15. Cited in 'The Light That Never Goes Out,' *The Guardian*, February 23, 2002.

espousing. In 'We'll Let You Know,' for example, it is surely hard to overlook the irony or 'exterior' perspective which laces the hooligan's utterances ('how sad are we? / and how sad have we been? / We'll let you know . . . Oh, but only if—you're really interested'). The same is true of its glancing self-reflexivity ('and the songs we sing / they're not supposed to mean a thing'), which interrupts identification by drawing attention to its fictionality.[16] Hence, in daring to take seriously the appeal of such views—which in so far as they attract adherents they must presumably possess—he reveals them to be ridiculous as well. (For this reason, it may be helpful to view Morrissey's character songs as dramatic monologues, comparable in kind to the first-person poetic utterances of Robert Browning's psychopathic speakers, which in a similarly disturbing way invite sympathy as well as judgement.[17]) This kind of mobility, which is a salient feature of Morrissey's writing, and which allows him to step outside of, renounce, or ironize from within, another's perspective, should also prevent us from attributing any of these positions to Morrissey.

The aim of this digression, it should be made clear, is not to try and make out that Morrissey is in fact a PC liberal humanist and the sort of writer that the bourgeoisie can safely like. On the contrary, Morrissey is, I believe, the greatest disturbance popular music has ever known, who has an instinctive sympathy for the marginalized or excluded (however unpalatable these may be) and a suspicion of all that seeks to establish itself as 'normal' (however worthy such things may appear), and whose favoured sport, like the decadents before him, is *épater le bourgeois*.

CHANGING PLACES

The foregoing discussion of 'We'll Let You Know' and 'The National Front Disco' has carried us towards a second kind of mobility, distinct from the more 'monadic' mobility identified in 'You're Gonna

---

16. 'The National Front Disco' is arguably even more blatant in its ironic distancing. Whilst Morrissey could use the word 'disco' in the 1980s with relative neutrality, as he does in 'Panic,' by the 1990s—when *Your Arsenal* was released—after the revolution of Acid House and Rave Culture, the word was becoming as quaint as the thing, and had come to signify an event at the village hall attended by readers of Enid Blyton. Even more obviously, the juvenile protagonist whose views are at issue is presented from the perspective of his hand-wringing mother and friends—who constantly refer to him as 'our boy' or 'my boy'—thus reinforcing the *Beano*-esque character of the events described and placing the singer at a further remove from the adolescent views he holds up for inspection.

17. These issues are discussed further in chapter 4.

Need Someone On Your Side' and 'Certain People I Know,' where
the movement was a turning of, or within, an individual speaker. To
illustrate this other, more 'dialectal' form of mobility, I wish to go
back to The Smiths' fourth album, *The Queen Is Dead,* and the song
'Cemetry Gates,' the middle section of which runs as follows:

> You say: 'ere thrice the sun done salutation to the dawn'
> and you claim these words as your own
> but I'm well-read, and I've heard them said
> a hundred times (maybe less, maybe more)
> if you must write prose or poems
> the words you use should be your own
> don't plagiarise or take 'on loan'
> there's always someone, somewhere
> with a big nose, who knows
> and who trips you up and laughs when you fall.

The passage begins with an apparently straightforward state of affairs
and a clear and stable opposition between an 'I' and a 'you.' The
latter is a writer who claims to have authored a piece of quoted text
'ere thrice the sun done salutation to the dawn,' which the 'well-read'
former has discovered to be an act of plagiarism,[18] which prompts the
'I' to challenge the 'you' and censure the act of plagiarism as such. But
in the course of this censure, there is a movement of sympathy and a
shifting of positions, as the 'I'—who seems to be a writer as well—
starts to sound more like the party being criticized, and the use of 'you'
in the later section appears to include quite a lot of the speaking 'I':
'there's always someone, somewhere / with a big nose, who knows /
and who trips you up and laughs when you fall.' By the end of the passage, then, it seems that we are being encouraged by the speaking 'I' to
sympathize with the victim of precisely what the 'I' was itself doing at
the outset. So in the space of a few short lines, the speaking 'I' appears
somehow to have crossed over from the position of antagonist into the
position of the victim or injured party. Whilst this chiastic shifting of
sympathy in one sense resembles the mobility we observed in 'You're
Gonna Need Someone On Your Side,' it is achieved by a more radical
'interpersonal' mobility, which sunders the opposition between the 'I'
and the 'you.' Let us consider another example.

---

18. The line is taken from *Richard III*: 'The early village cock / Hath twice done salutation to the
morn' (V, 3, 229–30).

On *Southpaw Grammar*, Morrissey's fifth solo album (excluding compilations and live albums), the singer returns to the subject of authorship and addresses another kind of criticism. Here is the first verse of 'Reader Meet Author':

> You don't know a thing about their lives
> they live where you wouldn't dare to drive
> you shake as you think of how they sleep
> but you write as if you all lie side by side.

Once again, the song appears to begin with a straightforward criticism of a given set of circumstances, and once again the speaker and addressee seem to be clearly on different sides of a fence—the latter being criticized precisely for a separation from the subject of which he writes. In this case, though, the speaker adopts a more omniscient perspective, as indicated by the absence of an explicit authorial or speaking 'I,' and narrates the relationship between a 'you' and a 'they,' in which he is apparently uninvolved. But something rather odd occurs when we arrive at the chorus and the singer resorts to direct speech in narrating the author's defence:

> Reader, meet author
> with the hope of hearing sense
> but you may be feeling let down
> by the words of defence
> he says: 'No-one ever sees me when I cry.'

Partly perhaps as an inevitable result of the lack of any other 'I' and partly too because this is exactly the sort of thing we have become accustomed to hearing Morrissey sing of his own circumstances, there appears to be an irresistible slide of Morrissey's persona over into the perspective being criticized by the speaker. This sense of a momentary shift in sympathies is reinforced when we bear in mind that the singer was himself publicly criticized for writing from the apparently removed perspective of popular celebrity about the very 'shipwrecked lives' that the song's author is criticized for presuming to know. At which point, the 'you' whose behaviour the song's speaker emphatically denounces starts to seem strangely close to Morrissey, and once again during the course of the song, the party being criticized by the singer subtly becomes something of a victim—and a *reflection* of the singer—and draws our sympathy shortly after being presented as an object of criticism.

GHOSTS, GUESTS AND PERMEABLE SUBJECTS

It wouldn't be difficult to multiply instances of this kind. Instead, however, since the general principle should already be clear, I wish to look at a couple of slightly different examples, in which it is not so much a shifting of sympathy that is of interest to our discussion, but rather what we might refer to as a fluid ontology. What I mean by this can be illustrated if we consider the single 'Boxers,' released in 1995 and included on the compilation *World Of Morrissey*.

The song has a clear and fairly detailed character focus: the boxer in question is fighting (and losing) in front of his hometown, which according to the sampled commentary at the end of the song is 'south London,' and in the audience are the boxer's 'weary wife' (who 'walks away'), his nephew (who remains 'true' and 'thinks the world of [the boxer]') and Morrissey (who has to 'dry [his] eyes'). For the whole song, Morrissey appears to remain in character, in the audience—like a Hitchcockian cameo in his own work—and only to allow himself into focus as such. Except for one moment. And it is that moment which is of interest to our discussion. Here are the lines in which it occurs:

> Losing in front of your home crowd
> you wish the ground
> would open up and take you down
> and will time never pass?
> will time never pass for us?

In asking the question 'will time never pass?' and especially in the lingering repetition, without in any way letting go of its specific contextual reference to the apparently interminable fight, the line allows Morrissey's wonted persona to float in and dilate the reference of the line by including the much more general sense he has frequently voiced of time not passing and of 'life [being] long when you're lonely' ('The Queen Is Dead').[19] We find a more sustained example of this sort of fluidity in 'A Rush And A Push And The Land Is Ours.' To illustrate this, it will be necessary to consider the whole of the opening section:

---

19. For other songs in which Morrissey's persona appears to float past the window, see 'The Teachers Are Afraid Of The Pupils' ('To be finished would be a relief') and 'November Spawned A Monster' ('But Jesus made me, so / Jesus save me from / pity, sympathy / and people discussing me'—the self-referentiality of which has been foregrounded in live performances, where Morrissey sings with vehement emphasis 'and *idiots* discussing me').

Hello
I am the ghost of Troubled Joe
hung by his pretty white neck
Some eighteen months ago
I travelled to a mystical time zone
but I missed my bed
so I soon came home
they said: 'There's too much caffeine
in your bloodstream
and a lack of real spice
in your life'
I said: 'Leave me alone
because I'm alright, dad
just surprised to still
be on my own . . .'
Ooh, but don't mention love
I'd hate the strain of the pain again.

At the beginning of the song, the singer takes the part of a ghost and speaks from a named perspective which is apparently distinct from that other ghost 'Morrissey.' Yet, in a way that is becoming familiar, during the course of his speaking, there appears to be a fluid movement from this character perspective into Morrissey's own perspective. To whom do the lines 'Ooh, but don't mention love / I'd hate the strain of the pain again' belong? It is hard to say with any security. If they belong to Morrissey's own persona—with which they undoubtedly resonate—at what point did this take over or emerge? And what sort of foothold does it have in being? None of the preceding uses of 'I' decisively indicates this as its source. In fact, to the contrary, it is becoming clear that whilst normally we expect speakers to precede and produce utterances, in a strange way in Morrissey's writing, utterances seem in reverse to conjure their speaker.

Taking stock of the examples we have looked at so far, it is possible to discern, across a range of songs, an 'unsleepable' mobility that continually disturbs and forces us to rethink our relationship with that which is given; which keeps us from lazy identifications and demonizations (and so is the *enemy* of the kind of dogmatism of which Morrissey has been accused); and which makes the singer's perspective and sympathies hard to establish (whilst perpetually enticing us to try and do just this). In addition, we find another, more extreme form of mobility or fluid ontology, which transgresses even the separation of persons, with ghostly appearances of Morrissey's persona within the spaces of other characters' utterances. This last form of mobility shades over into a more radical form of play and recalls the example of 'Sheila Take A Bow,' discussed at the end of the last chapter. There it was noticed that Morrissey's playing with signifiers ('I'm a girl and you're a boy') was obviously a coy sort of linguistic cross-dressing, but also, more interestingly, involved a destabilization of referentiality in that it made sport of the expressive or deictic function of language, treating words as funny hats that might be tried on and cast off without commitment. The mobility we have observed in Morrissey's writing similarly subverts the conventions of coherence, stability and transparency upon which realist art depends. The ending of 'Certain People I Know,' for example—which, in chuckling to itself in front of us, lets us know that the singer knows that we know that he knows it's all a matter of play—compromises the realism of what went before it. In a similar fashion, the lightly reflexive lines in 'We'll Let You Know' ('and the songs we sing / they're not supposed to mean a thing') subversively bring their own referentiality into disrepute. And, likewise, the apparitional emergence of Morrissey's persona within the spaces allocated to other characters breaks the illusionist spell that encourages us to believe we are dealing with people rather than artistic constructions (even as it reinforces a sense of more intimate presence). Morrissey's mobility therefore clearly has a variety of functions and effects, and is analogous to irony in that it may be seen as a sort of linear self-differing, which retroactively dissociates the singer from his utterance. It is, furthermore, a *constitutive* characteristic of the singer's persona. That is to say, his persona doesn't first of all exist as some kind of graspable, static essence, which then, like an excitable child, behaves differently in public; rather, it is constituted in part *by* its mobility. Many of these features of Morrissey's mobility have important and unavoidable but too often unnoticed implications for the interpretation of his work—problematizing, in particular, attempts to attribute utterances or positions adopted in songs to the singer and essentialist thinking which presupposes that everything must be categorically this or that—as does the second version of the oxymoronic logic that constitutes his persona.

II

MULTIPLICITY

There is a moment of subtle complexity in 'Stretch Out And Wait' that is not apparent in the lyrics as they are printed:

> Amid concrete and clay
> And general decay
> Nature must still find a way
> So ignore all the codes of the day
> Let your juvenile impulses sway
> This way and that way
> This way, that way
> God, how sex implores you
> To let yourself lose yourself
> Stretch out and wait.

The singer's injunction to an unnamed and apparently generalized addressee to 'Let your juvenile impulses sway / This way and that way / This way, that way' is typical of Morrissey in a number of ways. It seems to call, without exactly doing so, for sexual liberation—the singer's own professed celibacy notwithstanding—which suggests, again, without doing so explicitly, a bisexual or at least a plural orientation ('This way and that way').[20] Things are already somewhat complicated, then, given the tension between what's said and what's suggested, and between the divergent orientations proposed. These complications are further complicated, however, by the appearance on the recording of another 'shadowy' Morrissey doing backing vocals. It's hard to hear whether there's an accompanying 'that way,' but as the 'principal' Morrissey sings 'This way and that way,' another Morrissey sings 'This way' over the former's 'that way.' The effect of this, on the one hand, is that the shadowy Morrissey's 'This way' sunders the apparent generality of the principal vocal line with a sort of greediness or urgency that tilts its 'this' away from meaning 'one particular way' into meaning *Morrissey's* way. Yet on the other hand, and of more immediate interest to our discussion, the overlay figures a simultaneity of divergent orientations—encouraging the addressee,

---

20. It is notable that any such liberation—of self, from self—from Morrissey's point of view involves passing, as it were, through *two* locks ('let yourself lose yourself').

that is, not only to a linear or sequential multiplicity, identified in the previous section as an oxymoronic mobility, but also suggesting that it is possible to sway 'this way and that way' at the same time. This is the second version of the oxymoronic logic that operates in Morrissey's lyrics.

We have of course already seen something of this multiplicity in his persona and, in particular, in his singing style (his tendency towards both a dandyish refinement and the carnivalesque; the conflicting claims of the mind and the body that are played out in his falsetto; and its opening up of a 'third' space conjoining masculine and feminine codes). We have noted as well a related multiplicity at a textual level in 'Certain People I Know,' which passingly evinces a 'cartoon' oxymoronic tonality in its conjunction of light-heartedness and violence. In this second section, I wish to examine in more detail some of the oxymoronic tensions that have started to emerge at a textual level—focusing in particular on the pervasive tension between 'gravity' and 'levity.'

GRAVITY

The roar which lies on the other side of silence

The song 'Unloveable,' included on the compilation *The World Won't Listen* and B-side on the twelve-inch of 'Bigmouth Strikes Again,' circles around the subject of communication—something to which the latter two titles allude as well:

> I know I'm unloveable
> You don't have to tell me
> I don't have much in my life
> But take it—it's yours
> . . .
>
> I know I'm unloveable
> You don't have to tell me
> Message received
> Loud and clear
> . . .
>
> I wear Black on the outside
> Beause Black is how I feel on the inside
> . . .

And if I seem a little strange
Well, that's because I am
. . .

But I know that you would like me
If only you could see me
If only you could meet me.

The song begins, as it were, *in medias res*—the singer's 'I know' intimating that the story is already old—and is in a sense a reflection on the story itself. At the centre of its reflections are anxieties about the relationship between the interior and exterior, both respecting that which reaches the speaker from without ('Message received / Loud and clear') and, more problematically, the expression of that which is 'on the inside' ('if I seem a little strange / Well, that's because I am'; 'I know that you would like me / If only you could see me'; 'I wear Black on the outside / Because Black is how I feel on the inside'). These reflections seem, furthermore, to be 'performed' at a vocal level, as the song has *two* vocal lines—the principal 'lyrical' voice and a heavily reverbed ghostly moaning, which precedes and survives the main vocal line, floating in and out throughout the song, apparently with a will of its own, and which joins in on a single word: 'inside.' This shadowy, prearticulate voice, which strangely wakes into speech at the word 'inside,' as though at hearing its own name, gives the impression of an exteriorization of an interior self—or what George Eliot refers to as 'the roar which lies on the other side of silence'—and of an unmediated exposure of this interiority.[21] What such ideal communication would reveal in the singer's case, the song asserts, is a feeling of blackness. (There is a lovely ambiguity in the line 'Because Black is how I feel on the inside,' which presents this blackness as something that is experienced by or affects the 'I,' but which also suggests a detachment of self from itself, and the self as object as well as subject, 'feeling' in the sense of ascertaining the quality of a thing, as one might dip one's elbow in the bath.) What we find, then, in 'Unloveable'—a song in which Morrissey is teetering over into metalyricism, singing about his life as a singer—is a meditation on the qualities for which he became famous: sincerity, earnestness and melancholy.

---

21. 'If we had a keen vision and feeling of all ordinary human life, it would be like hearing the grass grow and the squirrel's heart beat and we should die of that roar which lies on the other side of silence' (Eliot, *Middlemarch*), p. 226. Morrissey quotes from Eliot's novel in 'How Soon Is Now' and the 'matrix message' on 'Piccadilly Palare' is 'George Eliot knew.'

The nightingale and the rose

As we saw in the last chapter, with the ardour of the Protestant reformers, The Smiths set themselves against what they deemed to be the pretension, the triviality and the hedonism of 1980s pop at a number of levels—in calling themselves The Smiths, in their opposition to certain instruments, in the foregrounding of their ordinariness, and most especially in Morrissey's lyrics. In these, we find an extraordinarily brave and profound study of the singer's melancholy—which conscripts for its cause the observer who appears in taking its likeness to tame it—which in interview and in the songs themselves Morrissey insisted was a matter of fact. Indeed, even fairly early on in his career, Morrissey was writing 'meta'-songs about his songs not being believed and songs which were about their own sincerity. Here, for example, is the first half of 'The Boy With The Thorn In His Side,' from the 1985 album *The Queen Is Dead*:

> The boy with the thorn in his side
> behind the hatred there lies
> a murderous desire for love
> how can they look into my eyes
> and still they don't believe me?
> how can they hear me say those words
> still they don't believe me?
> and if they don't believe me now
> will they ever believe me?

The song may well owe something to Wilde's fairy tale 'The Nightingale and the Rose,' which Morrissey cites in an early interview whilst explaining the influence of Wilde on his work.[22] In the story, the bird's most beautiful song is produced by pressing its breast against a thorn, until it pierces its heart and causes the lifeblood to flow out of it and into the rose tree. Prior to this, the nightingale sang of suffering it didn't feel, for which it is criticized by the young student, 'who only knew the things that are written down in books':

---

22. 'My mother, who's an assistant librarian, introduced me to [Wilde's] writing when I was eight. She insisted I read him and I immediately became obsessed. Every single line affected me in some way. . . . There was a piece called "The Nightingale and the Rose" that appealed to me immensely then. It was about a nightingale who sacrificed herself for these two star-crossed lovers. It ends when the nightingale presses her heart against this rose because in a strange, mystical way it means that if she dies, then the two lovers can be brought together. . . . As I get older, the adoration [of Wilde] increases. I'm never without him. It's almost biblical. It's like carrying your rosary around with you' (*Smash Hits*, June 21, 1984).

'She has form,' he said to himself, as he walked away through the grove—'that cannot be denied her; but has she got feeling? I am afraid not. In fact, she is like most artists; she is all style, without any sincerity. She would not sacrifice herself for others. She thinks merely of music and everybody knows that the arts are selfish. Still, it must be admitted that she has some beautiful notes in her voice. What a pity it is that they do not mean anything.'[23]

Whether or not 'The Boy With The Thorn In His Side' owes anything to Wilde's fairy tale, it is clearly concerned with the singer's suffering—which is evidently also the source of song—and emphatic in its insistence on the importance of sincerity. (The texts are obviously additionally linked by their invocation of religious imagery and their depiction of the artist as a Christ-like figure.[24]) Like 'Unloveable,' though, it is tormented by anxieties about the mediation of interiority ('how can they look into my eyes / and still they don't believe me?') and bespeaks a dream of ideal transparency, which experience controverts. This is plain enough, no doubt; but the way in which the predicament is *dramatized* tends to be overlooked.

The song has been criticized for running out of lyrics and resorting to yodelling, with over a minute to go, as if the singer had shortchanged the listener.[25] Yet, even if one takes no pleasure in the astonishing vocal performance of the final wordless section, this is surely missing the point. For the singer's baroque ululations, 'like water bubbling from a silver jar,'[26] appear to swerve away from speech in search of an alternative strategy for communication in the face of speech's failure. As we saw in the second 'shadowy' vocal line of 'Unloveable,' the singer attempts almost in desperation to express his interiority 'without' language; what we hear is the sound of feeling aspiring to communicate itself unclothed. Indeed, the singer seems to yearn for a sort of ecstatic speech—a 'stepping outside' of

---

23. Wilde, *Complete Shorter Fiction*, p. 15.
24. In one of his early lectures on aesthetics, Wilde makes the following remarks on the Christ-like sacrificial offering of the artist, which anticipate the narrative of the 'The Nightingale and the Rose': 'While the incomplete lives of ordinary men bring no healing power with them, the thorn-crown of the poet will blossom into roses for our pleasure; for our delight his despair will gild its own thorns, and his pain, like Adonis, be beautiful in its agony: and when the poet's heart breaks it will break in music' (Wilde, 'The English Renaissance of Art,' p. 135).
25. The following assessment was offered in the *NME*: 'Seems like Morrissey himself gives up the song half-way through when he stops the words and uses up the rest of the needle-time with yodelling. If it's too much to expect a revision of world music with every record, we could at least ask for something a little less enervating' (cited in Rogan, *Morrissey*, p. 79).
26. This is how the nightingale's song is described in Wilde's fairy tale.

the inside *as* inside. If this is the case, the elaborate wordless section ceases to be an anticlimactic padding out or treading of water and is revealed instead as an *intensification* of the song's concerns. It is, we might say, a shift from telling to showing, in the hope of achieving a greater immediacy. In this sense, the giving up of speech is itself expressive, and the final section becomes a kind of commentary on its own inarticulacy.

Things are no better on this side of the fence though either, as it is a yearning for expression that is continually encountering its own inadequacy, and the more it reaches out and tries to haul its heart into its mouth, the more it seems to be knocking against the ineffable (it is noticeable that where the vocal line seems most urgently to appeal to us 'with outstretched voice,' Morrissey sings what sounds like 'no'). And yet perhaps the communication of this failure is itself a sort of success. For if what the singer desires is a transparent communication of interiority (the 'murderous desire for love' that lies 'behind' the hatred), and if this is what he wishes to express, doesn't the song gesture obliquely towards this in showing us its falling short of its aim? Doesn't it bring the ineffability it faces more clearly into view, that is, *by virtue of* its renunciation *of* speech? Either way, we can at least see in 'The Boy With The Thorn In His Side' something of the intense earnestness, melancholy and emphasis on sincerity for which Morrissey became notorious.[27]

The sacred heart

This emphasis upon sincerity, along with the earnestness and melancholy we have seen in 'Unloveable' and 'The Boy With The Thorn In His Side,' runs throughout Morrissey's work. At times it is explicitly stated, as in 'I'll Never Be Anybody's Hero Now' ('It begins in the heart / And it hurts when it's true / It only hurts because it's true'). And sometimes it is a value that is missing, which the singer bemoans (in 'Glamorous Glue,' for instance, he sings 'First day with the jar you find / Everyone lies / Nobody minds / Everyone lies').[28] But it is

---

27. Having said this, it is worth noting that even here we find an oxymoronic yoking of seriousness and levity, as the singer's urgently plaintive vocal performance constantly modulates into and out of a comical yodelling, like someone circling a ticklish place.

28. Morrissey appears ostensibly to be singing about glue-sniffing—else what would the sense of the title be or the subsequent verse ('Third week with the jar you find / everything dies')? Yet it is, more generally, one example among many of an evangelical rage at the disingenuousness of polite discourse, for which Morrissey clearly has a deep animosity ('In my life / why do I give valuable time / to people who don't care if I / live or die?' ('Heaven Knows I'm Miserable Now').

perhaps most effectively communicated when it is something that is *performed*. One of the best examples of this occurs in 'America Is Not The World,' on *You Are The Quarry*. Here, he sings:

> And I have got nothing to offer you
> just this heart deep and true,
> which you say you don't need
> See with your eyes
> touch with your hands—please
> hear through your ears
> know in your soul—please
> for haven't you me with you now?

Unremarkable though it may appear on the page, this is an extraordinary passage. The song, at the most immediately apparent level, offers a description of sincerity—a 'heart deep and true'—and, indeed, claims to have nothing *other than* sincerity to offer. This description is crucially underwritten by the singing, which in its utterance of 'please' reaches out to the listener with a density of yearning as beseeching as anything in Morrissey's oeuvre and which performs the sincerity of which it speaks. What is so extraordinary about the passage, however, is that it doesn't just describe or vocally perform its sincerity, it presents itself as evidence of its own claims and points towards a presence which is born out of its own fabric. To be more specific, in saying 'I have nothing to offer you / just *this* heart deep and true' [italics added] and in enjoining the listener to 'see,' 'touch' and 'hear,' the singer gestures towards a disclosure of presence in the song itself—as though the song could be the agency of real relation and such things could be given and received in its space.[29] There is also an implicit religious aspect to these lines. The singer's initial showing of his 'heart deep and true' recalls the popular icons of the sacred heart (images of Christ with his heart surreally exposed, common in Catholic iconography) and the subsequent injunction to

---

29. This kind of exposure—which in making a claim to presence in spite of absence is a sort of 'ontological scandal'—is a recurrent topos in Morrissey's work. In 'Rubber Ring,' for example, a song about 'songs that saved your life,' Morrissey sings: 'I'm here with the cause / I'm holding the torch / In the corner of your room / Can you hear me?' In 'Angel, Angel, Down We Go Together,' the singer similarly promises presence: 'and when . . . they've broken you / and wasted all your money / and cast your shell aside. . . . I will be here / believe me.' And in 'Sunny,' another song addressed to someone *in extremis*, he sings: 'I'm here—I won't move / I'm here and I will not move.' In these and other songs, Morrissey makes a radical claim to be present in what he sings and to give himself in his songs *as he is*. He likewise seems to value relationships formed with or by means of such textual presence as highly as, if not higher than, relations formed otherwise.

'see,' 'hear,' 'touch' and 'know,' which coincides with the advent of a choirlike accompaniment, calls to mind Christ's offering himself to 'doubting' Thomas to be seen and touched, so that he too might believe.[30] (We find a visual corollary of this in the photographs for 'The Passion of Morrissey,' an interview in *Uncut* magazine in 2006, where Morrissey poses as St. Sebastian, pierced by arrows, and as Christ, with stigmata and a radiating heart of light.) The final line of the passage quoted—'For haven't you me with you now?'—is arguably the most extraordinary of all, with its odd locution but, more importantly, in combining both the song's 'presencing' of its speaker and its implicit religious character.[31] Like the 'this' of the earlier line, the 'now' points towards a presence that inhabits the atemporal space of the song and opens into the listener's 'now,' dismantling the separations of time and space, so that the song accomplishes the disclosure it describes in the moment and act of its description— 'for haven't you me with you now?' The suggestion of presence is of course phrased as a question—even though it appears at least to some degree rhetorical—and thereby indicates an awareness that this may not be the case; although whilst this significantly qualifies the assertion, it makes it all the more serious as well, in showing that the speaker is aware of and still wishes to venture the claim *in spite of* such objections. The song's presence thereby seems to acknowledge itself as a ghostly presence or 'a living sign,' which appears without material evidence or in spite of bodily absence. In this sense, the claim once again carries a curious religious resonance—in this case, it is strangely reminiscent of Christ's promise to be with his disciples after his Ascension (John 14:18)—a Presence onto which every 'now' opens and which traditionally you 'know in your soul.' What can we conclude from the foregoing analyses?

In the anguished desire to communicate interiority without the treacheries of mediation, apparent in 'Unloveable' and 'The Boy With The Thorn In His Side,' and in the communion that is promised in the 'here' and 'now' of the songs themselves—a radical 'presencing' and disclosure of self that is brought about in and by the act of speech—we can see an unignorable and recurrent importance

---

30. John 20:24–9. The song may also have behind it the first epistle of John: 'That which . . . we have heard, which we have seen with our eyes, which we have looked upon, and our hands have handled' (1:1).
31. The very unusual locution seems to go out of its way to figure the speaking subject as a grammatical object, perhaps to intensify the sense of presence and something that can be grasped.

accorded to sincerity and an unusual earnestness towards popular music as such. Leaving aside the singer's notorious melancholy for now, two other things emerged in the course of our analysis which add to this general impression of gravity. One is that the songs' concerns are often performed, rather than merely stated (as seen, for example, in the backing vocals of 'Stretch Out And Wait' and 'Unloveable,' the eloquent renunciation of speech in 'The Boy With The Thorn In His Side,' and the distended emotive delivery of the singer's plea in 'America Is Not The World'). The other is that it is possible to discern shadowy religious resonances and analogies in what purport to be wholly secular songs. This is, as we saw in 'America Is Not The World' and 'The Boy With The Thorn In His Side,' partly a matter of textual allusion but partly, and more strangely, also a matter of the kinds of claims that are being made with respect to the singer's presence in what he says and the communion offered in the space of the song.

This, then, is the Morrissey with whom many are familiar. And his earnestness, melancholy and insistence upon sincerity are the primary lineaments of the gravity he counterposed to the triviality, hedonism and escapist fantasies of mainstream 1980s popular music. All of this is important and even revolutionary. But it is only part of the picture. To gain a fuller and more faithful sense of his work, we need to bring into view the 'lighter' elements in Morrissey's writing with which such gravity coexists. But first of all, a qualification is necessary.

WELL, THIS IS TRUE . . . AND YET, IT'S FALSE

At various points in the study so far, we have come across tensions between the 'natural' and the 'artificial.' In the first chapter it was observed that the 'ordinariness' of The Smiths—the band's name, Morrissey's appearance and his valiantly unedited clumsiness, etc.—was opposed to the flamboyant cosmetic glamour of New Pop (although it was also noticed that the singer's use of flowers and ironized dandyism complicate this opposition). Similarly, it was noted that during the same period, synthesized music came to be set polemically over against guitar music, with one side seeing the latter as somehow more 'authentic' and the other side seeing 'authenticity' as a misnomer or irrelevance in art.[32] Such oppositions were even

---

32. The 'postmodern' New Pop position was espoused, for example, by Ian Craig Marsh—a member of The Human League, Heaven 17 and the British Electronic Foundation: 'That whole set of ideas to do with artistic and emotional expression, authenticity, contact with the audience, community. . . . I was against that right off the bat' (cited in Reynolds, *Rip It Up and Start Again*, p. 375).

more pronounced with respect to lyrics. Not surprisingly, therefore, a critical discourse of 'sincerity' arose to characterise the opposition of bands like The Smiths to the hedonistic fantasies and arch vacuities of the New Pop movement. And whilst Morrissey has long since distanced himself from the exploded antinomies of 1980s pop, an unreflective rhetoric of 'sincerity' continues to dominate commentary on the singer. Johnny Rogan, for example, speaks of Morrissey stripping 'the mask away to reveal his true, unadorned feelings' and makes the following more extensive claim in his introduction to *Morrissey: The Albums* (trying, as ever, to write himself into the story):

> As Vini Reilly once suggested to me, probably with a tinge of romantic overstatement: 'There's not a moment of untruth in Morrissey's life.' Applying that quote to his songwriting gets to the heart of Morrissey's appeal. Listening to such compositions as 'Suffer Little Children,' 'Please Please Please Let Me Get What I Want,' 'Half A Person,' 'The Headmaster Ritual,' 'Meat Is Murder,' 'I Am Hated For Loving,' 'Sorrow Will Come In The End,' 'At Last I Am Born' and countless more, it is difficult to escape the conclusion that you have a direct line to the singer's heart and soul.[33]

Rogan means this as praise, of course, yet there are problems with speaking in this way about art. If 'true, unadorned feelings' were all that mattered, the sentimental drunk would be our greatest poet. What about the artistry, one wants to ask, that vanishes in speaking of a 'direct line' to the singer's heart and soul' (and whose is the 'tinge of romantic overstatement'?)? To paraphrase Mallarmés famous retort to Degas: one doesn't make poetry with feelings but with *words*. How, then, can we avoid such aesthetic naivety? And if speaking of sincerity or immediacy in art is problematic, how can we distinguish what Morrissey was doing from other artists, for Rogan's comments are surely based on something? To understand better why this is a problem and how we might reconceive this 'something,' it will be helpful to draw a brief analogy between the revolution brought about in popular music by 'indie' bands and the artistic, cultural and ideological revolution that was romanticism.[34]

---

33. Rogan, *Morrissey*, pp. 53; 1.
34. Johnny Marr has referred to his writing partnership with Morrissey as 'incredibly romantic,' which Richard Carman a little shakily glosses as follows: 'This was not, of course, in the sense of *amour*, but romance with a capital "R." Heightened sensation, heightened perception, heightened emotional involvement typified the romantic poets—Keats, Shelley, Coleridge and Wordsworth—

There are of course enormous differences in the scale of what happened, the historical context in which they took place, and the agenda that lay behind the respective revolutions. Even so, in some of its most important features, the sea change brought about in the 1980s by indie music is indebted to—and inherits the tensions involved in—the romantic movement.[35] What are these features?

If we focus on literature—the genre of most relevance to Morrissey's writing—the following general points may be made.[36] English romantic poetry was essentially a reaction against neoclassical taste, which came to the fore with the publication of Wordsworth and Coleridge's *Lyrical Ballads* (1789) and its revolutionary manifesto Preface (1800). The principal feature of neoclassical taste of relevance to us here is the emphasis it places on art, as a matter of artifice—that is, a skilful contrivance, and decorous periphrasis of the quotidian, whose most esteemed characteristics were refinement, polish and a formal cunning within highly conventionalized spaces. Simplifying things considerably, we can say that Wordsworth and Coleridge reacted by championing 'language really used by men' along with 'incidents and situations from common life.'[37] This was partly an aesthetic matter, since what they strongly objected to was 'the gaudiness and inane phraseology of the many modern writers.'[38] Yet it was an ideological matter as well, since they also took exception to the typical narrowness of such poetry's concerns and—breaching the neoclassical dictates of decorum—dealt seriously with 'lowly' subjects, in particular in writing about vagrants, beggars, criminals

---

and this was the "romance" that the two writers experienced together' (Carman, *Johnny Marr*, p. 45). It is hard to know exactly how Morrissey is using the polysemous term 'romanticism,' however, the following assessment of what he achieved with The Smiths suggests he is in agreement: 'The fluffy elements of pop stardom, if you like, are not why I'm here. I'm generally very interested in the written word and changing the poetic landscape of pop music, and I think I've achieved that. I think, with The Smiths, I introduced a harsh romanticism which has been picked up by many people and which didn't exist previously' (*The Observer*, September 15, 2002).

35. In her illuminating discussion of the aesthetics and rituals of British indie music, Wendy Fonarow similarly argues that indie 'reproduces a significant and unresolved ideological conflict in Western culture,' although she traces this conflict further back to the cognate theological arguments of the Reformation—concerning the nature of 'authentic' experience—and observes that 'the core issues of indie music and its practices are in essence the arguments of a particular sect of Protestant reformers within the secular form of music' (Fonarow, *Empire of Dirt*, pp. 27–8).

36. The outline of romanticism offered here obviously leaves out many of its discontinuities and complexities; however, it is the caricature of cultural history that is inherited by the indie movement, rather than the plurality of practices it belies.

37. Preface to Wordsworth and Coleridge, *Lyrical Ballads*, pp. 21–2. In fact, Coleridge never really agreed with Wordsworth on this point and Byron derided the prosaic idiom of the latter as the *antithesis* of poetry.

38. Ibid., p. 20.

and outcasts.[39] In addition—though it was presented as following on from this—the romantics exalted 'the spontaneous overflow of powerful feelings,'[40] which became the ultimate impulse, arbiter and concern of art. This inevitably led on the one hand to a turning inwards and an elevation of the individual, and on the other to a concomitant valorization of sincerity or authenticity. The importance of these qualities has been usefully summarized by Hugh Honour:

> The substitution of an expressive for a mimetic theory of the arts put a new emphasis on the authenticity of the emotions expressed and, consequently, on the artist's sincerity and integrity. Spontaneity, individuality and 'inner truth' came in this way to be recognized as the criteria by which all works of art, literature and music, of all periods and countries, should be judged. It is here, perhaps, that one essential, distinguishing characteristic of Romantic art becomes evident—the supreme value placed by the Romantics on the artist's sensibility and emotional 'authenticity' as the qualities which alone confer 'validity' on his work. Instead of reflecting the timeless, universal values of classicism, every Romantic work of art is unique—the expression of the artist's own personal living experience.[41]

In spite of the vast historical and cultural divisions, the indie reaction of the 1980s against the confusingly entitled 'New Romantic' or New Pop movement was fought along surprisingly similar lines. As Matthew Bannister observes,

> The early UK indie pop scene [was] a reaction to the commercialized 'yuppie' hedonist consumerism of Thatcherite Britain, defining itself against the mainstream association of the New Right agenda with the hedonistic commercialism and artifice of dance music, New Romantics and New Pop.[42]

The demonized features of the New Pop movement were its flamboyance, polish, opulence and artifice; the hallmarks of the indie reaction were therefore amateurism, ordinariness and an avowal of 'authenticity' (the insignia of which were 'out-of-tune singing and guitars, onstage scruffiness and disorganisation, lack of cool and an

---

39. One of the aims in dealing with such 'avoided subjects' was what George Eliot would refer to as an 'extension of our sympathies' (Eliot, 'The Natural History of German Life,' p. 110).
40. Wordsworth and Coleridge, *Lyrical Ballads*, p. 22.
41. Honour, *Romanticism*, p. 20.
42. Bannister, *White Boys, White Noise*, p. 62.

accent on content ["the good song"] over presentation').[43] The indie reaction against the artifice of New Pop concomitantly involved a self-conscious 'infantilism' or a kind of faux naivety (manifest in the 'primary school' fashion of The Pastels et al.), a nostalgia that countered the fetishizing of the brand new, and a foregrounding of unworldliness, dysfunction and suffering—all of which obviously, if largely unwittingly, hark back to prominent currents within romanticism. The icon and most eloquent advocate this 'new kind of youth culture . . . based in romanticism and asceticism'[44] was of course Morrissey.

As we have seen, Morrissey's reaction was essentially a complaint about pop music's distance from everyday reality ('Most records portray life as it isn't lived by people').[45] Relatedly, he was opposed to the 'gaudiness' and 'inanity' of 1980s music, abhorring both its emphasis on slick production and the stylized visual glamour of its practitioners, which to the singer involved an elevation of finish and technical accomplishment over the things that really mattered.[46] Hence his parallel counterrevolutionary emphasis on ordinariness and the 'natural'—of which his flowers were a somewhat overdetermined synecdoche. Furthermore, again like the early romantics, Morrissey evinced a radical, egalitarian humanism in giving voice to and entering into the perspective of the outsider—in his case, the criminal, the damaged, the 'maladjusted' and 'unlovable.'[47]

43. Bannister, *White Boys, White Noise*, p. 61.
44. Reynolds, *Bring the Noise*, p. 17.
45. Haupfuhrer, 'Roll Over Beethoven, and Tell Madonna the News,' p. 106.
46. It's interesting to notice the ways in which Morrissey saw what were to become his own oppositional values reflected in the protopunk protest of the New York Dolls. He values, for instance, their 'crude musicality' and the fact that they were 'the most professional unprofessional band there ever was' as it is evidence of alternative priorities: 'The Dolls' musical ideals were to let the instruments express themselves rather than holding firm to academic regulations. There is a word for this. Imagination.' He similarly values the uncensored seediness of their realism and its embrace of 'the bleak realities of ordinariness.' He likewise praises their 'deliberately gauche' appearance and in certain respects concurs with their not always so articulate sexual politics: 'Kids are finding out that the sexual terms homosexual, bisexual, heterosexual, all those are just words in front of "sexual." People are just "sexual." ' But above all, what he seems to value is their defence of the 'outcast,' as articulated in 'Frankenstein' and 'Human Being' and announced in their 1973 tour publicity: 'We have come to England to redeem the social outcasts' (Morrissey, *New York Dolls*).
47. The ethical dimensions of indie music have been foregrounded by Wendy Fonorow: 'Indie extols local/independent authority, the direct experience of music in a live setting, simplicity, the ordinary, asceticism in consumption, and the nostalgic gaze that looks back at a mythologized past of childhood innocence. Indie calls for a return to an imagined "golden age" of music prior to its debasement by the corpulent Leviathan music industry. Indie views its own aesthetic practices and the practices of others through a screen of ethics. It demonstrates at its core that aesthetics is a matter of morality' (Fonorow, *Empire of Dirt*, p. 19).

Underlying this act of imaginative sympathy, in the first generation romantics and in The Smiths as well, we find a tendency to associate 'common life' or the experience of the 'underclass' with that which is more authentic or essentially human (though Morrissey has a tendency to demystify his own idealizing sympathies, by satirizing whilst simultaneously inviting us to enter into the feelings of 'The Ordinary Boys'). And, finally, there is a salient parallel in the revolutionary importance the singer accorded to the candid expression of the most urgent feelings (a whole and hugely influential aesthetic manifesto is condensed in the phrase 'the spontaneous overflow of powerful feelings,' which encompasses the concerns as well as the manner of art ['powerful feelings' and 'spontaneous overflow'], even as it conspicuously leaves art out of the account). What is the problem, then, with this polemical advocacy of sincerity and feeling as aesthetic values?

The essential difficulty such arguments face is that art is *always* a matter of artifice, which necessarily mediates—or produces effects—and thus renders problematic any talk of 'sincerity' and 'feeling' in art, which tends to give the impression that no translation is involved in attempting to communicate our interior selves (Wordsworth's 'overflow' suggests an escape of interiority—still in possession of its interior character—into the outside, rather than a process of mediation). Yet it is simply not possible to step outside rhetoric and speak 'without art.' Communication involves signs and signs stand for something other than themselves. This is true of all communication, and given the more or less openly intervening stages of production—writing, publishing, recording, etc.—is even more apparent in art, whether pop music or poetry. All art, therefore, including that which affects to speak most directly and in the most heartfelt way, is a matter of contrivance and manipulation.[48] This is of course something that is celebrated by Wilde: 'Every century that produces poetry is, so far, an artificial century, and the work that seems to us to be the most natural and simple product of its time is always the result of the most self-conscious effort.' The corollary of which is that 'all bad poetry springs from genuine feeling.'[49] Talking about 'authenticity' in pop music is thus

---

48. 'Authenticity,' as Lawrence Grossberg argues, 'is itself a construction' and 'is in fact no more authentic than any other self-consciously created identity' (Grossberg, 'The Media Economy of Rock Culture,' p. 206).
49. Wilde, 'The Critic as Artist,' I, p. 228; II, p. 270.

like the cartoon character that carries on running after it's sped off a cliff without realizing there is no ground beneath its feet.[50]

This is not to say, we should hastily add, that it makes no sense to draw distinctions with respect to style or the concerns of art. On the contrary, in rejecting the previously prevailing taste, the romantics and their indie counterparts were evidently reacting to something. Nevertheless, it needs to be emphasised that these are distinctions that exist at a *textual* level (and under 'textual,' we should include all stagings of subjectivity). Language is not something that erases itself on delivering us up to some other thing that appears to lie 'behind' it or which brought it into existence; it is language that brings this 'behind' into existence. 'Sincerity' and 'feeling' in art are effects—as is the speaker—and these are produced by texts. It is therefore naive to think that we can treat art as a sort of stethoscope, which collapses the intervening boundaries, and read unproblematically backwards from text to the 'heart and soul' of the author, as though there were no interval or medium in between—however much texts themselves may tempt us to do so. This, then, is the first problem, concerning art in general.

Speaking of sincerity in Morrissey's work is additionally misguided because he is clearly aware of such problems. Even if the singer did not advertise his devotion to Wilde, this should be plain, his writing is *full* of arch acknowledgments of its fictional status.[51] In some cases, this is explicitly declared, as in 'Such A Little Thing Makes Such A Big Difference,' where he jauntily protests 'Leave me alone—I was only singing' (the comedy of which depends on our knowing that he also holds, and notoriously holds, a contrary view of singing).[52] In other songs, the singer flaunts the fictionality

---

50. For a lucid discussion of 'the aesthetic of authenticity,' see Gilbert and Pearson, *Discographies*, in which the authors point out that distinctions with respect to authenticity 'almost always proceed by rendering the technological components utilized in their favoured forms *invisible as technologies*' and 'are founded on an order of the real within which aesthetic preferences are transformed into ontological distinctions' (Gilbert and Pearson, *Discographies*, p. 112). See also Simon Frith's article 'Art versus Technology: The Strange Case of Popular Music,' in which he not only challenges the opposition between technology in music and 'authenticity' but also argues that 'technological developments have made the rock concept of authenticity possible' (Frith, 'Art versus Technology,' p. 269).

51. Morrissey's love of self-conscious artifice is obviously also related to and revealed by his admiration for the glam-rock tendencies of Bolan, Bowie and the New York Dolls. For a good discussion of the willed and positive inauthenticity of glam rock, see Auslander, *Performing Glam Rock*.

52. The utterance's reflexive undermining of itself, after the manner of the Cretan paradox—in that, if he is 'only singing,' he is 'only singing' that he is 'only singing'—is therefore significant as well as vertiginously ironic, since it leaves teasingly in play both the suggestion that he doesn't 'mean' what he's singing and—in so far as this is implicated in its own disclaimer—the suggestion that he does.

of his writing by foregrounding the medium—by means of generic heterogeneity, or what I shall refer to as a 'cartoon ontology'; the conspicuous divergence between the performer and the speaking 'I' ('for working girls like me'[53]); or his habit of etceterizing, which lays bare the medium of signification with a gesture of exhaustion that speaks by means of semantic blanks or 'evacuated' signifiers.[54] On still other occasions, the textual status of his songs is more slyly declared by obliquely self-referential utterances ('don't you find this absurd?'; 'and the songs we sing / they're not supposed to mean a thing') as well as a whole range of vocal quirks (hammed impersonations, travestying pronunciations, carnivalesque noises, melisma and so on), which cloud the glass through which we look and keep us from supposing that language offers an 'unmediated, transparent, disinterested access to reality.'[55] Alongside these more dramatic exhibitions of its own textuality, we additionally find in Morrissey's writing recurrent references to songs and singing ('Stop Me If You Think You've Heard This One Before,' 'Paint A Vulgar Picture,' 'Get Off The Stage,' 'Sing Your Life,' etc.) and the act of writing or communication ('Sister I'm A Poet,' 'Girl Least Likely To,' 'Reader Meet Author' and so on). These ubiquitous references to the act of signifying, whilst in many cases innocuous enough in themselves, in conjunction with the singer's more overt self-referential gestures— which, like Oliver Hardy's turning to face the camera, draw attention to the medium that holds them in being—keep us queasily swaying in and out of awareness of the song's artifice (where this is part of the point and part of the pleasure). An illustration of what such 'queasiness' entails may help.

BENIGN ALIENATION

'Rusholme Ruffians' appears on the album *Meat Is Murder* alongside songs which purport to describe biographical experiences ('The Headmaster Ritual'), personal convictions ('Meat Is Murder'), and songs which aspire to a transparent communication of interiority ('That Joke Isn't Funny Anymore'; 'Well I Wonder'). If these other songs tend to keep their art in the background, however, 'Rusholme

---

53. 'Maladjusted.'
54. 'Blah, blah, blah, blah' ('At Last I Am Born'). This latter tendency is discussed in chapter 3.
55. Smith, 'Auden's Light and Serio-Comic Verse,' p. 100.

Ruffians' *foregrounds* its art. It is a song about the fair—which is a place, in Morrissey's experience, 'of tremendous violence, hate, distress, high romance and all the truly vital things in life.'[56] But it is also and obviously a place of artifice—of induced effects, such as fear and exhilaration, which are premeditated and paid for. The song signals its association with this element of artifice in a number of ways. Firstly, it is framed with sound effects which subtly determine its meaning: the entwined fade-in of the music and the fairground noise creates the impression that the song takes place within, rather than speaking from outside, the world of the fair; whilst the clunking lever-shifting with which it closes gives the impression that the song itself was a mechanically produced effect, as though it had been occasioned by the insertion of a coin. The music, too, is a blatant allusion to Elvis's '(Marie's The Name) His Latest Flame'—the first verse of which was frequently performed as a prelude to live versions of the song—which, in waving around its intertextuality, announces itself as a work of art, born in part of and doing homage to another work of art.[57] The lyrics, which similarly borrow from Victoria Wood's 'Fourteen Again' and 'Funny How Things Turn Out,'[58] are less overt in exhibiting their textuality, though they do thematize the issue of signification:

> An engagement ring
> doesn't mean a thing
> to a mind that lives by brass (money)
>
> . . .
>
> scratch my name on your arm with a fountain pen
> (this means you really love me).

There is a nice gentle irony in the second of these utterances concerned with things 'meaning' things, which at once communicates

---

56. Cited in Rogan, *Morrissey*, p. 51.

57. Brian McHale's comments on the unsettling effect of 'intertextual figures'—characters borrowed from other texts—are enlightening with respect to music as well: 'This is more radical than it sounds, for when one plagiarizes (or, more politely, "appropriates") a character from another text, that character comes trailing fragments of its own world, the world of its "home" text. To introduce realized intertextual characters in this way is to violate the norm of textual-ontological unity (one text/one world), in effect producing an ontologically composite or heterogeneous text, one that mingles or straddles worlds. It produces, in short, a characteristically postmodernist text in which multiple worlds coexist in uneasy tension' (McHale, *Constructing Postmodernism*, pp. 216–7).

58. I am grateful to Simon Goddard for this information.

the truth of the statement in its teenage context (doing so *does* 'mean' you 'really love' someone in this world) and its naivety outside this context. The irony in this way has a subtly alienating effect, in that it prevents us from remaining wholly within the narrative perspective and encourages us at the same time to step outside and reflect critically upon it. Such alienation—which is effective *because* it is intermittent and slight, for it keeps us see-sawing in and out of involvement and thus aware of the threshold, rather as fairground rides themselves do—is further elicited by the bizarre twists and turns of the singer's delivery, marvellously rolling the /I/ of 'money' and swerving midword into ham falsetto in 'mine' and 'devout,' as if his vocal acrobatics were part of the fair.

In all sorts of interrelated ways, then, the song draws attention to its artificial status. Importantly, however, it does so, gently, by insinuation, in a way that keeps us teetering in and out of awareness, inducing an oxymoronic queasiness rather than outright alienation. For Morrissey is too enthralled by 'the urgency of life'[59] to gaze perpetually at the medium in which he contemplates it, but too fascinated with art to refrain from interrupting his gaze with allusions to that which sustains it.

ART AND LIFE

It should now be obvious why it is problematic to speak, as Rogan does, of 'a direct line to the singer's heart and soul.' It should additionally be apparent that this naive view of art impoverishes what it seeks to praise, for not only does it fail to appreciate the irreducible role of mediation in art, it fails to see that Morrissey's writing is informed by and frequently thematizes such an awareness. (One of the singer's favourite aphorisms, which he attributes to Goethe, is: 'Art and Life are different, that's why one is called Art and one is called Life.'[60]) If, then, it is problematic to speak of 'authenticity' or 'sincerity' in art, does this not undermine what was said earlier about 'feeling aspiring to communicate itself "unclothed,"' 'the impression of an unmediated exposure of interiority' and 'a radical "presencing"

---

59. 'Angel, Angel, Down We Go Together.'
60. *The Face*, July 1984. The closest I've been able to come to tracing this quote—which is promiscuously recycled but never referenced—is: 'Es begreift, daß Kunst eben darum Kunst heiße, weil sie nicht Natur ist.' ('It [genius] realizes that art is art precisely because it is not nature' [my translation].) *Wilhelm Meisters Wanderjahre*, vol. 17, Book 2, 8, p. 480.

and disclosure of self' which is promised in Morrissey's songs? Does such a 'postmodern' reading of the sign not commit us to an 'ironic nihilism which refuses to valorize any single image, identity, action or value as somehow intrinsically better than any other'?[61] Not necessarily; since to argue that all art is a matter of signs does not mean that differences do not exist. However, it locates these differences at a textual level. It is therefore still possible to communicate values—even if signs have no intrinsic meaning—and speak of presence, sincerity and an impression of immediacy as textual effects. And that is precisely the argument at the centre of 'Unloveable,' where Morrissey sings 'I wear Black on the outside / Because Black is how I feel on the inside.' The act of wearing something, which in this case is an act of signifying, is a willed and 'artificial' gesture, which employs signs to stand for or point towards something with which they have no intrinsic relation (crucially, the word 'black' is used in Morrissey's lines in two different senses). The signification of interior 'blackness' is therefore, strictly, a fiction with no inherent connection with the singer's exterior 'blackness.' And the song is quite open about this. Yet at the same time, and in talking about the act of signification, the singer attempts to communicate an interior state—which here and elsewhere he insists is in accordance with something that holds in reality—*in spite of* this incommensurability and the artifice of the medium.

Overlooking the ineradicable metaphoricity of the sign, as commentary on Morrissey routinely does, means that we miss the anxieties and tensions—but also the possibilities—that are brought into play by the medium's artifice. It is to some of these neglected possibilities that we now turn.

THE HERESY OF PARAPHRASE

One of the most pervasive problems in commentary on Morrissey is an unreflective attachment to realism. In spite of the fact that the singer has repeatedly signalled an allegiance to other traditions— most obviously in his championing of Wilde—and in spite of the fact, as Terry Eagleton points out, that 'bending the rules of realism is as Irish as emigration,'[62] most commentators on Morrissey's

---

61. Grossberg, 'The Media Economy of Rock Culture,' p. 206.
62. Eagleton, Review of Joseph O'Connor's *Redemption Falls*, in *Saturday Guardian*, May 5, 2007.

work approach the artist with an unquestioned presupposition that everything must have an underlying realist 'aboutness,' into which his lyrics may be translated without loss or remainder.[63]

Presuming everything must have a realist 'aboutness'—and where it seems to be lacking, supplying their own or criticizing its absence—is a fault to which Bret, Goddard, Rogan and Simpson all in their different ways fall prey. David Bret, for example, seems to think that a lyric is an advert for its own 'aboutness'—and that it is this, rather than what the writer actually says or doesn't say that matters. Criticism, for Bret, thus means paraphrase—which dissolves, rather than sharpening our awareness of, the work itself—and any gaps or ambiguities are just so many dots for the critic to join. The result therefore tends to be either an exercise in vacuity ('In "You're The One For Me, Fatty," Morrissey champions obesity, the fact that big can really be beautiful') or else it replaces the lyric it purports to describe with a story of its own. Here, for example, is Bret's commentary on 'Alsatian Cousin':

> The song deals with the old chestnut of age-gap sex, to which is added a touch of voyeurism. The narrator has watched a pair of lovers in the forecourt, then later at a campsite where the tent-flap is deliberately left wide open. But there is a problem: the fact that, al fresco, sex is unsatisfactory because the older lover with the leather elbow patches has always been accustomed to doing it on his desk.[64]

Mark Simpson, by contrast, is less literalistic—though this in a sense is the problem—and more of a conspiracy theorist, in that he assumes that Morrissey's lyrics are reducible to a coded biography—of a coherent narrative kind—and that criticism means breaking this code. 'Billy Budd' is thus *really* about the singer's relationship with

---

63. *In The Well Wrought Urn* (1947), Cleanth Brooks put forward a polemical critique of the tendency to assume that a poem is reducible to what it is 'about,' which he referred to as 'the heresy of paraphrase.'

64. Bret, *Morrissey*, pp. 179 and 108. Rogan exhibits a similar flair, pointing out that 'The Edges Are No Longer Parallel' shows Morrissey 'successfully introducing geometry into the lexicon of songwriting' and helpfully informing us with regard to 'You're Gonna Need Someone On Your Side' that 'lyrically, the song stresses the need for friends' (Rogan, *Morrissey*, pp. 252 and 181). Rogan takes such reductive readings even further, however, with his penchant for repesenting the recurrence of incidental details as thematically significant. We are told, for example, that 'I Have Forgiven Jesus' echoes the theme of 'Friday Mourning' (because they both mention Friday) and that the theme of 'The Lazy Sunbathers' is 'not dissimilar to that evoked in "Everyday Is Like Sunday"' (since they both mention bombs).

Johnny Marr[65] and *Vauxhall and I* is actually 'about' Morrissey's relationship with Jake:

> Perhaps this new outlook . . . had something to do with the fact that by *Vauxhall and I* Morrissey seemed to finally really have the one that he couldn't have, in the form of a tattooed thirty-year-old suedehead boxer called 'Jake,' who tagged along at interviews, working as his driver and live-in general factotum and who may well have really, really opened his eyes. The same Jake is credited with taking the picture on the rear of the *Vauxhall* sleeve, showing what looks like Morrissey's paws on someone's muscular back with a swallow drawn on his right hand, a doodling habit, reportedly, of Jake's (hence the single 'Swallow On My Neck' is also probably a Jake-inspired work).
>
> Jake's inked torso is also on the rear of the single from the album, 'The More You Ignore Me,' and he is offered 'very special thanks' at the end of *Vauxhall*'s credits. It's even possible that the album title is itself a reference/tribute to Jake. . . . In interviews Morrissey reportedly referred to the name as the birthplace of 'someone I know.' In other words the ruffian that Morrissey had been looking for, calling for in his work all these years appeared to have finally materialized.[66]

Whatever the interest and validity of these speculations—and their 'perhaps,' 'may,' 'probably' and 'possible' do little to disguise the determination of its 'X is really Y' procedure—the problem is that the act of criticism again encourages a passing beyond what is or isn't actually said (a transition explicitly signalled by Simpson's 'in other words') and furnishes an 'aboutness' of the critic's imagining, which distorts or displaces the work itself and effaces its aesthetic character.

That all art must have a realist 'aboutness'—and that this is what we value or 'look for' in art—is a remarkably recalcitrant and unquestioned assumption.[67] Yet there are other traditions and other things that art can do or be, aside from existing for the sake of its 'aboutness' (indeed, art is arguably brought into being by that which in the act of communication exceeds its utilitarian 'aboutness'). One thing it can do or exist as is play.

---

65. Simpson, *Saint Morrissey*, p. 153.
66. Ibid., p. 152.
67. For a seminal account of how Western art became dominated by the idea of 'content,' see Susan Sontag's essay 'Against Interpretation.'

LEVITY

The telling of beautiful untrue things

A good example of what I mean by play is to be found in 'Is It Really So Strange?' the opening song on *Louder Than Bombs*. The song has a fairly conventional structure, consisting of three verses, with a chorus following the first two and a change section in its place to close. The verses begin in a parallel way—'I left the north / I travelled south'; 'I left the south / I travelled north'; 'I left the north again / I travelled south again'—and comprise two subsections, one describing the various journeyings and one envisioning the elaborate violence the speaker would be prepared to endure ('Oh yes, you can kick me / and you can punch me / and you can break my face'). These subsections then culminate in a parallel claim—'I can't help the way I feel'; 'But you won't change the way I feel'—which prompts the chorus that gives the song its title. What is interesting about the song, however, is that it moves in the direction of offering a conventional realist narrative, but stops short of actually doing so. It also includes other elements and discontinuities which likewise trouble any attempt to read for realist 'aboutness'—most obviously, the surreal lines 'I got confused—I killed a horse'; 'I got confused—I killed a nun'—which at the narrative level come out of nowhere and in a sense 'exceed' the story that contains them, but which are, structurally and formally, carefully paralleled and find a counterpart in the sublimely mundane parenthesis '(I lost my bag at Newport Pagnell).' In attempting to extract from the song or characterize it in terms of a realist 'aboutness,' commentary on 'Is It Really So Strange?' tends to travesty both this shortfall and this 'excess.' Here are a couple of examples:

> The song ['Sheila Take A Bow'] was coupled with 'Is It Really So Strange?' the story of a boy who relocates from the North to the South, experiences threats, prejudice and confusion, but only gets more of the same when he heads back to his roots.[68]

> Chasing the disinterested object of his desire from North to South and back again, in his lovelorn confusion Morrissey confesses to murdering first a horse and then a nun. The unrequited amour corrupting his

---

68. Bret, *Morrissey*, p. 85.

every move is, he claims, invincible enough to even withstand physical violence from his averse love-interest. Alas, this black comedy ends with the grim realisation that, with the blood of a Bride of Christ on his hands, just like Gene Pitney in Bacharach and David's '24 Hours From Tulsa,' he can 'never, never go back home again' (ditto The Shangri-Las' 1965 classic 'I Can Never Go Home Anymore').[69]

Apparently immune to matters of form, irony or voice, Bret offers a paraphrase of the song which elides all the things that make it interesting, and reduces it to a plot it doesn't quite have. Whilst Goddard, by contrast, is sensitive to the musical ironies of the song—speaking of its 'stylised . . . rock 'n' roll motifs' and its 'tongue-in-cheek Fifties feel'[70]—he is similarly constrained by realist presuppositions to read everything 'straightly' and see every line in the song, however bizarre, as having a literal representative function—which is to say, as existing solely for the sake of its 'aboutness' (although his almost apologetic attempt to 'write up' the narrative—'lovelorn confusion,' 'unrequited amour' and 'the blood of a Bride of Christ'—betrays a nagging anxiety about the reductiveness of such reading). What, then, is going on, if the song eludes and exceeds a realist aboutness?

What we can see in 'Is It Really So Strange?' is an unshackling of the referential function of language and the advent of what I am referring to as 'play.' This may sound somewhat abstruse, but what it means is that language is being used for a purpose other than imitation or representation. To understand what this purpose might be, it will be instructive to refer to the antirealist aesthetic theory of Morrissey's hero, Oscar Wilde, as brilliantly expounded in the singer's favourite text, *The Decay of Lying*.[71]

According to the principal speaker of Wilde's dialogue, Vivian, 'art never expresses anything but itself. It has an independent life, just as Thought has, and develops purely on its own lines.' This independent development is characterized as follows:

> Art begins with abstract decoration, with purely imaginative and pleasurable work dealing with what is unreal and non-existent. . . . Then

---

69. Goddard, *The Smiths*, p. 219.
70. Ibid., p. 218.
71. Wilde has a curious status in commentary on Morrissey, in which he seems to have become a kind of mascot for various vague causes, valued for almost anything except as a *writer*. Tellingly, Rogan, Simpson, Bret and Goddard all repeatedly refer to Wilde, without ever discussing any of his works.

> Life becomes fascinated with this new wonder, and asks to be admitted
> into the charmed circle. Art takes life as part of her rough material, rec-
> reates it, and refashions it in fresh forms, is absolutely indifferent to fact,
> invents, imagines, dreams, and keeps between herself and reality the
> impenetrable barrier of beautiful style, of decorative or ideal treatment.

Art is therefore—or should be—akin to lying, which he defines as
'the telling of beautiful untrue things,' the corollaries of which are:
a preference for 'whim' as opposed to consistency (which is for the
'dullard and doctrinaire . . . who carry out their principles to the bitter end of action'); a privileging of art *above* nature (as the former
reveals 'Nature's lack of design, her curious crudities, her extraordinary monotony, her absolutely unfinished condition'); and a frank
disregard for fact (which is the 'vulgar' preserve of the modern
novelist, who 'is to be found at the Librairie Nationale, or at the
British Museum, shamelessly reading up his subject'). Wilde's 'new
aesthetics' is thus polemically set over against realism or imitation,
which he describes as falling into 'careless habits of accuracy,' and
instead endorses the alternative principles of Orientalism, 'with its
frank rejection of imitation, its love of artistic convention, its dislike
of the actual representation of any object in Nature.'[72] (It is worth
noting that the butt of many of Wilde's jokes in setting out his 'new
aesthetics' is Wordsworth, whose manifesto preface to *Lyrical Ballads*
calls for precisely the 'return to Life and Nature' that *The Decay of
Lying* seeks to repudiate.)

Morrissey's aesthetic position—in so far as one can be deduced
from his practice—is plainly not as extreme as this (although neither, considering his whole oeuvre, is Wilde's). Indeed, it is part of
my argument that Morrissey's 'oxymoronic' writing is aligned on
the one hand to the aestheticism of Wilde, but also on the other
hand to the romanticism of Wordsworth.[73] Nevertheless, Wilde's
extremist aesthetic views helpfully cast light on certain aspects of
Morrissey's practice.[74]

---

72. Wilde, *The Decay of Lying*, pp. 191; 173; 192; 164; 163; 166; 167; 175.
73. Morrissey's early use of flowers—as something 'natural' but also as an *objet d'art*—interestingly
hovers between the antithetical attitudes of Wordsworth and Wilde.
74. The singer's manner of speaking in interviews also inherits the aestheticism of Wilde's Vivian:

> *Eleanor Levy*: What would be your favourite moment from *Brookside*?
>
> *Morrissey*: Oh, good heavens, there are so many. One's diary is just littered with moments
> from *Brookside*.

(*Record Mirror*, September 21, 1985).

Returning to 'Is It Really So Strange?': the song, to begin with, suggests a conventional narrative, which is encouraged by the approximate biographical correspondence (Morrissey moved from Manchester to London in 1984, and the theme of not belonging is central to his work). But by the time we get to the second verse, the lyrics seem to be driven more by aesthetic concerns and to have less to do with anything outside themselves. The generality of the journeying and the deadpan reversal of direction at the start of each verse, for example, whilst connoting a certain pointlessness, begins to seem more abstract and less referential, especially by the time we get to the third verse—'I left the north again / I travelled south again'—whose phonetically ungainly 'again' comically points towards a repetition at the level of discourse as well as story, turning the song's focus further in on itself.[75] This shift away from referentiality is even more apparent in the song's heterogeneous images of violence, which announce a kind of cartoon ontology—a universe, that is, of bloodless, deathless violence, in which the usual laws of cause and effect are suspended. A horse and a nun, like the sponge and the rusty spanner in 'The Queen Is Dead,' for example, appear to be selected for their very incongruity, and the second verse's description of the violence the singer is prepared to endure ('Oh yes, you can punch me / and you can butt me / and you can break my spine') evidently owes more to Morrissey's comical habit of introducing surprising variations into lists than any attempt to represent a realistic state of affairs.[76] In both cases, in other words, the lyrics are determined to a large degree by *aesthetic* criteria. Finally, the singer's Elvis impersonation (or impersonation of an Elvis impersonation) that follows ''Cause I love you' and which is of a piece with the plumy guffaw at the end of 'Certain People I Know,' similarly foregrounds the song's quotational character—which is to say, its self-conscious use of stock phrases—and, as a sort of intertextual gesture, suggests art speaking of other art more than of anything outside itself. (It is hard, in view of these oblique allusions to its own textual status, not to sense a self-reflexive wink in the song's title as well.)

75. 'Story' and 'discourse' are terms used in narratology to distinguish between 'what is told' and 'how it is told.'

76. Realizations of this 'cartoon ontology' are to be found throughout Morrissey's writing. Take, for instance, the first three songs on *Meat Is Murder*: 'The Headmaster Ritual' ('he does the military two-step down the nape of my neck'); 'Rusholme Ruffians' (in which he repeats, without differentiation, and with Punch and Judy impassivity, 'and someone falls in love / and someone's beaten up'); and 'Nowhere Fast' ('a tough kid who sometimes swallows nails').

We must be careful, however, not to push this too far. Morrissey's lyrics are rarely, if ever, a matter of 'abstract decoration . . . dealing with what is unreal and non-existent,' as we find, say, in 'The Cocteau Twins.' Rather, they retain a suggestive or flirtatious referentiality—which is at times abandoned and at times insisted upon—such that they hover between and are crucially different from purely imaginary dealings with the nonexistent as well as conventional realism. This is what I mean by 'play.' We can be more precise. Whilst his lyrics tend to 'make sense' locally—and do not in the main consist of nonsense sounds or phrases—they at the same time frequently eschew or are relatively uninterested in any underlying or coherent 'narrative' sense.[77] Thus they often play with meanings—staging a mobility, heterogeneity or reflexivity—and are shaped as much by aesthetic concerns as they are by a desire to express or represent a state of affairs outside themselves.[78] Again, this is by no means always or absolutely the case. Morrissey is this *as well as* that. But this fugitive, pervasive tendency towards play is one of the reasons why Morrissey's lyrics are invariably more than their 'aboutness.'

In defence of lightness

The realist exaltation of 'content' encourages a blindness to other aesthetic effects as well. Unquestionably, the quality along with play that has been most depreciated by commentators on Morrissey is lightness—which has in fact ceased to have a positive existence of its own and has instead become the gap in which 'aboutness' would have had its being. (Hence the dismissive assessments of his 'lighter' work as 'silly,' 'frivolous' and 'infuriatingly slight.'[79])

Lightness has had an extremely bad press and has oddly come to be a term of abuse. 'Oddly,' because whilst it's customary to describe some of the most valued works of art—such as Mozart's piano concertos, Shelley's lyrics, Fra Angelico's annunciations or the carvings in Southwell Chapter House—as 'light' without lightness being a pejorative term, it is commonly used nowadays to mean the opposite of

---

77. Morrissey has spoken approvingly of this tendency in other lyricists: 'New York Dolls songs are much better where there is no storyline' (Morrissey, *New York Dolls*).

78. One is again reminded of Wilde's green carnation, which was a celebration of sterility and the uselessness of art: 'It is superbly sterile, and the note of its pleasure is sterility. A work of art is useless as a flower is useless. A flower blossoms for its own joy' (cited in Bartlett, *Who Was That Man?* p. 46).

79. Bret, *Morrissey*, p. 248; Goddard, *The Smiths*, p. 171; and Reid, *Morrissey*, p. 7.

serious and a near relative of the superficial. Indeed, there seems to be a default assumption, which betrays a lingering 'Victorianism,' that earnestness is what matters in art (one recalls Bernard Shaw's remark about the comedy of an Englishman's seriousness). As a result, in line with the 'lite' of the food and drink industry, 'lightness' has come to be how we refer to something with an ingredient missing.

There is obviously something quite crazy about this. It is like criticizing Beaujolais for not being Claret. In many cases, lightness isn't a deficiency of seriousness or an anaemic version of something else, *it is its own thing*. Its delicacy, its mobility, its 'only' being this or that, its repudiation of gravity or heaviness may be—as it is in the finest china, the movement of Galina Ulanova or the passing of David Beckham—the result of the most exquisite skill and evidence of alternative aims.[80] Such lightness doesn't set itself alongside anything else as 'deeper.' And whilst few would wish lightness to be the only or even the supreme value, few would surely wish its achievements out of existence and deny it is an estimable *alternative* value.[81] As Susan Sontag observes of the exemplary lightness of camp: 'There are other creative sensibilities besides the serious' and one cheats oneself as a human being if one only has respect for the latter.[82]

Morrissey's particular brand of lightness once again clearly aligns him with Wilde, who was of course the nemesis of Victorian seriousness (and to whom Sontag's 'Notes on "Camp"' are dedicated). He has a fondness too, though, for *Carry On* film lightness and the kind of comedy—such as *Round the Horne*—which was broadcast,

---

80. G. K. Chesterton's comments on the subject are salutary: 'One "settles down" into a sort of selfish seriousness; but one has to rise to a gay self-forgetfulness. A man "falls" into a brown study; he reaches up at a blue sky. Seriousness is not a virtue. It would be a heresy, but a much more sensible heresy, to say that seriousness is a vice. It is really a natural trend or lapse into taking one's self gravely, because it is the easiest thing to do. It is much easier to write a good *Times* leading article than a good joke in *Punch*. For solemnity flows out of men naturally; but laughter is a leap. It is easy to be heavy: hard to be light' (Chesterton, *Orthodoxy*, p. 128).

81. For a consideration of lightness as a value rather than a defect, see Italo Calvino, *Six Memos for the Next Millenium*, chapter 1.

82. Sontag, 'Notes on Camp,' pp. 114–5. One might of course claim more for the aesthetics of lightness. Terry Eagleton, for example, argues that the playfulness of W. H. Auden—who edited a celebrated anthology of light verse and asserts in its introduction that 'lightness is a great virtue'— can be read 'not as a defeatist political withdrawal, but as an instance of that "carnivalesque" spirit, subverting the solemnities of bourgeois authority with the iconoclasm of humour and the body' (cited in Smith, 'Auden's Light and Serio-Comic Verse,' p. 99). In his consideration of the 'lighter' aspects of 'late style,' Edward Said relatedly contends that amusement is a 'form of resistance,' since it does not require reconciliation with a status quo or a dominant regime' (Michael Woods, Introduction, *On Late Style*, p. xiv). I am grateful to Marina Warner for bringing Said's argument to my attention.

appropriately enough, on the BBC's Light Programme. Such humour is a pervasive element in Morrissey's lyrics—as we shall see in the subsequent discussion of innuendo; however, it is apparent as well in his cast of eccentrics and character sketches, which include 'Dagenham Dave,' the 'vicar in a tutu,' 'Tony the Pony,' and the unconscionably abused window cleaner 'Roy.'

The song 'Roy's Keen,' on *Maladjusted*, has prompted some of the most patronizing commentary on the singer to date. For Rogan, it is 'banal,' laden with 'bad puns' and includes 'one of the most painfully strained metaphors in pop.'[83] For Bret, who revealingly thinks 'Sorrow Will Get You In The End' is 'brilliant' and should have been 'the focus point of the album,' it is 'rather silly' and nothing more.[84] Even the album's bassist, Jonny Bridgwood, has dismissed it as 'throw-away.'[85] Let us look again at this neglected song.

> He's romancing you
> and chancing his arm
> he'll be here
> smiling on time . . .
> Roy's keen, oh Roy's keen
> we've never seen a
> keener window-cleaner
>
> the ladder's a planet
> Roy is a star, and
> I am a satellite
> (but that's alright)
>
> He can hold a smile for as long
> as you require (even longer) . . .
> don't say you'll hold it steady
> then you let it go
> don't say you'll hold it steady
> then you let it go
>
> You're up the ladder
> into each corner
> foot in a bucket
> we trust you to wreck it

83. Rogan, *Morrissey*, p. 243.
84. Bret, *Morrissey*, p. 248.
85. Cited in Rogan, *Morrissey*, p. 243.

Even when it's under your nose
well, you just can't see it, can you?
well, it's here
right under your nose
and you just can't see it, can you?

'Even when it's under your nose / well, you just can't see it, can you?'
One of the many joys of 'Roy's Keen' is its reflexive allusion to its
own innuendos and the sense it gives one that it was lying in wait for
its obtuse criticism—whilst all the time keeping a perfectly straight
face. And it is this perfectly straight face that lies at the centre of
many of its other comic effects.

We are told very little about the song's 'star' Roy; however, it is a
sign of Morrissey's adroit characterization that so much can be communicated so economically. All we need to be told in fact is 'He can
hold a smile for as long / as you require.' We are given a gentle nar-
ratorial nudge in the ribs by the eccentric pronunciation of 're-quire,'
whilst the cutting parenthesis '(even longer)' puts one in mind of Jane
Austen's Mr Bennet, whose irony is all the more crushing for seeming so complementary ('You have delighted us long enough'[86]). The
earlier verse's 'smiling on time' is less overt in its irony, but its double
sense of 'arriving on time, smiling' and 'smiling on cue' conveys a
similarly withering impression. That there is little else to say about the
character is of course itself saying something (and one suspects that
the sublimely unreflective Roy would himself deem the song to be
'banal' or 'rather silly'). Perhaps what's most amusing of all, though,
about the song is its performance of his lack of irony. And it is in this
very straight-facedness that the song's own irony paradoxically consists. (Roy's artless good will is delightfully reflected by the barbershop
cheeriness of the backing vocals, whose spruce textbook 'la la la's are
likewise comical *on account of* their very straight-facedness. Similarly,
once one's got the general idea, even the verbatim repetition of the
song's first four lines seems to be an ironic impersonation of Roy's *lack*
of irony and immutable eagerness to please.[87])

---

86. Austen, *Pride and Prejudice*, p. 69.
87. In the same way, it seems to me that the song's flagrantly lame pun—which groans at its
own corniness—is intended to reflect something of the character of the protagonist (as we shall
see, Morrissey does something similar in 'Dagenham Dave'). And as for the 'painfully strained
metaphor,' we should notice that it is spoken by Roy's sidekick or at any rate someone at the level
of the song's characters. (Morrissey frequently speaks from the perspective of a sidelined observer
or a bit-part character.) Its inanity is thus staged and, like Dogberry's inarticulacy in *Much Ado
About Nothing*, tells us something about its speaker, and it is Rogan's attempt to interpret it that
is painfully strained.

Aside from the comedy of Roy's characterization, the other principal appeal of the song is the *Carry On* slapstick of its second half, which comically seeks out the archetypally corny gag ('foot in a bucket / we trust you to wreck it') and introduces an element of sexual innuendo.[88] Indeed, whilst neither Rogan nor Bret seems to pick up the joke, the passing around of the ticklishly unspecified 'it'—which includes a medial Frankie Howerd 'ooh-oh' in case we missed the innuendo—is rich with suggestive ironies. These multiply wonderfully in the final verse, which—again in an manner that reminds one of Frankie Howerd—manages to be brazenly salacious in reflexively speaking about picking up on things ('well, it's here / right under your nose / and you just can't see it, can you?') and in doing so vertiginously makes fun of its own processes.

'Roy's Keen' doesn't attempt to do much more than this. Though 'this' seems to me to be quite enough, and condensing a *Carry On* film into a three-minute pop song is surely not an inconsiderable achievement.[89] Of course, one might nevertheless persist in deeming such things 'silly' and maintain that art should deal with 'serious' subjects. But for Morrissey—as for Auden, Betjeman, Byron and others—such things have their place in art because silliness is 'part of the whole show.'[90]

Camp

The darkest place, according to a Chinese proverb, is underneath the lamp. In a certain sense, which seems to bear this out, as a result of the everyday ubiquity of the term, we have apparently become blind to camp; for the more it has become established in common usage, the more it seems to have passed out of sight as a critical or

---

88. The song also doubtless owes something to George Formby's 'When I'm Cleaning Windows,' whose speaker clearly differs from Morrissey's Roy, but whose sexual innuendo anticipates Morrissey's practice. Here are a couple of verses:

Pyjamas lyin' side by side
Ladies nighties I have spied
I've often seen what goes inside
When I'm cleanin' windows

She [a famous talkie queen] pulls her hair all down behind
Then pulls down her . . . never mind
And after that pulls down the blind
When I'm cleanin' windows.

89. See pp. 234–37 for a related discussion of 'Vicar In A Tutu.'
90. Smith, 'Auden's Light and Serio-Comic Verse,' p. 97.

aesthetic category. Morrissey has himself lamented this state of affairs in speaking of his attachment to camp:

> *James Brown*: What about camp flirting?
>
> *Morrissey*: I never do that.
>
> *Brown*: You do!
>
> *Morrissey*: I knew you'd stray. I knew as soon as I mentioned 'camp' you'd stray from the real meaning of the word. I knew you'd suddenly think of feathers and things like that. No, I don't flirt. You were there at Wolverhampton, you could see the steam, there was aggression.[91]

One of the unfortunate consequences of this critical blindness is that the space in which art of this kind is appreciated on its own terms comes to be filled by other, more familiar categories, alien to its reasons for being, according to whose standards or rationale it is then inappropriately judged. Manifestly, not all of Morrissey's work could be characterized as camp, yet a large amount of it—with The Smiths and as a solo artist—undoubtedly is or contains prominent elements of camp, and the lack of a corresponding critical category has shaped its reception and frequently led commentators to denigrate it as an inferior form of some other thing. *Kill Uncle* is an obvious case in point. Here is what Johnny Rogan has to say about the album:

> *Kill Uncle* was a puzzling record. Sparse and superficial, it had none of the momentum of *Viva Hate* nor the breadth of *Bona Drag*. At just over 33 minutes, it was insubstantial to the point of insult . . . an album bereft of passion, drama or any deeply held conviction or emotion. . . . The selection now looks embarrassingly lightweight, as if they were struggling to find enough songs to fill the album, which was not the case. While some tracks impressed, others were dull as dish water with sparse melodies and trite lyrics.[92]

No one, I think, would want to argue that *Kill Uncle* is Morrissey's greatest work. But I do wish to suggest that it has been widely criticized according to the wrong criteria and that its negative reception was in many cases mistaken in its failure to recognize the difference between criticizing a work as a deficient version of something one likes and a successful version of something one doesn't like. Thus, Rogan's

---

91. *NME*, February 25, 1989.
92. Rogan, *Morrissey*, pp. 163–5.

criticism of the album as 'superficial,' 'insubstantial' and 'bereft of passion, drama or any deeply held conviction or emotion' is wrong, I think, not because it isn't these things, but because this isn't necessarily a criticism. Indeed, the characteristics he identifies as faults—its lightness, its aloofness, its lack of depth and its celebration of surfaces—are the very aims of camp aesthetics and *positive* qualities from its point of view.[93] If we wish to appreciate such works on their own terms—which is only equivalent to considering the success of a comedy *as* a comedy, instead of deploring it as a failed attempt at tragedy—it will be helpful to refamiliarize ourselves with the typical features of camp art.

Descriptions of camp invariably advert to the way it eludes description (and frequently enact its excesses in attempting to define them). For Sontag, it is a 'fugitve sensibility'; for Medhurst, defining camp 'is like attempting to sit in the corner of a circular room'; and for Mauriès, it is 'an impossible object of discourse, a word—and, by that, an ethic, an aesthetic, a *savoir-vivre*—that exceeds description.'[94] Nevertheless, descriptions have been attempted, and there is a certain amount of agreement between them. Most commentators, first of all, agree that camp is not a thing (though there are popular icons and exemplary instances) but a sensibility, attitude or manner of comportment. This manner of engaging with things is, importantly, not fixed, but is instead a mobile, marginal or 'contrapuntal' posture, which is detached from, at odds with or in excess of its object (as Fabio Cleto puts it, camp is 'the crisis of identity, of depth, and of *gravity*'[95]—suggesting a nonessential 'logic of destabilization . . . on the move in "things themselves"'[96]). Everyone agrees that there is 'a peculiar affinity and overlap' between camp and homosexuality[97] but there is fierce disagreement about the origins, 'ownership' and commodification of camp.[98] In terms of style, there are a number

93. Steve Sutherland's vindictive review of the album in *Melody Maker* is likewise perfectly accurate in its characterization of *Kill Uncle* but similarly mistaken in assuming that this is necessarily something negative: '*Kill Uncle* is Morrissey comfortably slippered, feet on the pouffe, tea and scones, and a welcome guest in the home of the so-bad-it's-good Sally Army. *Kill Uncle* is Morrissey revelling in mediocrity. . . . *Kill Uncle* is such a tragic, turgid, pathetic record one can only assume it's an act of spite' (cited in Rogan, *Morrissey*, p. 167).
94. Sontag, 'Notes on Camp,' p. 106; Medhurst, 'Batman, Deviance and Camp,' p. 154; and Patrick Mauriès, *Second Manifeste Camp* (1979), cited in Cleto, *Camp*, p. 3.
95. Cleto, *Camp*, p. 34.
96. This is how Nicholas Royle describes deconstruction (Royle, *Deconstructions*, p. 11).
97. Sontag, 'Notes on Camp,' p. 117.
98. The attempt by Moe Meyers and others in the 1990s to supplant Sontag's 'apolitical' and 'aestheticized' account and 'reclaim' camp as 'solely a queer (and/or sometimes gay and lesbian) discourse,' fencing off and demoting any other manifestation as 'Pop camp' or a 'trace' of its 'original,' has itself been vigorously repudiated by Cleto and others (see Cleto, *Camp*).

of characteristics which tend to recur. Most critics point towards its love of artifice or the 'unnatural' and the way in which it delights in excess (which may be a matter of gratuitousness—as in the extravagant ornamentation of Gaudí's buildings or the musicals of Busby Berkeley; hyperbole—as in the use of overinflected diction, such as 'darling,' 'ghastly,' 'divine,' etc.;[99] or it may be the ironic 'too much' of parody).[100] Closely related to this love of artifice and 'excessive' style is a tendency towards theatricalization and 'dressing up'; as Susan Sontag famously observes: 'To perceive Camp in objects and persons is to understand Being-as-Playing-a-Role. It is the farthest extension, in sensibility, of the metaphor of life as theatre.'[101] We find a cognate multiplication of surfaces at a linguistic level in the wordplay and 'semiotic excess' in which camp delights—a semantic ambiguity which, at one time, was a form of protection that 'made the double life possible,' for it 'allowed men to construct a gay world in the midst of but invisible to the straight world,'[102] but which has become much more assertive and a way of *subverting* the dominant discourse of 'the straight world.'[103] This tendency towards 'duplicity' and theatricalization leads us onto another important feature of camp—namely, incongruity.

According to Philip Core's aphoristic 'Camp Rules,' camp is 'a disguise that fails.'[104] What this means, I take it, is that it is a masquerade or performance which advertises itself as such, and which wants us simultaneously to see through and go along with its illusion—to be aware of the performer as well as the performance (or to see the quotation marks around the performance).[105] In this way, as Richard

99. Cohan, *Incongruous Entertainment*, p. 16.

100. Steve Cohan suggests that the stylistic excess of camp is a 'homological' reflection of the social status of the 'queer': 'At its most affective, camp recognised the queer as social excess—the surplus value of straight culture, so to speak—while providing the rationale or alibi for his being "too much" through style, taste, and parody, the assertion of a dissident sensibility distinct from the mainstream yet located within it' (ibid., p. 18).

101. Sontag, 'Notes on Camp,' p. 109. Once again, it is possible to see stylistic elements of camp—such as its love of drag and cosmetic effects—as a reflection of debates about the 'performative' nature of sexuality and gender. Judith Butler, for example, argues that drag is not an 'imitation of gender' but instead 'dramatise[s] the signifying gestures through which gender itself is established' (Butler, *Gender Trouble*, p. viii).

102. Chauncey, *Gay New York*, p. 286.

103. In the words of Steven Cohan: 'Camp wit exploited the ambiguity of straight discourse in order to articulate a queer perspective of social as well as sexual relations. It provocatively challenged the legitimacy of perceived intent, exposing the larger cultural field in which words bore meanings beyond their confining straight context' (Cohan, *Incongruous Entertainment*, p. 13).

104. Core, *Camp*, p. 7.

105. The importance of quotation marks to camp has been highlighted by Sontag: 'Camp sees everything in quotation marks. It's not a lamp, but a "lamp"; not a woman, but a "woman," "person" and "thing"' (Sontag, 'Notes on Camp,' p. 109).

Dyer writes, '[Camp] holds together qualities that are elsewhere felt as antithetical: theatricality and authenticity . . . intensity and irony, a fierce assertion of extreme feeling with a deprecating sense of its absurdity.'[106] (Dyer is discussing the camp appeal of Judy Garland, whose 'oxymoronic' combination of involvement and detachment is exemplified in her performance of 'The Man That Got Away,' in *A Star Is Born*, a song invested with pathos and sung with conviction, at the end of which Garland winks at the band, appearing momentarily to signal a subjectivity outside the song's persona.[107]) Such incongruity is neatly summed up by Esther Newton as a 'double stance toward role, putting on a good show whilst indicating distance.'[108] The disjunction between involvement and detachment isn't always signalled by an abrupt dropping of the mask or breaking of the spell, however. Sometimes it's achieved by an aloof disposition—a languid alienation from one's own gestures—which, as Gary McMahon notes, is 'so emblematic of camp.'[109] (The novels of Ronald Firbank, with their exquisite doodling, their writerly browsing and their frank disinterest in the encumbrances of character or plot, are a superlative example.) There is an obverse incongruity, though, which is equally characteristic of camp. In her 'Notes on Camp,' Sontag distinguishes between the 'old-style dandy' who 'hated vulgarity' and the 'new-style dandy' or 'lover of camp' who 'appreciates vulgarity,' observing that where 'the dandy would be continually offended or bored, the connoisseur of Camp is continually amused, delighted.'[110] Sontag's comment reminds us that it is the subject's gaze that counts in camp; for a thing may be amusing and delightful *without* being camp. In order to attain the distinction of camp, there must be some sort of discrepancy between the object of appreciation and the subject's response—as if the camp gaze combined Sancho Panza's view of things as well as Don Quixote's—which crucially needs to be preserved, even as it is apparently elided in the wand-waving ennobling of camp tribute.[111] (This is the logic of Sontag's notorious final 'note'—'The ultimate

106. Dyer, 'Judy Garland and Gay Men,' p. 154.
107. Cohan, *Incongruous Entertainment*, pp. 24–6.
108. Newton, *Mother Camp*, p. 109.
109. McMahon, *Camp in Literature*, p. 35.
110. Sontag, 'Notes on Camp,' p. 117.
111. According to McMahon, 'Two opposite elements synthesise vitally in camp composition: the domestic banality of everyday life . . . and the fanciful daydream' (McMahon, *Camp in Literature*, p. 63).

Camp statement: it's good because it's awful'[112]—which illustrates why the loving gesture of camp may be seen as a sort of redemption or aesthetic salvation.)

There are two other typical features of camp which sum up many of the characteristics identified so far: firstly, the elevation of style over content (and surface over depth). Wilde, for example, will bestow lavish attention upon incidental objects in the midst of a narrative, converting the 'background' into a virtual protagonist, for the sake of decoration, as though he were a spectator of his own creativity, idly in love with the medium of his imaginings.[113] (Firbank would elevate this love of style and surface still further, increasing the camp discrepancy between the commonplace phenomenon and the extravagance of the subject's regard; as Siegfried Sassoon reports of one of their conversations, 'His most rational response to my attempts at drawing him out about literature was "I adore italics, don't you?"'[114]) The second overarching feature, which obviously follows on from this, is the flippancy or frivolity of camp. Indeed, as Sontag claims, the 'whole point of Camp is to dethrone the serious.'[115] This is much more subversive—and paradoxically serious—than it may at first appear; for, as Hugh Haughton argues—speaking of Wilde's *Decay of Lying*—the camp/aesthetic critique of seriousness is at the same time a critique of European realism, which 'calls into question the entire mimetic tradition in Western art and morality.'[116] At the heart of camp, then, is a radical overturning of conventional values, discreetly effected by a chiasmus of incongruities, which is typically identified as a matter of treating the serious trivially and taking the trivial seriously—though in doing so, it gives the foundations a shake and makes it hard to speak about 'the serious' and 'the trivial.'

---

112. Sontag, 'Notes on Camp,' p. 119. Camp, for McMahon, is thus a sort of benign category mistake, in which the everyday is seen through the lens of the fairy tale and coloured with 'the mythology and romanticism and pageantry of fantasy' (McMahon, *Camp in Literature*, p. 63).

113. Consider, for instance, the following description: 'They took their seats amidst a crowd of watchers. The tulip-beds across the road flamed like throbbing rings of fire. A white dust—tremulous cloud of orris-root it seemed—hung in the panting air. The brightly coloured parasols danced and dipped like monstrous butterflies' (Wilde, *The Picture of Dorian Gray*, p. 57).

114. Cited in Horder, *Ronald Firbank*, p. 151.

115. Sontag, 'Notes on Camp,' p. 116.

116. Haughton, preface to Wilde, *The Decay of Lying*, p. vii.

The importance of not being earnest

If we look again at *Kill Uncle* with the aesthetics of camp in mind, its lightness seems to make more sense and may be viewed as a positive achievement, rather than a lack of something else. This isn't to say that we have to like this kind of art; what matters is that we recognize it *as* a particular kind of art and judge it according to those terms.

Manifestos are of course beneath the indolent dignity of camp; however, the album's aesthetic agenda is clearly announced in the opening song. 'Our Frank' is a tartly lethargic rejection of thinking, depth, sincerity and seriousness, whose gratuitously punning title advertises its frivolity and a preference for surfaces—an effect that is dependent upon its very weakness. Here is the opening verse and the ad-libbed final section:

> Our frank and open
> deep conversations
> they get me nowhere
> they bring me down, so
> give it a rest, won't you?
> give me a cigarette
> God give me patience
> just no more conversation
>
> Won't somebody stop me
> from thinking all the time
> so deeply
> so bleakly . . .
> about everything—
> who I am, how I am
> and where I am.

The singer's request for a cigarette—and it's hard to tell whether 'Morrissey' is speaking, being spoken to, occupying both positions or in some sense moving between them—is of course part of the song's counterintellectualization and corollary elevation of the sensual. Yet it is also, in the canon of aesthetic literature, an emblem of idleness and 'pointless' pleasure and, as Gary McMahon points out, 'a popular performance accessory to the aloof poise of the camp perspective.'[117] This 'aloof poise' is reinforced by the use of genteel

---

117. McMahon, *Camp in Literature*, p. 137.

rhyming vocatives—here and elsewhere on the album ('blend, my friend'; 'your taxi is here, my dear'[118]) as well as overinflected epithets ('frankly vulgar')—a consistent feature of Morrissey's idiolect. This counterintellectual elevation of the sensual is extended in the middle section and chorus:

> Give us a drink
> and make it quick
> or else I'm gonna be sick
> sick all over
> your frankly vulgar
> red pullover
> now see how the colours blend.

Whilst being sick is, needless to say, far too much of an exertion to be camp, there is obviously something *very* camp about the extravagance of the singer's distaste for 'deep conversations' and the addressee's 'red pullover'—especially when, in the next breath, the end of the world is introduced and folded up into a prefatory 'although' clause[119]—an extravagance that is matched by the phonetic 'excess' of the three line rhyme ('all over / vulgar / pullover'). There is additionally something decidedly camp about the attention accorded to colour and the immediate swerve into the realm of fantasy it induces ('now see how the colours blend'). In all of which, we can see a conspicuous attraction to surfaces and style (and a concomitant disdain for 'depth'), a tendency towards gratuitous or 'excessive' gestures (in punning, rhyming and hyperbole), and a two-way tonal incongruity in the song's trivial treatment of the serious conjoined with a serious treatment of the trivial. These camp effects are accentuated by the aloof ennui of the singer's delivery and elements of theatrical whimsy in the accompaniment (chintzy piano, 'Madness' bass, and the cartoon echoing voices of the outro[120]). If we widen the semiotic frame still further, we find these camp effects are also reinforced by the album's artwork, which depicts the singer—statuesque and aloof, photographed from below—wearing heavy

---

118. 'Mute Witness.'

119. 'The world may be ending / but look, I'm only human.'

120. The carnivalesque conclusion seems to represent a schizophrenic unleashing of voices (which come to the fore as Morrissey slides into doing what he asks—and in the act of asking—somebody to stop him from doing) whilst at the same time advertising its representational effects as 'manufactured' by the conspicuous speeding up and slowing down of the vocals.

eyeshadow, with a prodigious quiff, and assuming obviously assumed poses (not gestures, but 'gestures').[121]

To be sure, the album isn't like this throughout; indeed, its swings of tone are more extreme than on most of Morrissey's recordings. Nonetheless, its keynote is camp, and the lightness of 'Sing Your Life,' 'King Leer,' 'Driving Your Girlfriend Home' and 'Tony The Pony' predominates and furthers the aesthetic of 'Our Frank.'[122] 'Sing Your Life,' for example—a song so exquisitely thin you can almost see through it (and whose thinness is its consummate achievement)—doesn't venture outside its self-reflexivity for any of its materials. Instead, it skims the surface of its own reflection—or *is* the skimming of its reflected surfaces—as though the artist were attempting to fashion a work which was solely concerned with its own medium, and was gazing at its gazing at itself in the glass. The song's camp wink, however—and the sign that its lightness is a *refusal* of the seriousness and 'depth' of realist aboutness—comes in the final verse, where the singer teasingly raises our expectations that he is after all going to step outside the song's reflexivity and say something 'about' something:

> and make no mistake, my friend
> your pointless life will end
> but before you go
> can you look at the truth?

But having taken us to the edge of what appears to be an imminent Morrisseyesque disclosure, the singer swerves away with the bathos of a 'knock, knock' punch line, and the camp 'truth' that he in fact imparts is: 'you have a lovely singing voice.' There is, finally, something camp as well about the pathos of the singing towards the end of the song (which has a pastiche of chorus-boys' backing vocals as its foil), where he repeats 'Oh sing your oh-oo-oh.' Recalling the camp tendency to treat the trivial seriously, John Clum has described Judy Garland's performance of 'The Trolley Song' (in *Meet Me in St. Louis*) as a 'classic camp moment' on account of 'the extreme

---

121. The phrase 'Nothing to declare but my jeans'—which is of course a wordplay on Wilde's famous wordplay, which flaunts its frivolity and renunciation of 'depth'—appeared on press advertisements for the album (see Slee, *Peepholism*, p. 111). It is worth noting as well that Morrissey insisted on changing or excluding the names of musicians who played on the album on aesthetic grounds (Roger Beaujolais is not credited and Steve Nieve becomes Steve Heart), reminding one of the decadent exaltation of the aesthetic in *The Importance of Being Earnest*.
122. 'Tony The Pony' is included on the American issue only.

anxiety she is projecting while singing an inane song.'[123] To refer to the 'contentless' reflexivity of Morrissey's song as 'inane' would be to misunderstand its 'light materials' (and to overlook the finesse involved in its achievement). However, there is in Morrissey's song, too, an intensity that is in excess of the lyrics' occasioning, which parallels the disparity in Garland's performance and which similarly seems to be a matter of the singer's emergence through and 'overtaking' of the song's persona. Rather than spoiling things, though, the singer's exposure of the role by overstepping the mark is a kind of 'fortunate fall,' for in the failure of realism—or the *staging* of its failure—lies the success of camp, which reverses the imperatives of classical mimesis ('*ars artem celare est*') and delights in exposing the illusion it fosters.[124]

The camp of 'King Leer,' by contrast, is less a matter of ironically self-alienating gestures (though the dip into stumbling extrametrical prose—'I can't quite remember'; 'and nothing much happened'—draws attention to, in falling behind, its own artistry) and is more simply a matter of whimsy, which is as much constituted by the music as the lyrics. (In the primary A-F#minor refrain, the music cultivates a sort of technicolor tweeness—whose major's too major and whose minor's too minor—which comes out the other side as something other than tweeness, and is the musical equivalent of the unoccasioned pathos in Morrissey's singing at the end of 'Sing Your Life.'[125]) The title of the song is the first sign of this whimsy and has been roundly abused as an 'appallingly bad pun'[126]—as if Morrissey hadn't noticed its corniness. But we miss the point—as well as patronize the singer—if we fail to see that its corniness serves a purpose and once again announces an alternative aesthetic.[127] The following remarks on Firbank's antirealist fiction may help us to recognize the genre in which Morrissey also seems to be working:

---

123. Clum, *Something for the Boys*, p. 150.
124. Gary McMahon highlights the correspondence between the Brechtian alienation or 'A' effect (when a play disrupts the audience's identification by drawing attention to itself as a work of art) and what he refers to as the 'Ahh' effect of camp, which similarly exposes its workings, but does so with more of a smirk (McMahon, *Camp in Literature*, passim). There are obvious differences, however, for Brecht seeks to dispel the illusion of the theatre, as he wants art to serve *extra*theatrical purposes, whereas camp desires to dissolve the distinction, so that *everything* becomes theatre.
125. The camp colouring is turned up even further in the first (nonvocal) chorus with the addition of what sounds like a flute, whose kitsch embroidery nudges the song in the direction of a children's TV theme tune.
126. Rogan, *Morrissey*, p. 172.
127. As Walter Redfern points out, 'wilful bad punning can ascend to a kind of high verbal camp' (Redfern, *Puns*, p. 20).

Brigid Brophy attributes the author's painterly technique of 'isolating a single image in space,' an aspect of his 'aerated' style, to the line drawings of Aubrey Beardsley. Beardsley framed images by lines or art nouveau motifs, in turn influenced by the isolated images in Japanese prints and Japanese poetry. Again, she notes, incongruous juxtapositions of images space themselves apart on Firbank's pages. 'The image is displayed in its importance during the pause the reader is forced to make as he negotiates its unpredictable relation to the image before it.' This dissociation of narrative time and distancing from content suspending plot to crystallize a moment, a look, a style, reveals the author plying his craft behind the scenes.[128]

Morrissey's title bears only a very oblique relation to the story's lyrics and is more of an isolated moment of play, recalling the self-sufficient aesthetic suspensions of Firbank, Beardsley, Wilde and others.[129] It seems to exist for the sake of its whimsy, like a marginal doodle, that distracts us from—rather than introducing—the narrative that follows, such as it is.[130] In revealing more interest in the serendipities of language than in telling us anything, the title thus announces a refusal of seriousness, 'depth' and the conventions of realism.[131]

The song itself unfolds in the same vein, with its tendency to move 'sideways,' according to aesthetic connections or 'cartoon' logic, rather than in a 'linear' narrative manner, following the conventional dictates of plot ('Your boyfriend, he / went down on one knee / well, could it be / he's only got one knee?') and its forced rhymes ('surprise you / Tizer'; 'Chihuahua / an hour'), which succeed in reminding us we're in an aesthetic realm *as a result of* their awkwardness (the Chihuahua is of course the perfect camp prop—as a creature transformed into an *objet d'art*—which appropriately causes the addressee to swing between the aesthete's poles of delight and boredom).[132] There is even a fleeting aspirate snigger in the instrumental middle section,

128. McMahon, *Camp in Literature*, p. 146. The quotations from Brophy are taken from her biography of Firbank, *Prancing Novelist*.

129. As a self-consciously throw-away and 'lowbrow' gesture—which irreverently recycles the surfaces of 'high art'—it has something in common as well with the levelling citational aesthetics of Pop Art and the elevated ephemera of Warholian camp.

130. Throughout his career, Morrissey has exhibited a camp penchant for gratuitous wordplay, which crops up repeatedly in his titles, credits and matrix messages ('Oscillate Wildly,' 'Terrace Stomp,' 'The impotence of Earnest,' etc.).

131. Morrissey has remarked, 'What's important to me are the vocal melodies, even more than the lyrical content' (*Melody Maker*, August 9, 1997).

132. 'With a homeless Chihuahua / you cooed for an hour / you handed him back and said / "you'll never guess / I'm bored now."'

as though the singer were idly observing his own performance from the wings, making light of his making light of things, in case there were any doubt about how to take the song's frivolity.

Kill Uncle is certainly Morrissey's campest album, and 'Our Frank,' 'Sing Your Life' and 'King Leer' most clearly illustrate its aesthetic. Yet it would be a mistake to see this as an isolated flowering of camp style. As we saw in chapter 1, the holding together of involvement and detachment which constitutes the 'double aspect' of camp is a characteristic feature of Morrissey's performance. Likewise, the consummate endorsement of camp's trademark elevation of surface and style over content and 'depth' is to be found in 'This Charming Man' ('Why pamper life's complexities / when the leather runs smooth on the passenger seat?')—a song which in its disregard for narrative coherence, its use of overinflected epithets, its baroque layerings of arpeggiated guitars and its flamboyantly overwrought melisma is undoubtedly one of the campest things Morrissey has ever done. And probably the most sublime example of camp tone is 'Girlfriend In A Coma,' which discovers a borderland between pathos and flippancy by superfluously insisting on the seriousness of an obviously serious subject. Indeed, the 'comedy' of the song—which made Bono almost crash his car he laughed so much the first time he heard it[133]—paradoxically derives from its very straight-faced-ness and its seamless pastiche of platitudinous seriousness.[134] (In this respect, the song might be compared to the Pop Art images of Roy Lichtenstein, whose pastiche of the clichéd pathos of comic strip characters, with accompanying speech bubbles ['I know how you must feel, Brad . . .'], have an ironic resonance in spite of their 'neutral' reproduction.) And lest we imagine that all this is behind him, it is worth remembering that in 2007 Morrissey initiated talks about taking part in the Eurovision Song Contest—that cardboard parallel universe of camp—to which he also pays tribute with affectionate parody in the video for 'You Have Killed Me.'

How does Morrissey's fondness for camp fit in with the larger argument of the study about him being a great 'disturbance'? Generally speaking, camp is associated with momentary effects, and is

---

133. Cited in *The Importance of Being Morrissey* (documentary broadcast on Channel 4 on June 8, 2003).

134. Nadine Hubbs describes the song's 'marriage of tragic seriousness with transparent artifice' as 'characteristically Wildean and quintessentially camp' (Hubbs, 'Music of the "Fourth Gender,"' p. 281).

seen as an instantly gratifying form of 'light' entertainment, which doesn't seek to exceed its surfaces, and is sensationally consumed in its own spectacle. As a result, it is frequently deemed to be an anodyne and unchallenging aesthetic, which is happily paralysed in the amber of its quotation marks and is emasculated by its very excess. To some extent, this is certainly true (though, as I have argued, it isn't necessarily a criticism). Yet such a reading overlooks the subversive character of camp and the ways in which its 'double stance,' its impersonations, and its ill-fitting 'oxymoronic' tone deconstructs the identities it performs and exposes their underlying ideological structures.[135] For what camp does, according to Caryl Flinn, is 'to take the signs of human identity and place them into a performative situation, distancing them from their "original" sites, or indeed, the notion of an original or natural condition at all.'[136] In this way, it raises questions about the relationship between the exterior and the interior—such as whether the latter is expressed by or a projection of the former; whether identity is an essence or a performative effect; whether the 'self' is a singular, stable and knowable entity; and what in any context it means to be 'authentic.' In fact, as Flinn argues, 'gay male camp helped set the stage for feminist formulations of masquerade and other, nonessentialist articulations of gender as a performative phenomenon underived from innate essence, soul, or anything "in" the body.'[137] Such 'disturbing' tendencies have aesthetic ramifications too. For example, camp's serious treatment of the trivial and trivial treatment of the serious, along with its habit of citation and its love of cliché, kitsch and 'trash,' calls into question the distinction between 'high' and 'low' or 'popular' culture and 'exposes taste and value as social constructions.'[138] (It is therefore curious that critics of pop music tend to be vociferous in their complaints about snobbery and hierarchies of taste, and yet so often reproduce exactly the same distinctions—between 'high' and 'low'—*within* popular music,

---

135. Camp may be said to 'deconstruct' the identities it performs in that its acts of quotation reveal that no sign (gesture or signifier) is able to control its own meaning, for its 'iterability'—which is what makes it a sign—allows it to be repeated in contexts which alter its meaning; or as Derrida puts it: 'No meaning can be determined out of context, but no context permits saturation' (Derrida, 'Living On,' p. 81). Morrissey's singing of 'Bye, bye, baby' in 'Girlfriend In A Coma'—which repeats The Bay City Rollers' repetition of The Four Seasons' utterance of an already hackneyed phrase—is a good example of such 'nonsynonymous' acts of citation.

136. Flinn, 'The Deaths of Camp,' p. 439.

137. Ibid., p. 440.

138. Drewal, 'The Camp Trace in Corporate America,' p. 177.

and exhibit the prejudice they claim to deplore in their disparaging attitude towards the aesthetics of camp.) It was additionally noticed that camp engenders a coy variant of the Brechtian alienation effect in adverting to the disparity between the performer and the performance. Indeed, at the centre of camp is what we might refer to as an aesthetics of tickling—a toying at the edges of things, which delights in short-circuiting the identification it invites and seeks to keep us teetering on the threshold of illusion. (Tickling, like camp, is a *tertium quid*, in that it is an approach which is simultaneously a holding off and, since it engenders a sensation between pleasure and pain, just as camp coquettishly exposes the illusion, it fosters and vexes the opposition between the serious and the trivial.) Camp is thus, like tickling, a form of flirtation, which calls into question the status of its own gestures and speaks from a place where in a sense it is not, whose insignia is a 'too much' that coincides with a 'not enough.' (Tickling is similarly the ghost of touching or a kind of tactile whispering—an 'almost nothing' which is itself only in being barely there—that comes into being insofar as it elicits a desire for more or less touching.) By staging its own signifying gestures and giving the impression that signs are things that come out of a wardrobe, camp gently precipitates a crisis of meaning and suggests that 'language is not the governable instrument of a speaking being.'[139] Quite to the contrary, camp seeks to keep in view the sign's polysemy and celebrates the infidelities of semiosis. Indeed, it gleefully surrenders to the inconstancy of the sign—whose meaning is determined by context but no context can exhaust—and revels in its exorbitance. To put this another way, camp delights in showing how the sign carries more meaning than it's using and thus always in some sense differs from itself.

Camp, I am suggesting, is therefore in various ways akin to deconstruction—which takes place discreetly *within* a system and on its own terms, like a parasite or virus, showing how they may mean 'more, less, or something other than' what their author indended them to mean,[140] and which does not annihilate the system or context it speaks within, but effects a trembling 'which nothing can calm' that spreads through 'the entire inherited order.'[141] (Derrida, as

---

139. Derrida, *Mémoires: for Paul de Man*, p. 96.
140. Derrida, *On Grammatology*, p. 158.
141. Derrida, *A Taste for the Secret*, p. 9; *Positions*, p. 42.

Nicholas Royle points out, is 'fascinated by the notion that what is most powerful is often the most disarming feebleness, which reinforces the foregoing comments about tickling and our earlier observations about the subversive 'weakness' of Morrissey's protest.[142]) Camp is likewise a practice that takes place parasitically *within* a given context, performing with quotation marks and speaking with borrowed terms.[143] In this way, by 'inhabiting otherwise' adopted signs—and showing, as the drag artist exemplarily does, that they may mean 'more, less, or other than' their author intended—camp destabilizes or brings to light the inherent instability of such signs. It is therefore in a sense a metadiscourse, since it is *about* its use of quotation marks, inviting us to reflect on what it means to do or to 'be' something within quotation marks, and—even more subversively—suggesting that what we do (or 'are') in other, nonartistic contexts might also be performed within quotation marks. In this sense, camp may serve an *ethical* purpose, for as Donna Haraway points out, 'Queering a specific normalized category' is not necessarily 'for the easy frisson of transgression,' but may instead be 'for the hope of livable worlds.'[144]

Morrissey appears to be drawn to camp partly because it is in this way discreetly and yet profoundly disturbing. There is, however, another reason why, I suspect, he finds it so appealing, which takes us back to a discussion at the centre of the previous chapter. According to Caryl Flinn, the 'disunified body, the funny body that doesn't quite fit with itself, is, of course, *the* body of camp, as any drag queen will attest.'[145] Flinn's astute observation exposes to view the connection between the aesthetics of camp and embarrassment; for, like embarrassment, camp involves a slight, benign insynchronicity of the performer and the performance, or as Flinn puts it, camp 'demands disphasure, not just of signifier and signified, but a more general being out of step, a lagging behind, a barrier between subject and object.'[146] The 'funny body that doesn't quite fit with itself' is an

---

142. Royle, *Jacques Derrida*, p. 29.
143. Camp is characteristically adjectival or adverbial and, in contrast to the modernist austerity of Ezra Pound, disdains the steadiness of nouns and verbs—which is to say, it turns up the volume of the 'in what way' and delights in the 'dressing up' of modification. As such, it invites entrance into a world of 'Being-as-Playing-a-Role,' in which identities are a matter of performance rather than essence.
144. Haraway, 'A Game of Cat's Cradle,' p. 60.
145. Flinn, 'The Deaths of Camp,' p. 446.
146. Ibid, p. 438.

apposite way of characterizing not only many aspects of Morrissey's early gauche performances (his clothing, his dance, his voice, etc.) but also a great deal of his subject matter. It is, for example, this preoccupation with the body that's not quite at home with itself that underlies his concern with the 'monstrous,' the alienated, the 'maladjusted' and the 'queer,' as well as his interest in 'spectral' lives that pass out of being before coming to an end or proceed without quite coming into being. It is this same preoccupation, I suggest, that lies behind his peculiar animosity towards conventional either/or categories and labels. And there is an obvious connection between the body that differs from or 'doesn't quite fit with' itself and the 'oxymoronic' self, whose multiplicities characterize so many aspects of Morrissey's work. Rather than being a slightly embarrassing but anomalous episode in the singer's career, camp would therefore seem to be the style that is most suited to Morrissey's perennial concerns. Indeed, just as one could say that there is a homology or internal analogy between the style and underlying attitudes of punk, it is possible to argue that there is a parallel homology between the self-alienating incongruities of camp and Morrissey's recurrent concern with 'the funny body that doesn't quite fit with itself.'

SCORCHING AND DRENCHING

The 'oxymoronic' persona that has emerged so far involves a conjunction of the glamorous and the gauche, the masculine and the feminine, the erotic and the asexual, 'Irish blood' and 'English heart,' aloof aestheticism and imaginative sympathy, and, as we have seen in the preceding section, a tendency on the one hand towards introspection, melancholy and unflinching candour, which coexists with a tendency on the other hand towards artifice, lightness, comedy and play. There is one further conjunction of 'oxymoronic' characteristics I want to highlight in this chapter—namely, Morrissey's mixing of lyrical and conversational modes. What this refers to is his tendency to employ an elevated, poetic idiom alongside a conspicuously colloquial voice and a realistic representation of everyday experience.[147] In Byron's day, such a mixing of modes—which was described as

---

147 'I still like the idea of songs being virtual conversation pieces,' Morrissey has claimed—' "Tell me, why is your life like this?" I like the idea of being the sympathetic vicar' (Robertson, ed., *Morrissey: In His Own Words*, p. 87).

'scorching and drenching at the same time'—attracted fierce criticism and prompted a wonderfully spirited defence.[148] In Morrissey's case, by contrast, it has passed largely without comment. It therefore seems appropriate to conclude this chapter on the 'oxymoronic self' with a discussion of the ways in which Morrissey speaks 'out of both sides of his mouth simultaneously.'[149]

It is commonly observed that Morrissey's writing is concerned with—and seeks to extend our sympathy towards—the outcast, the damaged, the delinquent and the 'unloveable.' But it has not been noticed that there is an intriguing congruity between his aesthetic elevation of such human subjects and his lyrical treatment of other 'unpoetic' phenomena—the mundane, the contingent, the kitsch and the ugly. For whilst Morrissey is a lyricist of human nature—in its irreducible multiplicity, however 'light,' dark, contradictory or 'queer'—he is also, importantly, a poet of 'things.' Indeed, in spite of the sense of dysfunction, affliction, alienation and privation that pervades so much of his writing, his lyrics may be said to celebrate and *save* the everyday.[150]

Morrissey is a poet of the mundane detail. His songs include references to: a Frisbee, a three-bar fire, leather elbows, a mouth full of pie, a double-decker bus, the Daily Mail, a Jensen Interceptor, 'Churchillian legs,' 'phlegm lapels,' the power cut in 1972, 'loafing oafs and all-night chemists' and 'standing round the shops with peas.'[151] His lyrics also frequently mention—and evince a peculiar sensitivity to the distinctive resonances of—particular places, such as: Whalley Range, Piazza Cavour, the Fulham Road, SW6, Earls Court, Sloane Square and the Newport Pagnell service station.[152]

---

148. See Byron's letter to John Murray, August 12, 1819, *Byron's Letters and Journals*, vol. 6, p. 207.
149. R. D. Altick, speaking of Robert Browning, in ' "A Grammarian's Funeral": Browning's Praise of Folly?' p. 449. Byron defends the 'scortching and drenching' of Don Juan by pointing out that life mixes experiences in this way, even though art conventionally separates them. Such an 'oymoronic' art—which speaks of fried eggs and sunsets—is therefore in one sense the antithesis of camp, which irons out these jolts in its aesthetic vision, and whose hallmark is a serenely alienated gaze of perpetual delight or boredom. What such scorching and drenching underlines, then, is that Morrissey, like Byron, is camp as well as *anti*camp.
150. 'I get ideas from almost everywhere,' the singer maintains, 'but especially from supermarket queues—I have a talent for eavesdropping and it's amazing what you learn while waiting to pay for your fruit juice' (*Melody Maker*, September 26, 1987).
151. 'Mute Witness,' 'Sweet And Tender Hooligan,' 'Alsatian Cousin,' 'Dagenham Dave,' 'There Is A Light That Never Goes Out,' 'The Queen Is Dead,' 'Teenage Dad On His Estate,' 'The Harsh Truth Of The Camera Eye,' 'Pregnant For The Last Time,' 'Late Night, Maudlin Street,' 'Now My Heart Is Full,' 'Girl Least Likely To.'
152. 'Miserable Lie,' 'You Have Killed Me,' 'Maladjusted,' 'Piccadilly Palare,' 'Hairdresser On Fire,' 'Is It Really So Strange?'

This acute sensitivity to local resonances is reflected as well in the diverse conversational idioms that his lyrics incorporate. As we have seen, Morrissey's speakers often adopt a cultivated camp idiom ('charming,' 'gruesome,' 'frankly vulgar'). However, he exhibits a particular fondness too for the cadences of colloquial speech ('it's just a run-around'; 'it was a good lay'; 'a dipper, a slider, a cart-horse provider'[153]). There are a number of things that link Morrissey's writing to the poetry of John Betjeman, such as the allusion to 'Slough' in 'Everyday Is Like Sunday' and the broadcast of recordings of 'A Child Ill' before concerts.[154] But the underlying connection that such overt links betoken is surely the way both writers—with affection and without flinching—embrace the 'everyday.' Philip Larkin, himself a great poet of the commonplace, has commented perceptively on this aspect of Betjeman's writing: 'he is an accepter, not a rejecter, of our time, registering "dear old, bloody old England" with robustness, precision and a vivacious affection that shimmers continually between laughter and rage.'[155] This is a fine observation and applies, I suggest, to Morrissey as well. In the singer's case, this 'vivacious affection' often exists in spite of a melancholy or pessimism that is perhaps closer to Larkin's own verse than it is to Betjeman's. Even so, Morrissey's writing is, like Betjeman's, vitally 'resigned to swallowing anything.'[156] John Powell Ward has argued that this aesthetic embrace of the everyday—or 'poetry of the unpoetic'—is a characteristic feature of what he calls 'the English line.' With Larkin particularly in his sights, he describes this as follows:

> It is melancholic and laconic; sited in a recognizable and familiar land-scape; written and indeed spoken in ordinary language; preoccupied with domesticity, love and death; searching unavailingly for where true knowing may be found; inward and self-anxious; stamped with unfulfilled desires and longings; and casting back to a secure lost world which, in [Larkin's] case, he sardonically laments never existed.[157]

---

153. 'Teenage Dad On His Estate,' 'Everyday Is Like Sunday,' 'Suedehead,' 'Teenage Dad On His Estate.'
154. There may also be an echo of 'I am bald, and old, and green' ('The Olympic Girl') in Morrissey's 'I am sick and I am old and I am plain' ('Still Ill').
155. 'The Blending of Betjeman,' in Larkin, *Required Writing*, p. 129.
156. Ibid., p. 132.
157. Ward, *The English Line*, p. 176.

If such characteristics are the insignia of the 'English line,' then Morrissey should certainly be included in it.[158]

Morrissey's embrace of the everyday undoubtedly aims to produce a frisson of pleasure at finding such 'incongruous' things in the aesthetic realm—and in doing so attempts poetically to reproduce the garish aura of the kitsch.[159] (His bringing of flowers into the absurdly separated world of pop music seems to have been motivated by a parallel impulse.) It therefore has behind it a subversive desire to force 'high' art to make room for the 'lowly,' and a determination—however bleak and incongruous the result—faithfully to represent contemporary reality. (Larkin responded to 'romantic reviewers' who criticized his work for depicting a 'uniquely dreary life' by saying 'I'd like to know how [they] spend their time. Do they kill a lot of dragons for instance?'[160]). The process works in reverse too, however; for if the aesthetic embrace of the everyday 'demeans' high art—in travestying the principle of decorum—it at the same time elevates, and may even epiphanically transform, the lowly. John Bayley has recently written well on this subject:

> It is even possible for a poet to give such a freshness and surprisingness to kitsch as the thing itself. Rather as Andy Warhol and other artists transformed the kitsch object by looking at it with a new and craftily reverent ebullience, so a poet like John Betjeman transforms the commonplace—the Romantic commonplace in particular—into his own sometimes comic and bizarre but always wonderfully new and lyrical enthusiasms. Things that to the bored and indifferent observer, and the unloving eye, seem merely ugly and vulgar are transformed into a landscape of new beauties. . . . The point worth emphasising is that John Betjeman, by drawing our attention to these humdrum things in his own ecstatically aesthetic way, is doing for poetry what Warhol and others did for visual art. He is making kitsch into something rare and

---

158. Michael Bracewell puts forward precisely this argument in *England Is Mine*, where he links Morrissey's ambivalent nostalgic vision of Englishness with the poetry of Auden, Betjeman and Larkin. Of course, pop music has its own version of Ward's 'English line,' which includes The Kinks, Bowie, Paul Weller, Madness, The Pet Shop Boys, Pulp, Blur, and Arctic Monkeys. (For an illuminating discussion of the 'scorching and drenching' in the character songs of David Bowie and The Kinks—that is, their 'use of music hall style to point up the quiet depression of everyday lives'—to which Morrissey's work is manifestly indebted, see Auslander, *Performing Glam Rock*, chapter 4.)

159. Such aesthetic affection for the kitsch quotidian is at the same time linked to an 'American line,' which includes the Pop Art of Warhol and others.

160. Interview with Ian Hamilton, 'Four Conversations: Philip Larkin,' p. 73.

new, transforming the fatigue of the too-much-seen daily object into what is suddenly rich and strange.[161]

Pop music, also, is able to turn a transformative gaze to the commonplace and the kitsch. Indeed, Jarvis Cocker has described 'Englishness' in pop as a 'sense of the romantic in the everyday,' citing The Kinks as his exemplar.[162] The superlative exponent of such 'romanticism' in pop music, though, is surely Morrissey.[163] Who else could—and would want to—interest us in all-night chemists, the alley by the railway station, the leather on a passenger seat, the grease in the hair of a Speedway operator, 'Trudging slowly over wet sand' or 'Drinking tea with the taste of the Thames'?[164] And here we come upon what is perhaps the most surprising 'oxymoronic' aspect of Morrissey's work. For, in spite of the sense of pathos and privation that pervades his lyrics, they are filled with moments in which everyday things and experiences are affectionately preserved, and elevated by their preservation; moments which, if they are not epiphanies, nonetheless allow such phenomena to 'put off' their ephemerality and exceed their commonplace appearances in the direction of an epiphany. In fact, I'm not sure Morrissey has ever sounded so full of affection as when, apropos of nothing, he sings of 'loafing oafs and all-night chemists'—an affection he transmits to the listener and which is *of itself* transformative; for in loving such things, he makes them loveable.[165] In aesthetically celebrating the kitsch, the everyday and the 'lowly,' and in the process uncovering what it is that makes them loveable, Morrissey is, we might say, glorying in their infirmity.

161. Bayley, 'Linguistic and Class Resource,' pp. 229–30.
162. *Select*, April 1993.
163. Simon Reynolds has drawn attention to this aspect of The Smiths' art: 'The Smiths reinstate both the strangeness of pop, its otherworldly elegance, *and* its connection with reality' (Reynolds, *Bring the Noise*, p. 6).
164. 'Now My Heart Is Full,' 'I Want The One I Can't Have,' 'This Charming Man,' 'Rusholme Ruffians,' 'Everyday Is Like Sunday,' 'Come Back To Camden.'
165. This is the moral, as Chesterton points out, of *Beauty and the Beast*—that a thing must be loved in order for it *to become* loveable (Chesterton, *Orthodoxy*, p. 55).

CHAPTER 3

———— ∞∞ ————

The Art of Coyness

My only weakness is . . . well, never mind.

—*Shoplifters Of The World Unite*

TELLING THE TRUTH BY MEANS OF A LIE

There is a famous scene in the Marx Brothers' *Duck Soup* in which Groucho defends his client by pleading his insanity in the following paradoxical fashion: 'Gentlemen, Chicolini here may talk like an idiot and look like an idiot—but don't let that fool you: he really *is* an idiot!' Groucho's joke brings into view the possibility of an odd kind of double deception whereby someone may pretend to be what they *are*. Slavoj Žižek clarifies this paradoxical logic with reference to another well-known joke, recounted by Freud, about two Polish Jews, one of whom says to the other: 'Why are you telling me that you are going to Cracow, so that I'll think you're going to Lemberg, when you are really going to Cracow?'[1] What this comical remark renders visible, according to Žižek, is the way in which *truth itself* may deceive us. These two jokes may help to introduce Morrissey's art of coyness.

The previous chapter drew attention to issues of mediation, artifice and play, which crucially complicate the naive but commonly held view that Morrissey's songs provide us with 'a direct line to the singer's heart and soul.'[2] This is not to say that what he artistically represents may not in some sense hold in reality. He may be—and indeed I believe he is—impersonating himself (even if this self does not exist apart from the performance). Like Groucho, we might therefore say, this man claims to be shy and acts in a shy way—but this shouldn't

---

1. Žižek, *Looking Awry*, p. 73; Freud, *Jokes and Their Relation to the Unconscious*, p. 161.
2. Rogan, *Morrissey*, p. 1.

deceive us: he is shy! The paradoxes involved in publicly performing shyness are of course not lost on Morrissey:

> *Interviewer*: Do you ever go out dancing, stuff like that?
>
> *Morrissey*: Heavens no! I can only do that in front of four thousand people.[3]

Which brings us to the second joke. Publicly talking about or 'revealing' one's shyness doesn't disperse the concealment to which it points—it deepens it, since one may, as Freud's joke illustrates, paradoxically hide behind the truth. We can see something of these paradoxes at play in 'Ask.'

Like a number of Morrissey's other lyrics, the 1986 single 'Ask' has suffered on account of its apparent lightness. According to Simon Goddard, for example, it is 'whimsy,' 'lightweight,' 'superficial,' 'froth.'[4] As we have seen, one of the problems with describing a work as 'light' is that it tends to be a way of terminating consideration of it. Hence, whilst Goddard is informative and happy to talk for pages when it comes to the instruments and special effects used to create the music ('a Rickenbacker twelve-string and a classic Stratocaster' and 'a simple harmonica vamp, purposely overdriven through a Seventies "Boom Box" stereo'[5]), he has little to say about the lyrics—as his multiplication of synonyms testifies—beyond describing them as 'light.'[6] Yet lightness is an aesthetic production too. And the nature of this lightness—how its effects are constituted, whether it is the complex lightness of irony, whether it is a making light of something serious or whether it is an attempt to represent that which is *of its nature* light—would seem to merit consideration as well. What, then, is going on in 'Ask'?

The first interesting oddity to note is that there is something coy about the singer's point of view. This is because he seems to be singing from both sides of the fence:

---

3. Cited in Simpson, *Saint Morrissey*, p. 124.
4. Goddard, *The Smiths*, pp. 202–3.
5. Ibid., p. 203.
6. Rogan is wholly at a loss to find anything whatsoever to say about the song, devoting a page and a half to describing the authorship wrangles with Craig Gannon, well documented elsewhere, and then adding in a final sentence: 'The disputes aside, "Ask" was a sprightly single which justly maintained the group's recent promising run of hits, peaking at number 14.' One might have expected a little more in a book of 340 pages that describes itself as 'a detailed study of the recordings of Morrissey.'

Shyness is nice, and
Shyness can stop you
From doing all the things in life you'd like to

...

So, if there's something you'd like to try . . .
ASK ME—I WON'T SAY 'NO'—HOW COULD I?

The singer is of course notorious for his shyness—which is often painfully apparent in televised interviews and is a recurrent subject in his lyrics ('Sixteen clumsy and shy / That's the story of my life' ['Half A Person']; 'I am the son / and the heir / of a shyness that is criminally vulgar' ['How Soon Is Now']). Furthermore, he sings in 'Ask' with an 'inside knowledge' of shyness ('Shyness is nice and / Shyness can stop you / From doing all the things in life you'd like to'), which likewise leads us to assume that the shyness he is talking about is his own. Yet, as the inferential conjunct 'So' suggests, he appears to be urging the addressee to indulge their desires and to be coaxing them out of *their* shyness—whilst he, by contrast, speaks as though he is standing in the open, wholly exposed and is shy of nothing ('Nature is a language—can't you read?').[7] Now it's easy of course to dismiss this as a game or an elaborate pretence. Logic, also, would seem to support this—for how can one be shy as well as not shy? But nature is obviously not answerable to logic, and—however paradoxical it may appear in the abstract—most of us are presumably familiar with the *experience* of feeling both this and that. Pointing this out doesn't explain what's going on—nor does it rule out the possibility that it's all matter of pretence—though it does create room for an alternative explanation.

The second thing to notice, which helps to bring this alternative explanation into visibility, is the shift from 'shyness' in the first verse to 'coyness' in the second:

Coyness is nice and
Coyness can stop you
From doing all the things in life you'd like to.

---

7. There is an increasing discrepancy betweem the lyrics as they are sung and as they are printed on the album sleeve. According to the former, the opening lines are: 'Shyness is nice and / Shyness can stop you,' whereas according to the latter they are: 'Shyness is nice but / Shyness can stop you,' as though the singer was in two minds about exactly how negative the impediment of shyness is.

This virtual repetition tends to be ignored or criticized as a lazy attempt to get a second cup of tea out of the same tea bag. However, it seems to me that the subtle shift in virtually repeating what was said earlier is significant as well as wonderfully sly, and crucial to our understanding of the song. Shyness and coyness are, to be sure, often used interchangeably. Yet the difference between them—especially when they are set next to each other—is that there is a wink in the eye of the latter (as the *OED* puts it, coyness means 'archly or affectedly shy'). Characteristically, Morrissey thus appears to be drawing attention to a self-consciousness within his performance—by winking at the camera—which lets us know that he is aware of the absurdity of publicly performing his shyness. The shift from 'shy' to 'coy' is therefore itself a coy gesture, which alludes to its own knowingness and exposes the paradoxes that structure its performance. To put this in terms of Freud's joke about deceiving by means of telling the truth, in 'Ask' the singer is telling us he is shy, aware that in making this public we will think he is *not* shy, when in fact he really *is* shy. In this way, he may be said to be hiding behind the truth.

EXPOSURE

In the early days of The Smiths, Morrissey frequently described what they were doing as a matter of radical exposure: 'We're naked before the world,' he said. 'We just rip our hearts open and this is how we are.'[8] 'We are four individuals, naked before the world.'[9] Nakedness was more than a useful analogy; it was something of a guiding principle around which The Smiths' aesthetic cohered. This is apparent in their militant insistence upon the importance of the song, unpromoted and 'stripped bare' of elaborate production;[10] it is evident too in their refusal of many of the conventional pretences of the music industry (as Andy Rourke points out, 'Morrissey was one of the first people to refuse to use a microphone on *Top of the Pops* and

---

8. *Zig Zag*, February 1984.
9. *Jamming!*, May 6, 1984.
10. Speaking of *Hatful Of Hollow*, an album of radio sessions 'in the raw,' Mick Middles notes: 'The simplistic edges succeeded in highlighting the strength of the songwriting, the virtuosity of Johnny Marr's guitar work and the gradual coming together of four musicians with one purpose. These were all traditionally "naked" plus factors, all perpetuating a certain purity and old-fashioned virtue. And yet there was *Hatful Of Hollow* doing business with the ultra smooth plastic perfection of Sade, the pop bubble and squeak of Wham! and the megahype of Frankie Goes To Hollywood. Yet again, The Smiths headed the forefront of the backlash' (Middles, *The Smiths*, p. 61).

pretend he was actually singing. He just sang it without one because obviously he was miming. Nobody's really credited The Smiths for that'[11]). There is of course also the literal nakedness on the cover of their first single (a male figure photographed from behind, who almost seems to be sculpted out of the wall against which he is leaning), on the cover of their first album (the torso of Joe Dallesandro in Andy Warhol's film *Flesh*), and Morrissey's own habit of losing his shirt onstage—which is at once a physical exposure and, however conventional it may have become, a symbolic baring of the self in a state of nature. (It is customary at Morrissey's concerts for there to be an 'antiphonal' display of emotion, with the singer laying himself bare to the audience—literally and metaphorically—and a stream of fans struggling onto the stage to kiss, embrace or simply touch him in return.[12]) In his solo work, as we saw in 'America Is Not The World,' his lyrics go one stage further and speak of an exposure or exteriorization of interior organs—usually the heart—'I carried my heart in my hand'; 'with my heart on a string'; 'my heart it left with you.'[13] This emphasis upon nakedness is clearly bound up with The Smiths' reaction to the aesthetics of New Pop. It is also another way in which Morrissey *embarrasses* his audience—as the singer himself makes clear:

> When we began, I thought there was a need to find somebody who was honest to fault. Nobody had been like that before, because all the popular figures had become like early Seventies rock stars. There was nobody out there putting their heart on the line. There was no one singing as though they would die if they didn't. I had to be boringly personal. I'm beyond embarrassment now.[14]

Whatever lies on the other side of embarrassment—and whether or not it is desirable and possible to remain there—these comments make clear that Morrissey was *aiming* to overstep the mark ('honest to a fault'; 'boringly personal'). From one point of view, as the singer acknowledges, such exposure is a social solecism. Yet to see

---

11. Cited in Goddard, *The Smiths*, p. 54.
12. Morrissey actively encourages such communion. At a concert in 1991, at the Pauley Pavilion in Los Angeles, he said to the audience, who had been separated from the stage for security reasons: 'We're fully grown adults. If you want to stay in your seats, that's okay with me—but you don't have to!' (cited in Bret, *Morrissey*, p. 168).
13. 'I Have Forgiven Jesus,' 'Dear God Please Help Me,' 'Sunny.'
14. *Jamming!*, December 1984.

this overstepping the mark as something negative, one must first of all assume that the social world whose protocol it transgresses is an absolute value and ignore the possibility that such impropriety may in fact be a fidelity to a more fundamental set of principles, from whose point of view the conventions of polite society are *themselves* a transgression.[15] From this point of view, fitting in is a failing, and transgression becomes an exercise of virtue. In which case, embarrassment loses its kinship with the pricking of conscience and is unmasked as one of the blandishments of conformity. Morrissey's polymorphous habit of exposure may therefore be seen as one of many ways in which he renders visible the cultural construction and discreet tyrannies of 'normality.'

THE MOMENT OF THE SONG

Morrissey's songs are unusually full of deictic or 'pointing' words, such as 'now,' 'here,' 'this' and 'these': 'I've seen this happen in other people's lives / and now it's happening in mine'; 'I've never felt quite so alone / as I do right now'; 'and here is the very last plea from my heart'; 'All men have secrets and here is mine'; 'this is the final stand of all I am'; 'stop me if you think you've heard this one before.'[16] We should notice as well that his songs are filled with a particular *type* of deictic word—namely, those which point to the *present* (as opposed to those which point away, such as 'then,' 'there,' 'that' and 'those'). What is the significance of this?

In the last chapter, attention was drawn to the ways in which Morrissey's songs establish a mode of relation and gesture towards a disclosure of presence which is born of its own utterance and takes place within the moment of the song, and in this way present themselves as evidence of their own sincerity. The insignia of such self-presencing are deictic words such as 'this,' 'now' and 'here.' These performative allusions to the moment of the song are also involved in the discourse or drama of exposure. At this point we need to slow down a little.

When, for example, Morrissey sings 'I've never felt quite so alone / as I do right now' ('Wide To Receive'), the song presents the

15. In interview, Morrissey approvingly quoted Fran Lebowitz's remark 'polite conversation is no conversation' (*The Face*, July 1984).
16. 'That Joke Isn't Funny Anymore,' 'Wide To Receive,' 'Come Back To Camden,' 'What Difference Does It Make?' 'Well I Wonder,' 'Stop Me If You Think You've Heard This One Before.'

moment of experience as coterminous with the act of description—he is presented, that is, as describing events *as they go on*. The song in this way dramatizes rather than merely describes the experience, and the emotional disclosure is presented as something going on before us. In other words, the song doesn't report an exposure that takes place elsewhere—it is the space in which the exposure occurs.

The act of utterance may play an even greater role in Morrissey's songs and may itself in fact form part of the experience. In 'Well I Wonder,' for instance, the events are again narrated as presently occurring:

> Gasping—but somehow still alive
> this is the fierce last stand of all I am.

In this case, though, the act of utterance isn't merely temporally involved in the experience—it becomes an active element within that experience. It is something which the speaker seems to cling to—perhaps the *only* thing he has left to cling to. 'This is the fierce last stand of all I am.' The assertion doesn't describe an act of holding on that takes place apart from itself; instead, it *constitutes* the act of holding on. In this sense, the 'discourse' becomes part of the 'story' and affects even as it describes the course of action. We find a rare positive version of this in 'Now My Heart Is Full.' Here, in what is perhaps the most epiphanic of Morrissey's songs, the verses' nostalgic reflections on metonymies of Englishness—which merge fictional and biographical worlds—give way to and seem themselves to engender the state of speechless emotional repletion that is described and *occurs* in the chorus:

> tell all the friends
> (I don't have too many
> just some rain-coated lovers' puny brothers)
> Dallow, Spicer, Pinkie, Cubitt
> rush to danger
> wind up nowhere
> Patric Doonan—raised to wait
> I'm tired again—I tried again, and
> now my heart is full
> now my heart is full
> and I just can't explain
> *so I won't even try to.*

Once again, the song exposes an emotional event that occurs in front of us (although, if in 'Well I Wonder' the act of utterance holds off the despair whose imminence it simultaneously signifies, in this case the song is the agency of its own epiphany). Furthermore, it in a sense *involves* us in that event—its 'now' conjoining the atemporal, textual presentness of the song and the 'now' of the act of listening. In this way, we are invited to witness the pageant of his bleeding heart.

I KEEP MINE HIDDEN

Whilst it is in principle difficult to verify Morrissey's claim 'The More You Ignore Me, The Closer I Get,' it's hard to escape the contrary impression that his exposure somehow coincides with concealment and the more you concentrate attention upon him, the further away he seems to get. As we shall see in the following section, this concealment is partly a matter of lack or what's left unsaid but also partly a matter of 'excess'—of telling us too much. Before separating out the part played by lack and excess in Morrissey's self-concealment—which exists as a counterpoise to his tendency towards self-exposure—it will be helpful to clarify the peculiar way in which such concealment and exposure may coincide. To do this, I want to look at the final song that Morrissey and Marr wrote together, 'I Keep Mine Hidden.'

As Simon Goddard points out, in the years immediately after The Smiths split up, Morrissey frequently drew attention to 'I Keep Mine Hidden' and claimed it was the song he 'always played first when reviewing their legacy.'[17] Nevertheless, the song was as hidden as it's possible for a recording on general release to be—tucked away as a B-side on twelve-inch and cassette formats only, and not included on any album. This simultaneous tendency towards concealment and exposure is a curious reflection of tensions that are played out in the song itself. Grant Showbiz, the song's producer, has the following to say about it:

> For me that is the *key* song that sort of says everything. There are very few songs where Morrissey says 'this is me,' a lot of the time they're just these wonderful vignettes, but I think 'I Keep Mine Hidden' is a very personal song, a very direct song from Morrissey to Johnny.[18]

17. Goddard, *The Smiths*, p. 254.
18. Ibid., pp. 253–4.

Sort of. Leaving aside the final point about it being 'a very direct song from Morrissey to Johnny' (the words 'you' and 'yours,' which the song consistently employs, are after all rather open), Showbiz's characterization of the song is both helpful and misleading, since if the song 'sort of says everything,' it also sort of says nothing. Let us look at the lyrics:

> Hate, love and war
> force emotions to the fore
> but not for me, of course, of course
> I keep mine hidden
> Oh . . .
>
> I keep mine hidden
> but it's so easy for you
> because you let yours flail
> into public view
> oh . . .
>
> Yellow and green
> a stumbling block
> I'm a twenty-digit combination to unlock
> with a past where to be 'touched'
> meant to be 'mental' . . .
>
> Use your loaf!

This is certainly a rather enigmatic saying of everything. Yet Showbiz is in a sense right to characterize the song in this way, for the singer is in fact saying 'this is me' and its 'this,' if it's true, has implications for all his writing. The problem, though, is that what he is showing us is of course his concealment. 'I keep mine hidden'; 'I'm a twenty-digit combination to unlock.' Indeed, the song even keeps hidden what precisely it is that it keeps hidden.[19] Both of these tendencies—his concealment and his exposure—are simultaneously in play and need to be kept in view, however paradoxical their coincidence may seem. Morrissey's lyrics in this respect resemble the poetry of Christina

---

19. Pat Reid tells us more than most of us want to know about himself, but his remarks make the song's coy ambiguity clear: 'We would sit around Hugh's trash-strewn ground-floor flat opposite Hippo Pizza in Tooting Broadway and analyse tracks like "I Keep Mine Hidden" ("He's referring to his emotions." Hugh opined with scholarly gravitas. "His genitals, surely." I quipped, a pseudo-baggy Evelyn Waugh wannabe' (Reid, *Morrissey*, p. 53).

Rossetti (1830–94), whose melancholic ruminations on unfulfilment, isolation and the sense of being 'Dead Before Death' have been described as an 'aesthetics of renunciation.'[20] A brief comparison may help to clarify the techniques by which their coyness is cultivated.

In her poetry, Christina Rossetti was a consummate flirt. Whilst *Goblin Market* is overflowing with sensual and similitive excess, and her devotional verse figures a passionate yearning for the divine in erotic language, redolent of the The Song of Songs, her shorter secular lyrics are remarkable for what they leave offstage and for their ability to *interest us* in what they leave offstage. She is in so many of these miniature dramas exquisitely skilled in awakening and sustaining a curiosity on the verge of satisfaction and is extraordinarily fertile in finding ways of alluding to without actually saying something. But what makes her of particular interest to us at this juncture is the fact that her lyrics are often *about* their own secrecy, and, like 'I Keep Mine Hidden,' are thus all the more flirtatious. Here, for example, is part of 'Winter: My Secret,' which has been described by Isobel Armstrong as 'almost a summa' of the poet's work:[21]

> I tell my secret? No indeed, not I:
> Perhaps some day, who knows?
> But not today; it froze, and blows, and snows,
> And you're too curious: fie!
> You want to hear it? well:
> Only, my secret's mine, and I won't tell.
>
> Or, after all, perhaps there's none:
> Suppose there is no secret after all,
> But only just my fun.
> Today's a nipping day, a biting day;
> In which one wants a shawl,
> A veil, a cloak, and other wraps:
> I cannot ope to every one who taps,
> And let the draughts come whistling thro' my hall;
> ...
>
> Perhaps some languid summer day,
> When drowsy birds sing less and less,

---

20. Gilbert and Gubar, *The Madwoman in the Attic*, p. 558.
21. Armstrong, *Victorian Poetry, Poetics and Politics*, p. 357.

And golden fruit is ripening to excess,
If there's not too much sun nor too much cloud,
And the warm wind is neither still nor loud,
Perhaps my secret I may say,
Or you may guess.

The poem teasingly puts something before us in the very same
gesture that takes it away—the opening line ventriloquizing our
interest and then closing the door in the reader's face, only to leave
it fractionally ajar in the following line, 'Perhaps some day.' The
next line or 'move' then reaffirms its refusal, without revoking—but
without furthering—the possibility of the 'perhaps' it raised: 'But
not today.' Whereupon it abruptly changes the subject and coyly
plays with the curls in its hair ('it froze, and blows, and snows'). This
alternating pattern of concealment and the suggestion of revelation is
reversed in the subsequent lines, where the reader is playfully rebuked
for the curiosity the poem has itself incited, which then appears to
relent again 'You want to hear it?' before apparently resolving to keep
itself to itself—'I won't tell.' Only apparently, though, because the
poem continues to feed the curiosity it refuses to satisfy by leaving
the possibility of disclosure open without actually disclosing anything (there are a lot of 'perhapses' as well as an 'or' at the start of the
second stanza, which retroactively countermands the resolution of
the preceding refusal, and a concluding repetition of 'may,' which—
like the tantalizing musical suspension of the tonic on which 'Please
Please Please Let Me Get What I Want' ends—leaves us wavering on
the conditional threshold of a 'perhaps').

Morrissey's coyness in 'I Keep Mine Hidden' is less a matter
of shifting perspective and lacks the 'shall I? shan't I?' teasing of
'Winter: My Secret.' (Having said that, we have already identified
a radical ambiguity that structures so many of his lyrics and renders
their point of view teasingly elusive.) The coyness in this case has
more to do with its tonal or generic heterogeneity; for in spite of its
apparently serious subject, the song is imbued with an oxymoronic
and ironizing cheeriness—most obviously by the hilariously straight-
faced chirpy whistling with which it begins and the offbeat lightness
in the final line ('Use your loaf!'). Such gestures recall the subversive
whimsy of 'Certain People I Know,' 'Is It Really So Strange?' and
'Sheila Take A Bow,' and in shrugging their shoulders at the song's
seriousness have the same effect as Rossetti's acknowledgement that

perhaps 'there is no secret after all, / But only just my fun.'[22] What the two writers share more generally, however, is an aesthetics of secrecy; an interest, that is, in writing *about* secrets, rumours, hiddeness, reticence and ineffability, but also a flirtatious tendency—which is something performed—to deepen their concealment even as they expose themselves. What both writers offer, in other words, is a sort of poetic striptease, in which garments are enticingly removed only to reveal further garments underneath (Rossetti archly speaks of the need for 'A veil, a cloak, and other wraps' as she stalls in her poetic removal of garments) and in which the secret is constituted rather than disclosed by the act of undressing. This is the case in 'I Keep Mine Hidden,' where the singer reveals the existence of a secret, instead of what that secret is.[23] We find a similar instance of this in 'What Difference Does It Make?':

> All men have secrets and here is mine
> so let it be known
> [for] we have been through hell and high tide
> I think I can rely on you
> and yet you start to recoil
> heavy words are so lightly thrown
> but still I'd leap in front of a flying bullet for you
>
> so, what difference does it make?
> it makes none
> but now you have gone
> and you must be looking very old tonight.

---

22. I cannot agree with Simon Goddard's view of the song, who seems to want to wish away or save the song from its irony: 'Resurrecting something of the thumping riposte of "Sheila Take A Bow," Marr's arrangement has often been dismissed as "music-hall," but is actually a standard Fifties rock 'n' roll pattern, very similar to that of Doc Pomus and Mort Shuman's "A Teenager In Love." Only in Morrissey's whistling milkman entrance does the track pass the point of no return into vaudevillian ham, though it was perhaps fortunate that a further "whistling-solo" was later removed and replaced by Marr's uncomplicated monophonic guitar break' (Goddard, *The Smiths*, p. 254). I don't think describing the arrangement as 'music-hall' is necessarily pejorative, and can't help regretting there isn't a little *more* milkman's whistling. Leaving matters of taste aside, the problem with Goddard's reading is that he brackets its irony as some sort of aberration—rather than a constituent element of the song—which leads him to the rather impoverishing conclusion that it 'relays a crippling inability to express emotion' (ibid, p. 253).

23. Even the description of the obstacles to exposure are somewhat ambiguous in Morrissey's lyric. I take it that the line 'yellow and green' is meant to imply cowardice and inexperience, and that these constitute 'a stumbling block.' Rather bizarrely, Simon Goddard sees this as 'a thinly veiled reference to the colour coding of temazepam capsules'—rewriting the line to support this ('a "yellow and green stumbling block"')—and, apparently glad to have a factual matter on his hands, provides a detailed footnote on the active ingredients, the highest permitted dosage, its controlled prescription and adverse side effects!

The song begins with what appears to be the announcement of an imminent disclosure—'All men have secrets and here is mine'—an impression that is immediately reinforced by the following line 'so let it be known.' And yet this disclosure never actually seems to come about. What part of the lines that follow is the disclosure itself? If we keep track of the syntax, the lines seem instead to circle around the act of disclosure. The 'for,' which I include in square brackets, is sung on *The Smiths* (but not on *Hatful Of Hollow*) and isn't included on the lyric sheet. However, it only underlines the apparent continuity of the prefatory frame, reminding the addressee of what they have been through together and rhetorically seeking to affirm his or her reliability—something one tends to do *before* disclosing a secret. The 'and yet' with which the following utterance begins, though, implies a continuation—in its qualification—of the preceding issue and suggests that we still haven't left the frame. The same is true of the 'but still' which begins the last line of the verse and the 'so' with which the chorus opens. We therefore seem to have arrived at the song's chorus without getting beyond the announcement of, and negotiations about, the disclosure of a secret. From this point of view, the initial deictic 'here is mine' appears once again to point towards a revelation that there *is* a secret rather than a disclosure of it. In a typically Morrisseyesque move, we then suddenly find out the relationship is over ('now you have gone') and find ourselves on the far side of disclosure, without anything other than the existence of a secret having been disclosed.[24]

'Reel Around The Fountain' presents us with an even more intriguing example, as a result of the even greater tension between revealing and concealing that it exhibits. Naturally, it is the revelations that attract attention and, as with 'What Difference Does It Make?' and 'I Keep Mine Hidden,' its concealment tends to be overlooked. And yet what is *not* said or revealed is a *positive* feature which structures the song and crucially contributes to its erotic character or *jouissance*. (Like any good tease, Morrissey knows exactly how many buttons to undo and how many to leave done up.) On account of this tension, the song additionally forms the perfect introduction to the story of The Smiths—as the first song on their first album—awakening

---

24. It could of course be objected that the subsequent verse involves the disclosure of the song's secret ('I stole and I lied, and why? / because you asked me to!'), but—apart from the fact that in this belated and unmarked position it would be a rather secretive disclosure of a secret—if the addressee asked the singer to do these things, it is presumably not a secret.

our curiosity with its partial exposures, its intimation of the imminence of further exposure, and its manifold veilings—whose allure
consists in showing us what they're concealing.

Like 'What Difference Does It Make?' the song begins with what
appears to be a prefatory announcement of a revelation: 'It's time the
tale were told / of how you took a child / and you made him old.' At
this point, however, 'Reel Around The Fountain' also stalls, telling us
about the story and its need to be told, rather than actually *telling* the
story. For what follows has a future-oriented or optative character,
so that suddenly we are looking forwards rather backwards, and no
account of how the song's 'you took a child and . . . made him old'
is in fact forthcoming. (That said, one might argue that the song
introduces the telling of a tale that continues beyond its own boundaries and is coextensive with Morrissey's writing career.) The song's
imperatives ('slap me on the patio'; 'Meet me by the fountain') and
the comical dream section ('I dreamt about you last night / and I fell
out of bed twice') certainly give us some idea of the singer's feelings
and teasingly offer what are possibly veiled or 'translated' reflections
of past events, but they don't tell us anything directly about what
occurred. In fact, if anything, they make it more mysterious, for the
desire they bespeak seems to run counter to the impression created
in the opening lines, which suggest that what happened was some
sort of fall and a source of sadness (assuming the 'you' of the song is
the same throughout). The song thus reels itself between elegy and
affirmation, and conjures up—in reverse, from effect to cause—an
experience that has given rise to desire and disclosed something of
value but is suffused with a sense of loss as well. (One is reminded of
'This Night Has Opened My Eyes'—'She took away your troubles /
oh, but then again / she left pain'—though if in this latter example
the ambiguous condition is more a case of 'neither-nor' ['I'm not
happy / and I'm not sad'], in 'Reel Around The Fountain' it is a case
of 'both-and.') In this way, condensed and fragmentary as it is, the
song belongs to a tradition that includes Blake's ambivalent mythological vision of the traumatic fall from innocence into experience,
which is at once a gain, an awakening, a corruption and a loss.

This reeling between elegy and affirmation is beautifully
expressed in the vocal line, which stretches itself out the first time
'you made him old' is sung, so that its melismatic folds finally come
to rest on the cheerful root of A major, but is then compressed when

the line is repeated, so that 'old' falls earlier on the much more disturbing and melancholic F♯ minor (nine). This combination of responses to the same event is figured more extensively later in the song—appropriately as Morrissey enigmatically sings 'they were half right,' and during the extended climactic 'I do'—where the guitars circle around picking the notes D-C♯-A, as the bass (in various instruments) moves between D and B, so that whilst something in one sense stays still, the melody as a whole swings between D major (seven) and B minor (seven/nine)—that is, between what are generally perceived to be cheerful and melancholic tonalities. To make things even more complicated, this oxymoronic combination of responses is even reflected in the word 'reel' itself, which might either be a lively and positively connoted dance or the more negatively connoted staggering of one who can barely walk.

What we find, then, in 'Reel Around The Fountain' is another song that brings a secret into view. Importantly, it doesn't disclose that secret—although it undoes a few buttons and covers itself up in a way that draws attention to what it's concealing. Instead, as we saw in 'What Difference Does It Make?' and 'I Keep Mine Hidden,' it announces that there is something to tell, but then circles, as it were, around the fountain and leaves it enticingly untold.

This kind of teasing doesn't just occur at the start of Morrissey's career, as a way of awakening curiosity. It is a recurrent habit that persists throughout his writing, in spite of all his exposure as a popular celebrity. Hence, in 'Speedway,' to take a single example, after ten years in the public gaze, he somehow manages to be as teasingly secretive about his life as an immensely famous artist as he was about his life as an unknown and introverted teenager:

> All of the rumours
> keeping me grounded
> I never said that they were
> completely unfounded.

Once again, the utterance has the character of a disclosure—indeed, it is a disclosure—yet it deepens rather than dispels the mystery, since it doesn't specify *which* rumours were 'keeping [him] grounded' (and there are many possibilities) and only states that he 'never said' they were 'completely unfounded'—which implies that some (unspecified) element of these (unspecified) rumours *may* have a basis in reality.

Furthermore, saying that you 'never said' a thing was 'completely unfounded' is not the same as affirming that it is in fact the case. The disclosure is therefore all but vitiated out of existence by a string of discreet perhapses.

The point of this section is not to imply that Morrissey is a sphinx without a secret, leading his audience on, rather as Iago dupes Othello, for his own entertainment or commercial interest. Such a reading cannot of course be ruled out, and the singer undoubtedly delights in the ironies of an art that brings into being the secrets it simultaneously reveals. But it is equally possible—and I think a more compelling explanation—that there is something at stake which is kept secret out of self-protection, in the face of hostile forces from without, or which cannot be told because it is of its nature in some sense ineffable—which is to say, incommensurate with the available categories—and would be falsified by the telling.

LACK

Innuendo

It will doubtless seem rather odd to suggest that there is something coy about a record cover featuring an image of a naked man. Yet the cover of the The Smiths' debut single, 'Hand In Glove,' presents us with what appears to be the first public example of Morrissey's love of innuendo.[25] It also shows us something about how innuendo works.

If by 'innuendo' we mean an utterance or act of signification in which, as Morrissey puts it in 'Handsome Devil,' we sense 'something more,' the innuendo of the phrase 'Hand In Glove'—which is the only UK Smiths single that featured its title on the front cover—is generated by its juxtaposition with the cover image, in the neighbourhood of which it seems to mean 'something more.'[26] Innuendo is typically generated by such seeming—in which exposure and concealment again coincide—since what is meant is usually perfectly transparent and yet in some manifest sense entirely

---

25. The coyness of the image seems to have been lost even on some of the other band members: 'I remember showing a copy to my dad, saying "This is my first record." He was mortified. He said to me "That's a bloke's bum," and I said "Yeah." But when he asked me why, I just didn't have an answer for him' (Andy Rourke, cited in Goddard, *The Smiths*, p. 38).

26. The title appears in the bottom left hand corner of the cover, adjacent to the figure's backside, across which one of his hands is draped.

lacking. (Innuendo tends to hide behind its ostensible innocence as cartoon characters hide behind objects that are narrower than they are.) Such lack is thus from another point of view a sort of excess and is clearly related to the 'too much' of camp. Yet, as in the case of 'Hand In Glove,' it is crucially dependent for its effect—for its 'excess' to come into being, that is—on something outside itself (an arched eyebrow, a wink, a tone of voice, a context which precipitates its suggestiveness).[27]

Morrissey's innuendo largely relies on the use of ambiguous words or phrases. On account of their referential openness, pronouns and other indefinite parts of speech are a particular favourite and fertile resource: 'well it's here / right under your nose'; 'I keep mine hidden'; 'you gave me something I won't forget too soon'; 'And if the lights were out / could you even bear / to kiss her full on the mouth (or anywhere?).'[28] For the same reason, 'things' is another favourite of Morrissey's (as it was of Alexander Pope[29]): 'these things take time'; 'he knows so much about these things'; 'All the streets are crammed with things / eager to be held'; 'Why do you come here / when you know it makes things hard for me?'[30] Innuendo is a kind of parasitic discourse, which leaves its eggs in other birds' nests, and so there are, as we might expect, all sorts of other words and phrases which are used in Morrissey's lyrics to carry a supplementary cargo: 'And when we're in your scholarly room / who will swallow whom?'; 'And Sorrow's native son, / He will not rise for anyone'; 'you can pin and mount me like a butterfly'; 'I've not been feeling myself tonight'; 'It was dark as I drove the point home.'[31] But perhaps the most interesting use of innuendo is to be found in 'Piccadilly Palare,' which is a song *about* innuendo and in which the discourse itself is suggestive ('palare' or 'polari,' as every Morrissey fan knows, is a subculture argot or sociolect formed of Romany, backslang, thieves' cant and sailors' patois, which came to be used as a way of codedly speaking of homosexual activity).[32] What is so interesting about 'Piccadilly Palare' is that if innuendo is ordinarily a sort of linguistic smuggling,

---

27. Morrissey frequently uses melisma as a kind of phonetic eyebrow raising, conspiratorially alerting the listener to the lyrics' covert import.
28. 'Roy's Keen,' 'I Keep Mine Hidden,' 'These Things Take Time,' 'November Spawned A Monster.'
29. See, for example, Pope, 'The Second Satire of the First Book of Horace,' 87–90.
30. 'These Things Take Time,' 'This Charming Man,' 'Handsome Devil,' 'Suedehead.'
31. 'Handsome Devil,' 'Pretty Girls Make Graves,' 'Reel Around The Fountain,' 'I Can Have Both,' 'That Joke Isn't Funny Anymore.'
32. Polari was popularized—and to some extent domesticated—by 'Julian and Sandy' (played by Hugh Paddick and Kenneth Williams) in *Round the Horne.*

in which apparently innocuous language is made to carry a (transparently) concealed cargo of something more risqué, in Morrissey's song the reverse is the case. That is to say, what the words denote is perfectly innocuous ('so bona to vada' means something like 'so good to look at' and 'your lovely eek and / your lovely riah' simply means 'your lovely face and your lovely hair'), whereas what is risqué is the language as such, which is a metonymy of an underground and 'outlawed' culture. (In structuralist terms, it is the 'langue'—the shared system of language—rather than the 'parole'—the individual's use of its resources—that imports an extra 'illicit' meaning.[33])

Sometimes Morrissey's innuendo is a matter of giving the words a nudge and is accomplished by means of enunciation. In 'These Things Take Time,' for instance, the possible meaning of the following line is teasingly modified by the singer's stretching and pausing after the word 'behind': 'You took me behind . . . a dis-used railway line.' There is (I think) another exquisite example in 'Ask,' where the singer's pronunciation of the word 'bomb'—whilst he repeats the lines 'if it's not Love / Then it's the Bomb / That will bring us together'—seems at one point to shade over towards Inspector Clouseau's 'berm,' which of course—unbeknown to the character saying it—mischievously borders on the word 'bum.'[34] If this last example seems to be more in the eye of the beholder—though we should bear in mind that innuendo protests its innocence like guilty schoolchildren—it illustrates the important underlying principle of contagion. What I mean by this is that the author's habit of innuendo generates an implicit perspectival context, which precipitates—and prompts us to look out for—certain possible meanings among others.[35] This is the case with many of Morrissey's comic heroes—such as George Formby, Frankie Howerd and the *Carry On* team—to whom his use of innuendo is manifestly indebted. (The interplay of innocence

---

33. Polari has an ad hoc grammatical structure (or lack of one), whose 'rules' have never been written down, and which tends to be used in different ways by different users. The literal translation of 'so bona to vada' is 'so good to look (at).' It could perhaps be glossed as 'so good-looking' (Mark Simpson's translation), but the phrase 'bona-vardering' is also possible, and a frequently repeated phrase on 'Julian and Sandy' was 'How bona to vada your dolly old eek!' which seems to lie behind Morrissey's usage. I am grateful to Paul Baker in the Department of Linguistics and English Language at Lancaster University for advice on this subject.

34. To give us a triad of backsides, we might also include the repetition of 'behind' at the end of 'Unhappy Birthday,' which after a while starts to sound less like an adverb and more like a noun.

35. An obvious example is the way attention drawn towards the backside—by cover images, the singer's wearing flowers in his trouser pocket and the references to the behind in his lyrics—circularly encourages us to look for such allusions. This 'contagious' tendency is borne out by Nadine Hubb's suggestion that there is a double entendre in Morrissey's melismatic extension of the word 'seat' in 'This Charming Man' (Hubbs, 'Music of the "Fourth Gender," ' p. 282).

and suggestiveness in innuendo is perhaps most apparent in Frankie Howerd, who used to affect not to get his own innuendos until after his audience had picked up on them, whom he would then chastise for their naughtiness. Over time, this process would comically overtake itself, so that he would often chastise the audience's sauciness *before* they had picked up on—and as a way of *signalling*—a double entendre. Morrissey does something similar in 'Never Played Symphonies,' where he sings 'You slipped right through my fingers / No not literally / But metaphorically.')

Innuendo in Morrissey is also importantly a matter of what is *not* said. This is particularly the case with respect to the issue of sexual orientation. We will come to the related subjects of interruption and excess in subsequent sections; nonetheless, it is worth noticing here the way in which the singer's lyrics frequently leave the gender of his addressee unspecified:

> you ask me the time
> but I sense something more
> and I would like to give you what I think you're asking for.

It is worth noting, too, the delicacy and skill with which Morrissey exploits the ambiguities of the word 'you.' Clearly, on one level, where characters are involved, it coyly leaves open whether the addressee is male or female. Yet, at the same time it irresistibly involves the third-party audience, which often feels itself addressed 'through' the act of particular address. There are other complicating currents as well. In a song such as 'I'd Love To,' for example (*My Early Burglary Years*)—which leaves *what* the singer would love to do unspecified—the ambiguity is less a matter of gender or the listener's involvement (although these, to be sure, are operative as well) and more to do with a tension between the impression the song gives that a particular individual is being addressed—and that it is obvious who this person is—and the absolute openness of what is actually said. (Grant Showbiz's comments on 'I Keep Mine Hidden' and the widely held—but uncorroborated—view that 'I Won't Share You' is addressed to Johnny Marr plainly reveal the force of such suggestiveness.[36]) In this, we can once again see how Morrissey's 'ghostly' biographical persona is subtly but crucially involved in the generation of the songs' meaning.

---

36. Andy Rourke's comment—which carries a kind of banker's privilege that it may not in matters of interpretation deserve—has encouraged this latter view: 'I always got the impression that ['I Won't Share You'] was obviously about Johnny' (cited in Rogan, *Morrissey*, p. 103).

If it's often unclear who the singer is talking about, things are rendered even more ambiguous by his parallel tendency to leave unclear *what* it is that takes place. Characteristically, this isn't a complete absence. Rather, as we saw in Rossetti's writing, the lyrics leak their own secrets and give the reader glimpses and suggestions, which allure without satisfying our curiosity (though there may of course be a 'sublime' satisfaction in being left wanting). Let us return to 'Reel Around The Fountain,' which exhibits a remarkable creativity when it comes to speaking indirectly and leaving things suggestively unsaid. Take, for example, the following lines:

> people said that you were easily led
> and they were half-right.

Morrissey's use of 'half,' which is foregrounded by the parallelism with the previous section, quietly complicates everything and encourages speculation by tantalizingly telling us much less than it appears to. It complicates not least the dynamics of the relationship, which are apparently clear at the start of the song, in suggesting that the seducer—who 'took a child' and 'made him old'—is to some extent in the power of the seduced, who suddenly seems less passive and more knowing. The dream section similarly invites and thwarts our speculation. Its opening line—'I dreamt about you last night'—implies that some kind of disclosure is looming. Yet the following slapstick description of the dream's effects—'I fell out of bed twice'—means that we remain outside the narrative, and are left to read backwards from effect to cause across a comical aporetic boundary. In this sense, the dream section mirrors the song's overall structure, as it too is a narrative about a further narrative that remains essentially untold. The lines that follow deepen the song's ambiguity in several respects. It is firstly unclear whether or not they belong to the dream section, which may be coextensive with the music's 'change' section—as the playful piano and the sudden shift to seaside-postcard bawdy might suggest—or which may be confined to the first two lines. Secondly, their cartoon bawdiness entails certain anatomical ambiguities, which leave the gender of the addressee and the sexual orientation of the speaker in doubt:

> you can pin and mount me like a butterfly
>
> ...
>
> two lumps, please.

The lines even tease us by telling us what the addressee *doesn't* say—in a manner that first of all leads us to think the utterance belongs to the speaker and is in fact being spoken—and in doing so offer us a negative clue as to what the speaker desires:

> but take me to the haven of your bed
> was something that you never said.

Finally, the title and central image of the song is itself somewhat ambiguous. In addition to the ambiguity noted earlier, the question arises: is the utterance a request or a description? The syntax of the song's parallel utterances—'slap me on the patio'; 'Meet me by the fountain / shove me on the patio'—incline us to read it likewise as an imperative; but it's a rather odd thing to ask someone spontaneously to do. If, however, it's more of a description—and it may of course float dreamily between the options—is it remembered or imagined? That is to say, is something of the kind supposed to have taken place in the narrative or is it a projection of desire? One might naturally respond that it doesn't matter; it is a beautifully resonant poetic image and should be appreciated as such. Which is true; but it does matter that we *don't* know, since its resonance is engendered by its ambiguity, and it is surely also of significance in a song that excels at interesting us in, whilst avoiding telling us about, what actually occurred.

So far, I have focused almost exclusively on innuendo as a matter of language. To conclude this section, it is worth reminding ourselves of the importance of extralinguistic innuendo in Morrissey's art. As we saw in the opening chapter, one of the most striking things about the early Smiths was Morrissey's appearance. When the band performed 'Heaven Knows I'm Miserable Now' on *Top of the Pops*, for example, in May 1984, Morrissey wore a pink blouse, a ladies' plastic broach, and had flowers growing out of him. Such things obviously communicate something, and certain items of clothing, colours and fashion accessories carry conventional connotations, which may then be deployed or played with as signs. This is manifestly something that Morrissey was doing. The point I am concerned with here, though, is not what such things mean, but how they mean. And it seems to me that, like his lyrics, his appearance makes use of innuendo. That is to say, it communicates indirectly in a manner that is at once screamingly obvious and yet wholly unstated. The same may be said of his early falsetto. In singing, as it were beyond, his own reach, he was flagrantly stepping over into the territory conventionally inhabited by the female, the prepubescent boy and the castrato. Yet the associations that are communicated in doing so are entirely implicit. This habit of indirectness and suggestion is likewise at play in The Smiths' covers and their 'matrix' messages—such as 'The impotence of Earnest' ('William, It Was Really Nothing,' side A) and 'Oursouls, oursouls, oursouls' ('That Joke Isn't Funny Anymore,' side A). Perhaps the most teasing example is on 'Hand In Glove,' where the matrix messages—'Kiss my shades,' by Morrissey, on side A, and 'Kiss my shades too,' by Johnny Marr, on side B—interact with the cover (the nude male), the song itself (in which, according to Simon Goddard, Morrissey sings 'Kiss my shades' during the bridge section—though I'm not convinced) and most obviously with each other. On account of their ambiguous orientation (who are they addressed to? what are their referents?), their equivocal status (do they belong to the work itself or to the work's frame?), their intertextual, parodic and often gnomic character ('You are believing, you do not want to sleep'; 'Tomb it may concern'), as well as their covert inscription (scratched on the run-out grooves of the record and only visible at a certain angle), matrix messages are perhaps the most teasing of all Morrissey's indirect communications.[37]

At all sorts of levels, then, we can see the importance of innuendo to Morrissey's art. Why might this be? What is it about innuendo that makes it so appealing? In the final section of this chapter, 'Flirtation,' I shall discuss the function of Morrissey's coyness in general. However, since, like lightness, innuendo has had a bad press, and unlike its more respectable relatives—such as metaphor—seems to be deemed beneath critical consideration, it may be worth pausing for a moment to reflect upon its function and appeal.

Redeeming vulgarity

In response to the question posed by Morrissey in 'Still Ill'—'Does the body rule the mind / or does the mind rule the body?'—innuendo would seem to imply the former, associated as it is with the tendency to see sexuality at play in everything. But it is also importantly directed towards the mind, since it has a gamelike character,

---

37. For a full list of The Smiths' matrix messages, see Goddard, *The Smiths*.

in challenging the audience to pick up on its covert meaning, and is an exercise—however primitive—in polysemy. In this way, innuendo reflects, even as it appears in its puerility to prescind from, the 'mind-body dichotomy.' This dual involvement of the mind and the body—which like Abbot and Costello are always getting further entangled with, in attempting to escape from, one another—is doubtless part of the appeal for Morrissey; as is the fact that, on this reading, it is at once esoteric and vulgar. Furthermore, if we recognize innuendo as a species of carnival laughter, we can see that it has an additional 'philosophical' aspect—in that it embodies a vision of man—in its preoccupation with the corporeal.[38] Like carnival laughter, innuendo has a democratic foundation: in pointing towards the drives and pro-cesses to which all human beings are subject, it involves a 'suspension of all hierarchical precedence' and reveals a realm of 'purely human relations.'[39] ('Vulgar' in its primary etymological sense means 'of the common people.') Such humour would therefore obviously appeal to Morrissey, whose work, as we have seen—both in its concern for the marginalized, the damaged, the fallen and the 'queer,' and in the animosity it evinces towards institutions, nations and individuals that appear to deny the claims of common humanity—is centrally bound up with the defence of the human. Its appeal might also lie in the fact that innuendo is the mirror image and hence perhaps the ideal opponent of hypocrisy—a vice for which the singer has a particular dislike—in that it intimates behind all fine appearances an 'embarrassing brotherhood' in corporeality.[40]

This last point helps us to see how, in spite of its lightness, innuendo has an implicit 'philosophical' dimension and 'embodies a vision of man.' Like carnival laughter, and unlike satire, innuendo is not 'an individual reaction to some isolated "comic" event.'[41] It is, instead, laughter at man's predicament—at finding ourselves at the mercy of our materiality. It is, as Bakhtin insists, 'the laughter of all the people,'[42] at what it means to be a person. Innuendo, in addition, is reflexive and, like carnival laughter, includes those who are doing the laughing. It therefore differs from satire in this respect as well, which as Swift observed, 'is a sort of glass, wherein beholders

---

38. In highlighting the implicit 'philosophical' dimensions of the carnivalesque, I am drawing on the seminal work of Mikhail Bakhtin in *Rabelais and His World*.
39. Ibid., p. 10.
40. See Ian Donaldson's discussion of 'levelling comedy' in *The World Upside-Down*, p. 7.
41. Bakhtin, *Rabelais and His World*, p. 11.
42. Ibid.

do generally discover everybody's face but their own,'[43] in that the innuendoer is not exempted from their own censure—even if the speaker and the audience playfully accuse each other of culpably accusing each other. Innuendo in this way—cheekily and lightly of course—invites us to perceive man and the world 'in its laughing aspect,'[44] and as such is a sort of 'philosophical' laughter.[45]

There are of course certain obvious differences between innuendo and the carnivalesque. Innuendo, for example, is much more playful and has something of a dialogical character. At one level, as we can see in Frankie Howerd or Dame Edna Everage, it is a way of handling the audience, by 'flirting' with meaning (you suggest something indirectly, the audience laughs, and then you tell them off for their dirty minds), in a way that incriminates all, though all claim exemption. As we have seen, something of this is evident in Morrissey's lyrics, which speak with a sense of a knowing audience, in spite of their ostensibly monological cast. More subtly, though, innuendo also involves the kind of play that was identified in songs such as 'Sheila Take A Bow' and 'Is It Really So Strange?' since its implicit multiplication of radically divergent meanings—which it authors but doesn't wholly own up to—subversively separates the powers of language from its truth-telling function. (Having said that, in taking advantage of the contingencies of language—and it is precisely because puns are in one sense the 'fault' of language that it possible comically to disown one's innuendo—such play carries us back in the direction of the carnivalesque, which likewise celebrates the comedy of being subject to the contingencies of material being.)

The other obvious difference between carnival laughter and innuendo concerns the degree of explicitness involved. Carnival is a festive occasion and is an open and much more dramatic celebration of a 'nonofficial, extraecclesiastical and extrapolitical aspect of the world, of man and human relations . . . and a second life outside officialdom.'[46] Its characteristic logic, as Bakhtin felicitously puts it, is 'the peculiar logic of the "inside out" (*à l'envers*), of the "turnabout,"

---

43. Swift, preface to *Battle of the Books*, p. 104.
44. Bakhtin, *Rabelais and His World*, p. 13.
45. If laughter, as Baudelaire suggests, is in essence 'satanic,' since it depends upon the abasement of its object ('On the Essence of Laughter'), carnival laughter—which has its roots in the religious world of the Middle Ages—is, by contrast, 'benevolent,' since it unites in uncovering a fundamental kinship and encourages what Edith Kern describes as 'a vision of man *sub specie aeternitatis*—quite in contrast to bourgeois notions of importance and obligations to standards of propriety' (Kern, *The Absolute Comic*, p. 8).
46. Bakhtin, *Rabelais and His World*, p. 6.

of a continual shifting from top to bottom, from front to rear, of numerous parodies and travesties, humiliations, profanations, comic crownings and uncrownings.'[47] In comparison, then, with the radical reordering of the festival, innuendo will appear decidedly tame and a timid kind of transgression. Yet innuendo keeps this 'second world' or 'second life outside officialdom' continually in view or only a wink away, and it is a haunting reminder of the persistence of the carnivalesque within the everyday. It is therefore in a way more subversive on account of its implicitness, for in contrast to carnival, which is in some sense confined by its licence, innuendo hovers out of the reach of prohibition and permanently threatens the 'official' civil order. Moreover, it inhabits the very structures of civility themselves, turning their resources to its own advantage, and suggesting that there is no space which is immune to the possibility of corruption.

Morrissey's use of innuendo is evidently indebted to a number of discrete traditions—such as music-hall, glam rock, the *Carry On* school, the sensibility of camp, the slang of gay subculture, and Irish literature's love of wordplay (Sheridan, Wilde, Joyce). And its appeal appears to be similarly diverse. All the readings canvassed so far would seem to be relevant to Morrissey's usage. However, they all share an implicit assumption that innuendo is a way of avoiding what can be more directly or more accurately expressed. On this reading, its indirectness is viewed as a sort of detour or a dilution of a more 'literal' way of speaking. But it might be asked, against this assumption, if this is always the case? *Is* innuendo always a roundabout way of saying something that can be said more directly? Are there not perhaps things that it is not possible to express otherwise or more 'literally'—especially where what is signified is a matter of 'becoming' or an interior impulse, which is to some extent ineffable or a secret, even to ourselves? Indeed, isn't *all* language radically metaphorical and a form of translation when it comes to signifying interiority? In which case, might not a form of utterance which foregrounded its indirectness be paradoxically more faithful to what it seeks to signify? And, if this is so, wouldn't its indirectness cease to be a sort of dawdling or obfuscation and instead positively contribute to the signifying process? As this is an issue that has a bearing on the whole chapter, I hope without being accused of coyness myself I can

---

47. Bakhtin, *Rabelais and His World*, p. 11.

call into question this underlying assumption and allude to without elaborating an alternative possibility, which will be considered in detail in the final section.

Interruption

A major component of Morrissey's coyness, which is closely related to innuendo, is interruption. Like innuendo, it offers a way of communicating by means of suggestion; but if innuendo hides behind its own polysemy, interruption is even more ambiguous as it may intimate things by means of a gap. This is of course something that primarily pertains to the lyrics. However, the cover of The Smiths' debut album provides us with a good illustration of the suggestive character of interruption and shows how Morrissey employs it in other media as well.

It has frequently been noted that the cover image of Joe Dallesandro in Warhol's *Flesh* is cropped from a larger image in which the seminaked Dallesandro—playing a male prostitute—is sitting on a bed with a male client (played by Louis Waldon), who is licking his lips in a tableau of sexual appetite.[48] Yet none of Morrissey's commentators has anything to say about the effect of such cropping and the strange way in which the manifest (homo-)sexual elements in Warhol's film are at once implied by and yet absent from Morrissey's cover image. It is this apparitional remainder—which opens up a third modality between presence and absence—that is brought into being by interruption and which suggests that there may be something paradoxically creative about the act of fragmentation.

Clearly, not all interruption is of this kind, and certain distinctions need to be made. We may, for example, distinguish between what is traditionally known as aposiopesis (breaking off suddenly and leaving a sentence unfinished) and anacoluthon (an utterance that abruptly changes direction, leaving its initial course incomplete). We might additionally distinguish between unmarked and marked interruption—that is, between utterances that are simply abandoned and those that are terminated by 'etceterizing' gestures which describe their own interruption (this latter type of interruption is considered separately below). All these different kinds of interruption are to be

---

48. See, for instance, Goddard, *The Smiths*, p. 296; Rogan, *Morrissey and Marr*, p. 191; and Bret, *Morrissey*, p. 51.

found in Morrissey's lyrics. Let us begin with aposiopesis—that is, 'becoming silent'—a good example of which can be seen in 'Sister I'm A Poet.'

At first glance, the song's 'becoming silent' seems innocent enough (although the interruption is oddly itself excised from the lyric sheet). This is what Morrissey sings:

> All over this town
> yes a low wind may blow
> and I can see through everybody's
> clothes with no reason to hide these words I feel
> and no reason to talk about the
> books I read
> but still, I do
> that's 'cause I'm a . . .
> sister I'm a . . .
> . . . all over this town

On the face of it, this isn't a difficult game of hangman. The chorus appears to be an elliptical version of the song's title, and what's missing would seem to be perfectly clear. But is it? Doesn't the omission function rather more creatively and bring other possibilities into play? One might additionally wonder if there are any clues in the vocative 'sister,' and whether being a poet is something you are (or do) 'all over [the] town.' The song gives us other reasons for pondering this refusal to say what he is. Here is the second verse:

> Along this way
> outside the prison gates
> I love the romance of Crime
> and I wonder: does anybody feel
> the same way I do?
> and is Evil just something you are?
> or something you do?
> sister I'm a . . .
> sister I'm a . . .
> . . . all over this town

We are manifestly in familiar Morrissey territory here, with its reference to the 'romance of Crime' and its meditation on the nature of evil. But the song's questions on the subject of the latter have another, more general dimension and seem to have a bearing on the becoming silent of the chorus. The question about 'being' and 'doing' obviously doesn't just pertain to evil. Rather, it may legitimately be asked of any characteristic: is X something we are or something we do? Which is another way of asking whether our predications (concerning identity and orientation, etc.) point towards essences or discursively produced 'effects'; that is, narrative constructs—rather than innate qualities— whose meaning is a matter of relational differences. Morrissey's question thus betrays suspicions about notions of given and immutable essences—in conceiving of a 'does' independent of any 'is'—which bring to light a more ideological construal of the chorus's interruption. Might the singer's becoming silent on the threshold of predication betoken an anxiety about essentialist descriptions—about the space of the 'is'—and represent a refusal of the available categories or categorization as such? This is not of course Morrissey's way of speaking, and we shouldn't lose sight of the song's casual and ironic character (undoubtedly, the singer is playing with—but also to some extent seeking to redeem—the frilly-shirt status of the 'poet' within the context of popular music). Nevertheless, his consistent and conspicuous tiptoeing around the space of predication is consonant with his relentless and outspoken rejection of categorizing labels throughout his career, including especially the descriptions of sexual orientation—which his silence invites—which dare not speak their name.[49]

If this reading is correct, the singer's refusal to say what he 'is' points towards a construal of his coyness that counters the widely held view that it is a sales ploy and/or a matter of cowardice. For, on this reading, the singer's silence tempts us to consider such labels in order to question the act of labelling. His coyness would therefore serve a critical purpose, and in repudiating the essentializing tendencies of either/or categories—which fix what may of its nature be fluid or ambiguous (or which may be a matter of discursive construction)— might paradoxically be seen as having a representational function in its very attempt to evade representation.

Aposiopesis has other, less complicated functions and produces a number of other effects as well. In 'Will Never Marry,' for example,

---

49. When asked in 2001 about Morrissey's approach to sexual politics, his friend James Maker replied: 'On the gender issue Morrissey is in agreement with Gore Vidal's assertion that one cannot be defined as either heterosexual or homosexual—there are only heterosexual and homosexual acts' (cited in Reid, *Morrissey*, p. 94).

the singer interrupts his repetition of the previous verse in the following way:

> I'm writing this to say
> in a gentle way
> Thank You . . .
> I will live my life as I . . . oh.[50]

In this case, the interruption figures a kind of swoon and a ballooning of emotion that breaks open the speech that seeks to express it. It is a linguistic wound, inflicted, as it were, from within, and as much a synecdoche—that reveals its speaker—as the act of speech. In other words, the interruption serves a dramatic function, and the singer's becoming silent is itself a sort of eloquence. There is furthermore something reflexive about the breakdown of speech which reinforces its dramatic effect. It is as though, in the act of repetition, the speaker is faced with and affected by what he has expressed, which then in a paradoxical reversal speaks back to and silences him. Thus, whereas in 'Well I Wonder' the articulation of incipient despair conjures up out of its own fabric the fragile means of resisting that despair, in 'Will Never Marry' the utterance seems to *bring about* its speaker's despair, in setting his predicament more vividly before him. Indeed, what we witness is the opposite of catharsis and the inability to keep darkness at bay. Just as the 'inbuilt guilt,' of which he goes on to sing, becomes personified and seems to torment him from without,[51] his words—as he comes round to singing them again—appear to loom up before him and make themselves felt from the outside. In this way, he is secondarily tormented by the reflux of his own utterance.[52] The sound of the children playing, which floats in and out—after the utterance of 'alone,' 'laughs in your face,' and as the song fades out—seems to figure a further haunting (of children he won't have? of being tormented as a child?), which again confuses the distinction between inside and outside, and dramatically complicates the song's silences. What began, then, as a polite attempt to lay something to rest ends up unleashing all manner of demons, which turn on

---

50. The first verse runs as follows: 'I'm writing this to say / in a gentle way / Thank You—but no / I will live my life as I / will undoubtedly die—alone.'

51. 'For whether you stay / or you stray / an inbuilt guilt catches up with you / and as it comes around to your place / at 5 a.m., wakes you up / and it laughs in your face.'

52. Such reflexive suffering—in which the subject becomes its own object and receives even more painfully from without what it knows from within—is a recurrent subject in Morrissey's writing, as seen for example in 'I Know It's Over' and 'The Harsh Truth Of The Camera Eye.'

their keeper and show no sign of going back in the jar. The silences of 'Will Never Marry'—which significantly exceed the passages of singing—are therefore anything but empty.

Undoubtedly the most dramatic and intriguing instance of aposiopesis in Morrissey's work is to be found in 'This Charming Man.' Not that one would be aware of any gaps in the text from reading most of the published commentary on the song. Here, for example, is David Bret's description:

> The song, preceded by a stirring introduction by Johnny Marr, is yet another tale of age-gap sex—the story of the 'jumped up pantry boy' (a later Victorian term for a rent boy) who, after his bicycle gets a flat tyre, finds himself being picked up by the nice man whose car has smooth leather seats, but who ultimately cannot understand why someone so handsome should care about him.[53]

It is difficult—pace David Bret—to say exactly what the song is a tale of. This is partly the result of its various ambiguities. Is 'this man,' who later on in the song says 'it's gruesome that someone so handsome should care' the same as 'this charming man'? Does the 'jumped up pantry boy,' spoken of in the third person, refer to the speaker? Which party utters 'why pamper life's perplexities / when the leather runs smooth on the passenger seat'? And what, if anything, does the utterance portend?[54] It is additionally difficult to say what happened, however, *because the song doesn't tell us.* There is an audacious gap in the text, which leaves the central events unnarrated:

> Punctured bicycle
> on a hillside desolate
> will nature make a man of me yet?
>
> when in this charming car
> this charming man
>
> why pamper life's complexities
> when the leather runs smooth on the passenger seat?

53. Bret, *Morrissey*, p. 45.
54. More subtly, one might wonder whether 'charming'—when applied to the man—implies an activity that's performed or a property that's possessed; that is, whether it is more something he 'is' or something he 'does'? It is likewise unclear how much innuendo is involved in the final refrain 'he knows so much about these things'—which is moved further and further away from its ostensible referent by its repetition—and which threatens to complicate the apparent innocence of the speaker (if, indeed, the speaker is the referent of the 'he').

> I would go out tonight
> but I haven't got a stitch to wear.

The interruption of the song's refrain is not graphologically marked on the lyric sheet (which doesn't use any punctuation), but it is manifestly an incomplete sentence: 'when in this charming car, this charming man. . . .' What is the significance of this interruption?

As we have seen in the other examples looked at so far, the space opened up by the act of interruption is not entirely empty but is instead a 'haunted' space. It is an emptiness which produces as much as it leaves out, and whose 'meanings' are neither exactly present nor absent. The space at the centre of 'This Charming Man' shimmers in precisely this way. There are, on the one hand, all sorts of cues which invite us to see it as a sex-shaped space: the apparently pre-scient opening question ('will nature make a man of me yet?'), which recalls that other tale of innocence and experience, 'Reel Around The Fountain'; the sudden shift to an interior perspective and what seems to be a seductive injunction to lead a less reflective and more sensual life ('why pamper life's complexities / when the leather runs smooth on the passenger seat?'); the epithets 'handsome' and 'charming,' which signal attraction but also idiomatically and in their prodigal-ity of delight have a suggestive camp quality; and paradoxically the silence itself, whose very decorousness is suggestive (one is put in mind of the blank chapters in *Tristram Shandy*—the quintessential narrative of interruption—which veil but also paradoxically 'repre-sent' uncle Toby's liaison with the widow Wadman[55]). On the other hand, however, the events at the centre of the song's narrative remain a complete mystery. We are told something about the who and the where, but nothing about the what. Absurd as it may seem to won-der about it, we don't even know how large the gap is (or how many it would take to fill the Albert Hall). And what are we to make of the consummately enigmatic line that might either surface in the midst of the gap or mark its outer perimeter? ('why pamper life's complexities / when the leather runs smooth on the passenger seat?') Is the reference to the appeal of the leather on the passenger seat a metaphor, a metonymy or even the event itself?

---

55. The story—which both proceeds and is prevented from proceeding by continually interrupting itself—begins with the 'interruption' of its narrator's conception, which with the mad performa-tive homology that governs the story is reflected at every level of its narration.

The tone of the song is ambiguous too. Whilst the music is unusually bright and bouncy, angularly hopscotching along in A major, there is a melancholic lethargy to the vocals, which allow the initial sparkling arpeggios to pass and join in at the emergence of the first minor chord. Thereafter, like an unwilling child taken for a walk, the singer's voice seems to pull against rather than follow the line of the music, creating its own folds and stretching itself across the contours of the melody. In timbre, as well, the song sets up a contrast between the ebullient picked notes of the multiple guitars and a voice which appears to be burdened with its own interior heaviness. The greatest divergence in the song and its most ambiguous moment, though, occurs as Morrissey sings 'this charming man.' At this point, the voice virtually stands still or intersects the 'horizontal' progression of the melody with 'vertical' melismatic scalings within the words 'charming' and 'man.' The gap is thus created—as much as it is left—by a dwelling within certain words, which take on an almost tactile quality. The utterance in this way seems to figure a kind of reverie, as the singer appears to be less interested in telling a story and more intent on stretching out the time spent dwelling on certain elements—caressing them interiorly, as one might affectionately stroke an image or feel that saying the name of one's beloved somehow brings them closer.[56] Yet there is at the same time something expressive about this melismatic treading of water—it is as if the singer were trying to tell the whole story in those two words alone. In which case, the phonetic convolutions of 'charming' and 'man' would cease to be merely an ornamental flourish and may be seen as an attempt to communicate a complexity, ambivalence or plenitude, which these words evoke but can't express, by making language itself stammer.[57] We came across something similar in 'The Boy With The Thorn In His Side,' where the singer seems to be tormented by an

---

56. One of the entries in Roland Barthes' *A Lover's Discourse* is 'the loquela': 'This word, borrowed from Ignatius of Loyola, designates the flux of language through which the subject tirelessly rehashes the effects of a wound or the consequences of an action' (Barthes, *A Lover's Discourse*, p. 160). Morrissey's melismatic protraction of the phrase 'this charming man'—which sounds as though the words are shaking him as much as he is shaking the words—seems to represent the speaker's 'tireless rehashing' of the narrative.

57. In speaking of making language stammer—as opposed to stammering in language—I am alluding to Deleuze and Guattari's remarks on major and minor languages ('make language stammer, or make it "wail," stretch tensors through all of language, even written language, and draw from it cries, shouts, pitches, timbres, accents, intensities'). Such 'creative' stammering is a communicative strategy, characterized simultaneously by 'an impoverishment, a shedding of syntactical and lexical forms' and 'a strange proliferation of shifting effects, a taste for overload' (Deleuze and Guattari, *A Thousand Plateaus*, p. 145).

'excess' to which language is inadequate, which results in a carnival of alingual stammering. If the extravagant melisma of 'This Charming Man' is viewed in this way—as the insignia of an interior excess and an attempt to make language itself stammer—its grinding to a halt with a kind of running on the spot would in another sense be a *continuation* of the utterance and communicate an *abundance* of meaning in advertising the failure of speech.

We can see from these examples of aposiopesis in Morrissey's work that interruption can serve a variety of functions. In 'Sister I'm A Poet,' for instance, the anxieties it bespeaks about the space of predication reveal an ideological dimension and suggest it may form part of a more general protest against essentialist thinking. In 'Will Never Marry,' by contrast, it appears to serve a more dramatic function—which is to say it points towards events that are coextensive with the act of speaking—and (in this particular case) represents a running aground of language in the face of overwhelming darkness. And lastly, in 'This Charming Man,' the singer's suspension of the narrative at a critical moment with an extraordinary melismatic excrescence might be seen as a violence inflicted on language itself or a creative mutilation, as a result of—and as a way of communicating—an excess that is incommensurate with language. What these examples all reveal, however, is that interruption may be a *constructive* gesture—in which cessation and continuation paradoxically coincide—which opens up a 'haunted' space that can produce effects and in which meaning coyly plays in spite of its apparent emptiness.

Let us turn now to our second type of interruption—namely, anacoluthon—a clear example of which is to be found in 'Shoplifters Of The World Unite':

My only weakness is a list of crimes
My only weakness is . . . well, never mind.

Morrissey's coyness, as we noted earlier, typically involves a conjunction of exposure and concealment, which at times coincide and on other occasions constitute a rhetorical 'ebb and flow' of the kind we see here. The first of the anaphorically parallel lines is something of a confession, owning up to the 'criminality' of his 'weakness.' Yet, in doing so, it raises more questions than it answers and slyly opens up a plurality within this 'only.' Returning to the subject in the following line then gives the impression that a further, more precise disclosure is imminent and inflames our curiosity. However, the utterance is interrupted on the threshold of disclosure and ebbs away, having told us even less, closing the couplet with a vowel rhyme that analogously haunts us with what it doesn't quite provide.

The second example I want to look at is less conspicuous—since it is an interruption that doesn't leave a gap—and is a recurrent gesture in 'Dear God Please Help Me':

> I am walking through Rome
> with my heart on a string
> dear God please help me
>
> And I am so very tired
> of doing the right thing
> dear God please help me . . .
>
> Then he motions to me
> with his hand on my knee
> dear God did this kind of thing happen to you?

Most of the verses in the song follow this 'amphibious' pattern, consisting of a couple of lines of description interrupted by an apostrophe (a 'turning away' in the act of address), in each case here invoking God. On the first few occasions, this involves a call for help, but in the latter two cases it is much cheekier and perhaps even blasphemous ('dear God, did this kind of thing happen to you?'; 'dear God if I could, I would help you'). Leaving aside the question of blasphemy for now, what we should notice is the way the act of apostrophe at once coyly suggests and conceals a moment of sexual intimacy—in that suddenly calling out to God suggests the advent of some sort of crisis or heightened experience, though it simultaneously draws a curtain across by interrupting the narration of that very experience.

Perhaps the most intriguing example of anacoluthon is to be found in 'At Amber'—a song that is *about* the singer's self-interruption. The first verse sets the scene in a seedy hotel, alluding to the behaviour of the other guests with wonderful litotes ('Where the men and women / are acquainted quite well') and conveying a sense of his own state with great economy and comedy: 'I'm disputing the bill / I will sleep in my clothes.' The second verse then offers an approach to an explanation of his noninvolvement:

> I'm calling you from the foyer
> of the Sands hotel
> Where the slime and the grime gel
> and I cannot—or, I do not . . .
> and oh, my room is cold.

In order to appreciate the significance of this interruption we need to notice how it ties in with a number of other interruptions at different levels in the song. Briefly, the *donnée* is a comparison between the physical disability of the singer's 'invalid friend' and his own inability to take part in things ('oh, my invalid friend / in our different ways / we are the same')—which tormentingly appears to coincide with a desire to join in ('I'm envying you / never having to choose') and which leaves him stalled 'At Amber.'[58] These different but similar 'suspensions' are then additionally reflected in certain narrative details. The phone call, which comments upon and to some extent occasions the singer's noninvolvement, is made in 'the foyer'—the entrance space, which is within and without, part of and yet not part of the main hotel—and the conversation is itself interrupted by the 'invalid friend,' who slams down the receiver saying 'if I had your limbs for a day / I'd steam away.' The anacoluthic hedging at the song's centre—which fails twice in its attempt to articulate the subject of its hedging—thus presents us with a linguistic equivalent of the stalling 'At Amber' it seeks to describe. Moreover, the hesitation between 'cannot' and 'do not' seems to be prompted by—and raises—questions about how far such noninvolvement is a matter of volition and how far it is a matter of ability or a 'given' (is it something we 'are' or something we 'do'?). In this way, and by incorporating into the narrative the invalid friend's angry response, the song calls into question its own comparison and disrupts the song's monological character, so that *as a whole* it is suspended between positions by what Bakhtin would refer to as its polyphony of voices. That the song reflects at a superordinate level the equivocation it describes—in presenting us with differing attitudes towards it—is of particular interest to our general discussion, since it shows the singer is prepared to ask questions about—and take seriously the critique of—his notorious

---

58. This might be contrasted with 'I Can Have Both,' in which the singer seems to *take pleasure in* remaining in the limbo of temptation ('Staring in the window of the shop that never opens / planning my selection from all the treats inside / should I take as I desire—oh shall I, oh shall I? / or should I hang around to be enticed inside?').

shyness. The fact that he doesn't hide from such accusations—that it is a pretence or a form of indulgence—and openly acknowledges that he doesn't know to what degree it is a matter of will suggests that his playful impersonation of himself is at the same time an uncensored engagement with complex realities.

EXCESS

Having it both ways

In *Jokes and Their Relation to the Unconscious*, Freud recounts the following delightful 'piece of sophistry':

> A. borrowed a copper kettle from B. and after he had returned it was sued by B. because the kettle now had a big hole in it which made it unusable. His defence was: 'First, I never borrowed a kettle from B. at all; secondly, the kettle had a hole in it already when I got it from him; and thirdly, I gave him back the kettle undamaged.'[59]

Each one of A's defences, as Freud points out, is valid in itself, but taken together they are absurd, as they logically exclude one another. In other words, there is an *excess* of explanation. In the preceding section, we saw that Morrissey's shyness to a large extent results from a *lack* of information and a strategic concealment, typically cultivated by the oblique pointing of innuendo and his habit of interruption. The opposite, however, is true as well: in a way that reinforces the oxymoronic picture of the previous chapter, not only do we not have enough information, we also have too much! In contrast to the comical scenario described by Freud, though, I wish to suggest that in Morrissey's case, the excess is sustainable and not simply absurd. The bewildering 'excess' on which I shall focus in this section pertains to his sexuality.

It will of course seem bizarre to contend that there is 'too much' sexuality in Morrissey. The singer has clamed to live 'a life that befits a priest,' and probably the most recurrent subject in his lyrics and interviews is the radical lack of intimacy. Yet, rather like the defendant in Freud's piece of sophistry, Morrissey appears to adopt a number of other positions as well, each of which in itself is unexceptional, but which taken together are logically problematic. On *Hatful Of*

---

59. Freud, *Jokes and Their Relation to the Unconscious*, p. 100.

Hollow, for instance—an album that played a crucial part in fashioning the singer's persona—we find lyrics that suggest a homosexual orientation ('This Charming Man'), a heterosexual orientation ('Handsome Devil') and an inclination towards celibacy ('These Things Take Time'). His manner of singing also adds to the confusion, in its adoption of a multiplicity of gendered positions—male, female and androgyne—with its sudden irruptions of flamboyant falsetto (in 'What Difference Does It Make?' and 'You've Got Everything Now,' for example). It is, to be sure, vital to remember that we are dealing with suggestions and to bear in mind all of the other provisos to do with the discreet metaphoricity of the pronoun 'I' and the singer's playful use of signs ('I'm a girl and you're a boy,' etc.). Nevertheless, as all of these qualifications problematize rather than preclude any connection between what's voiced in the songs and the singer's persona (which is itself a discursive construct), what emerges from Morrissey's early lyrics is an 'excess' of sexual orientation.[60]

It is naturally tempting to explain such 'excess' as a result of carelessness or indecision, or else dismiss it as a matter of play (and in thus divesting it of its seriousness, furtively turn it into something else). Yet Morrissey's comments in interviews on the subject of sexuality consistently and stubbornly refuse the exclusivity of the conventional categories and insist upon a more open space which is consonant with his songs' 'excess':

> It's crucial to what we're doing that we're not looking at things from a male stance. I can't recognise gender. I want to produce music that transcends boundaries. . . . I refuse to recognize the terms hetero-, bi- and homo-sexual. . . . People are just sexual, the prefix is immaterial.[61]

How is this consonant with his songs' excess? Morrissey's art, it was noticed earlier, is in many respects an art of refusal, which characteristically entails a withholding of consent, a nonparticipation, an abandonment of conventions, and an obstinate no-saying. However, another way of refusing alternatives is by saying yes *to all of them*. And it is in precisely this way that Morrissey's 'excess' may be seen as a performative refusal which corresponds to and furthers by other

---

60. I should perhaps make clear that this is a matter of logic rather than prudery—for whilst with regard to sexual orientation it is obviously not a contravention of logic to favour this as well as that, it is rather more problematic to maintain a position that favours both as well as neither.

61. *Melody Maker*, September 3, 1983; *NME*, December 1984. Morrissey's comments clearly echo those of the New York Dolls (cited below, p. 83).

means his explicit refusal—by dint of no-saying—of the normative categories of sexual identity. (We have already come across this paradoxical confluence of all and nothing in our discussion of the 'androgynous' and 'neuter' chords that pervade the music of The Smiths.)

But even explaining Morrissey's 'excess' as a performative refusal and the mirror image of his no-saying is misleading if it implies a premeditated stepping outside categories which are accorded an anterior reality. Instead, the underlying argument seems to be that gender identities are performatively constituted cultural constructs and such categories are retroactively imposed upon something much more fluid and ambiguous. It is this more fluid and ambiguous space—'without' gender—towards which Morrissey's performance gestures in both renouncing and encompassing all conventional gender positions. And it is on account of this that with legitimacy he has described himself as 'a kind of prophet for the fourth sex.'[62]

Et cetera

Earlier in the chapter, a distinction was made between 'unmarked' and 'marked' interruption—that is, between utterances which are simply abandoned and etceterizing gestures which describe this abandonment. Such etceterizing gestures are common in Morrissey's work: 'I could say more / but you get the general idea'; 'And there is no point saying this again'; 'from difficult child / to spectral hand / to Claude Brasseur / blah, blah, blah, blah'.[63]

Usually, as in the foregoing examples, they play a fairly minor part in the song, ironizing the song's subject, the singer's own practice or the conventions of the medium. In 'Dagenham Dave,' for example, the obviousness—which is emphasized by the singer's litotes—belongs to the subject of the song (Dave), whose unreflective predictability is communicated by the interruption of his description. (Commentators on the song tend to criticize it for its lightness or vacuity—having first of all assumed that lightness is a fault. Rogan, for instance, characterizes it as 'tired' and 'insubstantial.'[64] However, it seems to me, firstly, that the song's foregrounded vacuity—witness the degeneration of its outro chorus into a playground chant of Dave's name—effectively and amusingly conveys the character of its subject; and, secondly, that

---

62. *Sounds*, June 4, 1983.
63. 'Dagenham Dave,' 'You Have Killed Me,' 'At Last I Am Born.'
64. Rogan, *Morrissey*, p. 226.

this is quite an achievement. It is hard to write about things that lack depth; yet they also have their place in the world. And it is to Morrissey's credit—and a sign of the breadth of his sympathy—that he wishes with affectionate irony to document their existence too.) In 'At Last I Am Born,' on the other hand, the singer's etceterization—'blah, blah, blah, blah'—seems to be at his own expense and a yawn at the familiarity of his own story. But, as in 'You Have Killed Me,' it also appears to involve a metafictional dimension as well; that is to say, its yawn is partly directed towards the act of narration as such (in 'You Have Killed Me,' this is more obvious, and ironic rather than weary, in that during the final chorus—conventionally a space of repetition—Morrissey sings (and indeed repeats) 'there is no point saying this again').[65]

On other occasions, the etceterizing gesture plays a much more integral part in the song, and it is in such cases that it may be seen as a figure of 'excess.' We can illustrate this with two examples—one light or positive and one dark. The first occurs in 'Now My Heart Is Full.'

> I was tired again, I tried again, and
> now my heart is full
> now my heart is full
> and I just can't explain
> *so I won't even try to.*

The song's chorus involves two interruptions. In the first instance, as we noted earlier, the singer abandons the narrative in order to express the feelings it has engendered ('and / now my heart is full'). The 'discourse' thus turns into the 'story' and the song's drama moves into the present. It is, we might say, a metafictional epiphany, since he is overcome with emotion in and as a result of the act of narration. The subsequent etceterization—which is an interruption of this interruption—announces what appears to be an even more radical abandonment of narration in signifying a failure of speech ('and I just can't explain / *so I won't even try to*'). And yet the narrative is in a sense saved by its confession of unworthiness and its failure is turned into a sort of success, for the singer's refusal to explain his inability

---

65. We additionally find sexually suggestive etceterizing gestures in Morrissey's lyrics, as in 'A Swallow On My Neck' ('He drew a swallow on my neck / and the more I will not say') or 'Boy Racer' ('he's just too good looking and . . . and . . . and . . . ').

to explain signifies the advent of an overwhelming excess—an excess that would be *reduced* by speech but which may be preserved and paradoxically communicated by the *failure* of speech. The utterance is therefore a kind of negative performative in that it does what it says it is *not* doing in the act of disavowal. There is of course something comical about this—which doesn't annul but coexists as an arch awareness in tension with the surfeit of emotion it represents—for once again we have a chorus, or an 'antichorus,' which consists of a refusal to sing a chorus. However, the crisis of language—which on this occasion is provoked by an overflow of the heart's affections— also recalls the anguished running aground of speech in 'Will Never Marry' and the urgent attempt to communicate 'without' language in 'The Boy With The Thorn In His Side.'

It is hard to imagine any further escalation of the song's epiphanic speech, following the interruption of an interruption with a disavowal of the adequacy of language. But this is precisely what occurs in the final climactic chorus, which runs as follows:

> now my heart is full
> and I just can't explain
> so . . . so . . . so . . . so . . . so . . . so . . . so . . .

The beauty and the drama of this final welling over is obviously lost on paper, though something may be said about how its effects are achieved. The singer's stalling on the word 'so' figures a kind of benign collapse—which is yet perfectly poised—and a slowing down to epiphanic stillness. It represents an overflow of feeling that coincides with an *effacement* of speech: whereas earlier he told us that he couldn't explain and so wouldn't even try, now the singer can't even explain that he just can't explain. And yet the very collapse of speech is itself communicative, for this is the speechlessness of repletion, the suspended animation of someone in ecstasy, and a stammering which intimates a plenitude beyond speech. This 'still point of the turning world'[66] is in part melodically figured, as the singer's 'so' holds a tremulous $C^\sharp$ over the guitars' circling movement between A, D-E, expressively wresting the D into a D major seventh in the process. The interruption also dilates the utterance's meaning, for whilst the 'so' synecdochically preserves and continues to signify the etceterized clause ('I won't even try to'), it at the same time opens up

---

66. Eliot, 'Burnt Norton,' II, 16.

a supplementary adverbial sense of 'to an extreme degree'—so that it appears to describe even as it refuses to explain the experience—and perhaps even an arch suggestion of 'so there,' which recalls the teasing swings of defiant privacy in Rossetti's 'Winter: My Secret': 'You want to hear it? well . . . my secret's mine, and I won't tell.'

Two general points from this discussion should be brought to the fore. First, the etceterizing gestures in 'Now My Heart Is Full'—'I just can't explain / so I won't even try to'—signal an excess rather than a shortfall of givenness, a surfeit of interiority which is incommensurate with language. Second, this overwhelming experience—whose 'excessive' character is preserved and communicated by the breakdown of speech—is an occasion of ineffable *joy* and a fullness of the heart which overthrows the self that 'contains' it. Such epiphanies are of course common in romantic and modern literature—and especially prominent in the work of Wordsworth, Proust and Joyce, for example. It is much more remarkable, though, to stage the advent of a romantic epiphany within the parameters of a three-minute pop song. And it is more remarkable still that it should be Morrissey—a writer whose work is synonymous with misery—who does so. To avoid any further damage to his reputation, let us turn to our 'et cetera' of excessive darkness.

'Sweet And Tender Hooligan' is a miniature black comedy, whose irony, antirealism and mobility of voice have led to a certain amount of flat-footed commentary.[67] Also, the most interesting, radical and bizarre part of the song—which involves what are surely some of Morrissey's most brilliantly strange and subversive lyrics—has passed virtually without comment. I am referring of course to the etceteras, which take up almost half of the song. Here is a transcript of the final section—which, with the instrumental outro, lasts longer than the 'narrative' section of the song:

---

67. Goddard, for example, observes that the singer's 'derisive counsel that "he [the sweet and tender hooligan]'ll never, never do it again—at least not until the next time" expressed a lack of faith in the British penal system that was strangely conservative, especially when contrasted with the graphic horror of the young lad's misdeeds' (Goddard, *The Smiths*, p. 220). And Bret, apparently missing the intertextuality of the song's ending and sublimely oblivious to its use of irony, describes it as follows: 'Morrissey's hard-hitting but honest appraisal of a violent youth who swears that he will never get into trouble again—at least not until the next time. He tries to convince us that the bludgeoning of an old man with an electric fire was an accident; that the woman he strangled was old and would have died anyhow. The narrator begs the jury to look into the boy's "mother-me" eyes before reaching its verdict—after all, he only turned to crime because he was in debt!' (Bret, *Morrissey*, p. 85).

And in the midst of life we are in death et cetera

And in the midst of life we are in debt et cetera

Et cetera, et cetera, et cetera, et cetera
In the midst of life we are in death et cetera

Et cetera, et cetera, et cetera, et cetera
In the midst of life we are in death et cetera

Et cetera, et cetera, et cetera, et cetera
Et cetera, et cetera
In the midst of life we are in death et cetera

Before commenting on Morrissey's proliferating etceteras, we need to say something about the intertext from which they appear to spawn. The line, as it is given on the lyric sheet, is 'In the midst of life we are in debt.' However, Morrissey's lyric sheets are somewhat unreliable and the first time round it sounds as if he sings 'In the midst of life we are in death.' Either way, the former is obviously a play upon the latter, which is taken from 'The Burial of the Dead' rite in *The Book of Common Prayer* (which is itself a translation from the Latin liturgy *'Media vita in morte sumus'*).[68] Whilst clearly arising out of the preceding narrative, the line thus also links the song, in spite of its parody, with the fundamental facts of life and death and our attempts to come to terms with them. Quite a lot is therefore at stake. In pointing this out, I'm not trying to evaporate its irony or the play of its imagining. On the contrary, I think such elements have been underplayed in commentary on the song and crucially contribute to the tonal heterogeneity that is one of the hallmarks of Morrissey's writing. The other side of this heterogeneity, however, is a darkness which we domesticate if we reduce it to 'the young lad's misdeeds.' What, then, is the significance of Morrissey's 'et cetera'?

In the first place, it is of course ironic—which is to say, somehow at odds with itself or its context. Conventionally, in narrative, song and art in general, we expect something to be given, created or disclosed to us. Yet the etceterizing gesture is a *refusal* to narrate; and in a work of art, it is thus a refusal of its own reason for being. Morrissey's extended singing of 'et cetera'—especially where for a whole verse he sings nothing but 'et cetera'—may therefore be seen as an

---

68. The parody 'In the midst of life we are in debt' is first recorded in *The Cynic's Calendar* (1902) by Ethel Watts Mumford.

'antilyric' and a form of art which is a refusal of the enterprise of art. Earlier, we saw that the singer's yawning at his own practice is indebted to the ennui of the Byronic-Wildean dandy. Here, however, his flamboyant boredom seems to have a darker and more embittered character, and is closer to the gestures of exhaustion which we associate with punk or the Theatre of the Absurd. In both of which, this is at once an aesthetic as well as an existential protest—'a gob of spit in the face of Art,' as Henry Miller puts it,[69] and a cry whose very inarticulacy is an expression of helplessness, alienation and the apparent absurdity of life. Furthermore, there is a homology in the aesthetic of both these movements—that is, a correspondence between the views or attitudes expressed and the form or style of their expression (the guitar solo in The Buzzcocks' 'Boredom' is indeed boring, and, as Estragon remarks in *Waiting for Godot*, 'Nothing happens, nobody comes, nobody goes, it's awful!'[70]). Relatedly, there is a prominent metafictional element in their performances (one thinks, for example, of John Lydon onstage in New York in 1978 singing 'This is no fun,' and Hamm in *Endgame*—premiered in French in 1957—remarking 'This is deadly'[71]). Morrissey's protracted 'etcetera' likewise exposes its own textual status and performs the exhaustion of which it speaks. It is, as it were, a blank signifier, which renders visible the space of signification with a gesture of deferral. In fact, the phrase offers us a miniature allegory of deconstruction, for what it signifies is the mechanism of signification and the logic of différance. (It is no wonder that Derrida wrote an essay on 'et cetera.'[72]) Morrissey's use of the phrase should therefore be related to a range of other subversive gestures in his work—such as his playful use of signs and his generic heterogeneity—which call attention to its fictionality. His 'excessive' repetition of 'et cetera' seems in a sense to beget itself, however, and give way to something much darker. Indeed, it is arguably the most nihilistic moment in Morrissey's oeuvre. There are two interrelated aspects to this.

On the one hand, Morrissey's 'et cetera' might be seen as a form of *Sprachskepsis*—a radical linguistic scepticism or crisis of

---

69. Miller, *Tropic of Cancer*, p. 10.
70. Beckett, *Waiting for Godot*, Act I, p. 34.
71. Beckett, *Endgame*, p. 25.
72. 'Et Cetera . . . (and so on, und so weiter, and so forth, et ainsi de suite, und so, überall, etc.),' in Royle, *Deconstructions*.

language.[73] Such a reading is supported by the earlier narrative, which is a courtroom testimony ('so jury you've heard every word / but before you decide') that associates itself with a context in which language is supposed to be stable, transparent and a tool of law. Yet its apparently innocuous ironies wrench words so far away from their conventional meanings that they float free and cease to make sense: 'he swore that he'll never, never do it again / and of course he won't / urr . . . (not until the next time) / poor old man / he had an 'accident' with a three-bar fire . . .' The natural consequence of this unhinging of language or revealing of its lack of any fixed or intrinsic connection with extralinguistic reality is the kind of delighted complicity in the play of signification that takes place, for example, in 'Sheila Take A Bow'—which was the A-side to 'Sweet And Tender Hooligan' and whose 'la la la' is the obverse of its 'et cetera'—or the terrifying sense of disconnection that leads Hofmannsthal's Lord Chandos to feel he has 'lost completely the ability to think or speak of anything coherently.'[74] It is this latter, dark alternative which appears to be signified by Morrissey's 'et ceteras.'

On the other hand, though, there is something manic or deranged about the song's furious stasis, which seems to descend into what Jean-Jacques Lecercle describes as an experience of *délire*. According to Lecercle, délire is an experience of madness or possession in language, in which it 'ceases to be controlled by the subject but on the contrary rules over him,' and where 'articulated speech gives way to incantation and animal noise, the scream (*le cri*).'[75] Morrissey's 'excessive' utterance—which is excessive precisely because it *doesn't* move—is manifestly not a literal scream, nor is it as psychotic as the majority of Lecercle's examples. Nevertheless, in its bizarre proliferation and vehemence in excess of its apparent occasion, its degeneration into indecipherable consonantal slurring, backed by violent slashing guitars and the way in which its speaker seems to get 'carried away,' it is closer to the voice of délire that it is to conventional speech. Moreover, there is something peculiar about etcetera that conspires to subvert its speaker's mastery. What is it?

---

73. The phrase *Sprachskepsis* or *Sprachkritik* alludes to a radical loss of faith in language, which results in a sense of existential estrangement, the celebrated account of which is Hugo von Hoffmanstahl's *The Letter of Lord Chandos*.

74. Hofmannsthal, *The Letter of Lord Chandos*, p. 133. As he puts it later: 'Words floated round me; they congealed into eyes which stared at me and into which I was forced to stare back—whirlpools which gave me vertigo and, reeling incessantly, led into the void.'

75. Lecercle, *Philosophy through the Looking-Glass*, pp. 7; 35.

Etcetera is of course a conventional way of signalling a projected continuity of familiar data, which literally means 'and the others' and is tantamount to saying 'you can finish the list yourself.' Yet it discreetly harbours a mischievous openness—for who can set a limit on that list of others? It is in this sense a shorthand for a sort of infinity. (For Derrida, it 'in one go swallows everything into its gulf.'[76]) This mischievous openness is dizzyingly radicalized when that which is etceterized is etcetera.

In 'Sweet And Tender Hooligan,' what is initially etceterized is large enough already ('in the midst of life we are in death'—or the parody, which is itself a kind of etcetera). However, the subsequent repeated etceterization of etcetera involves an exponential dilation as it were of infinity, such that each etcetera includes everything that the previous utterance etceterized *and* its etceterization. In this way the utterance at once insanely encompasses everything, and yet in its blanket surfeit of referentiality it also entails an *evacuation* of significance. The etcetera is thus self-perpetuating, in that it says nothing but leaves nothing to say, except to etceterize the previous etcetera. (One is put in mind of a remark by Samuel Beckett—whose work is enthralled by the negative infinities of etcetera—'there is nothing to express, nothing with which to express, nothing from which to express, no power to express, no desire to express, together with the obligation to express.'[77]) In this sense, we can see Morrissey's manic repetition of etcetera as a délire 'loss of mastery by the subject who is compelled to give in to this proliferation,'[78] and as an utterance that gives way to 'incantation and animal noise'[79] as Morrissey seems to be 'carried away' in a negative ecstasy, singing a verse of nonsensical sounds, out of which emerges a dislocated repetition of etcetera, which locks into the violent driving cycle of the music. In the words of Lecercle: 'At this point language is no longer an instrument of communication . . . , the privileged vehicle of social practice, it has become the bearer of the violent passions of the human body: no longer the word, but the scream.'[80] Whilst Morrissey's utterance is in a way obviously staged—in that he is in a recording studio—and presumably to some degree at least premeditated, there is a sense in

---

76. Royle, *Deconstructions*, p. 285.
77. Beckett, 'Three Dialogues,' p. 139.
78. Lecercle, *Philosophy through the Looking-Glass*, p. 38.
79. Ibid., p. 35.
80. Ibid.

which he seems eventually, through his etceterization, to be screaming at his own scream.

The song that follows 'Sweet And Tender Hooligan' on *Louder Than Bombs* is 'Half A Person,' which tells the story of a Charles Hawtrey–esque speaker, who 'booked [himself] in at the Y . . . WCA,' and asked ' "do you have a vacancy / for a Back-scrubber?" ' It is with a similar lurch that we must turn our attention to the findings of the chapter in general.

FLIRTATION

Flirtation, according to Adam Philips, is 'the (consciously or unconsciously) calculated production of uncertainty.'[81] Leaving aside the oxymoronic difficulties of an 'unconsciously calculated' action, it seems fair to say on the evidence of this chapter that Morrissey's art is essentially 'flirtatious' in Philips's sense. The advantage of characterizing his work in this way is that it keeps in view the mobility and lightness as well as the elusiveness that is crucial to so much of his art. (Of course, Morrissey's art involves exposure too, but what could be more flirtatious than being exposed *as well as* elusive?) The disadvantage of describing it in this way is that flirtation is held in rather low esteem, and tends like lightness to be viewed as the trifling shade of some other thing. And yet, as Philips astutely points out, 'Flirting may not be a poor way of doing something better, but a different way of doing something else.'[82] It is this more positive sense of flirtation that I wish to invoke in drawing some conclusions about Morrissey's 'art of coyness.'

The singer is of course routinely criticized for his 'flirtatious' art, and his 'calculated production of uncertainty' is frequently interpreted as a matter of cowardice or an elaborate sales ploy. In particular, his refusal to define himself sexually, in terms of the customary categories—by identifying with a multiplicity of positions, whilst at the same time remaining aloof from all of them—has proved to be persistently troubling. Richard Smith, for example, writing for *Gay Times* in 1990, responded to the release of 'Piccadilly Palare' as follows: 'If you're not gay, then get your hands off our history. You can't steal the very words from our lips just so that you can embellish your

81. Philips, *On Flirtation*, p. xvii.
82. Ibid., p. xxii.

songs with (pardon the pun) a bit of rough.'[83] This response has been endorsed by David Bret:

> And *Gay Times*' Richard Smith had a valid point: if he was gay, the gay press wanted him to come out properly and offer strength and support to all those fans who had shut themselves up in bedrooms—seeking solace in his music to help them come to terms with being gay. And if he was not totally gay, then they wanted him to say so, leave off their culture and stop flaunting it in their faces. 'Being gay isn't for making money out of unless you're a fully paid-up member of the company,' Kris Kirk admonished. 'Otherwise you get out of the theatre and find yourself another job.'[84]

Such responses seem to me to be misguided for two principal reasons: firstly, they involve a whole range of unquestioned essentialist assumptions concerning the nature of sexual identity; and secondly, they fail to appreciate the political value—not least for the cause for which they purport to speak—of Morrissey's refusal to chain himself to a particular category. Let us consider each of these in turn.

If a thing eludes our conventional categories—in refusing to commit itself to any of them or in claiming allegiance to more than one—there are two basic ways of interpreting this. On the one hand, we can assume that such categories correspond to essences and distinctions that exist in and exhaustively constitute reality, and thus explain the mismatch as an aberration on the part of the thing. In which case, the implication is that such elusiveness is abnormal (it *shouldn't* be like this) or disingenuous (it isn't *really* like this). Alternatively, however, it is equally possible to see such a mismatch as calling into question the adequacy of our categories, which would thereby be exposed as cultural constructs imposed upon a reality which is in fact more fluid. In this case, such elusiveness would take on a more positive 'deconstructive' function, since it not only lays bare the artificial character of our conventional categories but also reveals the coercive, regulatory nature of essentialist thought, which implicitly outlaws—by deeming them either to be counterfeit or 'abnormal'—things which may *of their nature* be neither this nor that or both this *and* that.

---

83. Cited in Bret, *Morrissey*, p. 137.
84. Ibid., pp. 137–8.

The responses of Bret and Smith, which are fairly representative critiques of Morrissey's elusiveness, seem to assume without a second thought that homosexuality is something you 'are'—rather than something you 'do'—and that this essentialized identity is unified, fixed and transparently knowable. (Bret's luminously gauche phrase 'totally gay' begs all sorts of questions it apparently hasn't occurred to him to ask.) Maintaining such views is possible of course. However, it involves an heroic ignoring of the major currents in modern and postmodern thought concerning the 'death' or dissolution of the traditional subject, which is more commonly viewed as radically disintegrated (if not self-differing), an identity-in-process, more an 'effect' or cultural production than a cause, and sublimely unknowable to itself. It also involves a thorough ignoring of what Morrissey's work has to say about such matters.

As we have seen, the singer explicitly rejects out of hand—as falsifying—the conventional categories of sexual orientation ('I refuse to recognize the terms hetero-, bi- and homo-sexual') and has referred to the mobile, siteless, open position of which he is the 'prophet' as the 'fourth gender.' More subtly, his lyrics are consistently suspicious of all kinds of essentialism ('is Evil just something you are? / or something you do?') and his habit of behaving as though he's quoting his own gestures exposes his identity as a performative construct.[85] Relatedly, his work also explores—in light and dark registers—the ways in which the self exceeds itself and 'contains' more than it can express, or is not wholly in control of itself and its products, or is haunted, as it were, by itself from without. In such ways, his lyrics raise all sorts of questions about the autonomy, the knowability and the parameters of subjectivity.

In outlining the problems with the governing assumptions of the standard critique of Morrissey's elusiveness—which his work calls into question in advance of their articulation—we have already passed over into the second objection: namely, that such a critique fails to appreciate the political or ethical value of Morrissey's 'flirtatious' aesthetics. For the singer's deconstructive refusal of the normative categories of sexual identity isn't simply a matter

---

85. It was noted earlier that camp is typically adjectival or adverbial, and thus foregrounds a posture or manner of performing, as opposed to an essential characteristic or state. This obviously corresponds to Gore Vidal's view—which is apparently shared by Morrissey—that 'there is no such thing as a homosexual person, any more than there is such a thing as a heterosexual person. The words are adjectives describing sexual acts, not people' (Vidal, 'Sex Is Politics,' p. 550).

of realism—that is, an objection to their noncorrespondence with
the more fluid, heterogeneous and veiled nature of how things are;
it is also born of a vigilant sense of the strategies of power which
produce and discipline the gendered subject,[86] and is an attempt, in
the words of Judith Butler, 'to counter the violence performed by
gender norms.'[87] As the singer has himself insisted, 'These words
[heterosexual, homosexual, bisexual] do great damage, they confuse
people and they make people feel unhappy so I want to do away with
them.'[88] Morrissey's work—and this needs to be stressed in view of
the heavy words that are so lightly thrown—is thus crucially engaged
in a defence of difference.

Making all of this clear doesn't of course disprove the critique of
Morrissey's elusiveness put forward by Bret and others. However, in
revealing such elusiveness to be a consistent symptom of something
more fundamental, it represents a more compelling alternative explanation uncountenanced by such critics.[89] This more fundamental
elusiveness has been the overarching subject of the first three chapters of the study, and so shouldn't need rehearsal here; though it is, at
this intermediate juncture, worth emphasizing the centrality of the
principle itself.

One of the extraordinary things about Morrissey's work is the
number of sites or directions from which his meanings come. There
are naturally the lyrics themselves, but there are as well his frequent
alterations of them in live performances, his correlative comments
on the same subjects in interviews, the pregnant images that often
accompany them, his appearance and the act of singing them, and
the matrix messages which speak from elsewhere but which also
form part of this suggestive polyphonic coalescence of meaning.
What makes such 'meaning'—which constitutes his persona—all the
more elusive, however, is the fact that there is no site of authority.
What in this rhizomic web of meaning trumps what? Do the lyrics,
as they are printed (which sometimes differ from how they are sung),

---

86. Since an early age, Morrissey has been interested in and influenced by the views of radical
feminists, such as Susan Brownmiller (see *Sounds*, June 4, 1983; and Rogan, *Morrissey and Marr*,
p. 90).
87. Butler, *Gender Trouble*, p. xxv.
88. *Smash Hits*, June 21, 1984.
89. Mark Simpson, to his credit, is sensitive to the antiessentialism of the singer's elusiveness and
pours scorn on the either/or dogmatism of his more obtuse critics in *Saint Morrissey* (chapter
9). But, like the rest of the book, his discussion is unfortunately marred by the overpowering
aftershave of his preening self-consciousness.

have ultimate authority? Do his live alterations, with their apparent immediacy, carry more conviction? Or do his 'real life' comments, outside an aesthetic space, have a superordinate jurisdiction? The answer of course is that in a classic poststructuralist fashion we are delightfully led from one signifier to another without ever arriving at an ultimate signified—which is a spectral effect or a 'living sign' created by the chain of signifiers themselves.

But perhaps we ought to conclude by acknowledging one further possibility, which is brought into view by Hegel's famous pronouncement that 'the secrets of the ancient Egyptians are also secrets for the Egyptians themselves.'[90] One plausible explanation that is never countenanced by critics of the singer's elusiveness— and which is why I doubt that the rumoured autobiography would answer the questions—is that the secrets of Morrissey may also be secrets for Morrissey himself.

---

90. Žižek, *The Parallax View*, p. 234.

CHAPTER 4

⸙⸙⸙

Maudlin Street

This story is old—I KNOW
but it goes on.

—*Last Night I Dreamt That Somebody Loved Me*

THE DARK WOOD

Woody Allen's *Annie Hall* begins with two jokes that are intended to explain how his character feels about life and his relationships with women. The first is an exchange between two elderly ladies at a Catskills resort, one of whom says: 'Boy, the food at this place is really terrible'; to which the other replies: 'Yeah, I know, and such small portions.' The second is attributed to Groucho Marx and is paraphrased by Allen's character, Alvy Singer, as follows: 'I would never want to belong to any club that would have someone like me for a member.' What can these two jokes tell us about Morrissey?

The view of life expressed by the first is glossed by Singer himself: 'Full of loneliness and misery and suffering and unhappiness, and it's all over much too quickly.' This bleak view of things—whose proliferation of near synonyms suggests a tendency to dwell on or wallow, even as its speaker insists upon the awfulness of it all—is consonant with Morrissey's. On every album the singer has produced, as a solo artist and with The Smiths, we find an obstinate insistence upon the presence, the reality, and the *infinity* of suffering,[1] as well as a constant sense that whatever else may come and go, death is always 'at one's elbow.' In Morrissey's case, too, there is something 'excessive' about this insistence—its repetition, its hyperbole and

---

1. Writing from prison in the letter to Lord Alfred Douglas which was later given the title *De Profundis*, Wilde claims: 'Better than Wordsworth himself I know what Wordsworth meant when he said—"Suffering is permanent, obscure, and dark, / And has the nature of infinity."' (Wilde, *De Profundis and Other Writings*, p. 48).

the embarrassing exposure it involves. And yet, as we have seen, his work is also full of whimsy, lightness and play, and—as it is in *Annie Hall*—the darkness is often conjoined with humour.

The relevance of the second joke is perhaps less apparent. We find, of course, in Morrissey as well the kind of paradoxical suspicion of the very belonging he seems to crave, which underlies Singer's allusion to the joke. In 'How Can Anybody Possibly Know How I Feel?' for example, he sings:

> She told me she loved me,
> which means
> she must be insane . . .
> they said they respect me,
> which means
> their judgement is crazy.

We have additionally seen how Morrissey's tendency to do things within ironic or camp quotation marks means that he seems paradoxically to differ from himself, and is thereby able to suspend his membership of the club to which he simultaneously belongs. There is a further sense, though, in which we might say that the singer would never want to belong to any club that would have him as a member. Morrissey is crucially an *oppositional* artist, whose songs, in many cases, are less an expression of personally held views and more a 'tactical' adoption of outsider perspectives. For, like William Blake, he is deeply suspicious of anything that seeks to install itself as 'normal' and is alert to the danger of things turning into what they oppose—which is one reason we find him apparently relinquishing positions once his point has been made (as seen, for instance, in his renunciation of 'the art of weakness' or the softening of his opposition to synthezised music). This instinctive, mobile suspicion of the established is also, I suspect, tied up with the singer's fascination with violence, which he sees to some extent as a product of the 'normality' that cowers in its shadow.[2] More disturbingly still, violence, to Morrissey, seems to possess a kind of vitality or authenticity that is lacking in 'civilized' society. Charles Guignon has written helpfully about the aesthetic 'appeal' of violence in modern culture more generally:

---

2. 'Under every *Good* is a hell,' wrote Blake, who saw the need for 'Contraries' and hence had a sympathy for the latter, as he believed the Good's attempt to establish itself has an innate tendency to produce the hell it purports to oppose (annotation in Swedenberg's *Heaven and Hell*, in *The Complete Poetry of William Blake*, p. 602).

Of course, there is another reading of the significance of the heart of darkness within, a reading that has shaped a sort of counter-culture to the dominant culture of authenticity in contemporary society. This counter-culture encourages us to accept the fact that what lies within is characterized by aggression, cruelty and violence, and holds that authenticity is precisely a matter of getting in touch with and expressing those dark impulses and cravings. The idea that being authentic is a matter of venting all that is brutal and ugly in the inner self, originating in the work of such pivotal figures as the Marquis de Sade, Arthur Rimbaud, Georges Bataille and Antonin Artaud, now has come to play a central role in certain lifestyle enclaves of Western culture. It appears in the 'Theatre of the Absurd' and the 'Theatre of Cruelty,' in the Beat poetry of the fifties—for example, in Allen Ginsberg's 'Howl'—and it shows up again and again in Heavy Metal and punk rock, in gangsta' rap and slam poetry, and in styles of art that quite consciously set out to be a 'slap in the face' to the bourgeoisie.[3]

Clearly, Morrissey's lyrics should be included in this list, which exhibit an 'infernal' sympathy for the rebellious, the contrary or the adversaries of 'normality,' and with extraordinary bravery and fidelity attempt to speak from within the heart of darkness.

NO'S KNIFE

One of the most subtle but telling signs of Morrissey's quarrel with popular music and the difference he made is his replacement of pop's cheery ad lib 'yeah, yeah, yeah' with an insistent 'no, no, no.' In some cases, this no-saying merely reinforces a manifest negative orientation, as in 'America Is Not The World': 'and I have nothing to offer you / no, no, no, no'; whilst on other occasions it signals a resistance to a counter-orientation, as in 'Shakespeare's Sister': 'No, Mamma, let me go.'[4] Sometimes, however, Morrissey's no-saying seems to arise out of nowhere and have nothing to do with the narrative in whose cracks it flowers. This is the case, for example, at the end of 'This

---

3. Guignon, *On Being Authentic*, pp. 104–5.
4. We also find mixed litanies of yes and no, in which Morrissey swings between positions, as in 'Tomorrow,' where at one point he sings, 'I never said I wanted to' [pause] 'Well, did I?' and then later ad libs 'no-yeah, no-yeah' or in 'Whatever Happens, I Love You,' where he stretches the principle to a comic extreme ('But when all is said and done / it's you I love / yes, yes, yes, yes, yes, no, yes, yes, yes . . . ').

Night Has Opened My Eyes' and even more clearly in 'William, It Was Really Nothing':

> The rain falls hard on a humdrum town
> this town has dragged you down
> no, no-oh-oh
> and everybody's got to live their life
> and God knows I've got to live mine.

In such cases, it's unclear what, if anything, is being resisted. It is likewise unclear, if something is being resisted, whether this 'something' is within or without the self. And, further, if this something is within the self—as the lack of any manifest agency outside may suggest—it is unclear what exactly is doing the resisting.[5] Such questions are complicated by matters of intertextuality and the involvement of the singer's personae, which multiply the possible orientations of his no-saying. It may, for instance, be a 'sideways' address to other texts and a saying 'no' to the 'yeah, yeah, yeah' that customarily takes up such space in popular music. Alternatively, it might represent a dropping of the mask—or the melancholy equivalent of a camp wink—and the emergence of a more direct relation between the singer and the audience (though, to be sure, this unmasked self is itself a mask or textual construction).[6] Such irruptions are important for other effects too.

As we noticed in the previous chapter, Morrissey's songs frequently dramatize the event or state they describe, presenting it as something occurring in the moment of the song. Morrissey's no-saying frequently takes on a dramatic character in just this way, and rather than being a mere description, seems to be *an act* of resisting or holding on. In 'You Know I Couldn't Last,' for example, when

---

5. William Empson once pointed out that the speaker of Keats's 'Ode on Melancholy' must in some sense want very much to go to Lethe, if it takes so many negatives to restrain him ('No, no! go not to Lethe, neither twist / Wolf's-bane, tight-rooted, for its poisonous wine; / Nor suffer thy pale forehead to be kissed / By nightshade'). If the principle holds for Morrissey too, his no-saying would suggest an immense latent counterimpulse to something, which is precisely what he argues in 'The Boy With The Thorn In His Side' ('behind the hatred there lies / a murderous desire for love'). This subject is taken up again in chapter 5, pp. 261–5.
6. One might further distinguish between a no-saying that remains in character, as in 'Best Friend On The Payroll' ('It's not gonna work out / no, no, no, no') and a no-saying that seems to respond dialogically from another perspective, as in 'Boy Racer' ('He thinks he's got the whole world in his hands / And I'm gonna kill him / oh no, oh no, oh no, oh no . . . '), both of which differ in turn from the no-saying that appears to come from a perspective outside the narrative, as we saw in 'William, It Was Really Nothing.'

Morrissey sings 'so don't let the good days / of the gold disks / creep up and mug you / no, no, no, no,' he sounds as if he's trying to fight off the presently encroaching forces he describes. Similarly, in 'Rubber Ring'—a song about the way songs can keep one afloat—the first chorus's slurred singing of 'no' appears to take on precisely such a supporting function, as though the utterance itself were holding something at bay. Perhaps the most poignant example, however, occurs in 'I Won't Share You,' where just before the final heartrending refrain—which sounds more like a plea for something the singer feels is slipping through his fingers than an assertion of something within his control—there is an irruption of no-saying within the homonym 'know,' as if he's desperately trying to hold onto what's departing in and *by means* of the act of singing:

> Life tends to come and go
> Well, that's okay
> Just as long as you know no, no, no, no, no, no, no . . .
> I won't share you.

Morrissey's no-saying rarely makes it to the lyric sheet and isn't always as conspicuous as the examples I've cited. (It has, however, been powerfully reinforced by preconcert recordings of Maya Angelou's 'No No No No.'[7]) Indeed, what we often find are borderline lexical utterances that verge on or shade over into a 'no,' as in 'The Boy With The Thorn In His Side' or the falsetto middle sections of 'Pretty Girls Make Graves.' It is perhaps less articulate, too, than my remarks so far have suggested. Yet it is for this reason all the more significant. For Morrissey's no-saying seems to be something underlying, like an underground stream, that is uncovered by the cessation of speech or which wells up in its interstices. If we return to the no-saying in 'William, It Was Really Nothing,' for example, it has no apparent connection with the narrative in which it occurs—which is bleak but comprised of affirmative utterances—and tonally introduces a gravity that the narrative lacks, which seems to pull it in another direction. (There is a comparable gravitational pull in the lines that follow—away from the addressee's perspective, which

---

7. It is also something of which the singer is clearly conscious. When asked by Paul Morley, 'How do you resist that particular pressure to succumb to the straightforward?' he replied: 'It's very hard. You get bored hearing yourself say the same old things time and time again. Hearing your voice say no, no, no . . .' (*Blitz*, April 1988).

ostensibly governs the song—towards the speaker's own perspective: 'and everybody's got to live their life / and God knows I've got to live mine.')

If, then, there is a form of no-saying in Morrissey's lyrics which 'exceeds' or seems to speak from outside the narrative in which it occurs, what might it signify? What is he saying 'no' *to*?[8] One possibility is that he is not in fact saying 'no' to anything—or at least to any *particular* thing—and that it is instead what Slavoj Žižek refers to as a '*No as such*'; that is, not 'a "No" to a particular content' or even 'a signifying "No" but, rather, a kind of bodily gesture.'[9] This is certainly a helpful way of thinking about Morrissey's no-saying, which often seems to detach itself from referentiality or sing from a place that has no language.[10] Another possibility, however, is that it is more like a Hitchcockian camera shot, where we are shown the person screaming rather than what they are screaming at. In which case, the singer's apparently 'contentless' negations may, on the one hand, be an instance of what Samuel Beckett memorably describes as 'no's knife in yes's wound'[11]—a preemptive attempt to escape suffering by stifling the 'murderous desire for love.'[12] On the other hand, the singer's 'excessive' no-saying might signify the advent of something more sinister and a more uncanny assailant.

The final verse of 'Ammunition,' on *Maladjusted*, is enlightening in this connection:

I've been crying
it comes back on these salient days
and it stays
and it says:
'We've never really been away.'

---

8. Morrissey's ad-libbed no-saying is too frequent and consistent with the other refusals in his work to be a matter of chance or meaningless decoration. His refusal may be brought into focus by comparison with Paddy McAloon's avoidance of the 'yeah, yeah, yeah' ad lib. In both cases, a sense of 'belatedness' effects a swerve in their practice, but whereas for the latter this results in a more sanguine exploration of aesthetic variations, for the former it is a more antagonistic and 'ideological' taking issue with the tradition.

9. Žižek, *The Parallax View*, pp. 83–4.

10. For a suggestive discussion of this subject in general, see Michel de Certeau, *The Practice of Everyday Life*, pp. 162–4.

11. Beckett, *Texts for Nothing*, XIII, in *Complete Shorter Prose*, p. 113.

12. This would be appropriate if 'The Boy With The Thorn In His Side' is indeed influenced by Wilde's 'The Nightingale and the Rose,' in which the bird *seeks out* the thorn and the wound is self-inflicted. (The curious choice of the adjective 'murderous' might also imply a reflexive violence and a lack so great it destroys the self.)

In the space of these few short lines, an uncanny 'it' emerges out of the singer's sadness—an 'it' which seems to be both unnameable and familiar—which first of all turns into a person or something capable of 'saying,' and then even more peculiarly becomes plural and omnipresent ('We've never really been away'). It is this amorphous, plural, unnameable darkness—which is present even when it's not apparent and which paradoxically exceeds its particular—that frequently seems to elicit the singer's no-saying.

To be more precise, Morrissey's evocative 'no, no, no' betokens, I suggest, the seeping in of a darkness that lies everywhere in wait; that speaks in the name and with the voice of its victim; that separates everything from everything; that is ingenious in its torments and tireless in its persecutions; that turns every defence to its own advantage—including the art that would capture its likeness; that wrestles without giving itself to be wrestled with; that is not dispelled but is *intensified* by the knowledge that it exists in the eye of the beholder; that is not tempered but is rendered more appalling by repetition; that has no place of refuge; that answers no call; that gathers everything up into a sterile epiphany and makes of everywhere one little room. This is the darkness that laps at the edges of Morrissey's vision in so many of his songs, whose ingress is registered by the half-articulate cries of 'no' that recurrently irrupt in their crevices—a darkness which, like Banquo's ghost, is invisible to all but the haunted.[13] Then how is it possible, it may be asked, to say so much about a darkness that remains at the edge of vision? Because it is a darkness that the singer also directly confronts.

IT

Undoubtedly one of the most direct confrontations of darkness in Morrissey's work is 'I Know It's Over,' on *The Queen Is Dead* (1985). Since I shall focus on the song in some detail, it will be helpful to have the entire lyric in front of us.

> Oh Mother, I can feel the soil falling over my head
> and as I climb into an empty bed
> Oh well, enough said

---

13. In her essay, 'I am Christina Rossetti,' Virginia Woolf observes that 'death, oblivion, and the rest lap round your songs with their dark wave' (Woolf, *Collected Essays*, p. 59).

I know it's over—still I cling
I don't know where else I can go
Oh Mother, I can feel the soil falling over my head
see, the sea wants to take me
the knife wants to slit me
do you think you can help me?
10 Sad veiled bride, please be happy
handsome groom, give her room
loud, loutish lover, treat her kindly
(although she *needs* you
more than she *loves* you)
and I know it's over, still I cling
I don't know where else I can go
I know it's over
and it never really began
but in my heart it was so *real*
20 and you even spoke to me, and said:
'If you're so funny
then why are you on your own tonight?
and if you are so clever
why are you on your own tonight?
if you're so very entertaining
why are you on your own tonight?
if you're so terribly good-looking
then why do you sleep alone tonight?
because tonight is just like any other night
30 that's why you're on your own tonight
with your triumphs and your charms
while they are in each other's arms . . .'
It's so easy to laugh
it's so easy to hate
it takes strength to be gentle and kind
it's so easy to laugh
it's so easy to hate
it takes guts to be gentle and kind
love is Natural and Real
40 but not for you, my love
not tonight, my love

love is Natural and Real
but not for such as you and I, my love
Oh Mother, I can feel the soil falling over my head
Oh Mother, I can feel the soil falling over my head
Oh Mother, I can feel the soil falling over my head
Oh Mother, I can feel the soil falling over my head . . .

The lyric consists of a series of acts of address or calling out, beginning and ending with an address to the singer's mother, which
conventionally the audience is allowed to overhear. Some of the
addressees are made explicit—the 'Sad veiled bride,' the 'handsome
groom,' and the 'loud, loutish lover'—whilst some are ambiguous
(the 'you' in line nine and line twenty, 'my love' in line forty and
following). It is helpful to identify these shifts of address to try and
keep track of the contours of this lyrical drama. But it is at least as
important to notice *that* the singer is calling out—and calling out
repeatedly in different directions—for the call is a vocal reaching
out, a crying 'with out-stretched voice,' which typically bespeaks a
desperate attempt to establish relation, but which reveals—in thus
attempting to repair—a radical alienation.[14]

There is a restlessness, too, in the shifting between metaphorical
and apparently more literal registers in the first two verses, suggestive of mental agitation and a mind trying at once to hold onto and
escape itself. (Having said that, the distinction between metaphorical and literal is hard to draw in the second verse, for whilst the sea
and the knife seem to appear before him, as the dagger does to
the unhinged Macbeth, and are manifestly figments of a troubled
imagination—in taking on a volitional life of their own—the bride,
the groom and the lover are presumably presented as imaginary as
well. Indeed, set next to each other, with their parallel syntax, they
appear to be 'stock' figures and more abstract than real, so that there
is something peculiarly moving about his giving them advice—in a
way that sounds like he's taking his leave—'as one incapable of [his]
own distress.'[15]) The song even seems to be trying to bring itself to
an end in the first few lines ('Oh well, enough said'), only to meet

14. The fact that the singer calls out to his mother—something he also does in 'Rubber Ring' and
'Shakespeare's Sister'—obviously reinforces this sense of desperation by resituating the speaker in a
relation of radical dependency.
15. The allusion is to Ophelia in *Hamlet* (IV, 7, 177).

an opposing force within itself that keeps speaking.[16] This pattern of interior conflict is reflected in the line that follows—'I know it's over—still I cling'—which precisely conveys the tragic groundlessness of the countermovement of the 'still' clause, in the use of 'cling' without anything to cling *to*. (This sense of clinging, with nothing to cling to, is even more conspicuous on the lyric sheet, where as a result of the linebreak, the place of the object is filled by empty space.) Thus shorn of its object, it becomes a reflexive clinging onto clinging itself.

The restlessness betokened by the conflictual syntax—and at another level by the shifts in register and addressee—coexists with the awful sense of paralysis that the song's central image conjures up ('Oh Mother, I can feel the soil falling over my head'), a paralysis that has the quickened vitality of despair at its centre. For most of the song, the singer's delivery is uncannily poised, and this despair is kept in check, even as it is lyrically expressed. Yet it has an air of abstraction, in the midst of extremity, that presages an imminent and violent eruption.

Before there is any eruption, though, there is a further twist of the knife, as if the mind is seeking its own emetic—or more frighteningly, preying upon itself. But first there is a joke—of sorts. The second time the singer attempts an explanation of the title's 'It,' we discover that the unnamed thing that's over—and that we expected the song to tell us about—'never really began.'[17] This isn't a joke that yields many laughs. It is important, however, that we recognise the unfolding of the narrative has the shape of a joke—building up and then suddenly puncturing our expectations. This is because the discrepancy between the 'norms' that our expectations bring into play—the title and genre encouraging us to expect the end of a melodramatic love affair—and what actually turns out to be the case underlines the wretchedness of the latter. It also reminds us that the singer is of course aware—and more aware than anyone—of the absurdity of his predicament. As a Beckett character in an ash can observes, 'Nothing is funnier than unhappiness.'[18]

---

16. This is the first sign of the song's 'Beckettian' character and its concern with haunting interior voices that speak to and for but appear to have their origin *outside* the self.

17. The 'really' introduces a slight degree of equivocacy, since it allows both 'not to any significant extent' and 'not in fact,' and thereby leaves open the possibility that the whole affair—such as it was—was entirely imagined, as the 'real' of the following line implies.

18. Beckett, *Endgame*, p. 20.

The joke's punch is largely packed into the little word 'even,' in line twenty, which is in fact an 'only' that has comically puffed itself up to fill the space of its opposite. In this way, as it were single-handedly, the 'even' resuscitates our expectations and thus sets the stage for the remorseless, slow-motion torture that follows. For what was said, about which the 'even' brags, was this:

> 'If you're so funny
> then why are you on your own tonight?
> and if you are so clever
> why are you on your own tonight?
> if you're so very entertaining
> why are you on your own tonight?
> if you're so terribly good-looking
> then why do you sleep alone tonight?
> *because tonight is just like any other night*
> that's why you're on your own tonight
> with your triumphs and your charms
> *while they are in each other's arms . . .*'

This, then, is the 'It' whose passing away the song laments. This brutally direct and relentless interrogation of the singer on the subject of his loneliness is what the 'It' consists in and what he clings to for comfort! In fact, it's far less merciful than an interrogation, as the tormentor asks rhetorical questions, accompanied by knife-stabbing staccato violins, not to find out anything about the speaker but to reveal the unsustainability of the only things that apparently made his loneliness supportable. At which point, it all starts to look undeniably like an inside job—and a mind spitefully turning its venom on itself.[19] For surely no one else—and least of all a virtual stranger—could know with such unerring precision where to strike in order to destroy someone's last means of support. The

---

19. It is at this point that the song once again starts to resemble a Beckettian drama, and in particular *Eh Joe*, in which the lone protagonist is tortured from within by questioning voices:

> Thought of everything? . . . Forgotten nothing? . . . [. . .] Why don't you put out that light? . . . [. . .] What's wrong with that bed, Joe? . . . [. . .] You know that penny farthing hell you call your mind . . . That's where you think this is coming from, don't you? . . . [. . .] Anyone living love you now, Joe? . . . Anyone living sorry for you now?

In a letter to Alan Schneider, Beckett wrote of the drama: 'Voice should be whispered. A dead voice in his head. Minimum of colour. Attacking. Each sentence a knife going in, pause for withdrawal, then in again' (Harmon, *No Author Better Served*, p. 201).

voice's rejoinder—*'because tonight is just like any other night* / that's why you're on your own tonight'—likewise bears the hallmark of the self-tormenting mind, as it makes use of the kind of facetious mis-answering of questions one finds in *Alice's Adventures in Wonderland* in order to get in a final blow, generalizing the present misery of the speaker to a constant condition. The grotesque joke at the centre of the song therefore is that the singer is mourning the end of an affair (because it's all he's got) which consisted in someone—perhaps even an imaginary someone—cruelly making clear to him that he is—and ordinarily is—alone and taking from him any sense of self-value that he could possibly hold against such loneliness.

Setting things out in this way makes the narrative sound ludi-crous of course; and I do so only to reveal the overarching ironies that distance Morrissey the writer from the singer or speaker, and which allow the former to explore whilst at the same time reflect-ing critically upon the mind's encounter with excoriating darkness. Such irony, however, is importantly not incompatible with realism; so whilst Morrissey invites critical reflection by distancing himself from the character-perspective of the song, he is nonetheless able to present us with a harrowing first-person account of despair which simultane-ously invites identification. Locally, therefore, the song's ironies do not obtrude or palliate its lyrical depiction of darkness. On the contrary, the bleeding of the singer's heart and the fraying of the very threads of his being are represented to us with extraordinary vividness.

In previous chapters, we have looked at Morrissey's dramatiza-tion of presence in the moment of the song and how in this way he creates a peculiar sense of intimacy. In some cases, this is a benevo-lent, quasi-religious offering of communion, which is vitally uplift-ing. There is a dark equivalent of this, however—a presentness of suffering that involves us in its agonies. For Morrissey doesn't merely write *about* darkness, 'recollected in tranquillity';[20] he writes from within it. We have none of the safety or distance of an afterwards; instead, his songs dramatize being *in extremis*—the ongoing, pres-ent moment of suffering: the first-person consonant cry of someone being buried alive, of a mind violently turning on itself, and of a heart haemorrhaging in front of us.[21]

---

20. Wordsworth, preface to *Lyrical Ballads*, p. 42.
21. One is again reminded of Beckett's depiction of the self-lacerating consciousness or 'thinking,' as he calls it—'if that is the name for this vertiginous panic as of hornets smoked out of their nest' (Beckett, *Molloy, Malone Dies, The Unnamable*, p. 322).

Yet in the midst of 'I Know It's Over' and before the final climactic refrain, there is one further extraordinary move. Pulling against the unleashing of the musical drive towards the explosive conclusion, and, even more dramatically, reversing the relentless gathering and sharpening of darkness, the singer suddenly holds his ground and responds to his tormentor's persecution with what is surely the most eloquent, courageous and steadfast defence of love in his writing:

> It's so easy to laugh
> it's so easy to hate
> it takes strength to be gentle and kind
> it's so easy to laugh
> it's so easy to hate
> it takes guts to be gentle and kind
> love is Natural and Real
> but not for you, my love
> not tonight, my love
> love is Natural and Real
> but not for such as you and I, my love.

Musically, the turning point of the song occurs as Morrissey sings the first three lines quoted above. From this point on, the song is on the way to or *already in the throes of* its tempestuous conclusion. Except for Morrissey.

To be sure, the irresistible onward rush of the music towards its conclusion lets us know that the battle has in a sense already been lost and the darkness that has been closing in since the beginning of the song is the only possible end of things (like the lyrics, the melody ends up exactly where it began—only where it was restrained and muted to begin with, it is unfettered and violent at its close). But, in another sense, Morrissey's heroic standing still as the tumultuous chorus starts going on around him arguably inaugurates a larger victory, since the terrible undoing of the singer brings into view that which may yet withstand such undoing.[22] (There is, I think, a subterranean but nonetheless crucial connection between the Love

---

22. This kind of 'sacrificial' logic evidently appeals to Morrissey, as we know from his praise of Wilde's fairytale 'The Nightingale and the Rose,' in which the nightingale sings as she sacrifices herself of 'the Love that is perfected by Death, of the Love that dies not in the tomb' (Wilde, *Complete Shorter Fiction*, p. 16). Like Wilde, Morrissey appears to identify the artist's 'sacrificial' suffering—whose 'thorn-crown . . . will blossom into roses for our pleasure'—with the redemptive suffering and the self-sacrifice of Christ.

that Morrissey stands up for here and the Light whose existence he defends in the midst of darkness on the same album.[23])

With wonderful subtlety, the song points towards the logic of this overthrow in its transvaluation of the central word 'over.' Early on in the song, the second time Morrissey sings 'I don't know where else I can go,' he bridges the space into the following section by singing 'over, over, over, over'—carrying forward the 'over' of 'I can feel the soil falling over my head' and anticipating the 'over' of the coming line. Later on in the song, during the defence of love passage, Morrissey once again bridges the gap between the end of one utterance and the beginning of another by singing 'over, over, over, over . . .' However, in this case, the word takes on an entirely different meaning, as with beautiful calm he sings, 'it takes strength to be gentle and kind—over, over, over, over.' And if only for a moment, the word at the epicentre of the song's darkness is made instead to speak for the good. And suddenly in the midst of darkness we are in light.

The song of course doesn't end at this point. The light is eclipsed and darkness, it seems, finally has dominion. Yet all this time, whilst the music has been urging the song towards its climax of darkness, Morrissey has calmly and with great deliberation been moving in the opposite direction. In the course of which, we should notice another reversal that has been quietly accomplished. Attention was drawn earlier to the singer's restless acts of address, reaching out desperately in the act of calling, in an attempt to establish relation. Now, just before the waters close over him, his act of address ('my love')—presumably to the listener—offers the very communion for others that was lacking and whose lack occasioned the song's despair. Having resisted the pull of the music into its final darkness, and having established in the timeless moment of the song that which may be held against this darkness, he then *chooses*—when he is ready—to go into the night.[24]

This doesn't of course do away with the darkness or mean that night is not night. Indeed, whilst the first utterance of the extended fade-out refrain carries forward the dignity and composure of the preceding section, it's not long before the singer's voice starts to buckle and strain, and he seems to be staring into the abyss. To be sure, in one sense, the final refrain appears to add very little to the

---

23. 'There Is A Light That Never Goes Out.'
24. As Slavoj Žižek notes, 'The highest act of freedom is the display of *amor fati*, the act of freely assuming what is necessary anyway' (Žižek, *The Parallax View*, p. 17).

song. And this is certainly the case, if we only look at the repeated utterance on the page. Yet it's in these lines that the hitherto muted despair of the song bursts forth so affectingly in Morrissey's singing.

Whereas at the outset of the song, the singer's delivery reveals little of the despair the lyrics express—and his failure to stitch them into a single utterance bespeaks extreme enervation or resignation ('Oh Mother—I can feel—the soil falling over my head')—in the final refrain, his voice seems to be warped from within by a despair that's too big, too wild and too unwieldy for the lyrics, which steers his voice like a shopping trolley and barely lets him take any breath at all—even between the utterances, which are now virtually stitched together. This loss or surrender of absolute control—around the fifth repetition—is by no means a fault. Rather, it is aesthetically successful *because of* its technical imperfection. It is this impression of being carried away—of language being mastered by what it seeks to express—which is conveyed by the voice's straining at the seams that is crucial to the song's dramatization of a mind losing hold of itself. And it is this overburdened straining that once again effectively conveys the impression of something going on in the present.

There is also, finally, something dramatically appropriate about the song's returning to its beginning and the repetition, over and over again, of a single line. Speaking of the radical stasis of his very particular wretchedness in *De Profundis*, Oscar Wilde writes: 'Suffering is one very long moment. We cannot divide it by seasons. We can only record its moods, and chronicle their return. With us time itself does not progress. It revolves.'[25] There is a general truth in this, as Wilde well knew, and the formal circularity of Morrissey's lyrics—which are of course *about* not getting anywhere and not finding a way out—reflects the 'revolving' timeless character of suffering. Likewise, the distraught repetition of a single line—which fades out but doesn't come to an end—is expressive of the way in which depression reflexively fuels its own malaise (one is depressed partly because one is depressed). As Morrissey writes elsewhere: 'there is no law of averages here / if you feel down, then you're bound to stay down.'[26] The ad lib 'over, over, over, over' therefore appears in some sense also to be about itself and to locate the articulation of despair within the predicament, as something that adds to its causes, rather

---

25. Wilde, *De Profundis and Other Writings*, p. 30.
26. 'The Edges Are No Longer Parallel.'

than situating it on the outside or seeing it as a way of escaping them. Morrissey, it seems, like Wilde before him, knows what Wordsworth meant when he wrote:

> Suffering is permanent, obscure and dark,
> And shares the nature of infinity.[27]

LIVING DARKNESS

'When you gaze long into an abyss,' as Nietzsche discovered, 'the abyss gazes back at you.'[28] In his confrontations of darkness Morrissey, similarly, finds the darkness looking back at him. As we saw in 'Will Never Marry,' guilt is experienced as an external and personified agency, which haunts the singer with a life of its own. And as we have just seen in 'I Know It's Over,' a volitional animating agency is attributed to the sea and the knife, which 'want' to take the singer's life—even as in a rhetorical sense he has already given it to them. In Morrissey's lyrics, the darkness is continually turning into something living or personal. It appears not as a background or an abstraction, but as an adversary (or an alluring siren). And whilst in 'The Hand That Rocks The Cradle' this is affectionately presented as a childish anthropomorphism, albeit one that seems to preoccupy the singer, elsewhere it is a much more disturbing effect.[29] Let us consider a couple of examples.

'The Headmaster Ritual,' the opening song on *Meat Is Murder*, is at once comical and sinister in its descriptions of violence:

> mid-week on the playing fields
> Sir thwacks you on the knees
> knees you in the groin
> elbow in the face
> bruises bigger than dinner plates.

---

27. Wordsworth, *The Borderers*, Act III, 1543–4.

28. Nietzsche, *Beyond Good and Evil*, maxim 146, p. 102.

29. We additionally find in Morrissey's lyrics anthropomorphic gestures that bespeak affection ('Goodbye house, goodbye stairs,' he sings in 'Late Night, Maudlin Street') as well as more conventional extended personifications, as in 'America Is Not The World' or 'Trouble Loves Me.' Some of the most interesting cases, though, are the ambiguous quasi-personifications that crop up in his work, frequently in his descriptions of place. In 'Suffer Little Children,' for example, the refrain 'Oh Manchester, so much to answer for' has a densely apostrophic resonance, even though it lacks explicit marking as such. Similarly, the streets in 'On The Streets I Ran' possess an anthropomorphic quality whilst in another sense remaining an inanimate 'it' ('you never have them / but they always have you . . . And all these streets can do / is claim to know the real you / and warn: *If you don't leave / you will kill, or be killed*').

There is a similarly disconcerting slipperiness in its subsequent anthropomorphic descriptions:

> please excuse me from gym
> I've got this terrible cold coming on
> he grabs and devours
> he kicks me in the showers.

The ostensible slide into personification—referring to the cold as a 'he'—appears to be a *reversal* of the personifying process, since it transforms what we presume is in fact a human agency—who 'grabs and devours' and 'kicks [him] in the showers'—into a nonhuman phenomenon, in a parody of a schoolboy's protective discretion. Yet the 'devours' introduces something excessive or uncanny into the description, which makes it hard to say if the cold is a transparent disguise for a merely human agency or if the latter isn't itself a personification of some other unnamed darkness.[30] It's also interesting to note that as in 'I Know It's Over,' where the loss of life entailed in the singer's state of suspended animation is reversed in the corollary ascription of life to inanimate objects, there is in 'The Headmaster Ritual,' too, a chiastic exchange of animism, for the personification of the singer's 'cold'—which may mask a further personification—finds a dispersonifying counterpart in the opening description ('Belligerent ghouls') of those who inhumanly 'run Manchester schools.'[31]

One of the most intriguing illustrations of 'living darkness' in Morrissey's writing is to be found in 'Shakespeare's Sister.' Here are the lyrics to the first section:

> Young bones groan
> And the rocks below say:
> 'Throw your skinny body down, son!'
> But I'm going to meet the one I love
> So, please don't stand in my way
> Because I'm going to meet the one I love
> No, Mamma, let me go!

---

30. Freud's foremost example of the uncanny is 'doubt as to whether an apparently living being is animate, and, conversely, doubt as to whether a lifeless object may not in fact be animate' (Freud, *The Uncanny*, p. 135).

31. In 'I'm Throwing My Arms Around Paris,' the singer explains that his anthropomorphic affection is prompted by a lack of human relations: 'In the absence of your love / and in the absence of human touch / I have decided / I'm throwing my arms around / around Paris because / only stone and steel accept my love.'

'Shakespeare's Sister' is certainly not as dark as 'I Know It's Over,' but it is perhaps more uncanny. Most obviously, the rocks, like the sea and the knife in 'I Know It's Over,' take on a life of their own and call to the speaker, whose suicide—so the narrative presents it—is desired by its instruments. Once again, the darkness wants the singer.[32] Yet there is something uncanny about the opening line as well. The singer's bones—and not the speaking subject—appear to initiate or respond to the call of darkness with semiarticulate groaning—an impression that is reinforced by the parallelism of the first two lines (grammatical subject followed by verb of communication). This is rather odd. The groaning of the singer's bones, if the line can be read in this way, brings to light a division within the subject and a source of orientation more powerful than the conscious self. (In leaving the flesh of the subject aside, the description also partially dispersonifies the speaker, so that again the lyrics figure a chiastic exchange of animism.) The vocative 'son' has a casual quality; but, if rocks can speak and wish to take the life of the singer, it's not so fanciful to see it as set over against the other vocative ('Mamma') so that death also in some sense claims the speaker as its own, who is pulled in different directions by what Freud refers to as Eros and Thanatos. Even more so than in 'I Know It's Over,' then, what we find in 'Shakespeare's Sister' is that the darkness *lures* the singer, claiming kinship with him and speaking to something deep inside him, which corroborates its call. (As a cliff-edge utterance, the song thus seems quite literally to represent the act of gazing into the abyss only to discover it returning one's gaze.[33])

The lure of darkness does not, however, hold absolute sway. And whilst the singer pleads with his mother to let him go, as though she were the only obstacle, the 'But' of line four appears to pull against its own assertion in suggesting the impulse to go and meet 'the one [he] love[s]' exists in the face of a counterimpulse, of which it is the only evidence.[34] (If, as it seems we are led to assume, 'the one I love' is death, the tenor of the line is in agreement with what precedes it; the

---

32. We find a similar situation in 'Speedway' where the singer asserts—of the unnamed addressee who also wills his destruction—'You won't sleep / until the earth that wants me / finally has me.'

33. In Virginia Woolf's fictional reconstruction of the life of the 'dead poet who was Shakespeare's sister,' from which the title of the song is taken, the protagonist does in fact kill herself 'one winter's night' (Woolf, *A Room of One's Own*).

34. The lecture in which Virginia Woolf tells the story of Shakespeare's sister pointedly begins with 'But' ('But, you may say . . . '), with no anterior position in view, and repeatedly begins sentences in this way, as if the act of articulation were a counterstatement made in the face of an invisible opposing force, which of course is the underlying argument of the lecture.

'But' therefore ushers the utterance across an impediment it has itself brought into the narrative.[35]) This conflict is brought into the open in the trancelike middle section of the song, where for a few bars, everything suddenly slows down, and a wonderful multicoloured space opens up, as the song's monochrome rhythmical backing is interrupted by a radical key change (from E major to C major) and a sequence of resonating luminous chords, throughout which Morrissey sings 'no, no, no, no, no, no, no.' Of course, it's extremely hard to say what's going on at this point, and it's perhaps a mistake to look for any kind of realist interpretation—especially given the bewildering change of subject in the final verse. Nevertheless, the singer's somnolent repetition of 'no,' coupled with the sudden radiant stasis of the music, suggests a kind of undertow or a dreamlike surfacing of a countervailing inclination—something resisting the 'erotic' lure of death; a no-saying, as it were, to his characteristic no-saying.

That Morrissey is more than 'half in love with easeful death' is obviously no news. Nor is it surprising to find an element of conflict in his response to the lure of darkness. What it is surprising to discover, though, is that in spite of the commitment to realism in his work, Morrissey habitually thinks in allegorical terms. That is to say, he explores and represents states of mind, conditions of being, predicaments and ideas by means of symbolic agents—as opposed to thinking in abstract terms. This doesn't mean that we find in his lyrics characters like Hopeful, passing through the Slough of Despond; though we do occasionally encounter personified abstractions, such as Sorrow, Trouble, Despair and Disappointment.[36] But what makes his tendency to allegorize states and ideas so unusual is the fact that his narratives involve *uncanny* agents—shadowy presences embodying peculiar ontologies, which on account of being in some sense 'too much' or 'too little' are best described as in-between phenomena or 'becomings': a becoming-human of abstractions or inanimate objects and conversely a becoming-inanimate or -ghostly of the human.[37]

---

35. There is additionally something 'excessive' about the dance of levity that succeeds these lines the second time they occur ('But I am going to meet the one I love / La-de-da, la-de-da'). Like the soliloquies of Hamlet which suspend in speaking about what he purports to desire the moment the possibility of fulfilment is offered, these lines make one wonder, if the speaker is so overjoyed at the opportunity that's arrived, why does he stand around for so long talking about it?

36. 'Pretty Girls Make Graves,' 'Trouble Loves Me,' 'Come Back To Camden,' 'That's How People Grow Up.'

37. In speaking of 'becomings,' I am drawing on the work of Deleuze and Guattari (see, in particular, Deleuze and Guattari, *A Thousand Plateaus*).

Recall, for example, the 'it' in 'Ammunition,' which emerges like a kind of incubus. Similarly, guilt, in 'Will Never Marry,' is a personified and persecuting agent that 'comes around to your place / at 5 a.m. . . . wakes you up / and . . . laughs in your face'; despair is a state in which inanimate objects take on a sinister life of their own or the darkness assumes an erotic lure; and loneliness is a dispersonifying condition of preceding one's life or surviving one's decease in the manner of a ghost. And it is by means of such uncanny agents that Morrissey explores and reveals the radical existential drama of mundane experiences such as loneliness, privation, longing and disfigurement.

MONSTROSITY

There is an extraordinary moment in the video for 'November Spawned A Monster,' which features Morrissey miming in a state of choreographed derangement in Death Valley, in the Nevada desert.[38] In between the first and second verse (1:37–40 and 1:43–45) and again towards the end of the song, there is an interrupted tracking shot of the singer in the middle distance, as he slowly turns towards the camera, his face grotesquely disfigured by computer manipulation, and who appears as a result to have been transformed into a Francis Bacon portrait of himself. The shot only lasts for a few seconds and is easy to overlook.[39] Yet it deserves to be as famous as—and is manifestly related to—his earlier 'impaired' appearance wearing a hearing aid and National Health glasses. In this brief moment, which is the visual equivalent of the mobile textual appearances considered in chapter 2, the singer boldly identifies himself with and as the 'monster' of the song.

'November Spawned A Monster' lies at the imaginative centre of Morrissey's writing. 'It was a pinnacle,' he has said. 'In its invasion of the mind of a "poor twisted child, so ugly," trapped and unloveable in its wheelchair, it expresses me most accurately. It's the record I have striven to make.'[40] Why is the song central to Morrissey's work and what is it about the song that 'expresses [him] most accurately'?

Monstrosity is the other of normality, and in its various senses is one of the most persistent subjects in Morrissey's lyrics. One sense

---

38. The video was directed by Tim Broad, who died in 1993.
39. The clearest view occurs between 3:50 and 3:54, when the tracking shot is concluded.
40. Cited in Rogan, *Morrissey*, p. 194.

of 'monstrous' is 'a huge or outrageous thing.' Typically, of course, this is understood in a physical sense (Frankenstein's monster, it will be recalled, is a being of 'gigantic stature,' whose 'yellow skin scarcely covered the work of muscles and arteries beneath'[41]). But it clearly applies to nonphysical 'things' too, such as feelings or affection. (The real tragedy of *Frankenstein*, to stay with this example, is the 'monstrous' ballooning of the creature's emotions that results from their lack of reciprocation.) And Morrissey, more than anyone in pop music, is the chronicler of 'oversized' feelings—of emotions that exceed articulation but defy containment, and overwhelm the experiencing subject; of feelings, as in *Frankenstein*, that find no response and as a result swell gigantically to fill the space of the absent object; of *embarrassing* feelings that make their audience flinch and squirm, and are a scandal to 'polite' discourse.[42]

Another sense of 'monster' is an imaginary and usually frightening creature, which relates to the shadowy allegorical presences that recur throughout Morrissey's writing. Such monstrous presences are the uncanny 'becomings' of inert objects, which disturb the 'normal' order of things, since their life appears to be borrowed from within and yet they seem to haunt from without, and because such phantom or 'excessive' life paradoxically appears to differ from and yet belong to the object. In this way, the monstrous shadow of inanimate phenomena confuses the distinction between the living and the lifeless, the inside and the out, as well as the self and that which is not-self. (The same is true of the uncanny becoming-human of places in Morrissey's writing—most notably Manchester—which seem to haunt him as living presences.) There is something 'monstrous' too, in this second sense, about Morrissey's spectral persona, which escapes and even 'exceeds' its creator without, however, having an independent existence. Indeed, the tangled relationship between Morrissey the creator and 'Morrissey' the persona—a 'living sign' created in his own image—in some ways returns us again to *Frankenstein*, whose eponymous hero spends the rest of his days after creating the monster—who is constantly confused with and given the name of its creator—by turns pursuing and fleeing his creation,

---

41. Shelley, *Frankenstein*, pp. 54; 39.
42. 'I tell listeners in words outside the accepted dictionary of [pop] language. They sometimes find it unacceptably honest. Mention of sexual rejection is a reminder of when it happened to them, and they don't really want to know.' (Morrissey cited in Haupfuhrer, 'Roll Over Beethoven, and Tell Madonna the News,' p. 105).

which is an uncannily elusive and haunting figure that for so much of the narrative is neither fully absent nor present.

The primary meaning of 'monstrous,' though, is 'mishapen or abnormally formed,' and it's this kind of 'monstrosity' that Morrissey's lyrics most daringly confront—and nowhere more directly than in 'November Spawned A Monster,' which is, he has claimed, 'in a sense . . . my version of the New York Dolls' "Frankenstein."'[43]

The New York Dolls were a singularly disturbing band, whose sublime disregard for taste meant that they didn't fit in with anything, but were assertive in not fitting in. And 'Frankenstein' is a characteristically disturbing song, which is itself a lumbering work of 'trash,' roughly stitched together and spilling out all over the place. (I should perhaps add that these are terms of approbation.) Yet 'November Spawned A Monster' is a far more daring song—not only because in refusing to euphemize or soften the awkwardness of its subject it risks offence, but because conversely in seeking to extend our sympathies it risks sentimentality. The song avoids being either offensive or sentimental, however, *because it risks both.*

The opening lines conjure up and confront us with the worst, but conjoin this with a gesture of vehement sympathy that doesn't flinch at or paint over any of its unpleasantness:

> Sleep on and dream of Love
> because it's the closest you will
> get to love
> poor twisted child
> so ugly, so ugly
> poor twisted child
> oh hug me, oh hug me.

The chorus or subsequent section of the song involves a shift from second-person address ('you') to a first-person voice, which is crucial to the song's drama:

> one November spawned a monster
> in the shape of this child,
> who later cried:
> 'But Jesus made me, so
> Jesus save me from pity, sympathy
> and people discussing me'

---

43. *The Face*, March 1990.

> a frame of useless limbs,
> what can make GOOD
> all the BAD that's been done?

The shift to a first-person utterance is pivotal as well as dramatic, as it allows a self-referentiality into the song—which, as we have noted, is emphasized in live performances, and is even more emphatically reinforced in the video.[44] One further moment in this remarkable video is worth highlighting at this juncture. At the end of the song, as the music fades (5:05–5:07), slightly out of breath and certainly out of character, the singer smiles and presses something back into his ear, which the following frame, shot from beneath, reveals to be some sort of in-ear monitor or hearing aid. Either way, this glimpse of the singer out of character breaks the illusion and draws attention to the song as a staged performance, in the manner discussed earlier in the section on camp. However, this breaking of the illusion is itself staged—in that it is filmed and edited—and the singer's stepping out of character only reveals another character (the persona 'Morrissey'), since whatever it is behind his ear recalls his wearing of a hearing aid, which was, he claimed, 'a symbol that spoke for downtrodden and lonely people' and an advertisement of his own infirmity. In this way, the singer's separation of himself from the character he is performing paradoxically *reinforces* a sense of connection between the performer (behind the song's performer) and the subject of the song. It's as if he's saying, I know I may have been acting as though the monster of the song *is* me, but don't let that fool you—it really *is* about me.[45] Why is this important?

---

44. The opening frame of the video features Morrissey wearing a straw hat which has 'VILE' stencilled on the underside of its rim. He additionally gestures to his own body as he sings 'a frame of useless limbs' and, somewhat bizarrely—perhaps as a kind of semiotic litotes or reflexive irony—has a plaster over his left nipple.

45. For Morrissey's allusions to his illness, ugliness and disability, see, for example, 'Still Ill,' 'Late Night, Maudlin Street,' and 'At Amber' ('Oh, my invalid friend, / In our different ways we are the same'). The singer has also spoken repeatedly in interviews about the malady that blighted his adolescence, which hovered between a mental and a physical condition: 'It was like living through the most difficult adolescence imaginable. But all this becomes quite laughable, because I wasn't handicapped in a traditional way. I didn't have any severe physical deformity. I just about survived it, let's just say that' (March 1984); 'Before I joined the group I was in a serious medical condition' (May 1983); 'I never had an adolescence. I went straight from six to 46. . . . I suppose I've now regressed, but I wouldn't call it a second childhood, because it's my first' (May 1984); 'Some unwritten law states that you're not supposed to admit to an unhappy childhood. You pretend you had a jolly good time. I never did. I'm not begging for sympathy, but I was struggling for the most basic friendships. I felt totally ugly' (1984); 'I spent my entire childhood with my head buried in a pillow' (1984); 'I was 17, and biologically inferior to everyone else.' All quotations, except for the last, are taken from Morrissey: Robertson, *In His Own Words*; the final quotation is from Morrissey's entry, We Are Your Thoughts, in Sterling, *Work: 1976–2006*, p. 101.

At a general level, the singer's identification of himself with and as the 'monster' of the song is a powerful reminder that the 'glamorous turn' in his career was not an absolute break, but somehow coexists with his earlier persona and its associations with infirmity and alienation. More particularly, in 'November Spawned A Monster,' it allows him to bear the brunt of his own abrasiveness, in a way that renders it less unpalatable. (In a song that presents the subject's predicament as a theological issue, it is perhaps not out of place to see his decision to assume 'the features of the mutilated human'[46] as another 'sacrificial' gesture, especially in view of the crucifixion pose the singer assumes each time he sings 'Jesus' in the song's video.)

What Morrissey had in mind, I suppose, when he said that 'November Spawned A Monster' was his version of the New York Dolls' 'Frankenstein' is its challenging conclusion:

> I've gotta ask you one question:
> Do you think that you could make it with Frankenstein?[47]

And this is, to be sure, the donnée of the second verse. But once again, 'November Spawned A Monster' goes even further:

> And if the lights were out
> could you even bear
> to kiss her full on the mouth
> (or anywhere?)

Whilst in one sense asking if the listener could 'make it' with Frankenstein appears to go further than Morrissey's question about kissing, the realism of Morrissey's lyric—asking us to imagine being intimate with a concretely realized 'ugly' and 'twisted' individual, rather than a Hollywoodized mythological monster—is surely far more disturbing. Similarly, whilst the coyness of Morrissey's indefinite pronoun in one way keeps a discreet distance, compared to the directness of the New York Dolls, in another way the innuendo of 'anywhere' allows Morrissey to smuggle in a far more intimate and disturbing suggestion.

The first two choruses—or sections beginning with the words of the title—address the subject of sympathy and help us to understand the singer's disturbing, unsentimental posture. In the first case, the

---

46. Lacoste, 'Liturgy and Kenosis,' p. 251.
47. Sylvain Sylvain appears to confuse the monster with its creator (Frankenstein). The fact that the creator is the *real* monster and the 'monster' exhibits more humanity complicates but doesn't alter this.

'monstrous' subject calls out to Christ, though what she complains about and asks to be saved from is not her physical condition but rather 'pity, sympathy / and people discussing me.' The lines thereby introduce a pointed self-referential resonance, which turns the song in a sense inside-out, as the lines furnish a 'meta' critique of the song's discursive practice as a whole.[48] In the second chorus, we are presented with this startling figure of speech:

> one November spawned a monster
> in the shape of this child,
> who must remain
> a hostage to kindness
> and the wheels underneath her.

Formally, these lines culminate in what's known as a zeugma or 'yok-ing,' since the subject is a 'hostage' both to kindness and to the wheels underneath her. In holding together two wholly different categories of thing—'kindness' and 'the wheels underneath her'—the lines function as a kind of metaphysical conceit, which invites us to look for unnoticed analogies in dissimilar things. And what Morrissey's brilliant figure economically suggests is an ambivalent sense of kind-ness as something that constrains even as it benefits the subject. At the same time, in speaking elliptically of 'the wheels underneath her,' the lines convey a sense of the radical precariousness of her embodied existence and an impression of the body as something that the subject simultaneously has mastery over and is at the mercy of (which is to say, the mind at once rules and is ruled by the body). In the process, the description also daringly figures the becoming-mechanical of the prosthetically assisted subject, in a way that literalizes and confronts the listener with dehumanizing attitudes towards the disabled.

Prior to the song's conclusion, there is a remarkable hiatus in the lyrics, which instead of an instrumental solo features the deranged vocals of Mary Margaret O'Hara. Like the grotesquely mutated image of Morrissey in the video, her manic babbling or windings of voice are redolent of a monstrous amorphous consort of the alien, animal and human. In one sense, this hybrid 'becoming' may obviously be seen as an expression, by different means, of the

---

48. It is notable that something similar occurs in 'At Amber'—another song in which the singer riskily compares himself to an 'invalid.'

monstrosity of the song's subject (the 'poor twisted child'). Yet, along with the becoming-monstrous of the singer—present in the lyrics and conspicuous in the video—and on account of its irreducible idiosyncrasy, her singing seems to bring into being a *multiplicity* of monstrous becomings. In this way—for then everyone in the song is touched by monstrosity—Morrissey subtly effects a radical inversion, and within the world of the song presents the monstrous as normal. Which is another way of asserting that 'there is no such thing in life as normal.'

In a song of such extremity, violence, revulsion and monstrosity, it's hard to imagine how it can have another shock up its sleeve. How can it possibly disturb us further? The song's final shock is its delicacy. It disturbs us with diminuendo:

> Oh one fine day
> let it be soon
> she won't be rich or beautiful
> but she'll be walking your streets
> in the clothes that she went out
> and chose for herself.

Throughout the song, until now, there have been subtle echoes and coincidences of sound at the end of lines—partial rhymes and repetitions, which are not immediately apparent in the lyrics as they are printed (ugly/hug me, November/monster, child/cried, made me/save me, out/mouth and bear/anywhere). The final lines, however, step away from the satisfactions of end rhyme, and offer instead an imperfect crossed rhyme—clothes/chose—which almost trips us up with its prematurity and is a beautiful phonetic corollary of the scaling down of the aspirations they touchingly describe.

Discussing the dangers of confronting monstrosity, Derrida has written: 'Monsters cannot be announced. One cannot say: "Here are our monsters," without turning the monsters into pets.'[49] The great achievement of Morrissey's song is that he manages to extend our sympathies towards a 'monster' without turning her into a 'pet.'

---

49. Derrida, 'Some Statements and Truisms about Neo-Logisms, Newisms, Postisms, Parasitisms, and Other Small Seisisms,' p. 80.

ON NOT GETTING NO SATISFACTION

Is there life before death?

'Deprivation is for me,' Philip Larkin once said, 'what daffodils were for Wordsworth.'[50] Whether or not in saying this he was acknowledging the involvement of a certain pleasure in poetically recollecting his deprivation is hard to tell. Nevertheless, it is clear that his fine epigrammatical utterance holds true for Morrissey as well. Indeed, more so than daffodils were for Wordsworth, loneliness, lack and deprivation—to a degree that erodes the very existence of the self—is probably Morrissey's central subject.[51]

The comparison with Larkin is worth pursuing a little further. Along with their unremitting concern with deprivation, we have already noted the two authors' delight in the 'unpoetic' and their mixing of lyrical and conversational modes. Something else that links their writing and relates to the subject of deprivation is what we might refer to as the shadow of the ideal. To explain what this is, let us look at an example from Larkin first, who was described by Eric Homberger as 'the saddest heart in the supermarket':[52]

> Coming up England by a different line
> For once, early in the cold new year,
> We stopped, and, watching men with number plates
> Sprint down the platform to familiar gates,
> 'Why, Coventry!' I exclaimed. 'I was born here.'
>
> I leant far out, and squinnied for a sign
> That this was still the town that had been 'mine'
> So long, but found I wasn't even clear
> Which side was which. From where those cycle-crates
> Were standing, had we annually departed
>
> For all those family hols? . . . A whistle went:
> Things moved. I sat back, staring at my boots.
> 'Was that,' my friend smiled, 'where you "have your roots"?'
> No, only where my childhood was unspent,
> I wanted to retort, just where I started:

---

50. Larkin, *Required Writing*, p. 47.

51. We can see this emerging even in his monograph on James Dean, the second chapter of which is entitled 'Is There Life Before Death?'

52. Homberger, *The Art of the Real*, p. 74.

By now I've got the whole place clearly charted.
Our garden, first: where I did not invent
Blinding theologies of flowers and fruits,
And wasn't spoken to by an old hat.
And here we have that splendid family

I never ran to when I got depressed,
The boys all biceps and the girls all chest,
Their comic Ford, their farm where I could be
'Really myself.' I'll show you, come to that,
The bracken where I never trembling sat,

Determined to go through with it; where she
Lay back, and 'all became a burning mist.'
And, in those offices, my doggerel
Was not set up in blunt ten-point, nor read
By a distinguished cousin of the mayor,

Who didn't call and tell my father There
Before us, had we the gift to see ahead—
'You look as though you wished the place in Hell,'
My friend said, 'judging from your face.' 'Oh well,
I suppose it's not the place's fault,' I said.

'Nothing, like something, happens anywhere.'

The poem falls into two not quite symmetrical parts, and is concerned with a lack of symmetry. In the first part, stanzas one to three, the conventions of nostalgic recollection are introduced, whose inherited character is signalled by quotation marks: 'the town that had been "mine"'; 'where you "have your roots"?' (The title itself is an allusion to a nostalgic romantic poem of recollection by Thomas Hood, and so carries invisible quotation marks.) The second part of the poem, stanzas four to seven, then parodically elaborates these conventional romantic expectations and measures or negatively defines what actually happened against them ('did not invent,' 'wasn't spoken to,' 'never ran to,' etc.). The curious thing—and the point of particular interest to us here—is that his past is teeming with the shadows of what did *not* take place, all of which is imagined in considerable detail. And it is the difference between the shadow of the ideal and what actually occurred—or the tormenting hint of symmetry between them—that is the cause of pain.[53] It is, in other words, its likeness to 'something' that turns 'nothing' into deprivation.

Morrissey rarely writes this explicitly about his past, and many of his ironies or tonal inflections are communicated extralinguistically in singing. Nevertheless, the pervasive sense of deprivation in his writing is similarly informed and given added piquancy by the shadow of the ideal. (The climactic refrain of 'The Edges Are No Longer Parallel'—in which he insists 'there is no law of averages here' and 'if you feel down, then you're bound to stay down'—is 'My only mistake is I'm hoping.') Perhaps the clearest example of this is in 'The Never Played Symphonies,' one of the extra B-sides on *You Are The Quarry*:

> Reflecting from my deathbed
> I'm balancing life's riches against the ditches
> And the flat gray years in between . . .
>
> I can't see those who tried to love me
> All those who felt they understood me
> and I can't see those who very patiently put up with me
> All I can see are the never-laid
> Or the never-played symphonies.

Morrissey represents the rumour of the ideal that torments the actual with what it's not in a range of ways. On *Strangeways, Here We Come*, for example, he sings 'Last night I dreamt / that somebody loved me . . . Last night I felt / real arms around me'; and whilst he afterwards claims 'no hope—no harm / just another false alarm,' the dream itself gainsays his denial and bespeaks a hope that shapes the subsequent anguished questions: 'so, tell me how long / before the last one? / and tell me how long / before the right one?' Similarly, in 'Christian Dior,' the singer sketches the life of the French couturier, and counterposes what he did with what he 'could have' done:

> Christian Dior
> you wasted your life
> on aroma and clothes
> fabric and dyes . .

---

53. The poem's recurrent erratic rhyming likewise hints at without ever providing the symmetry of a conventional rhyme scheme.

you could have run wild
on the backstreets of Lyon or Marseille
reckless and legless and stoned
impregnating women
or kissing mad street boys from Napoli
who couldn't even spell their own name.

In this case, in a characteristic inversion of values, Morrissey depicts the glamorous world of success as a 'waste,' when measured against the seamy shadow of the 'could have.' (In the final verse, the transparent analogy is made explicit and the focus shifts to Morrissey himself, for whom the idealized world of success is but a continuation under other conditions of his previous alienation.[54]) In 'How Soon Is Now,' to take a final example, it's hard to tell whether the ventriloquized voice that elicits hope comes from within or without ('There's a club if you'd like to go / you could meet somebody who really loves you'). Either way, the hypothetical realm of the 'could' that contrapuntally accompanies what 'is' renders the singer's sense of loneliness even more acute ('so you go, and you stand on your own / and you leave on your own / and you go home, and you cry / and you want to die').

Whilst in Larkin's poem, the speaker sits back, stares at his boots, and looks as if he 'wished the place in Hell,' in Morrissey's writing the experience of deprivation is frequently presented as an *existential* problem—as something that eats away at being itself—as though existence were not an 'either/or' matter, but admitted of degrees, such that one's being could be emaciated or impaired without being annihilated.[55] This is what leads him to speak of being 'Half A Person' or of a 'half-life' and why he speaks of a perspective that is within being but prior to life ('At Last I Am Born'; 'Rubber Ring'; 'The Boy With The Thorn In His Side,' etc.). It is likewise what is at stake in describing himself as a ghost: 'They who should

---

54. The quietly elegiac first few bars of the introduction beautifully evoke a moment of private sorrow, which is then swallowed and 'forgotten' by the rest of the song—until it turns into a first-person narrative, that is, and the singer sinks back into elegy at the thought that 'years alone will never be returned.'

55. Biographical remarks to this effect are legion: 'I had a foul teenage existence. Except you couldn't call it an existence' (*Sounds*, November 9, 1983); 'You can look into a mirror and wonder —where have I seen that person before? And then you remember. It was at a neighbour's funeral, and it was the corpse' (*Blitz*, April 1988); 'My life never started at any stage—which I know you won't believe, but its true—so it never really got stopped at any point' (*Melody Maker*, March 12, 1988).

love me / walk right through me / I am a ghost / and as far as I know / I haven't even died.'[56]

Speaking of ghosts or pre- and postanimate states would doubtless be too gothic for Larkin's taste and apt to conflict with his militant commitment to a certain kind of realism. (Having said that, in poems such as 'Vers de Societé,' 'Aubade' and 'Next Please,' death is represented as a haunting and quasi-living presence.) For Larkin, there is a stage after tears, which doesn't continue to escalate into violence or tragedy, but rather sinks down into a kind of lame gloom, from which any undulations out of its pessimism—including tears themselves—are part of the problem they purport to express, as a melodramatic holidaying from realism and an indulgence of idealistic expectations.[57] That is to say, for Larkin, what's saddest of all is that life is less than tragic. Indeed, to his mind, tragedy is secretly a modality of hope, for the extremity of its complaint is seen as a sort of covert refuge whereby our suffering is accorded a significance it doesn't deserve and thus surreptitiously 'redeemed.'

There is an obvious and admirable bravery involved in Larkin's determination to be 'the less deceived' (the title of his second collection). And, seen in this light, the desperate cries, the violent protests and the descriptions of inchoate or emaciated being in Morrissey's lyrics are bound to seem excessive, if not a little silly. But Larkin's realism is an aesthetic preference—shaped by his aversion to what he saw as 'excesses' in art—rather than an inevitable form of mimesis. We might therefore legitimately ask whether the limits of this kind of realism are the limits of our experience. Are there not experiences which are of their nature so extreme—so chaotic, violent or destitute—that they would be 'tamed' by or beggar realistic description? Certainly, the modernists thought there were. The point will probably be readily conceded when it comes to the extremity of war (one thinks of Picasso's 'Guernica' or the violent breakings of Paul Celan's poetry). But the formal experiments of modernist art were of course extended to the violence of everyday experience. In fact, the representation of the angst and existential suffering of day-to-day life may be said to be its forte. Samuel Beckett, for instance, a

---

56. Morrissey describes the lives of others in this way too: the addressee of 'Reel Around The Fountain,' for example, is said to be 'virtually dead'; the subject of 'He Cried' is described as 'stoned to death / but still living'; and the 'she' in 'What She Said' asks, 'How come someone hasn't noticed / that I'm dead / and decided to bury me / God knows I'm ready.'

57. See, for instance, 'Love Songs in Age' or 'Born Yesterday.'

virtuoso of privation, has characters encased in urns, buried in sand, trapped in ash cans and mired in mud.[58] Obviously, from one point of view, there is something excessive or 'silly' about this. But the excess—and the silliness—belongs to the *experience*. Which is to say, it is a measured description of something excessive, rather than an excessive description of something moderate. More precisely, Beckett has recourse to an extremity of aesthetic form—a pairing away to the purity of lessness—as a way of representing a chronic penury of being or what Terry Eagleton aptly refers to as 'ontologically famished figures.'[59]

Morrissey's first-person descriptions of being buried alive, of 'half-dying,' of being 'killed by life' or 'stoned to death' and being 'half a person' are in certain respects a long way removed from the virtual insentience of Beckett's characters and the lacerating blankness of their privative worlds. Nonetheless, both writers are attempting to represent, by means of 'excess,' lives that never quite come into existence or Being losing something of itself to the darkness. What's more, the comparison helps us to see that there is a truth which may paradoxically be captured by hyperbole and which may even require a 'going beyond' in order to signify it accurately.[60] When seen in the light of Beckett's practice, as opposed to the fastidious disenchantment of Larkin's realism, Morrissey's paradoxical descriptions of death-in-life or life-in-death states seem to be less of an affectation and appear, instead, to form part of a serious and coherent vision of a privation that preys upon being itself.

Achilles and the tortoise

There is another, antithetical kind of melancholy in Morrissey's writing—as though the singer had been precluded from having his cake *or* eating it—the clearest articulation of which occurs in 'Heaven Knows I'm Miserable Now':

---

58. *Play, Happy Days, Endgame, How It Is.*
59. Eagleton, *Sweet Violence*, p. 67. Beckett's work represents a world in which all is 'corpsed' (*Endgame*, p. 25), and is filled with descriptions of ossified, atrophied and perpetually deferred life: 'The trouble with her was that she had never been really born!' (*All That Fall*, p. 37), 'As for her, it was almost as though she had suffered the inverse change. She had died in part' (Draff, *More Pricks Than Kicks*, p. 273); 'I shall never get born and therefore never get dead' (*Malone Dies*, p. 206); 'I can't get born' (*The Unnamable*, p. 353); '*Clov*: Do you believe in the life to come? *Hamm*: Mine was always that' (*Endgame*, p. 35). Beckett himself once remarked in conversation 'I have always sensed that there was within me an assassinated being' (Juliet, 'Meeting Beckett,' p. 10).
60. See Žižek's discussion of 'truth in the excess of exaggeration' in *The Plague of Fantasies*, p. 90.

> I was looking for a job, and then I found a job,
> and heaven knows I'm miserable now.

In this case, it is not that the object of satisfaction is absent or withheld; on the contrary, the singer gets what he wants. The problem, more disturbingly, is that satisfaction itself seems to be unsatisfying. Is there any sense in this?

According to Slavoj Žižek, it is the melancholy fate of desire circularly to seek its own perpetuation. Hence, instead of satisfaction, what desire desires is desire:

> We mistake for postponement of the 'thing itself' what is already the 'thing itself,' we mistake for the searching and indecision proper to desire what is, in fact, the realization of desire. That is to say, the realization of desire does not consist in its being 'fulfilled,' 'fully satisfied,' it coincides rather with the reproduction of desire as such, with its circular movement.[61]

Of course, desire conceals its tautological telos beneath the craving it wishes to preserve, double-crossing us in wanting to retard the attainment of the object it incites us towards. The paradoxical corollary of this reading of desire is that satisfaction in a certain sense ceases to exist and is revealed to be a chimera invented to sustain the cunning plan of desire.[62]

Whilst we might be suspicious of the cartoon fluency of such a theory, it nonetheless accords with the commonplace accounts of the slapstick whimsies of desire itself. And whether or not it adequately explains what's going on, it helps us to discern certain patterns of nonsatisfaction in Morrissey's lyrics.

Žižek illustrates his Lacanian reading of the subject's 'impossible relation to the object cause of its desire'[63] with reference to Zeno's paradoxes on the impossibility of movement, two of which are particularly relevant here. The first concerns Achilles and the tortoise

---

61. Žižek, *Looking Awry*, p. 7.
62. Žižek's argument was anticipated by that well-known proto-Lacanian Mick Jagger in his burden about continually not getting 'no satisfaction,' whose double negative gives the assertion a paradoxical twist: to claim that one 'cannot get *no* satisfaction' is, taken literally, to assert that one cannot get entirely *outside* satisfaction or arrive at a state which involves no satisfaction (it doesn't seem to have occurred to the singer that the reason he 'can't get no satisfaction' might be *because* he tries and he tries), and yet the utterance's dominant colloquial sense bewails a condition of ceaseless desire, implying by holding these two readings together that desire secretly satisfies itself in the avoidance of satisfaction.
63. Žižek, *Looking Awry*, p. 6.

and the inability of the former to catch up with the latter, which illustrates the dream paradox of 'a continuous approach to an object that nevertheless preserves a constant distance.'[64] The crucial point, as Žižek shows, is that whilst Achilles can easily *overtake* the tortoise, he cannot *attain* it, for he is always either too fast or too slow.[65] What this paradox elucidates, from a Lacanian perspective, is

> the relation of the subject to the object cause of its desire, which can never be attained. The object-cause is always missed; all we can do is encircle it. In short, the topology of this paradox of Zeno is the paradoxical topology of the object of desire that eludes our grasp no matter what we do to attain it.[66]

The second claim of relevance to us concerns the impossibility of covering a given distance—because to do so we must first of all cross half that distance, and before we do this we must cross half of that distance, and so on, ad infinitum—which illustrates the paradox that 'a good, once reached, always retreats anew.'[67] According to Žižek, what this makes clear is that

> the real purpose of the drive is not its goal (full satisfaction) but its aim: the drive's ultimate aim is simply to reproduce itself as drive, to return to its circular path to and from the goal.[68]

Both of these paradoxical patterns recur throughout Morrissey's writing.

We find versions of the first—the continuous approach to an object that nevertheless preserves its distance—hinted at in a range of titles: 'Nowhere Fast,' 'I Want The One I Can't Have,' 'Seasick, Yet Still Docked,' etc. It is also a recurrent narrative topos. In 'There Is A Light That Never Goes Out,' for example, he sings:

> and in the darkened underpass
> I thought *Oh God my chance has come at last*
> (but then a strange fear gripped me and I just couldn't ask).

---

64. Žižek, *Looking Awry*, p. 6.
65. Žižek draws a parallel with Brecht's claim in *Threepenny Opera*: 'Do not run after luck too arduously, because it might happen that you will overrun it and that luck will thus stay behind' (ibid.). One is again reminded of Jagger's trying and trying.
66. Ibid.
67. Ibid., p. 5.
68. Ibid.

In 'Girl Afraid'—whose elliptical formulation leaves it unclear whether it refers to a girl's fear or a fear of girls—we are presented with two characters whose anxious advances seem to consolidate their separation. And in 'Pashernate Love,' he sums up his relationship to that elusive quality saying: 'I'm always there, / it's always elsewhere.'[69] The superlative example, though, is 'How Soon Is Now,' where the singer laments the paradoxical impossibility of entering into the 'now,' which perpetually seems to recede at his approach whilst haunting him with its imminence.[70]

The second, closely related pattern—in which a goal once reached retreats anew—is an overarching concern in Morrissey's lyrics, which speak about fame as 'all [the singer] ever wanted from life.' Yet when it's achieved, it turns out to be a mirage or a teasing herald of its own arrival, for which he must always wait 'slightly longer' ('You Just Haven't Earned It Yet Baby').[71] This pattern is found at a local narrative level as well. In 'Handsome Devil,' for instance, he sings: 'There's more to life than books, you know, / but not much more'; and in 'Still Ill,' he similarly reasons: 'if you must go to work tomorrow, / well if I were you I wouldn't bother / for there are brighter sides to life / and I should know because I've seen them / but not often.' In both cases, the logic of the utterance comically undermines itself as it unfolds—leading us away from one alternative only to pull the rug from beneath the feet of the other. This 'Sisyphean' journeying of desire is most effectively represented in 'Heaven Knows I'm Miserable Now':

> I was happy in the haze of a drunken hour
> but heaven knows I'm miserable now
>
> I was looking for a job, and then I found a job
> and heaven knows I'm miserable now
>
> In my life
> why do I give valuable time
> to people who don't care if I live or die?

---

69. More subtly, the elusiveness of love is impressionistically suggested by the recurrent difficulties the singer has in saying the word—which turns into an 'Ow' and a mournful 'O' in 'November Spawned A Monster,' for example.

70. 'In The Future When All's Well' makes fun of such perpetual deferrals and 'the sad game' in which desire itself conjures the impediments of which it complains.

71. Speaking to Michael Bracewell in 1999 of his apparently glamorous life of exile in LA (living next-door to Johnny Depp in a house designed for Clarke Gable), the singer remarked: 'I think we're all lonely, and . . . I think that personal happiness is simply a mirage to keep us all going' (*The Times* magazine, November 6, 1999).

'Heaven Knows I'm Miserable Now' is a song of exile. It describes the singer's endless wandering as a result of a perpetual eviction from, or evaporation of, the place of satisfaction—whilst all the time subtly keeping alive a rumour of such a place by means of the apparently casual reference to 'heaven' in its refrain. Both work and an escape from work lure the singer out of passivity but fail to provide a place of refuge.[72] Yet passivity offers no sanctuary either ('two lovers entwined pass me by / and heaven knows I'm miserable now'). And of course sexual relations are even more unsatisfactory:

> What she asked of me at the end of the day
> Caligula would have blushed
> 'You've been in the house too long' she said
> and I naturally fled.

Either because one isn't wanted or because one is *excessively* wanted, relationships fail to provide satisfaction as well. Achilles is always too fast or too slow.[73]

A FOREIGNER ON THE EARTH

The perpetual exile of desire discernable in 'Heaven Knows I'm Miserable Now' is part of a more pervasive pattern in Morrissey's writing of radical nonbelonging. We have seen something of this already in our discussion of embarrassment and eccentricity; the 'homelessness' of his wandering voice; 'the funny body that doesn't quite fit with itself'; the mobility of the speaking perspective; his 'oxymoronic' Anglo-Irish identity; and the literal vagrancy that has characterized his career.[74] It is therefore no surprise to find that his lyrics are filled with a sense of being what Michel de Certeau refers to as a 'foreigner *at home.*'[75]

---

72. The cover of the single reinforces this idea, which depicts a disconsolate Viv Nicholson, who won the pools, escaped a life of poverty and lived unhappily ever after.

73. The melancholy comings and goings of satisfaction are suggested by the song's melody, too, which is poignantly glutted with major sevenths and whose final instrumental loop is a sublimely beautiful evocation of going somewhere and standing still, of delight flooded with melancholy, 'And Joy, whose hand is ever at his lips / Bidding adieu' (Keats, 'Ode on Melancholy').

74. When asked on returning to Britain in 2006 if he felt like an exile, he replied: 'I always felt like an exile, even as a teenager. It is a state of mind' (*The Times*, May 30).

75. Certeau, *The Practice of Everyday Life*, p. 13. The phrase 'a foreigner on the earth' is borrowed from George Eliot (*The George Eliot Letters*, vol. 1, p. 335), and is an allusion to Psalm 119 and the letter to the Hebrews (11:13).

Morrissey articulates this sense of nonbelonging in a variety of ways. On some occasions, it is explicitly stated it:

> driving in your car
> I never never want to go home
> because I haven't got one;
>
> I've zig-zagged all over America
> and I cannot find a safety haven;
>
> etch on a postcard
> How I Dearly Wish I Was Not Here.[76]

It is apparent, too, in the recurrent descriptions of leaving home ('Late Night, Maudlin Street'; 'Friday Mourning'; 'London'; 'Is It Really So Strange?'), which is taken to an extreme and turns into a cross between a gothic persecution and a Benny Hill chase in 'Panic':

> On the Leeds side-streets that you slip down
> I wonder to myself
> Hopes may rise on the Grasmeres
> But Honey Pie, you're not safe here
> So you run down
> To the safety of the town
> But there's Panic on the streets of Carlisle
> Dublin, Dundee, Humberside.[77]

We even find such nonbelonging imaginatively extended into the next world:

> Satan rejected my soul
> as low as he goes
> he never quite goes this low
> he's seen my face around
> he knows heaven doesn't seem
> to be my home

---

76. 'There Is a Light That Never Goes Out,' 'Let Me Kiss You,' 'Everyday Is Like Sunday.' Rogan mentions an unreleased song entitled 'Home Is A Question Mark' (*Morrissey*, p. 269).

77. One might additionally see Morrissey's uncanny descriptions of himself as a ghost or a 'not-yet-being' as a way of pointing towards a sense of nonbelonging so extreme it takes on an *existential* character. ('Uncanny' is the English equivalent for 'unheimlich,' which literally means 'unhomely' or having an 'unhoused' quality.)

> so I must find
> somewhere else to go.[78]

But perhaps the song that sheds most light on the singer's non-belonging is 'I Am Hated For Loving,' on *Vauxhall And I*. On the face of it, the song is a fairly unadventurous reworking of a by now familiar theme. And, indeed, it is dismissed as such by Johnny Rogan, who describes it as 'less than convincing' and an 'average composition' (although somewhat confusingly he describes it earlier on in the book as one of the songs that make it 'difficult to escape the conclusion that you have a direct line to the singer's heart and soul').[79] However, the song is odder, it seems to me, than either his praise or dismissal suggests. Here are the lyrics to the first section:

> I am hated for loving
> I am hated for loving
> anonymous call, a poison pen
> a brick in the small of the back again
> I still don't belong
> to anyone—*I am mine*
> and I am hated for loving
> I am haunted for wanting.

There is a curious lack of otherness in these lines. The framing passives elide their agent (who it is that is doing the hating and haunting); the specification of what this consists in is similarly lacking in grammatical subjects ('anonymous call, a poison pen / a brick in the small of the back again'); and in the central italicized assertion, '*I am mine*'—which is oddly poised between dejection and pride—the singer takes up a position on both sides of the copula, as that which is possessed and that which is doing the possessing. It's as if in the absence of reciprocating relation, the 'I' has swollen into the empty space. And yet the self doesn't seem to fill the space completely either ('I am falling,' he sings in the next verse, 'with no one to catch me'). Furthermore, the 'I am' of the song's refrain is strangely set adrift by the midline caesura ('I am . . . hated for loving'), which subtly raises the stakes of the singer's predicament by activating the existential sense of 'to be' latent in its auxiliary usage, and once again presents alienation as something that poses a threat to being itself. In this way,

---

78. 'Satan Rejected My Soul.' This appears to overturn the singer's prediction on *Kill Uncle* that 'There is a place / a place in hell / reserved for me and my friends,' where he hoped he wouldn't be in the way.
79. Rogan, *Morrissey*, pp. 209; 1.

the song furnishes us with a glimpse of the baroque interior contortions and tumescence engendered by the loneliness of nonbelonging.[80]

LILIES THAT FESTER

One of the things for which Morrissey is routinely criticized is his tendency towards self-parody. If we think, for example, of the child who joined the band onstage during the premier performance of 'Panic,' wearing a hearing aid with some foliage sticking out of his back pocket,[81] or the video for 'I Started Something I Couldn't Finish,' which features a number of look-alike Morrisseys—all wearing NHS glasses—cycling around Manchester with the singer, there can be no doubt that such a tendency exists. Moreover, there is perhaps something inevitable about this. As John Harris recently observed on *Newsnight Review* in a discussion about the self-referential turn on the Arctic Monkeys' second album, one of the odd things about the pop industry—as opposed, for example, to the literary world—is that writers who become famous for their chronicling of everyday life tend to be removed, as a result of their fame, from the very environment by which it is nourished. Which may explain, in part, why so many pop writers dry up creatively once they become famous. What's so unusual in Morrissey's case, however—and why I think his self-parody doesn't result in the soup of the soup of the soup—is that almost as soon as he started writing, his life as a pop star became part of his subject. Needless to say, this isn't in itself a guarantee of interest. But why it's interesting in Morrissey's case is because, far from transporting him into a world of inane plenty, becoming a pop star added further convolutions to and *deepened* his misery. Indeed, it oddly returned him to—whilst providing him with a new form of—the exclusion and loneliness he hoped it would assuage. For what could make you more of a 'foreigner at home' than fame?

Morrissey's lyrics of postfame misery tend to focus on a few recurrent themes, such as the ineluctable involvement in the corrupt and corrupting commercial world ('Paint A Vulgar Picture'), the sadistic self-interest of his business associates ('Why Don't You Find Out For Yourself'), the unforgiving gaze of fame ('The Harsh Truth Of The Camera Eye'), his pop-star colleagues ('The World Is Full

---

80. The existential character of the singer's loneliness and nonbelonging is reinforced by the concentric widening in the song's conclusion, firstly from 'I still don't belong / to anyone' to 'I still don't belong / to anywhere,' and then still further to an absolute condition: 'I still don't belong.'

81. Channel 4, Eurotube, July 5, 1986.

Of Crashing Bores'), malevolent critics ('You Know I Couldn't Last')
and—most interestingly of all—'the squalor of the mind.'[82]

The first surfacing of 'meta'-suffering in Morrissey's lyrics appears
to be in 'Frankly, Mr Shankly' (recorded in December 1985):

Frankly, Mr Shankly, this position I've held
it pays my way, and it corrodes my soul.

Fame, Fame, fatal Fame
it can play hideous tricks on the brain
but still I'd rather be Famous
than righteous or holy, any day

but sometimes I'd feel more fulfilled
making Christmas cards with the mentally ill
I want to live and I want to Love
I want to catch something that I might be ashamed of.

One of the most striking things about 'Frankly, Mr Shankly' is the elusiveness of its tone—which is heterogeneously constituted by the music,
the singer's delivery and the lyrics, which are themselves a compound
of the serious and the farcical. (The song appears to be notionally cast
as a parodic dramatic monologue uttered by a disaffected footballer to
his manager. But the fiction is so thinly maintained and the specifics of
the speaker's complaint so openly reveal it to be a fiction that the irony
of its framing has a nebulous significance.[83]) In fact, Morrissey seems to
be as interested in saying something the tone of which cannot be pinned
down as he is in saying that 'something.'[84] Nevertheless, the song voices
a complaint about pop-star life, which is itself held up for criticism but
which isn't cancelled out by its ironies. Indeed, the song's ironies arguably protect even as they complicate the singer's complaints, which may
paradoxically have been harder to take seriously had they been delivered

---

82. Sometimes the singer's complaints are much more generalized and aimed at an unnamed
doubting or hostile adversary, as in 'Bigmouth Strikes Again' or 'The Boy With The Thorn In His
Side.' But occasionally, as in 'Sorrow Will Come In The End,' his target is transparently particular.
And on still other occasions, as we saw in 'Reader Meet Author,' Morrissey becomes his own
adversary, satirizing his critics whilst simultaneously criticizing his role as author.
83. The irony of the song's fictional frame is most effective in the final utterance—'Oh, give us
your money!'—in which two antithetical voices coincide: on the one hand, in the voice of the
song's character, it appears to signify an exasperated agreement to take the money and continue in
his 'position,' whilst on the other hand, in the voice of a singer on an album which he naturally
wants us to buy, it ventriloquizes the inherent commercial nature of the aesthetic undertaking—
which includes aesthetic undertakings that complain about their inherent commercial nature.
84. I think Simon Goddard is barking up the wrong tree in describing Morrissey's rhetoric as
'almost Marxist' and concluding that the song is a 'comforting catharsis for long-suffering workers
the world over' (Goddard, *The Smiths*, pp. 183; 185).

straight. The darkest and most revealing reflections on this kind of suffering occur in 'You Know I Couldn't Last.'

The song begins with a description of the suffering that is inflicted from without:

> The whispering may hurt you,
> but the printed word might kill you . . .
>
> The teenagers who love you,
> they will wake up, yawn and kill you.

We can see in these lines a recurrence of Morrissey's tendency to speak about suffering—here, perhaps, with an allusion to Wilde[85]—in existential terms, as a death that cruelly doesn't bring an end to life (although the 'kill' in the second case may obviously be literal). What is of significance to us here is that this figurative topos is extended to the suffering of his postfame life, and thereby tacitly seems to equate the radical privation of which he sang in his earlier songs with a different form of alienation—which the success of such songs has paradoxically helped to bring about.[86]

In the final verse, the singer turns to the suffering that is inflicted from within, and the torment that is strangely engendered by comfort:[87]

> Then in the end, your royalties bring you luxuries,
> your royalties bring you luxuries,
> oh but—the squalor of the mind,
> the squalor of the mind,
> the squalor of the mind.

To complain about suffering that is caused by luxury is obviously a risky thing to do, in spite of the almost proverbial precedents.[88] It's apt, for a start, to invite the rejoinder 'I wish *I* had all that suffering.' Yet Morrissey's complaint escapes this natural but facile dismissal partly because it doesn't seek to conceal that this *is* a decadent form

---

85. Wilde, 'The Ballad of Reading Gaol,' 37–42.
86. Morrissey seems to have had a sense of such suffering—'in other people's lives'—ahead of its happening in his. In 'You've Got Everything Now,' for example, the singer contrasts the 'terrible mess' he's made of his life with the addressee's success, but then adds: 'so who is rich and who is poor? / I cannot say.' In *De Profundis*, Wilde similarly speaks of 'the strange poverty of the rich' (Wilde, *De Profundis and Other Writings*, p. 165), as Morrissey semi-ironically speaks of 'the riches of the poor' ('I Want The One I Can't Have').
87. There is an eerie languor to the song's verses—in their instrumentation and the repetition of their lyrics—that is suggestive of an anesthetizing comfort and puts one in mind of the sensual trance of the lotus eaters.
88. Shakespeare, for instance, memorably asserts: 'Sweetest things turn sourest by their deeds; / Lilies that fester smell far worse than weeds' (Sonnet 94).

of suffering—which is by no means the only or worst form of suffering, but is no less a real form of suffering for all that[89]—and partly because it manages to convince us, with its precisely expressive image of squalor, accompanied by the garish, harmonically 'overproximate' chord change between D seven and G seven, that something putrid born of luxury has planted in his mind its black flag.[90]

AVOIDED SUBJECTS

The darkness we have looked at so far has had personally to do with Morrissey. It is a claustrophobic, vampiric darkness—a darkness that summons him, that preys on being; or else it is already *inside* the house—the darkness of his own deformity or something festering within. But there is another darkness that informs his work, which also appears to be omnipresent and is inebriate with destruction. And that is the darkness of human evil.[91]

Such darkness, for many, is the most disturbing feature of Morrissey's work, and his interest in it has often got him into considerable trouble. I don't wish to deny or in any way diminish how disturbing this is. On the contrary, it is the study's central contention that Morrissey is a radically disturbing artist. But I do wish to argue that his unsqueamish treatment of certain politely avoided subjects is a sign of his seriousness and courage as an artist. For whilst Morrissey clearly sees the limits of and is often uninterested in realism, he at the same time seems to view it as the obligation of the artist to speak, without flinching, about that which is. And to exclude such darkness would entail a diminution of the reality his work seeks to represent. (Samuel Beckett once remarked, 'I started writing for the theatre because I hated it.'[92] Morrissey, it seems, was similarly driven as a writer by his hatred of the avoidances and cheerful disingenuousness of popular music.)

Death at one's elbow

Morrissey's lyrics are full of violence—arbitrary and senseless but also, even more disturbingly, glamorized and *carefully reasoned* violence. It

89. When asked in an interview 'Do you ever think that the problems of fame are fantasy problems that you tend to overindulge in?' Morrissey replied: 'No, they're very real problems. Absolutely real' (*Blitz*, April 1988).
90. The final image alludes to Baudelaire's 'Spleen' (IV).
91. This is the word that Morrissey uses in 'Last Of The International Playboys,' 'Yes, I Am Blind,' and 'Sister I'm A Poet.'
92. Cited in Alvarez, *Beckett*, p. 16.

is a world of hammers, hatchets, bicycle chains and screaming knives; of 'smashed human bone' and 'bespattered remains.'[93] It is a world in which goodness doesn't prevail and often backfires;[94] in which violence is infectious and even seems natural. Most disturbingly of all, it is a world, like ours, in which parents are brutally killed by children, and children (God save us) are killed for pleasure. Let us consider a couple of examples.

The first song that got Morrissey into serious trouble was 'Suffer Little Children,' on *The Smiths*. The song addresses the subject of the Moors murders, which took place in Morrissey's hometown of Manchester whilst he was a child, and a potential victim.[95] The pathos and delicacy of the song's performance—which are an essential aspect of anything that's said—obviously vanish when we look at the words alone on paper. However, we may in this way point towards some of its lyrical effects.

> Over the moor, take me to the moor
> dig a shallow grave
> and I'll lay me down
>
> Lesley-Anne, with your pretty white beads
> oh John, you'll never be a man
> and you'll never see your home again
> oh Manchester, so much to answer for
>
> Edward, see those alluring lights?
> tonight will be your very last night
> A woman said: 'I know my son is dead
> I'll never rest my hands on his sacred head'
>
> Hindley wakes and Hindley says:
> 'Oh, wherever he has gone, I have gone'
>
> But fresh lilaced moorland fields
> cannot hide the stolid stench of death.

---

93. 'First Of The Gang To Die,' 'Death At One's Elbow.'
94. See, for example, 'The Youngest Was The Most Loved.'
95. 'I happened to live on the streets where, close by, some of the victims had been picked up. . . . Within that community, news of the crimes totally dominated all attempts at conversation for quite a few years. It was like the worst thing that ever happened, and I was very, very aware of everything that occurred. Aware as a child who could have been a victim. . . . You see it was all so evil; it was, if you can understand this, ungraspably evil' (*The Face*, May 1985).

The song is an intimate and moving elegy which sympathetically entwines the singer with its subject. What makes its immensely risky act of imaginative sympathy so effective and tactful, though, is the way in which it recreates and memorializes within the miniature world of the song the haunted world it seeks to describe. The opening utterance—'Over the moor'—introduces a strangely disembodied perspective, which travels across and views the moors without any manifest subjectivity. (The phrase is repeated at the end of the song in a way that ambiguously blends the singer's voice with the ghostly voice of one of the victims: 'Over the moor, / I'm on the moor / the child is on the moor.') The line then unfolds into an expression of grief, which daringly describes the singer's mortifying sense of sadness in terms that recall what was done to the children. The lines thus bespeak a brave imaginative confrontation of the atrocities and an attempt at sympathetic participation in the suffering of the children. The following lines address each of the victims in turn by name and, in speaking to them as if they were able to hear, conjure a disturbing presence in the atemporal moment of the song that doesn't belong either to the living or the dead. In doing so, the song keeps agonizingly in view the unlived life that was tragically taken away from the children, in a way that a detached, nonimaginative tribute could not.[96] The song's confrontation of evil, therefore, evidently serves a larger benevolent, memorializing purpose, and seeks to disturb us, as it were, for the good. This isn't always the case, however.

'Ambitious Outsiders,' on *Maladjusted*, is another a song about the murder of children. And whilst in this case it is a fictional narrative, and its violence is threatened rather than actual, it is in certain respects at least as disturbing. Here is the first verse and chorus:

> Bolt-lock your doors
> alarm your cars
> and still we move in closer every day
> Top of the list

---

96. The song reinforces this sense of spectral presence in having the final verse spoken by the ghost of one of the victims, but also more subtly, in local ways, by means of the 'hanging' notes created by the guitars' chorus-pedal arpeggios, and the temporal 'enjambment' enforced by the singer in the following lines:

> we may be dead and we may be gone
> but we will be, we will be, we will be right by your side.

The singer's suspension of the second line with the repetition 'we will be' allows in a much more emphatic sense of the continuity in spite of death that the line goes on to proclaim.

is your smiling kids
but we'll be smiling too
so that's OK
oh, and by the way
thank you, because you're
giving, giving, giving
and we're receiving—
No, no, we're taking
keeping the population down.

The violence threatened in 'Ambitious Outsiders' is, like that of 'Suffer Little Children,' arbitrary and something we cannot guard against; worse still, it is something its perpetrators take pleasure in.[97] Yet there is nothing redeeming about the confrontation with evil in 'Ambitious Outsiders.' There is no memorial, no apparent moral, and every glimmer of innocence is engulfed in a wider darkness. In fact, innocence is the explicit target. But what makes the song especially disturbing is the fact that its violence is in league with civility.

The evil of 'Ambitious Outsiders' lies unrecognized within the civil order (We're on your street, but / you don't see us / or, if you do / you smile and say Hello) and speaks with the voice civility ('oh, and by the way / thank you'). Like the speaker of Swift's 'A Modest Proposal,' it even presents itself as 'reasoned' and logical ('well, it's your own fault / for reproducing / We're just keeping / the population down') and indulges in irony in discussing its intentions ('Top of the list / is your smiling kids / but we'll be smiling too / so that's OK'). In Swift's case, the 'Modest Proposal' put forward by his speaker—to ease the economic crisis in Ireland by selling the children of poor people for food—is clearly a satire, which aims at correction and disturbs us for a humanitarian purpose. In Morrissey's case, there are no such redeeming features. It doesn't appear to exist for the sake of 'correction' (in contrast to 'A Modest Proposal,' it is surely addressed to the victim rather than the perpetrator—who would doubtless nod along with us in bewailing how awful things are) or any underlying benevolent purpose. Instead, the singer seems to imagine and want us to confront unmitigated darkness simply because such darkness exists.

97. Both songs involve a disturbing use of laughter: whereas in 'Suffer Little Children,' the laughter of Myra Hindley—performed by Annalisa Jablonska—'illustrates' the line 'we will haunt you when you laugh,' the laughter in 'Ambitious Outsiders'—which occurs towards the end of the song, amidst a torrent of threatening noises—appears to be *about* its suggested acts of violence.

Once again, it is helpful to recall the context in which he started writing. What Morrissey detested most of all about 1980s pop music was its insanely disingenuous optimism—its turning away from the serrations of ordinariness and its denial of pervasive and unmitigated darkness, which had hardened into a prescriptive etiquette. For Morrissey, there was something grotesque about pop music's 'twee-ification' of the real. In fact, for him, there is something immoral about its turning away from darkess; and, in his eyes, its artists are like 'The Lazy Sunbathers':

> Religions fall
> children shelled
> '. . . *children shelled? That's all*
> *very well, but would you*
> *please keep the noise*
> *down low?*
> *because you're waking*
> *the lazy sunbathers.'*

Inviting the world to contemplate its darkness in a glass is of course nothing new in art (although pop music, seemingly enthralled by its own vacuity, has been slow to enter 'the chamber of maiden thought'[98]). What's so peculiarly disturbing about Morrissey's treatment of such darkness, however, is his tendency to represent it from within; to 'invade the mind' and speak with the voice of the criminal, the hooligan and the murderer. (It's illuminating to compare Morrissey's disturbing use of first-person perspectives with the characterization in the films of Quentin Tarantino, who encourages disconcerting identification with some of the most brutal people imaginable, by first of all presenting them as ironic, urbane and engagingly concerned with everyday trivia, such as the meaning of Madonna's lyrics or the metric equivalent of a Quarter Pounder.) In this way, like Tarantino, Morrissey demystifies the 'otherness' of evil, by showing it to exist much closer to home, embodied by people with whom we share something and entangled with mundane or more positive qualities. And in doing so, he dares us—as Baudelaire challenges his 'Hypocrite reader—fellowman. . . twin'—to identify in some way with the evil he represents.

---

98. Keats, letter to J. H. Reynolds (*Letters of John Keats*, p. 95).

Sympathy for the devil

One may have thought that confronting the darkness of murder and adopting the perspective of someone who presents it as a matter of civility would be the most incendiary thing the singer could do in a three-minute pop song. But there is another kind of darkness that Morrissey explores which got him into even more trouble, and that is the darkness of racism.

The subject has become so overdetermined, and commentary on it so out of proportion, one is loath to say anything about the matter. Yet if, as I am arguing, the refusal to avoid the most troubling subjects is one of Morrissey's virtues as an artist, it would be unbefitting—and selling him short—to pass over the matter in silence here.

There are two things which have come to light in the course of the study that should be borne in mind throughout such discussions. Firstly, there are a number of other 'offences' that need to be taken into consideration. This is because Morrissey doesn't only explore or 'invade the mind' of nationalistic hooligans. As we have seen, he also enters into the perspective of the child murderer, the parricide, the gang member, a 'working girl,' a somewhat unorthodox member of the clergy, and someone who in a moment of confusion kills a horse and then a nun. (The fact that Morrissey wasn't, to the best of my knowledge, investigated for the last two crimes reminds us that utterances in an aesthetic space are not the same as utterances outside it.) It's important to bear in mind all the other perspectives the singer adopts, as it reveals a wider and consistent interest in the marginalized, 'aberrant' or eccentric—in whose light the individual character sketches need to be assessed. The second thing follows on from this. Like Robert Browning's *Dramatic Lyrics*—whose first-person speakers were time and again mistakenly identified with their author—Morrissey's lyrics frequently inhabit imagined perspectives and speak with an 'I' that is not his own. And whilst sometimes of course Morrissey sings in his own voice (which is to say he sings in the character of 'Morrissey' or impersonates himself), the disclaimer with which Browning's first collection was prefaced pertains to Morrissey's lyrics as well:

> Such Poems . . . though for the most part Lyric in expression, [are] always Dramatic in principle, and so many utterances of so many imaginary persons, not mine.[99]

99. Browning, preface to *Dramatic Lyrics* (1842), Appendix B, p. 472.

The songs that are usually cited in connection with the darkness of racism are: 'Panic,' 'Asian Rut,' 'Bengali In Platforms,' 'We'll Let You Know' and 'National Front Disco.' The first, however, can be dismissed immediately.[100] For most of the 1980s, the word 'disco' was used in Britain as the generic term for what is now referred to as a 'club,' 'rave' or 'bop,' etc. It does not in this context refer to a type of music (how exactly would you burn this down?).[101] The word 'DJ,' likewise, did not refer to the cult figure of the subsequent rave scene, but rather the bumbling parochial character brilliantly parodied by Harry Enfield and Paul Whitehouse's 'Smashie and Nicey.'[102] 'Asian Rut' can be dealt with more summarily, too, for if anything it is an *anti*racist song, which is clearly critical of the violence it describes and seeks to arouse sympathy for its Asian victim. The other three songs are more problematic.

'Bengali In Platforms,' 'We'll Let You Know' and 'National Front Disco' are problematic because they involve and speak from within racist perspectives. As we saw earlier, however, in the latter two cases the songs' offensive first-person utterances derive from a delimited character perspective (in the first instance a football hooligan, and in the second a juvenile adherent of the National Front), which crucially separates them from the author of the song.[103] Moreover, the songs include an internal critique of the views they put forward, which further distances the author from their focalized, character perspectives. (In 'We'll Let You Know,' we find a version of what's known as free indirect discourse, but one which reverses its usual emphases, so that instead of a third-person or 'omniscient' narrative with a 'colouring' of the character's point of view, we have a first-person utterance coloured by the external irony of an omniscient perspective.[104] And in 'National Front Disco,' the offensive first-person perspective is set

---

100. The 'offending' lines are: 'Burn down the disco / Hang the blessed DJ.'

101. Johnny Marr's comment at the time similarly clarifies the neutrality of the word 'disco': 'You can't just interchange the words "black" and "disco," or the phrases "black music" and "disco music." It makes no earthly sense' (Goddard, *The Smiths*, p. 196).

102. The lyrics were apparently provoked by the Radio 1 DJ Steve Wright, who after a news report about the Chernobyl disaster recommended the programme with Wham!'s 'I'm Your Man' (cited in Goddard, *The Smiths*, p. 194).

103. The speaker in 'Asian Rut' is also clearly dissociated from the author and likewise identified as a juvenile ('There's peace through our school').

104. The opening utterance, for instance 'How sad are we / and how sad have we been'—carries in its use of 'sad' the slang sense of contemptible and ridiculous. Similarly, the claim 'honest, I swear, it's the turnstiles that make us hostile,' which is formally ascribed to the character-speaker, is clearly a parody of a lame excuse, which turns its speaker into a 'flat' cartoon character, and whose aesthetic patterning (turnstiles / hostile) keeps the superordinate involvement of the ventriloquizing artist in view.

alongside a number of other counterperspectives, which relativize and derisively reveal it as that of a young boy.[105])

'Bengali In Platforms' is the most problematic of the songs that deal with the darkness of racism. This is because the song's disturbing first-person refrain ('It's hard enough when you belong here') doesn't appear to proceed from a character perspective, and thus—by default—ends up in the author's mouth. One might, as some have, seek to defend the singer by pleading a lesser charge that, without malice aforethought, he is exploring his own congenital sense of nonbelonging in a transplanted context, so that it is the vehicle rather than the tenor that is the cause of offence. But this would only reduce the charge from witting to unwitting racism, for it still presupposes that as a Bengali, the subject does *not* belong here. This doesn't seem to me to be much of a saving or to explain what's going on.[106] But it does provide us with a clue, in reminding us of the singer's nonbelonging. What does this matter?

If we think back to our discussion of the singer's radical nonbelonging—his sense of being a 'foreigner at home'—which is apparent at so many levels of his work and is a constant subject throughout his career, there *is* no 'here' to which he belongs. As he sings in 'I Am Hated For Loving': 'I still don't belong / to anywhere.' It therefore seems wholly implausible that we would suddenly find him singing of his belonging and proudly defining his standpoint against another's nonbelonging. For this reason, I think it would be a mistake to identify the speaker of the song with Morrissey.

---

105. Johnny Rogan—who fanned the flames and then deplored the racist controversy that arose—concludes his comments on 'National Front Disco' with the following uncharacteristically cogent remark: 'What the composition demonstrated most forcibly was the songwriter's continued fascination with the disenchanted outsider whose world-view, however questionable or hopeless, was marked by pyrrhic defiance' (Rogan, *Morrissey*, p. 184).

106. A less problematic version of this defence has been put forward by Nabeel Zuberi, who writes about his own experiences as a 'Pakistani Brit,' and who suggests that the song is about a *particular* Bengali rather than Bengalis as such (Zuberi, *Sounds English*, p. 62): 'In "Bengali In Platforms" . . . the Bengali who wears unfashionable platform shoes is trying to make the English love him through a (failed) impersonation of Westernness. He's a pathetic creature, hoping to gain friends by dressing like a Britisher. I have to admit that Morrissey's description of the sartorial inadequacies of the Bengali reminds me of the recent Asian migrants we saw in postpunk Birmingham and Bradford, who always seemed to dress in unfashionable seventies gear (dodgy colour-coordination, bell-bottoms, and platforms) and about whom my brothers, my sister, and I had a supercilious middle-class assimilated laugh.' Commenting more recently in the *New Statesman* on Morrissey's public denunciation of racism, Rupa Huq—author of *Beyond Subculture: Pop, Youth and Identity* and herself 'a Bengali not in platforms'—endorses this view: 'The [singer's condemnation of racism] and his explanation of "Bengali In Platforms" as addressing a specific case and not all Bengalis is good enough for me to bury the hatchet' (*New Statesman*, December 10, 2007).

(The glaring parallels between the awkwardness of the 'Bengali In Platforms' and the singer's early gauche persona—whose own Ill-Fitting and incongruous clothes were an advertisement of his nonbelonging—also suggest that there is more of Morrissey on the side of the Bengali than on the side of the speaker.) If this is the case, as it is in 'National Front Disco' and 'We'll Let You Know,' the song's disturbing first-person utterance would turn out to proceed from a character perspective after all.

This doesn't of course do away with the problems. Whilst seeing his lyrics on the subject of racism as 'so many utterances of so many imaginary persons, not [his]' crucially separates Morrissey from the views their first-person speakers express, the singer is undeniably interested in such perspectives and for some reason leaves his own viewpoint open to debate.[107] One person for whom this is a problem is Nabeel Zuberi:

> As a studious fan I want to concede to Morrissey the escape clause of irony—that he doesn't really mean it, and he's just provoking Brits to think about the past, juggling the images, sounds, notions and potions of our collective memory. This is the attraction of tricksters. Listening to the songs repeatedly suggests to me that Morrissey is a ventriloquist, posing different voices against each other. You're never sure which voice belongs to him. On the other hand, the ambiguities of this kind of queer English tricksterism also leave me frustrated. I sometimes feel that it's about bloody time the English got beyond irony as a device to deal with their limited repertoire of the national. As much as an ironic mode has the potential to critique certain versions of history, irony can serve to evade realities and new possibilities as it takes apart the same decaying body of national cultural concerns again and again with its blunt scalpel.
>
> I remain caught in a bind: irony can be exasperating, but then again, who wants politically correct music? The ironies of being English or British are hard to escape whether one is Morrissey, a skinhead, or a Paki. And maybe irony is a necessary mechanism through which

---

107. At least in his lyrics, that is; for he has stated his views unambiguously in public: 'I abhor racism and oppression or cruelty of any kind and will not let this pass without being absolutely clear and emphatic. . . . Racism is beyond common sense and has no place in our society' (*The Guardian*, December 4, 2007). To be opposed to limitless immigration and to lament the disappearance of distinctive ways of doing things is, as Rupa Huq points out, wholly consonant with the current British (Labour) government's views and does not make him a racist (*New Statesman*, December 10, 2007).

certain versions of the national must be invoked and thus disempow-
ered, before being eventually disavowed.[108]

I admire Zuberi's sober, perceptive and scholarly discussion of
national identity in Morrissey's writing. However, I take a more positive view of irony. In adopting the form of the dramatic monologue,
Robert Browning was not being evasive, a 'trickster' or seeking 'the
escape clause of irony.' It had more to do with his suspicion of the
romantic gesture—the 'simple verticality of visionary aspiration'[109]—
and marked a scaling down of ambition from universal and eternal
Truth to the truth of a particular perspective. More positively, this
scaled-down attempt to capture 'prismatic hues' rather than pursue
'the pure white light' involved a *widening* of vision, for which he
needed an art that was equal to the contradictoriness of things—that
could faithfully represent the fugitive convolutions of subjectivity,
with its intertwinings of insight and delusion—an art that could
'speak out of both sides of its mouth' (or say of a given perspective
'Well, this is true . . . and yet, it's false'). The equivocal voice of the
dramatic monologue is peculiarly suited to such complex realities.[110]

Morrissey's dramatized first-person lyrics similarly allow him to
communicate contrary views of a given perspective. Moreover, such
'ironic' or equivocal imaginings may be seen—pace Zuberi—not as
an evasion but on the contrary as an attempt to capture as faithfully
as possible a reality which is of its nature complex. This eschewal
of the univocal voice on such a problematic issue reveals something
vital to our understanding of Morrissey's art.

Morrissey, as we know, has a singular aversion to that which sets
itself up as 'normality'—and forgets or effaces the power relations on
which it is based.[111] He therefore has an instinctive sympathy for the
outsider, the 'deviant' and the dispossessed (and the more such intimacy
makes us flinch, the more certain we can be that we are actually facing
the outsider). What happens, however, if such oppositional 'outsider'
perspectives are linked to or consist in violence? How can you signal

---

108. Zuberi, *Sounds English*, p. 64.
109. Leslie Brisman, 'Back to the First of All,' p. 56.
110. As Isobel Armstrong observes of the form: the dramatic monologue or 'double poem' is 'a
deeply sceptical' and 'inveterately political' mode, which enables the poet 'to explore expressive
psychological forms simultaneously as psychological conditions *and* as constructs, the phenom-
enology of a culture, projections which indicate the structure of relationships. . . . To re-order lyric
expression [in this way] is to give it a new content and to introduce the possibility of interrogation
and critique' (Armstrong, *Victorian Poetry, Poetics and Politics*, pp. 12–13).
111. As he sings in 'The World Is Full Of Crashing Bores': 'educated criminals / work *within*
the law' (italics added).

support for something to which you are also opposed? Irony—or the equivocal voice of the dramatic lyric—allows the singer to communicate a sympathy for the outsider or an oppositional stance, whilst simultaneously dissociating himself from its values.[112] In 'Glamorous Glue,' for example, Morrissey would seem to have sympathy with the speaker's critique of polite society ('Everyone lies/nobody minds') without endorsing the glue-sniffer's perspective. In this way, he is able to challenge the 'normal' by strategically speaking from a perspective that is opposed to it, without in the process enthroning its antagonist.[113]

If this is roughly what's going on in these songs—in which Morrissey speaks from within whilst differentiating himself from a range of oppositional perspectives—far from signalling a sort of cowardly evasion, the singer's use of the equivocal voice would turn out to have an *ethical* force, since its eschewal of explicit or univocal critique would be a function of its more thoroughgoing twofold critique. This critique isn't just opposed to the covert ideologies of the 'normal,' but is at the same time reflexively opposed to what it must strategically support in order to oppose the tyranny of the 'normal.'[114]

If such a conclusion is in one sense surprising—since it carries us a long way from the negative readings with which this section began—in another sense it is not, for what these reflections additionally reveal is an underlying connection between Morrissey's deployment of an equivocal voice and the pervasive antiessentialist and deconstructive tendencies in his work. In all three cases, underlying his practice, there is a vigilant suspicion of anything that seeks to install itself as 'normal' and a concomitant sympathy for the alien or eccentric.[115] These decentring tendencies are clearly reflected in the singer's diverse identifications with the 'monstrous,' the 'maladjusted,' the criminal and the excluded. They are apparent too in his

---

112. In Robert Langbaum's terms, the equivocal voice allows him to communicate both sympathy and judgement (Langbaum, *The Poetry of Experience: The Dramatic Monlogue in Modern Literary Tradition*), *passim*.

113. Morrissey's equivocal sympathy for the violent outsider in some ways resembles Blake's daring, ambivalent recasting of Milton's Satan as a hero, whom he sympathetically imagines—as a salutary contrary—without morally endorsing.

114. Such 'disturbing' tendencies make Morrissey an 'agitator' in Wilde's sense: 'Agitators are a set of interfering, meddling people, who come down to some perfectly contented class of the community and sow seeds of discontent amongst them. That is the reason why agitators are so absolutely necessary. Without them, in our incomplete state, there would be no advance towards civilization' (Wilde, *The Soul of Man under Socialism and Selected Critical Prose*, p. 131).

115. This may help to explain why Morrissey has such a huge following amongst Mexican-Americans, which, as Pat Reid has shown—in his examination of individual fans' testimonies—argues against xenophobic readings of his work and testifies to the singer's 'cross-cultural significance' (Reid, *Morrissey*, p. 43).

early, radically eccentric appearance—damaged, destitute, vulnerable and gauche—the archetypal 'other' of the 1980s hedonistic,
upwardly mobile ideal.[116] In other words, at the centre of Morrissey's
art—and forcibly countering accusations of racism—is a daring and
deep-seated defence of difference.[117] And it is on account of this that
Armond White can legitimeately speak of 'Morrissey's unique, musical human rights effort.'[118]

FIDELITY TO FAILURE

In his 'eulogy' for the group, written in 1987 and reprinted in the
recent collection *Bring the Noise*, Simon Reynolds attempts to explain
the significance of The Smiths:

> Why were The Smiths 'important'? Because of their misery. Never for-
> get it. Around *Meat Is Murder* the critics suddenly discovered Morris-
> sey's humour—George Formby was trundled out as a reference point.
> If you ask me, The Smiths could have afforded to be more *humourless*.
> The Smiths' finest moments—'Hand In Glove,' 'How Soon Is Now?'
> 'Still Ill,' 'I Know It's Over'—were moments of reproachful, avenging
> misery, naked desperation, unbearable reverence—free of the 'saving
> grace' of quips and camp self-consciousness. If there was laughter it
> was black, scornful, scathing. If The Smiths had only produced sunny,
> cuddly stuff like 'Heaven Knows I'm Miserable Now,' 'Ask,' 'Vicar In A
> Tutu,' they would have merely presaged the perky negligibility of The
> Housemartins, the sound that grins itself to death. The Smiths were
> heroic party-poopers at the *Top of the Pops* office do, glowering at the
> forced jollity; they were like those gauche youths who turn up to house
> parties only to cling to the dark corners in chaste disdain, driven by the
> naive, vaguely inhuman conviction that all merriment is a lie.[119]

---

116. As Morrissey pointed out at the time of the controversy: 'I think that if the National Front
were to hate anyone, it would be me. I would be top of their list' (*Select*, May 1994). This was in
fact confirmed by the response of skinheads to his notorious concert in 1992 (supporting Madness
in Finsbury Park), who abused and threw bottles at the singer, forcing him to abandon his performance. Contrary to a number of inflammatory reports, the incident suggests that bottle-throwing
skinheads are more sensitive readers of Morrissey's lyrics than certain journalists at the *NME*.
117. It is, I presume, on account of Morrissey's bold, consistent and subversive sympathy for the
dispossessed others of bourgeois 'normality' that the music journalist Tony Parsons declared 'Morrissey could invade Poland and I still wouldn't believe he was a racist' (*Vox* April 1993).
118. White, *The Resistance*, p. 223.
119. Reynolds, *Bring the Noise*, p. 43.

Whilst I can't agree entirely with this—for I think Morrissey's humour is stranger, more significant and more subversive than he allows—Reynolds deserves praise for reminding us of the unconventionality of Morrissey's dark imaginings and also for seeing something important in the very thing for which the singer tends to be criticized: namely, the *stubbornness* of his misery.[120] This is one of the reasons why it doesn't seem to me to be a sales ploy or a pretence (with the usual proviso of course: he may look like he's miserable and sound like he's miserable, but we shouldn't let this fool us—he actually *is* miserable!). For Morrissey the aesthete places so much value on not being boring, it's hard to imagine that he would tolerate such repetition—having made the point once and well—if it wasn't for something more urgent, more obstinate and more important than his aestheticism. (Another reason is that the darkness is so vividly expressed in his lyrics and communicated by his voice that he is able to convince us he's speaking of something seen from within.)

The stubbornness of the singer's representation of misery is important for several reasons. At the end of 'Last Night I Dreamt That Somebody Loved Me,' Morrissey sings:

> This story is old—I KNOW,
> but it goes on
> and on
> and on.[121]

The repetition—'it goes on / and on / and on'—allows the enfolded senses of 'going on' to fan out, and in doing so offers an explanation of the singer's stubborn depiction of misery. In the first or most obvious sense, the lines acknowledge that Morrissey has told this story before (the preceding song on the album is 'Stop Me If You Think You've Heard This One Before'), but point out that there is another reason for carrying on in spite of this—namely, the continuity of the singer's sadness. Alongside this, the lines make a more fundamental assertion that even though the story of loneliness is in general old, it is nonetheless something that actually takes place (the refrain 'I've seen this happen in other people's lives / and now it's happening in mine' registers a similar shock at the actuality of a familiar

---

120. Reynolds includes an editorial postscript in which he apologetically acknowledges that the eulogy is about Morrissey rather than The Smiths.
121. The final lines—'on / and on / and on'—are repeated in importunate falsetto, more clearly live than on *Strangeways, Here We Come* (see *Live At Earls Court*).

occurrence). Finally, the repetition 'and on / and on'—which is sung over a sequence that winces from C major seven into C minor, and in doing so figures a kind of grimace—carries a sense of tiresomely going on about something. The utterance thus involves a self-reflexive critique *as well as* a defence of what the singer is saying (and the realization that he is tiresomely 'going on' of course only further fuels that which is going on about).

The fact that we live belatedly in a world where the primary stories have already been told in no way makes suffering any less. Rather, again, it provides *further* cause, in taking something of its significance away (and here we are back with the sadness of Larkin 'after' tragedy—which is in a sense worse because it is less). That is to say, our familiarity carries us *away* from it, and renders the telling of the story more urgent whilst at the same time depriving us of the means for doing so. As Beckett puts it in the last words of *The Unnamable*: 'You must go, I can't go on, I'll go on.'[122] The stubbornness of Morrissey's representation of misery bears witness to the ways in which it infinitely exceeds expression; the way, that is—in spite of our familiarity, in spite of its repetitive nature and in spite of anything we might say about it—it goes on. In this sense, as it was noted earlier, the excess of hyperbole has a representative function, since it points towards that which is of its nature excessive ('Suffering is permanent, obscure and dark, / and shares the nature of infinity').[123] Similarly, the singer's tendency towards self-parody draws attention to the ways in which the act of expression in a sense 'overtakes' its subject and becomes part of the problem—which only elicits further attempts at expression. (This is the nightmare logic of the 'et cetera' witnessed at the end of 'Sweet And Tender Hooligan.')

There is of course, as there is in Keats, an element of indulgence in Morrissey's exploration of misery (just as Keats gluts himself on melancholy like a connoisseur, Morrissey becomes the spectator of his own misery, watching from without what he suffers within).[124]

122. Beckett, *Molloy, Malone Dies, The Unnamable*, p. 418.
123. Leaving aside pronouns, articles and the like, one of the most frequently occurring words in Morrissey's lyrics is 'never'—which threatens to turn into a subject of its own and has to be continually repeated, as though the lack he was pointing to could not be sufficiently signified by simple negation and was somehow infinite. ('Never Had No One Ever,' which circles around the phrase 'No I never . . . had no one ever,' as if the words were worry beads, seems to be an attempt to see how much negation you can get into a single utterance.)
124. There is in Morrissey's case a strong sense of its ridiculousness as well. Maudlin Street— where the singer's persona was born and raised—is borrowed from and presents his suffering as a *Carry On* film.

This 'voyeuristic fold' within the experience is not, however, an infidelity to what he describes; it is *part* of the experience. And in not editing this out—in allowing us, that is, to contemplate his contemplating his own experience—Morrissey is being more rather than less faithful to it. Indeed, it would be a kind of vanity to leave *out* his indulgence—like pretending we never look in the mirror. In this way, he transmits the whole of the experience—including his movement outside the experience within the experience, which paradoxically constitutes the experience.

The phrase 'fidelity to failure' is Samuel Beckett's and occurs in one of his last dialogues with George Duthuit:

> To be an artist is to fail, as no other dare fail, that failure is his world and the shrink from it desertion, art and craft, good housekeeping, living. . . . I know that all that is required now . . . is to make of this submission, this admission, this fidelity to failure, a new occasion, a new term of relation, and of the act which, unable to act, obliged to act, he makes, an expressive act, even if only of itself, of its impossibility, of its obligation.[125]

It is of course Beckett and not Morrissey who sought and perfected an art that expresses solely itself, its impossibility and its obligation. Nevertheless, Morrissey's great achievement—and what makes him a serious artist rather than merely a pop star—is that in Beckett's sense he has *dared to fail.* From the moment Steven Patrick Morrissey was put in a box on top of his wardrobe and he became 'a living sign,' Morrissey has made that failure his world and has never shrunk from it into 'art and craft, good housekeeping, living. . . . '

The aim of this chapter has been to display and celebrate this 'fidelity to failure'—his fidelity, that is, to the faultiness, the weakness, the brokenness of things; to the violence, the suffering, the blankness and the lack, whose sway we wish into the margins of existence, but which, he insists, lie at the heart of the everyday. I have also in the process attempted to show that the repetition, the hyperbole, the self-parody and the indulgence, for which the singer is commonly criticized, are in fact part of this 'fidelity to failure.' My final claim is perhaps even harder to swallow.

---

125. Beckett, *Proust; Three Dialogues*, p. 125. In the passage quoted, Beckett is talking about the Dutch painter Bram van Velde.

This is not a matter of pessimism; but, rather, an act of conscience, a keeping vigil, a 'memento mori,' and thus a matter of *sanity*. For within the three-minute spaces of popular music—without flinching or turning its monsters into pets, and however unconventional, embarrassing or disturbing it may be—Morrissey's art stubbornly bears witness to the darkness that is.

CHAPTER 5

———❦———

The Light That Never Goes Out

Andrew Male: Which songs are most obviously a result of your
  Catholic upbringing?
Morrissey: Everything. There's absolutely nothing else.

—*Mojo,* April 2006

TURNING TOWARDS ROME

The signpost featured on the back of The Smiths' last studio album,
Strangeways, Here We Come, offers directions towards five places,
each of which has some serendipitous significance for the band: the
prison, to the right, from which the album takes its title; Salford, in
the same direction, where twenty years later Johnny Marr would be
made a visiting professor of music; Ancoats, to the left, which was
used as a pseudonym for the backing singer on 'Bigmouth Strikes
Again';[1] Piccadilly, straight ahead, whose counterpart in London
inspired the single 'Piccadilly Palare'; and finally, also straight ahead,
St Peter's Square. What chance significance does this have?

In 2005, Morrissey moved to Rome, where, according to Mark
Beaumont, he 'discovered sociability, belonging and perhaps (whis-
per it) even *happiness* at last.' 'It's affected me,' the singer explained:

> I can see it, I understand it and for me it's quite well timed.
> I spent so many years on the journey inwards and I was very
> relieved to be led to Rome.

Beaumont: Have you found a home here?

———

1. The voice is in fact Morrissey's speeded up through a harmonizer.

Morrissey: [A tentative nod, a sniff of the city] I hope so, but since I never intended to be in Los Angeles and I never intended to be here and I do feel mysteriously led, then I can't tell.

Beaumont: And a muse?

Morrissey: [Another nod, firmer] I have certainly found a muse, and the way the album occurred here, how all the components jumped into place, I simply followed. When I came to Rome just over a year ago it grabbed me, I was whooshed and I just knew I had to stay and record the album here. . . . I came here accidentally, for no reason. It was a calling.

Beaumont: A voice in your head said, 'Go to Rome' and you went?

Morrissey: That's exactly what happened. You hear that voice and it's clear. . . . You simply sit back . . . and wait to be called.[2]

There is another sense in which the singer may be said to be 'turning towards Rome.' Morrissey is a child of Irish Catholic immigrants, who were married in Our Lady of Perpetual Succour in Moss Side, and who sent their son, to be brought up a Catholic, first to St. Wilfred's Primary School and then to St. Mary's Secondary Modern in Stretford.[3] Their household, as the singer would later describe it, was 'quite vividly Catholic. Then it became vaguely Catholic.'[4] Morrissey's adult writing, however, exhibits the opposite trajectory.

The religious has always been 'vaguely' present in Morrissey's work, even with The Smiths. In 'Miserable Lie,' for example, on their debut album, he refers to his 'flower-like-life'—a phrase he borrows from Wilde's description of Christ in *De Profundis*—and at the end of 'What Difference Does It Make?' the singer declares in consummately maladroit falsetto 'I'm a sacred one.'[5] As we have seen, in 'The Boy With The Thorn In His Side,' he overtly invokes Christian imagery, again perhaps via Wilde (who at the end of his life converted to Catholicism), and in 'Bigmouth Strikes Again,' he compares himself to the martyr Joan of Arc.[6] Elsewhere on *The Queen Is Dead*, he refers

2. *NME*, March 4, 2006.

3. Morrissey took his first Holy Communion in 1966 and was confirmed in 1968.

4. *NME*, June 8, 1985. When the singer's parents separated, just before Christmas in 1976, he lived with his mother, who is a devout Catholic and apparently the only person with whom the singer has had a constant, close relationship. According to Morrissey, it was his mother who introduced him to the work of Oscar Wilde, who 'always supported me in an artistic sense, when many people around her said she was entirely insane for allowing me to stay in and write,' and who was 'instrumental in engineering the way I feel about certain things' (*The Face*, July 1984).

5. The title 'Suffer Little Children' is also of course a biblical allusion (Matthew 19:14).

6. The matrix message on *Strangeways, Here We Come* eulogises another Catholic revolutionary ('Guy Fawkes was a genius').

to the church (critically) in the title song, and (more light-heartedly) in 'Vicar In A Tutu.' There are also obvious religious resonances in 'There Is A Light That Never Goes Out.' In 'Sweet And Tender Hooligan,' the singer alludes to *The Book of Common Prayer*, and in 'These Things Take Time,' he similarly cites and playfully modifies the opening line of a nineteenth-century Christian hymn.[7] Alongside these illusions, it is possible to discern in a number of songs what I have described as a 'sacrificial logic' and even a kind of religious ontology—on account of the communion that is offered in the space of the song—as well as a taking on of others' vulnerability in his iconic early persona.[8] More conspicuously, in 1985, he appeared on the front of the *NME* with a halo and realistic stigmata, and was described in the interview's prefatory comments as the 'Pope of pop,' who 'is still walking on water.'[9] All of these apparently disparate associations were underwritten by his 'scandalous' asceticism, which was typically characterized by the singer and others in religious terms:

> I live a life that befits a priest virtually. . . . I live a saintly life.[10]
> I lead somewhat of a religious lifestyle.[11]

Paul Du Noyer: Are you still the same monastic figure you've been portrayed as being?

Morrissey: I don't really know what monastic means—oh yes, from a monastery . . .

Du Noyer: Self-denying, ascetic.

Morrissey: Well, I suppose I was . . . This is a yes or no question, really. But yes.[12]

In recent years, without letting go of his antagonistic feelings, Morrissey's work has become 'quite vividly Catholic.' On *Ringleader*

---

7. 'Mine eyes have seen the glory of the coming of the Lord' ('Battle Hymn of the Republic,' by Julia W. Howe, 1861).

8. These 'vague' religious resonances were recognized and reflected in the behaviour of Morrissey's fans; as John Harris notes: 'His disciples, clad in a uniform usually acquired from charity shops, would dance to The Smiths' music using steps that amounted to cartoon gestures of self-pity: hands placed on the heart, eyes cast skywards in the manner of the crucified Christ' (Harris, *The Last Party*, p. 5).

9. The interview is illustrated with another picture of the singer with a halo, accompanied by the caption 'Tour Of Deity: Moz Crucified By The Press, In Glorious Colour, Every Wednesday' (June 8, 1985).

10. *NME*, September 24, 1983.

11. *Time Out*, March 7–13, 1985.

12. *Q*, August 1987.

Of The Tormentors, he calls out in prayer to God in three songs ('dear God please help me'; 'dear God when will I be where I should be'; 'Lord, these words I beg of you / as I kneel down at my bed'),[13] and he compares himself to the 'Catholic Marxist' Pier Paolo Pasolini.[14] In May 2006, shortly after the album's release, Morrissey appeared in a series of photographs in *Uncut* magazine, posing as St Sebastian, and as a Christ-like figure, once again with stigmata, in a crucifixion posture, and in another offering up a heart of supernatural light.[15] The most dramatic manifestation of this increased engagement with the religious, though, was the release in 2004 of 'I Have Forgiven Jesus,' on *You Are The Quarry*, which the singer promoted and performed dressed as a priest.[16] So, when in the tour that followed, the singer made the sign of the cross during 'There Is A Light That Never Goes Out,' it all seemed in some strange way to make sense. This final chapter examines Morrissey's treatment of religious subjects and considers whether his apparently nonreligious writing may have a submerged religious dimension or provenance. In doing so, I wish to explore why it might be that this recent turn towards the religious—however temporary, tentative or contradictory it may prove to be—seems 'in some strange way to make sense.'

I

∽

TENEBRAE

It behoves us to begin with darkness. As we saw in the previous chapter, Morrissey consistently writes about a world that is flooded with darkness—a world of dereliction, evil, radical privation and

13. 'Dear God Please Help Me,' 'On The Streets I Ran,' 'I Just Want To See The Boy Happy.'
14. Morrissey was asked about his identification with Pasolini and the two writers' Catholicism by Andrew Male:

> *Male*: Might there be another point of connection? Do you feel that even if you don't practice, you'll always be a Catholic?
>
> *Morrissey*: I don't think you have any choice. It's sandblasted into you. And it will take one hell of a blowtorch to get rid of it. That will never happen, regardless of what your feelings are, regardless of what your intentions are.

(*Mojo*, April 2006).
15. The photographs accompanied an interview by Paul Morley, announced on the front cover as 'The Passion of Morrissey' (on which the singer appears wearing a conspicuous crucifixion pendant) and entitled 'The Last Temptation of Morrissey.'
16. As if he were preparing for this, two years earlier when the singer played at the Royal Albert Hall, he came onstage to the sound of pealing church bells.

perpetual exile; in which goodness backfires and becomes a mask, accomplice or *target* of darkness; in which satisfaction is an alluring yet elusive goal that retreats upon arrival, and desire seems circularly to seek its own reproduction and to sustain us in a state of infinite longing. How can such a world be described as religious?

Because darkness is part of religion's story also.[17] It is the believer who prays 'mourning and weeping in this vale of tears.'[18] It is Jacob who wrestles all night with an unnamed and unknown adversary and who 'prevailed not against him' (Genesis 32:24–7). The phrase 'a foreigner on the earth' alludes to the radical exile of the psalmist, whose sense of desolation is articulated as follows:

> My days are consumed like smoke, and my bones are burned as
> an hearth.
> My heart is smitten, and withered like grass; so that I forget to eat
> my bread.
> By reason of the voice of my groaning my bones cleave to my skin.
> I am like a pelican of the wilderness: I am like an owl of the desert.
> I watch, and am as a sparrow alone upon the house top.
> Mine enemies reproach me all the day; and they that are mad against
> me are sworn against me.
> For I have eaten ashes like bread, and mingled my drink
> with weeping. . . .
> My days are like a shadow that declineth; and I am withered
> like grass.
>
> My soul is full of troubles: and my life draweth nigh unto the grave.
> I am counted with them that go down into the pit: I am as a man that
> hath no strength:
> Free among the dead, like the slain that lie in the grave, whom thou
> rememberest no more: and they are cut off from thy hand.
> Thou hast laid me in the lowest pit, in darkness, in the deeps. . . .

---

17. As Terry Eagleton recently observed, 'Christianity is . . . considerably more pessimistic than secular humanism, as well as immeasurably more optimistic. On the one hand, it is grimly realistic about the recalcitrance of the human condition—the perversity of human desire, the prevalence of idolatry and illusion, the scandal of suffering, the dull persistence of oppression and injustice, the scarcity of public virtue, the insolence of power, the fragility of goodness and the formidable power of appetite and self-interest. It is this condition which it dubs "original sin," meaning those flaws which appear to be structural to the cultural or linguistic animal, and which pace all naive historicism, are continuous in one form or another throughout the human narrative' (*The Gospels*, introduction, p. xxviii).

18. The phrase is taken from 'Salve, Regina' (Hail, Holy Queen), one of the four Marian antiphons.

> Thou hast put away mine acquaintance far from me; thou hast made
>   me an abomination unto them: I am shut up, and I cannot
>   come forth. . . .
> LORD, why castest thou off my soul? why hidest thou thy face
>   from me? . . .
> They came round about me daily like water; they compassed me
>   about together.
> Lover and friend hast thou put far from me, and mine acquaintance
>   into darkness.
>
> —Psalms 102 and 88

It is the lovesick bride of The Song of Songs who wanders around in the darkness desperately seeking her vanishing beloved, lamenting:

> By night on my bed I sought him whom my soul loveth: I sought him, but I found him not. I will rise now, and go about the city in the streets, and in the broad ways I will seek him whom my soul loveth: I sought him, but I found him not. . . . I opened to my beloved; but my beloved had withdrawn himself, and was gone: my soul failed when he spake: I sought him, but I could not find him; I called him, but he gave me no answer. The watchmen that went about the city found me, they smote me, they wounded me; the keepers of the walls took away my veil from me. I charge you, O daughters of Jerusalem, if ye find my beloved, that ye tell him, that I am sick of love.
>
> —The Song of Songs 3; 5

And it is of course Christ, who 'deeply grieved, even unto death,' in the garden of Gethsemane, calls out repeatedly to his Father in agony, and who cries from the cross in dereliction—'My God, my God, why hast thou forsaken me?'—as the sun is blacked out and darkness comes all over the earth (Matthew 27:46; Luke 23:44–45).[19]

In pointing out all of this, I am not attempting to claim that the darkness in Morrissey's work is a religious darkness or even necessarily has a religious dimension (although it is remarkable how many of his lyrics are punctuated with interjections of a religious cast—'God knows,' 'heaven knows,' 'God give me patience,' 'Oh my soul,' 'O Christ,' 'Dear God,' etc.—and how frequently in moments of crisis his speakers call out to and relate their predicament to God: 'Jesus

---

19. This darkness is commemorated with a ritual extinction of lights during Holy Week in the services known as 'Tenebrae' (which means 'darkness').

made me so / Jesus save me'; 'God come down / if you're really there / well, you're the one who claims to care'[20]). What I do wish to make clear, however, is that such darkness is by no means opposed to, and in no way sets Morrissey apart from, the religious.[21]

STUMBLING BLOCKS

Before we can attempt to talk about the light, we need to consider another, more pointed objection. Even if we are prepared to concede that the darkness in Morrissey is not opposed to the religious, and even if we accept that it may in certain respects resemble a religious darkness, surely his virulent, bitter and ironic references to the subject make clear his animosity towards religion? Yes; though I wish somewhat paradoxically to suggest that such animosity not only towards the institutions and earthly representatives of religion but also towards the divine itself may not be incompatible with belief.

The former is probably obvious enough and doesn't need much explaining. The criticism and fun-poking in 'The Queen Is Dead,' 'Vicar In A Tutu' and 'Yes, I Am Blind,' for example, are directed at fallen or aberrant representatives of religion, according to the church's own norms: in the first case, the alleged rapaciousness of the church; in the second, the—what shall we say?—eccentric wonts of one of its vicars (but to be fair, if the only thing the 'monkish monsignor' has against him is his fondness for dancing and sliding down the banister in a preposterously skimpy tutu, it is hard to see what wrong he is doing); and in 'Yes I Am Blind,' it is the laity or the supposed believers

---

20. 'November Spawned A Monster,' 'Yes, I Am Blind.' The cry to God in the latter appears to echo the opening line of Wilde's poem 'E Tenebris' [Out of Darkness]: 'Come down, O Christ, and help me!'

21. Wilde, it seems, wants to go further than this in *De Profundis*, in which he cites Dante's remark that 'sorrow re-marries us to God' (*Purgatorio*, xxiii, 81) and where he turns towards without yet wholly embracing the religious as a result of what he refers to as 'the purple pageant of my incommunicable woe' (p. 141). It is worth noting too that the lines he quotes from Wordsworth on suffering are not the poet's last word on the matter (though it is significant that Wilde only quotes the first part):

> Suffering is permanent, obscure and dark,
> And shares the nature of infinity.
> Yet through that darkness (infinite though it seem
> And irremoveable) gracious openings lie.

For Wordsworth, not only is there a 'yet' after the infinity of suffering—in view of which such suffering turns out only to 'seem' infinite and irremoveable—it is precisely through this darkness that 'gracious openings lie.' Leonard Cohen—who is obviously closer than Wordsworth to Morrissey—concurs: 'There is a crack in everything,' he sings in 'Anthem.' 'That's how the light gets in.'

who are criticized ('Little lamb / on a hill / run fast if you can / good Christians / want to KILL you / and your life has not even begun!'). In all three cases, then, nothing at all is said against the divine as such; neither is anything said which in any way impugns the claims of belief. We can be more positive. In 'The Queen Is Dead,' the singer's complaint paradoxically accords with the views of the church, since what he criticizes is against its own teaching (the complaint is therefore either one of hypocrisy—which is a criticism of its failure to uphold its teachings and not of these teachings, which it in a sense preserves—or else it is a mistaken impression). In 'Yes, I am Blind,' the situation is similarly complicated by the fact that the persecuted 'Little lamb' may of course suggest Christ (with whom the singer insistently identifies himself), which would only underline what is in any case apparent—namely, that what the Christians are doing is *un*christian. The singer would thus once again, albeit implicitly, turn out to be defending Christianity from itself in attacking some of its professed adherents.[22]

Things are even more complicated in 'Vicar In A Tutu,' which has been unjustly denigrated as 'an amusing but lightweight filler.'[23] Let's take another look at the lyrics.

> I was minding my business
> lifting some lead off
> the roof of the Holy Name church
> it was worthwhile living a laughable life
> Just to set my eyes on the blistering sight
> of a vicar in a tutu
> he's *not* strange
> he just wants to live his life this way.
> A scanty bit of a thing
> with a decorative ring

---

22. For Rogan—who seems to assume that such things must either be black or white—the song's suggestive presentation of Christ as the victim of Christians' violence is simply 'odd': 'The anti-Christian sentiments in the last verse are undeveloped, just at the point when they are getting interesting. Oddly, Morrissey uses the lamb—a symbol of Christianity—as the object of slaughter by Christians rather than Romans' (Rogan, *Morrissey*, p. 159). Yet as we have seen, Morrissey is able to stand at once within and without a given perspective and to feel sympathy as well as animosity towards its point of view (the 'equivocal voice' of the dramatic monologue—which conjoins sympathy and judgement—is the obvious illustration of this). In 'Yes, I Am Blind,' we are in any case dealing with two distinct things, whose difference tends to be elided, for Christ of course was not a Christian.

23. Goddard, *The Smiths*, p. 182.

that wouldn't cover the head of a goose
as Rose collects the money in the canister
who comes sliding down the banister
the vicar in a tutu.

. . .

The monkish monsignor
with a head full of plaster
said: '*My man, get your vile soul dry-cleaned*'
as Rose counts the money
    in the canister
as natural as Rain
he dances again, my God
the vicar in a tutu.
The next day in the pulpit
with Freedom and Ease
combating *ignorance, dust and disease*
as Rose counts the money in the canister
as natural as Rain
he dances again, and again, and again and
and the fabric of a tutu
any man could get used to
and I am a living sign . . .

The song is like a miniature *Carry On* film, with a cast of momentary but memorable characters: the eccentric vicar, his assistant Rose, the 'monkish monsignor' and the petty criminal who is the song's speaker.[24] It also contains one of Morrissey's finest comic couplets—'the fabric of a tutu / any man can get used to'—and is filled with delightful comparisons and descriptive precision: 'the head of a goose'; 'as natural as Rain'; 'combating *ignorance, dust and disease*.'[25] The song's greatest subtlety, though, and the feature of particular interest to us here is the final climactic repetition of 'I am a living sign' (which lasts for thirty seconds in a song of a little over two minutes). Why is this so significant?

---

24. As is often the case in Morrissey's songs, the ostensible speaking perspective is not consistently or prominently sustained and is subverted by a species of free indirect discourse (the line 'it was worthwhile living a laughable life' seems to involve a leaking into the character's perspective of an exterior ironizing point of view). The repeated lines defending the vicar—'he's *not* strange / he just wants to live his life this way'—likewise suggest the involvement of a supplementary 'omniscient' perspective.

25. There is more wit in the wonderful unobviousness of Morrissey's reference to 'the head of a goose' than in any of the patronizing commentary on the song.

The first thing to notice is the complexity of its 'I,' which dilates to include the singer as well as the song's vicar (and arguably its putative speaker too). Related to this, we should also notice the line's self-reflexive allusion, on the one hand to the textual status of the vicar, and on the other to the spectral persona of the singer, which is itself discursively constituted, and the ventriloquizing means by which the former sign 'lives.' The utterance is thus crowded with a multiplicity of distinct speakers, whose divergent voices resonate simultaneously (we at once hear 'Morrissey' singing 'I am a living sign' whilst the vicar utters the same words differently). The line's self-referential resonances—which further complicate this plurality of voices—enrich and exist in ironic counterpoint to the theological claim which is the utterance's ostensible import: namely, that the vicar is 'a living sign' of God.[26] And yet here too there is a wonderful promiscuity of reference, for if, as the Bible teaches, man is made in the image of God (Genesis 1:26), the claim extends to the 'private' person who fulfils the role of the vicar—whose quirky divergence from his public identity adds yet another voice to the polyphonic utterance—and to the singer's persona as well, who with all *his* eccentricities is also 'a living sign' of his Creator. In this respect, the utterance resembles the 'aberrant' falsetto cry of 'I'm a sacred one' at the end of 'What Difference Does It Make?' which insists upon a participation in a divine economy whilst foregrounding a radical eccentricity. In both utterances, therefore, the singer seems to be insisting not only that there is no individual outside the human, but also that there is no humanity untouched by the divine.

Manifestly, there is a cheekiness and a *Carry On* scurrility about this audacious straining of orthodox religious teaching that undoubtedly appeals to Morrissey. But the claim has a serious dimension as well and is consonant with the defence of the human that runs throughout the singer's work. (The song's refrain 'he's *not* strange / he just wants to live his life this way,' which appears to proceed from a perspective that transcends the level of its characters, undergirds the 'apologetic' character of the claim.) Moreover, for all its apparent irreverence—in holding up the scurrilous vicar as a sign of God—the invocation of the principle of *imago Dei* (the doctrine that man is made in the image of his Maker) is arguably not a straining of the

---

26. 'Vicar' literally means 'substitute' or 'in place of another,' and is used to designate an earthly representative of God.

doctrine at all; for if it is true, it is true of *all* mankind—however unpalatable their predilections to bourgeois sensibilities. Indeed, are we not aligning ourselves with the Pharisees who were scandalised by Christ's consorting with sinners (Luke 7:37–47), if we imagine the vicar's behaviour places him outside the workings of divine Providence? In this sense, like many of Christ's parables—*because* and not in spite of its audacity—the song challenges the reach of our charity.[27]

Of course, none of this sabotages the lightness of the song or obtains at the expense of its pervasive humour. But we sell it short—and domesticate Morrissey's ambivalent imaginings—if we fail to see that its lightness has a questioning underside, which challenges our squeamishly foreclosed sympathies in a manner that accords with Christian teaching, even as its facetiousness bespeaks a scepticism towards it.

FORGIVING JESUS

If the hostility towards the religious considered so far turns out on closer inspection to be much more ambivalent than it initially appears and to be directed towards the institution of Christianity, which is subtly dissociated from Christ himself, what are we to make of the animosity the singer evinces towards the divine? We find a sustained instance of this—and Morrissey's most serious lyrical engagement with the religion he claims influenced everything he's written—in 'I Have Forgiven Jesus':

> I was a good kid / I wouldn't do you no harm
> I was a nice kid / with a nice paper-round
> Forgive me any pain / I may have brung to you
> with God's help I know / I'll always be near to you
> but Jesus hurt me / when He deserted me but
> I have forgiven Jesus / for all the desire
> he placed in me when there's nothing I can do / with this desire
>
> I was good kid / through hail and snow I'd go / just to moon you
> I carried my heart in my hand / do you understand?

27. There may be a correlative elliptical allusion to the parable of the Good Samaritan (Luke 10:33) in 'Now My Heart Is Full,' where the singer asks repeatedly, out of nowhere in the middle instrumental section, 'Would you pass by?' and also perhaps in 'How Can Anybody Possibly Know How I Feel?' where he sings ironically 'look / see pain / walk away.'

Jesus hurt me / when He deserted me but
I have forgiven Jesus / for all of the love / He placed in me
When there's no-one I can turn to with this love

Monday—humiliation / Tuesday—suffocation
Wednesday—condescension / Thursday—is pathetic
by Friday—life has killed me

Why did you give me / so much desire?
when there is nowhere I can go / to offload this desire?
Why did you give me / so much love / in a loveless world?
when there is no one I can turn to / to unlock all this love?
Why did you stick me in / self-deprecating bones and skin?
Jesus—do you hate me?
Why did you stick me in / self-deprecating bones and skin?
Do you hate me? do you hate me? / do you hate me? do you hate me?

At the centre of the song is a bitterly ironic reversal of the relation-ship between Christ and man, respecting forgiveness, which appears to verge on, if it doesn't in fact pass over into, blasphemy. What this if-clause leaves open is, however, the vital question: what are we to make of the song's complaint? Is it blasphemous? Is it religious? Is it possible to be both?

To keep us from prematurely ruling out the second possibility, it is worth reminding ourselves that bitter and angry complaints that God is unjust, and has deliberately caused the speaker's suffering, frequently occur in the Old Testament and, most vehemently, in the book of Job, where the protagonist curses the day he was born:

Let the day perish wherein I was born, and the night in which it was said, There is a man child conceived. Let that day be darkness; let not God regard it from above, neither let the light shine upon it. Let dark-ness and the shadow of death stain it; let a cloud dwell upon it; let the blackness of the day terrify it. As for that night, let darkness seize upon it; . . . Let the stars of the twilight thereof be dark; let it look for light, but have none; neither let it see the dawning of the day: Because it shut not up the doors of my mother's womb, nor hid sorrow from mine eyes. Why died I not from the womb? . . . I will say unto God, Do not condemn me; shew me wherefore thou contendest with me. Is it good unto thee that thou shouldest oppress, that thou shouldest despise the work of thine hands? . . . Thine hands have made me and fashioned me together round about; yet thou dost destroy me. Remember, I beseech thee, that thou hast made me as the clay; and wilt thou bring me into dust again? Hast thou not poured me out as milk, and curdled me like cheese? Thou hast clothed me with skin and flesh, and hast fenced me with bones and sinews. . . . See thou mine affliction; For it increaseth. Thou huntest me as a fierce lion: and again thou shewest thyself marvellous upon me. . . . Wherefore then hast thou brought me forth out of the womb? . . . Are not my days few? cease then, and let me alone, that I may take comfort a little, Before I go whence I shall not return, even to the land of darkness and the shadow of death; A land of darkness, as darkness itself; and of the shadow of death, without any order, and where the light is as darkness.

—Job 3:3–11; 2–22

Clearly, Job doesn't pull any punches in his complaint to God. Like Morrissey, he attributes his exorbitant suffering to his Creator, who is perceived as an adversary ('Thou huntest me as a fierce lion'), and whose creation of the speaker in view of his treatment seems to make no sense at all ('Thine hands have made me and fashioned me together round about; yet thou dost destroy me').[28] What is perhaps most surprising to the modern mind, however, is that Job's conviction that his suffering is excessive, senseless and unjustified exists within a relationship of faith. As Walter Brueggemann points out in his commentary on the Psalms,

> The remarkable thing about Israel is that it did not banish or deny the darkness from its religious enterprise. It embraces the darkness as the very stuff of new life. Indeed, Israel seems to know that new life comes from nowhere else. . . . The gamut of expressions employed [in the Psalms of 'disorientation'] never escapes address to Yahweh. What is said to Yahweh may be scandalous and without redeeming social value, but these speakers are completely committed, and whatever must be said about the human situation must be said directly to Yahweh.[29]

To be sure, the psalmist and Job affirm a faith in the God they accuse of incomprehensible cruelty in causing their affliction, whereas

---

28. The book of Job, like Morrissey's lyric, begins by establishing the innocence of the protagonist and argues that his suffering is unjustified: 'There was a man in the land of Uz, whose name was Job; and that man was perfect and upright, and one that feared God, and eschewed evil' (Job 1:1).

29. Brueggemann, *The Message of the Psalms*, p. 53.

Morrissey apparently does not. Yet the comparison at least allows us to see that such feelings are not at all incompatible with belief— especially when *addressed* to God, as Morrissey's are.

Even so, we should be careful not to smooth away the evident differences. Morrissey's song involves a characteristic conjunction of humour (in his use of the dozy-schoolboy nonstandard 'brung' in speaking to God and in being presumably the first pop star to speak of doing a paper-round in a song) and urgent existential complaint (feeling that God must have hated him in creating him, he suffers so much from being himself).[30] Moreover, the singer seems to be making fun of religious teaching in a way that the psalmist and Job do not, ironically repeating back to Christ the promises he feels have been broken or seem meaningless ('I'll always be near to you').[31] In this respect, Morrissey's complaint is closer to the provocative and radically sceptical 'religious' poetry of Paul Celan, who enjambs a bitterly sardonic laugh in the midst of an orthodox act of praise—

> choirs at that time, the
> psalms. Ho, ho-
> sanna
> ('The Straightening')

—and who even more provocatively risks blasphemy in 'Tenebrae,' where we find a reversal of the relationship between Christ and man that parallels Morrissey's:

> We are near, Lord,
> Near and graspable.
>
> Grasped already, Lord,
> clutching one another, as if
> the body of each of us were
> your body, Lord.

---

30. There is an illuminating parallel between Morrissey's bitter complaint to Christ and the companionless monster's complaint to its maker in *Frankenstein*, which in turn recalls Adam's request for a mate in *Paradise Lost* and his questioning of God concerning the reasons for his creation (X, 743–5). Here are a couple of examples of the former: 'You, my creator, detest and spurn me, thy creature, to whom thou art bound by ties only dissoluble by the annihilation of one of us.' . . . 'From you only could I hope for succour, although towards you I felt no sentiment but that of hatred. Unfeeling, heartless creator! you had endowed me with perceptions and passions, and then cast me abroad an object for the scorn and horror of mankind. But on you only had I any claim for pity and redress, and from you I determined to seek that justice which I vainly attempted to gain from any other being that wore the human form' (Shelley, *Frankenstein*, pp. 74; 104).

31. Having said this, Job does employ irony in his complaint to God and parodies the language of the Psalms in his bitterness (see Gibson, *Language and Imagery in the Old Testament*, pp. 19–20).

Pray, Lord,

pray to us,

we are near.

In taking on the role of the comforter and promising to be near to Christ in his suffering, both speakers appear to mock the claims of Christian faith. (There is additionally in Celan's poem a mocking wink in the line break's exposure of the subjunctive—'as if'—which obliquely but contemptuously calls into question the surrounding narrative.[32]) And yet this apparently blasphemous bitterness is in Celan's text articulated by way of a compassionate gesture that takes seriously the suffering humanity of Christ and is in Morrissey's lyric accompanied by what seems to be an unironic sense of dereliction ('but Jesus hurt me / when He deserted me'), which implies a prior and latent state of relation.[33]

There are a number of other factors in Morrissey's case that need to be weighed against the appearance of blasphemy. In the first place, we should notice that the singer is doing exactly what from a Judeo-Christian point of view one is supposed to do—namely, turning towards and unveiling all one's cares before God in prayer—a term it would surely be uncharitable to refuse for a passionate utterance addressed to the divine, from whom its speaker seeks understanding, and whom its speaker sees as the source of his being. (At the centre of the song, there is an unscripted beseeching cry of 'oh pretty one,' which seems to be addressed to Christ—who else could it be?—and which corroborates the earlier sense of an underlying or latent state of relation.) Furthermore, there is an odd sort of orthodoxy to Morrissey's utterance, which employs carefully capitalized third-person pronouns in its references to the divine: partly in his deference to God the Father—whom he seems properly to distinguish from God the Son, and whose intercession he is aware of needing ('with God's help');[34] and partly in the fact that his blasphemous act—if

---

32. 'Gegriffen schon, Herr, / ineinander verkrallt, als wär / der Leib eines jeden von uns / dein Leib, Herr.'

33. Morrissey's song may owe something to Patti Smith's 'Gloria (In Excelsus Deo),' which Morrissey claims changed his life (*Blitz*, April 1988). Smith's song begins with an apparently blasphemous gesture—'Jesus died for somebody's sins but not mine'—and a defiant romantic attachment to her transgressions, which constitute part of her: 'my sins my own / They belong to me.' As in 'Dear God Please Help Me,' it is sexuality—and in both cases possibly same-sex relations—that provokes the turn towards the divine, and in both songs the speaker seems audaciously to question the reach of Christ's redemption of human nature.

34. Morrissey's line exchanges the roles traditionally attributed to Father and Son, respecting intercession.

blasphemy it is—strangely preserves even as it parodies in chiastically reversing the roles of the those parties involved in the orthodox conception of forgiveness. We might additionally note that Morrissey's wrongdoing—if wrongdoing it is—is also complicated by the fact that forgiveness is an act of piety, even if it is wrong from an orthodox perspective to suggest that Christ did anything that required forgiveness. This last point helps us to see why it is so hard to decide whether the song is blasphemous or not, for the problem—if problem it is—is that Morrissey is behaving *like* Christ *towards* Christ (and surely it isn't a coincidence that it is on Friday—after the 'stations' of humiliation, suffocation and condescension—that life is said to kill him?).[35] The singer is thus doing at once and inextricably what according to Christianity he should and should not be doing (and insofar as he expects his listeners to pick up on the apparent allusion to Good Friday, he seems to encourage his audience to collude with Christianity understood from within).

This leaves us with a number of interpretative possibilities. The whole thing could of course be a casual use of a narrative he knows but doesn't believe in, invoked as a novel way of exploring his usual concerns. The problem with this reading, however, is that the singer doesn't sound very casual, and as we have seen, the Christian story haunts his work—as it does that of his hero Oscar Wilde—in a way that suggests it is more than just another narrative option.[36] (We might also note that there is no sign of irony or casualness in the video, in which the singer—dressed as a priest and wearing a crucifix—calls out to God and makes the sign of the cross with apparently anguished earnestness.) A second possibility is that it is in fact blasphemy—that his utterance makes a mockery of the divine and sets him decisively *against* the religious. Though this reading too is troubled by the prayerlike character of the utterance and its

---

35. There is possibly another allusion to Christ—and the sacred heart—earlier on in the song where Morrissey sings, 'I carried my heart in my hand.'

36. For too long, Wilde's eleventh hour conversion to Catholicism was dismissed as the product of an unhinged mind or as one last aesthetic act, a view which is unsupported by the account of his ministering priest, Father Cuthbert Dunne, C.P., and ignores the evidence of a lifetime's fascination—if not flirtation—with the Catholic faith. As his close friend and contemporary at Magdalen W. W. Ward explains, 'His final decision to find refuge in the Roman Church was not the sudden clutch of the drowning man at the plank in the shipwreck, but a return to a first love, a love rejected, it is true, or at least rejected in the tragic progress of his self-realization, yet one that had haunted him from early days with a persistent spell' (cited in Holland, *Son of Oscar Wilde*, pp. 251–2). For a reassessment of Wilde's relation to religion, see Jarlath Killeen, *The Faiths of Oscar Wilde: Catholicism, Folklore and Ireland*; Mark Knight and Emma Mason, 'Taking Catholicism Seriously,' in *Nineteenth-Century Religion and Literature*; and O'Malley, 'Religion,' in *Palgrave Advances in Oscar Wilde Studies*.

orthodox gestures as well as the peculiar way as an act of piety it benignly subverts its own hostility. It is also, finally, worth bearing in mindwhat the singer doesn't call into question—namely: (i) that he was made by God; (ii) that God might be addressed in spite of his apparent absence; (iii) that the love he feels was given by God; (iv) that desire is a theological issue; (v) that God might have a plan for us ('why did you give me so much love . . . '); (vi) that God might care about our actions ('Forgive me any pain / I may have brung to you'); oh, and (vii) that there *is* a God.

To be sure, this doesn't do away with the charge of blasphemy. But if, as T. S. Eliot argued, 'Genuine blasphemy, genuine in spirit and not purely verbal, is the product of partial belief, and is as impossible to the complete atheist as to the perfect Christian,'[37] blasphemy would paradoxically turn out to be a sign of religious orientation. Of course, no one would contend that Morrissey is a 'perfect Christian,' if indeed such a thing is possible. Yet it is surely falling off the horse on the other side to see him as 'a complete atheist.'[38] Obvious as this may appear in the light of the assembled evidence, Morrissey's religious orientation remains something of a taboo subject in commentary on the singer—a thought that critics of this most disturbing author are not prepared to think. Simpson and Rogan, for example, both seem dogmatically to presuppose that faith is not a rational possibility, and so in spite of the evidence to the contrary take for granted that Morrissey does not believe in God—even in some incipient, conflicted or residual way.[39]

Returning to Eliot's illuminating comment, we might see blasphemy as a desperate or inchoate modality of faith—a complaining about that is also a turning towards. (It will be recalled that in the Bible even the experience of anger and despair or the sense of dereliction have to do with God.) Thomas Hardy—that arch sceptic, who was so sceptical he couldn't entirely believe in his scepticism—has a comment about the need for a kind of 'via negativa' which may be helpful here. In 'In Tenebris II,' the second of his triptych of poems on darkness, he insists 'if way to the Better there be, it exacts a full look at the Worst.' Hardy's utterance implies in the subjunctive positing of its if-clause that he speaks, like Morrissey, from within darkness

---

37. Eliot, 'Baudelaire,' in *Selected Essays*, p. 421.

38. When asked 'Do you believe in God?' the singer replied 'I try to' (*Q*, January 1995).

39. This is especially regrettable in the case of Mark Simpson's *Saint Morrissey*, since its author repeatedly invokes religious subjects without ever really taking them seriously on their own terms or showing any inquisitiveness about how seriously Morrissey takes such issues.

(and in contrast to Wordsworth, who speaks from the other side, of 'gracious openings' that lie *through* that darkness). But it insists as well that an unflinching confrontation of this is a necessary preamble to any light that may lie beyond it, and in doing so—without letting go of its hypothetical status—he identifies darkness as a step *on the way* to the light.[40] Moreover, in referring to the darkness within which he speaks as 'Tenebris'—as we have seen Wilde and Celan do—Hardy tacitly situates this darkness within a larger religious narrative, even if the moment of darkness remains unpierced by what he posits beyond it.[41] This attempt to affirm or remain open to the possibility of something that is nonetheless lost to him is a characteristic gesture in Hardy's writing. One of the most evocative examples of which is to be found in 'The Darkling Thrush.' Here is the concluding stanza:

> So little cause for carolings
> Of such ecstatic sound
> Was written on terrestrial things
> Afar or nigh around,
> That I could think there trembled through
> His happy good-night air
> Some blessed Hope, whereof he knew
> And I was unaware.

Morrissey of course doesn't have a song bearing the title 'Tenebrae.' However, in 'Yes, I Am Blind,' which obviously announces a benighted perspective, we find a subtle negative positing of the existence of a light outside the darkness encompassing the speaker, which parallels the logic of Hardy's Tenebrae poems ('Yes, I am blind / no I can't see / the good things / just the bad things . . . there must be something / horribly wrong with me?').[42] We find something similar in 'I Know It's Over,' where the speaker is sinking ever deeper

---

40. In *De Profundis*, Wilde even more confidently claims 'where there is sorrow there is holy ground' (p. 143).

41. At the end of 'In Tenebris I,' Hardy's speaker claims to wait in 'unhope.' Yet the apparent absolutism of this powerful coinage is relativized by the poem's title and the epigraph from Psalm 102 ('My heart is smitten and withered like grass'), which once again locates this darkness within a larger religious space.

42. Hardy reaches the same conclusion in 'In Tenebris II,' whose epigraph is taken from Psalm 142 ('I looked on my right hand, and beheld, but there was no man that would know me; . . . no man cared for my soul'):

> When the clouds' swoln bosoms echo back the shouts of the many and strong
> That things are all as they best may be, save a few to be right ere long,
> And my eyes have not the vision in them to discern what to these is so clear,
> The blot seems straightway in me alone; one better he were not here.

into excoriating darkness ('Oh Mother, I can feel the soil falling over my head') and is forced—through the torturous journey of the narrative—to accept that love is not 'for such as [him],' *and yet* he insistently affirms its reality (and in doing so brings it into being):

> love is Natural and Real
> but not for you, my love
> not tonight, my love
> love is Natural and Real
> but not for such as you and I, my love.

At the close of George Steiner's brilliant *Real Presences*, the author turns to the subject of Tenebrae. 'There is one particular day in Western history,' he writes, 'about which neither historical record nor myth nor Scripture make report.'[43] This is the dark Saturday between the day of crucifixion (Friday) and the day of resurrection (Sunday). It has become, he says, 'the longest of days.'[44] In speaking from a perspective after the Friday on which life has killed him, Morrissey, like Hardy, seems to identify the darkness in which he stands as the Tenebrae of the 'long Saturday.'

II

THE ULTIMATE SCANDAL

In his thoughtful chapter on Oscar Wilde and religion, Patrick R. O'Malley observes:

> In a life still more famous for its scandals than for its works, Wilde's deepest scandal—as perhaps it has ever been—is the scandal of the Cross. Indeed, Wilde's obsession with religion throughout his life reminds us that by far the earliest uses of the English word 'scandal' refer to religion rather than sexuality. . . . Wilde's scandalous religious yearnings are both: they challenge religious orthodoxy even as they serve as a stumbling-block to those who would read Wilde as the prophet of a gleefully atheistic queerness.[45]

Something similar could and should be said about Morrissey. For perhaps even more so than in the case of his hero Wilde, Morrissey's

---

43. Steiner, *Real Presences*, p. 231.
44. Ibid.
45. O'Malley, 'Religion,' p. 167.

'scandalous religious yearnings' have been ignored or domesticated in commentary on the singer. And yet, if, as the singer claims, everything he has written is in some sense a result of his Catholic upbringing, we would expect there to be some kind of underlying religious basis to his writing—that goes deeper than the references we have considered so far—which unites and helps to explain his central concerns. That such an underlying influence exists will be the contention of this second section.

HOLY FOLLY

In the opening paragraphs of *De Profundis*—which takes its title from the first line of Psalm 130—Wilde explains to its addressee, Lord Alfred Douglas, that it was 'according to the wisdom of this world' that the author sought to help him, and a few lines later he enjoins Douglas to 'remember that the fool to the eyes of the gods and the fool to the eyes of man are very different.'[46] In saying these things, Wilde is implicitly alluding to St. Paul's letters to the Corinthians and making the first of several attempts in the text to compare himself to Christ.[47]

In chapter 1, it was suggested that at the centre of Morrissey's art is a radical awkwardness or an embarrassing not-fitting-in, which encompassed his appearance, his singing style, his lyrics and his 'scandalous' asceticism. The singer, we might say, was making himself 'foolish' as a way of protesting against 'the wisdom of the world.'[48] Morrissey's witting foolishness, like the foolishness of which Wilde speaks in *De Profundis*, has a religious model behind it. And the singer is evidently aware of this:

---

46. Wilde, *De Profundis and Other Writings*, p. 98.
47. St Paul writes: 'hath not God made foolish the wisdom of this world? . . . Because the foolishness of God is wiser than men; and the weakness of God is stronger than men. . . . But God hath chosen the foolish things of the world to confound the wise; and God hath chosen the weak things of the world to confound the things which are mighty' (1 Corinthians 1:18–27).
48. It will be recalled that in the 1980s Morrissey was frequently characterized—and valued—as an 'idiot.' Here is David Stubbs's assessment: 'It's tempting to say we don't need Morrissey anymore, that his ghostly grey presence in the relentlessly gaudy pop terrain has faded as it has persisted. But Morrissey is needed, not as an ombudsman, or a figure of the Eighties but as a horrified figure against the Eighties, who has turned his back on the march of pop time as the last keeper of the sanctuary of self-pity, apartness, exile . . . . And *Viva Hate* is . . . another great album by our last star, our last idiot' (*Melody Maker*, March 19, 1988).

Interviewer: Another thing I've heard is, um, you lead a saintly life.
Morrissey: Yes . . .
Interviewer: Um, could you, sort of, explain a bit more about that?
Morrissey: Well, it's really . . . I'm just simply inches away from a
    monastery and I feel that perhaps if I wasn't doing this, that I
    probably would be in one.[49]

In what sense precisely does Morrissey's persona resonate with a religious model? What might it mean to be a pop star and yet 'inches
away from a monastery'?

In stepping outside society's norms, and in attempting to expose
the folly of the world's ways by being embarrassingly otherwise, Morrissey resembles a traditional and subversive but now largely forgotten figure: the holy fool. Given the distance of such a figure from our
contemporary situation, it will be helpful to remind ourselves of this
'embarrassing' tradition.

Daring to take seriously St Paul's teaching that the wisdom of
God is foolishness in the eyes of the world, the holy fool is 'a clown
for Christ's sake,' who is 'in a society yet not of it.' He is 'a nomad,
who never settles anywhere in the present world but wanders.' He
is ascetic, since this helps 'to resist the lure of worldly respect and
honour' and involves an 'emancipation of the senses, whereby man
ceases to be an automaton, a victim of compulsive behaviour, pulled
now this way, now that, by his passions and instincts, and attains
a sovereign freedom in his relations with others, refusing to regard
them as objects of possession, exploitation, and domination.' By
means of this 'sage-folly' and 'monastic marginality,' the holy fool
attempts 'to shock the people into perceiving the truth of their situation' and demonstrates 'solidarity with the outcasts of society.' He is
not content with 'social work' but 'identifies himself completely with
the wretched of the earth' and 'glories in infirmities.'[50] In showing
solidarity with the marginalized—the pauper, the idiot, the weak and

---

49. *Picture Disc* (Red Door Records, 1983) (*http://www.compsoc.man.ac.uk/~moz/quotes/quotesin.htm*).
50. The last phrase in quotation marks is taken from St Paul's letter to the Corinthians: 'Of such
an one will I glory: yet of myself I will not glory, but in mine infirmities. . . . And lest I should
be exalted above measure through the abundance of the revelations, there was given to me a
thorn in the flesh, the messenger of Satan to buffet me, lest I should be exalted above measure. . . . And he said unto me, My grace is sufficient for thee: for my strength is made perfect in
weakness. Therefore I take pleasure in infirmities, in reproaches, in necessities, in persecutions,
in distresses for Christ's sake: for when I am weak, then am I strong. I am become a fool in
glorying' (2 Corinthians 12:5–11).

the infirm—the monk 'does more than idealize the outcasts: he discovers a special relationship with them, with all those on the margin, all excluded from the centre of life, activity, and power. The monk voluntarily goes to the margin in order to realize a closer relationship with other "marginals," and also, indeed, with those at the centre; he withdraws from all men to be more closely united to all men.' Thus, 'while he flees human society, his influence . . . is ultimately beneficial to the community.'[51]

Morrissey of course is not a monk, and it would be ludicrous to ignore the obvious ways in which his lifestyle, insofar as it's available for scrutiny, differs from that of a religious. He is a wealthy celebrity; he is fiercely independent; he is vehemently opposed to institutions, systems and that which is established; and even his religious views are difficult to ascertain. Nevertheless, in a number of respects that have an implicit coherence and have remained largely constant, Morrissey's avowed lifestyle and views resemble those of the 'holy fool'—to such a degree that, as we have seen, it is commonplace for journalists to describe him as 'monastic.' This is genuinely extraordinary. Whatever one's views on matters of taste, it has to be acknowledged that carrying elements of monasticism over into the world of popular music—at a time when hedonism was celebrated *über alles* and in a way that transformed the context into which these elements were introduced instead of vice versa—is an extraordinary achievement. The details of this surprising resemblance are worth laying out explicitly.

Like the holy fool, Morrissey may in a sense be described as 'in a society yet not of it.' He was, in Paul Morley's words, 'watching from the inside but on the outside of everything.'[52] And as Mark Simpson has pointed out, The Smiths 'were relentlessly opposed to the world.'[53] This was most apparent in Morrissey's keeping himself outside sexual relations, which obviously set him physically apart, but also allowed him to transcend the categories of particular orientation. The same may be said about his courting of an 'anti-essentialist' androgyny—especially in his use of a 'borrowed voice' and his frequently genderless lyrics—which similarly enabled him to inhabit a position outside conventional categories. In tandem with

51. The foregoing unattributed quotations are taken from John Saward's study *Perfect Fools: Folly for Christ's Sake in Catholic and Orthodox Spirituality*, pp. 51; 17; 27; 29; 20; 80; 31; 1; 29; 77; and 41, respectively.
52. *Observer Music Monthly*, May 21, 2006.
53. Simpson, *Saint Morrissey*, p. 98.

these renunciations, the singer set himself apart from society—and gave visibility to a transgression of its values—with his notorious asceticism.[54] (In an article for *The Guardian*, entitled 'The Light That Never Goes Out,' Zoe Williams examined the visual impact of The Smiths, and commenting on Morrissey's extreme thinness, noted that this was prior to the contemporary cult of emaciation and belonged to a period when 'the rejection of food still counted as a synecdochic rejection of consumerism in general.'[55])

The singer's hermitic solitude and ceaseless wandering from place to place is manifestly a world away from the destitute wandering of the holy fool. Yet as we have seen, Morrissey has always sung about a radical homelessness—that amounts to an existential condition—and about being 'a traveller to the grave,' which points towards an underlying parallel in spite of this difference.[56] Likewise, the singer's aim in 'going to the margin'—both in terms of the lives he writes about and the advertisement of his own failure to fit in—seems on the one hand to be an attempt 'to shock the people into perceiving the truth of their situation' and on the other hand to show solidarity with the outcast. Morrissey's vociferous advocacy of animal rights is manifestly related to this and resembles the 'embarrassing' sympathy with other creatures exhibited by one of the most famous holy fools of all: St Francis of Assisi, the patron saint of animals and the environment.[57] Finally, there is a crucial correspondence between the holy fool's identification

---

54. Lacoste, 'Liturgy and Kenosis,' p. 250.

55. February 23, 2002. Needless to say, after living in LA for years, in a house designed for Clarke Gable—which, according to Michael Bracewell, had a huge crucifix above its living room mantelpiece—it's hard to maintain an antimaterialistic stance (although as we saw in the previous chapter, the singer complains from the other side of the fence about 'the squalor of the mind' that comes with a life of luxury). Nonetheless, this was a vital element in Morrissey's persona: 'There's something so positive about unemployment,' he once remarked. 'You don't get trapped into materialism, you won't buy things you don't really want' (*Sounds*, June 4, 1983). 'I've got no desire to possess anything at all. I can't fathom the idea of going to Madrid to shop. Which is why I'm not really successful as a pop star, if you like. . . . I don't really want to own anything at all. Not even a moped' (*Q*, August 1987).

56. In 'The Hand That Rocks The Cradle,' Morrissey alludes to 'The Pauper's Drive,' by Thomas Noel (1799–1861), and sings 'rattle my bones all over the stones / I'm only a beggar-man whom nobody owns'—a description he claims fits him 'like a glove.'

57. Wilde singles out St. Francis in *De Profundis* as the only Christian since Christ: 'God had given him at his birth the soul of a poet, as he himself when quite young had in mystical marriage taken poverty as his bride: and with the soul of a poet and the body of a beggar he found the way to perfection not difficult. He understood Christ, and so became like him. We do not need the Liber Conformitatum to teach us that the life of St. Francis was the true *Imitatio Christi*, a poem compared to which the book of life is merely prose' (Wilde, *De Profundis and Other Writings*, p. 179).

with the outcast and what I have referred to as Morrissey's 'art of weakness'—his iconic embodiment of vulnerability and his making himself weak to protest against the strong—which has behind it Paul's 'glorying in infirmity' and his 'scandalous' claim that 'my strength is made perfect in weakness' (2 Corinthians 12:9).[58] The clearest echo of the Apostle's 'foolish' inversion of values in the so-called 'Tearful Letter' occurs in 'I Know It's Over,' where Morrissey sings:

> It's easy to laugh
> it's easy to hate
> it takes strength to be gentle and kind

—a correlative of which is to be found in the singer's monograph *James Dean Is Not Dead*, where he praises the star for being 'strong enough to be gentle.'[59] (It was also noted in chapter 1 that Morrissey's use of flowers—which were certainly foolishness in the eyes of the world[60]—were part of a protest whose strength was its weakness.)

In all sorts of respects, then, in the eyes of the world Morrissey's behaviour is embarrassing and a matter of 'foolishness'—an impression that seems to be consciously accentuated by his 'motley' dress, his manic dance, his deranged and carnivalesque noises and in assuming 'the features of the mutilated human.' Such folly, however, as St Paul reminds us, is relative: just as the wisdom of God is foolishness to the world, the wisdom of the world is foolishness to God. So, whilst rejecting the ways and wisdom of the world from one point of view is an act of folly, from another point of view such weakness is strength and such foolishness is wisdom, and someone who 'deliberately chooses to be a fool in the eyes of the world becomes a sign to that world of the real madness of worshipping Mammon.'[61] In the words of Lacan, it is the nonfools who err.[62]

---

58. By including a hearing aid in his icon of the martyred Joan of Arc, the singer seems to be making fun of—by exaggerating—his sense of persecution, but at the same time to be according a religious significance to his own 'sacrificial' identification with the suffering of others.

59. Morrissey, *James Dean Is Not Dead*, p. 4.

60. 'People stop me in the street and say, "Where's your bush?" which is an embarrassing question at any time of the day' (*Jamming!*, December 1984).

61. Saward, *Perfect Fools*, p. 68.

62. Lacan, *Le Séminaire de Jacques Lacan, Livre XXI: Les non-dupes errant* (unpublished typescript).

EROS AND AGAPE

Don't mention love

There is something else in Morrissey's writing which resonates with a religious model, without which his other virtues are as sounding brass or a tinkling cymbal. It is something which surpasses all else, which abides throughout his writing and which he holds onto in spite of and even within darkness. It is something, we might say, that suffers long; that bears all things, believes all things, hopes all things and endures all things; something that—whilst all else shall pass away—never fails. This something is of course love.[63]

A likely objection arises immediately. At various points throughout the study, it has been suggested that the singer has recurrent and elaborate difficulties saying the word 'love.' How does this fit in with the contention that love is an all-surpassing value in his work? As Dr. Johnson remarked about a dog walking on its hind legs, the wonder isn't so much how, but *that* it does so. Before attempting to explain this apparent tension, it is therefore perhaps more important to affirm simply that it is the case. Here is the testimony of Danny Kelly, interviewing the singer in 1985:

> In all Morrissey's bleak urban mindscapes of isolation, disappointment, iron bridges, razor boys, illness and mistrust the one word that keeps blinking out is 'love.' Love as an adjective, a noun, a verb; love with a sigh, a groan, a sneer; love as sustenance, as torturer, as celebration and desecration. And yet there's this creature who claims—yawn—to sleep with no one (thus eschewing the notion that love equals the achievement of orgasm, rock's commonest definition), so what the hell is he on about? Has he ever *been* in love?

Morrissey: Do you mean actually experiencing relationships?

Kelly: No, not really, I mean the spiritual, mental delirium of being in love.

Morrissey: Not the physical thing?

> *Paranoia is not a pretty sight.*

Morrissey: Oh well, in that case I can easily answer. I am constantly in that state of desire and admiration for things, words.

---

63. When asked to pick five words that describe himself, Morrissey responded: 'Loving, lovable, lovely, lovelorn, loveless' (*Q*, January 1995).

Kelly: What's your conception of this thing called love?

Morrissey: It's very difficult to put into words because for each individual it's something quite different. Being in love is something I would never claim to fully understand.

> *Now the Morrissey voice is low; these are answers rather than public notices, words from somewhere other than the tip of his tongue.*

Kelly: You seem to be talking about loving things rather than people.

Morrissey: Well it's largely things other than people that I do become in love with. I must say that I'm even more bored than you, bored to nausea, with the word 'celibacy.' But I do think it's actually possible to go through life and never fall in love or find someone who loves you.

Kelly: You look and sound unbearably sad when you say that. Do you find a lack of human love a problem?

Morrissey: I *do*, but this word 'love'—*the head shakes slowly from side to side*—people can quite easily say that they love marmalade or they love mushrooms or they 'love' people.

Kelly: Oh come on, that's clutching at evasive straws. Don't you wish you loved people, and that people loved you?

> *The famous bogbrush haircut tilts back, his eyes fix a spot on the ceiling.*

Morrissey: Yes, yes I do.

Kelly: Do you think you'd be happier, more content, then?

Morrissey: Well yes. I'm convinced that once it happens, if indeed it ever does, there will be a tremendous turnabout in my life and that's captivating and riveting to me. I'm waiting for it to happen.[64]

Love, with a sigh, a groan, a sneer—but blinking out through everything is love. The difficulty Morrissey has in saying the word, on the evidence of this interview, seems partly to be a linguistic wincing ('Ooh but don't mention love / I'd hate the strain of the pain again') which recalls the dramatic failure of speech in 'Will Never Marry.'[65]

---

64. *NME*, June 8, 1985.

65. In contrast to the all too witting inability of Willy Wonka to say the word 'parents' in Tim Burton's facile 'darkening' of the character, Morrissey's lyrical difficulties with the word 'love' are expressive because they are *not* consistent.

But it is evidently also in part a response to the word's devaluation—and even here, in interview, he starts shaking his head as soon as he's said the word.[66] Rather than constituting some kind of tension, then, the difficulties the singer has saying the word 'love' would seem to be a *sign* of its all-surpassing importance, and his stammering, travestying and quotation-marked usage appears to be an attempt to *redeem* its value, by gesturing towards the corruption of its signifier ('as Barbara Cartland would say . . . ').[67]

Philip Larkin has a poem on a related subject called 'Love Songs in Age,' in which a widow comes across the songbooks of her youth and re-encounters the promises they make about love from the other side of experience:

> The glare of that much-mentioned brilliance, love,
>   Broke out, to show
> Its bright incipience sailing above,
> Still promising to solve, and satisfy,
> And set unchangeably in order. So
>   To pile them back, to cry,
> Was hard, without lamely admitting how
> It had not done so then, and could not now.

The experience of disappointment, 'then' and 'now,' for the character in Larkin's poem, results in a lame disillusionment concerning love. What is remarkable in Morrissey's lyrics, by contrast, is that the singer's 'faith' in 'that much-mentioned brilliance, love' remains constant *in spite of* its corruption and perpetual failure to come into being ('I might walk home alone,' he sings in 'Rusholme Ruffians,' 'but my faith in love is still devout'). The singer's attitude—and the contrast with Larkin—is most clearly illustrated in 'Yes, I Am Blind':

> Love's young dream
> 10 I'm the one who shopped you

---

66. The Swedish band The Cardigans have a song about the problems of saying the word 'love' entitled 'For What It's Worth,' on *Long Gone Before Daylight*. It speaks of 'a four letter word [that] got stuck in my head / the dirtiest word that I've ever said,' and ends with a lovely pastiche of Morrissey's falsetto. (Nina Persson, the band's singer and lyric writer, has described Morrissey as 'the best lyricist in the pop world.')

67. In *A Lover's Discourse*, Roland Barthes speaks of 'love's obscenity'—by which he means the embarrassing sentimentality of the amorous subject—and quotes Thomas Mann as an illustration of this 'modern' view: 'The word did not seem to him to repay such frequent repetition. The slippery monosyllable, with its lingual and labial, and the bleating vowel between—it came to sound positively offensive; it suggested watered milk or anything else that was pale and insipid' (Barthes, *A Lover's Discourse*, p. 175).

I'm the one who stopped you
'cause in my sorry way I love you
Love's young dream
aren't you sorry
15 for what you've done?
well, you're not the only one
and in my sorry way I love you.

These lines are odder than they initially appear. The first two 'stages' in these parallel sections recall the movement from youthful dreaming to disillusionment traced in Larkin's poem. But there is an unexpected third stage in Morrissey's lyric, which comes after and in a sense *countermands* the discrediting of 'Love's young dream,' since the surprising reason he gives for 'shopping' it is ''cause in my sorry way I love you.' The song thus suggests that the singer discredits and yet is nonetheless committed to 'Love's young dream.' (The paradox of this is sharpened the second time around, where the 'sorry' of line seventeen takes on the colouring of the preceding use in line fourteen, and subtly shifts in meaning from something like 'shameful' to something more like 'regretful.') In Morrissey's lyric, then—and this would seem to be generally the case—the dream somehow survives its exposure *as* a dream. This is explained—and one further twist is added—by the song's refrain, 'Yes, I am blind / no, I can't see / the good things / just the bad things,' which as we saw earlier, negatively posits the existence of a Good *in spite of* its being lost to the speaker, and in doing so it turns the tables on its own scepticism; for in attributing his pessimism to a failure of perception, he holds open the possibility that 'Love's young dream' might in fact be a reality.

Infinite desire

With the possible exception of the lighthearted refrain 'my faith in love is still devout,' love in Morrissey's lyrics has no explicit religious connotations. It is nonetheless the superlative name of God and does in its singular endurance and elevation appear to have something of a transcendent character. It is also worth adding that it is a puritanical secularism and *not* an orthodox Augustinian or Thomistic Christianity that sets eros over against agape.[68] Yet perhaps the most interesting

---

68. Whilst it's true that Christianity has a lingering reputation for censuring or being squeamish about eros, and whilst certain Christian theologians—such as Anders Nygren—have attempted to set enmity between eros and agape, there is a rich and powerful Christian tradition with a biblical

thing about love in Morrissey's lyrics, and what seems to bring it closest to a theological understanding of that preeminent virtue, is what might paradoxically seem to distance it from the religious, and that is the pain of infinite desire it involves. Indeed, Morrissey himself seems to see this as an argument against the divine, as witnessed by the climactic burden of 'I Have Forgiven Jesus' ('why did you give me / so much desire? / when there is nowhere I can go / to offload this desire?'). The funny thing about this complaint, however, is that it is in fact three-quarters of an orthodox theological argument.

In the previous chapter, we considered the melancholy fate of desire in Morrissey's lyrics, in which paradoxically a goal once reached retreats anew or else preserves its distance in spite of the subject's continual approach. From this it was concluded, in the light of Žižek's persuasive reading, that desire secretly seeks its own perpetuation in whispering of an ever offstage satisfaction. Yet to claim that desire radically exceeds its possible objects and survives its own satisfaction is not merely the nightmare of libidinal desire as construed by Lacanian psychoanalysis, it is also a *theological* reading of desire.

According to Augustine and Gregory of Nyssa, for example, following the argument of Plato's *Symposium*, the excessive and self-perpetuating character of desire is supposed to teach us—in giving us a taste of that which ultimately eludes us—the inability of any finite thing exhaustively to satisfy our desire, which in turn is supposed to lead us towards the divine by leading us to realise that only an infinite object—though object it isn't—can satisfy an infinite desire: 'Our hearts are restless until they rest in you,' as Augustine puts it at the start of *Confessions*.[69] Morrissey thus concurs with a theological reading of desire when he complains 'why did you give me / so much love / in a loveless world / when there is no one I can turn to / to unlock all this love'—no one, that is, except the person he turns to in saying that he has no one to whom he can turn.

---

foundation—that includes Dionysius the Areopagite, Gregory of Nyssa, Hans Urs von Balthasar, and was forcefully affirmed in the recent encyclical *Deus Caritas Est*—which holds to the contrary that eros and agape are intimately entwined, and that the former incites *religious* activity, and may carry us towards as well as away from the divine.

69. Morrissey's excessive saying of 'never' ('excessive' since its repetition adds nothing to 'not ever') might be seen as a corollary of infinite desire—and the obverse of the difficulties he has with the word 'love.' Speaking of 'a negative image of transcendence' in his fine study of tragedy, Terry Eagleton observes that in 'weighing how drastic things are with us, we take the measure of their potential remedy.' In this sense, Morrissey's infinite lack may be seen as 'a negative image of transcendence' (Eagleton, *Sweet Violence*, p. 60).

Melancholy ecstasy

This ambivalent turn towards the divine—which seems to involve a simultaneous holding onto the self—is also apparent in 'Dear God Please Help Me' on *Ringleader of the Tormentors*. Here too it is the exigency of desire that prompts it, but in this case it seems to be less hostile and more coy:

> I am walking through Rome
> with my heart on a string
> dear God please help me
>
> . . .
>
> Will you follow and know
> me more than you do
> track me down
> and try to win me?
>
> Then he motions to me
> with his hand on my knee
> dear God, did this kind of thing happen to you?
>
> . . .
>
> And now I am walking through Rome
> and there is no room to move
> but the heart feels free
> the heart feels free . . .

The opening image depicts the singer, walking through Rome, bizarrely with his heart 'on a string.' Whilst it's hard to say what exactly the image betokens, he seems to be imagining his heart as something outside himself—with a 'will' of its own or at least as a semiautonomous subject—as if it were a balloon or, more likely, a dog he was taking for a walk. What are we to make of this?

The song's wonderfully impressionistic image appears to make more sense when we recall that ecstasy, literally, means 'standing outside oneself,' and is a kind of erotic exodus or 'overflow' in which we are drawn away from ourselves and towards the other. This para-doxical sense of escaping oneself—in spite of our self-enclosure—would seem to fit in with the final refrain 'there is no room to move / but the heart feels free.' As we all know, taking a dog for a walk is a matter of being taken as well, and in this respect too the image corresponds to the dynamics of ecstatic experience, which is conventionally described as a matter of being rapt or ravished—that is, seized or snatched away.

The plot thickens when we further recall that ecstasy is a traditional religious discourse, in which eros and agape are benevolently confused,[70] and which refers—in the Christian tradition—to God's 'erotic' stepping 'outside' himself in his love for creation and the answering ecstasy of the created.[71] Such accounts of course in their idiom but also in the confidence of their faith are clearly a long way removed from Morrissey's lyric. However, in 'Dear God Please Help Me,' the singer's ecstasy—which has a complicating melancholy hue—is manifestly presented as a *theological* matter. Moreover, the sense of being ecstatically drawn outside oneself in Morrissey's lyric is an experience in which the lure of the divine and the worldly are *both* involved and are hard to tell apart. (The singer sounds as if he is speaking aside to a jealous lover—or trying to provoke jealousy—when he says to God, whilst his inamorato has a hand on his knee, 'did this kind of thing happen to you?[72]) Johnny Rogan goes even further and claims that 'the lyrical interpretation hinges upon a fascinatingly ambiguous third verse in which the narrator addresses either God or alternatively a mortal suitor to track him down and win his heart.'[73] I'm not sure how convincing this is—since the subsequent 'Then he' suggests a continuity of subject, in spite of the shift in pronouns, and in the latter utterance this is clearly revealed to be his worldly suitor. Nevertheless, Rogan's point reflects the general situation in the song—which is appropriately set in 'the eternal city'—in which the divine and the worldly both exert an erotic lure, and the singer's ecstatically adventuring heart appears to waver between them.

---

70. In the words of Gregory of Nyssa, 'Love [Agape] that is strained to intensity is called desire [Eros] (Gregory of Nyssa, *From Glory to Glory*, p. 44).

71. We can discern a benevolent slippage between eros and agape in Morrissey's most powerful defence of love: 'Love is natural and real, / but not for such as you and I, my love' ('I Know It's Over'). Formally, the lines constitute a chiasmus, in returning to where they began in 'love.' Yet the love of which they initially speak appears to be aligned with the erotic lack of the earlier verses, whereas the love with which the lines conclude is tendered in the direction of the anonymous listener and seems to be more akin to agape.

72. It is, to be sure, an old and not necessarily irreverent question to ask about the ways in which Christ participated in human experience. Yet, as in 'I Have Forgiven Jesus,' Morrissey's question has a cheekiness that nudges it in the direction of blasphemy.

73. Rogan, *Morrissey*, p. 297.

This reading, if viable, suggests a further explanation of the song's intriguing melancholy hue (and surely only Morrissey is capable of experiencing melancholy ecstasy); for the very event that sets his heart 'free' and carries him ecstatically away from himself leaves him suspended in a space which is as unresolved as the self he left behind. What's more, the separation of 'the heart' from the speaking self—which seems to allow the former feelings of its own and underwrites the sense of self-transcendence—divides the focalization of the narrative between the discreetly experiencing subjectivities, which keeps that which is left behind in view. The song thus complicatedly presents us with an image of the singer holding onto himself in observing himself escaping himself. And it is this impression of a holding on within a letting go that perhaps most accurately characterizes his ambivalent religious orientation.

The unlovable

Love in Morrissey's lyrics isn't solely a matter of eros—even if it is this that attracts the most attention. There is another kind of love of which he recurrently sings, which is less likely to make the headlines of the *NME*—but which is in fact even more subversive—and which resembles the preeminent Christian virtue agape. Plainly, such love is never cast in explicitly religious terms, and the singer is far from optimistic about its chances of prevailing this side of the hereafter: 'Love, peace and harmony? / very nice, very nice, very nice / . . . but maybe in the next world.'[74] Furthermore, such love in Morrissey's lyrics is obscured by—even though it is to some extent manifest in—his fascination with seediness, criminality and violence. Nevertheless, the radically unsqueamish charity that is evinced in his lyrics is arguably Christian in all but name. What is particularly striking—and particularly Christian—about this is its orientation towards the unloved or 'unlovable.'

There are two ways in which such charity is promoted in Morrissey's lyrics. Firstly, it is encouraged in a more abstract way, as a general principle ('It's so easy to laugh / it's so easy to hate / it takes strength to be gentle and kind'[75]), by keeping in view 'people who

---

74. 'Death Of A Disco Dancer.'
75. Tony Parsons once remarked that someone capable of writing these lines 'can only be on the side of the angels' (*Vox*, April 1993).

are weaker than you and I,'[76] or by insisting upon a common humanity, which no 'deviation' can put one outside of ('There is no such
thing in life as normal'; 'he's *not* strange / he just wants to live his
life this way'; 'still I maintain there's nothing / wrong with you').[77]
Secondly, it is promoted by speaking from within—and encouraging the listener imaginatively to inhabit—a range of 'semi-perilous
lives.'[78] By means of this characteristic aesthetic strategy, there seems
to be in Morrissey's lyrics an attempt to extend our sympathies—
alongside the play and the determination to document faithfully
how things are, however frightening, senseless or offensive this may
be—not just for 'easy' and obviously deserving cases, but for those
whom it is *really* hard to love, such as the hooligan, the thief and the
murderer—those, that is, whom Christ came to save and dared us to
love.[79] (Morrissey seems to be doing something similar in urging us
to care about nonhuman creatures by way of an anthropomorphic
imagining of their existence.[80] One is reminded again in this connection of St. Francis of Assisi, who spoke of and related to nonhuman
creatures as 'brother' and 'sister.') Let us consider an example of this
attempt to extend our sympathies.

Hidden away on the B-side of 'Dagenham Dave,' as if to under-
line the neglect of its protagonists, is a song called 'Nobody Loves
Us,' which deserves much more recognition than it has received.[81]
The first verse and chorus run as follows:

Nine times fined
never mind
things can only improve

---

76. 'A Rush And A Push And The Land Is Ours.'

77. As we saw earlier, this all-inclusive embrace of the human is given a *theological* underpinning,
as the singer seeks out and stands in 'eccentric' perspectives, and then insists in their name that he
is 'a sacred one' and 'a living sign.'

78. 'Maladjusted.'

79. Such imaginative sympathy is the preeminent characteristic of the romantic humanist Christ
of *De Profundis*: 'He realised in the entire sphere of human relations that imaginative sympathy
which in the sphere of Art is the sole secret of creation. He understood the leprosy of the leper,
the darkness of the blind, the fierce misery of those who live for pleasure, the strange poverty of
the rich. . . . With a width and wonder of imagination that fills one almost with awe, he took
the entire world of the inarticulate, the voiceless world of pain, as his kingdom, and made of
himself its eternal mouthpiece. Those of whom I have spoken, who are dumb under oppression,
and "whose silence is heard only of God," he chose as his brothers. He sought to become eyes to
the blind, ears to the deaf, and a cry in the lips of those whose tongues had been tied. His desire
was to be to the myriads who had found no utterance a very trumpet through which they might
call to heaven' (Wilde, *De Profundis and Other Writings*, pp. 165; and 171).

80. See 'Meat Is Murder.'

81. The song is included on the compilation *My Early Burglary Years*.

we are just stood here
waiting for the next great wound
and we just can't wait to make more mistakes
and to fluff our breaks, and to stuff our faces with cake
All in all, imagine this:
Nobody loves us
dab-hands at Trouble
with four days of stubble, we are
never loosen the grip on our hand
call us home
kiss our cheeks
nobody loves us
So we tend to please ourselves.

The song speaks from within an unnamed collective perspective of 'useless,' 'shiftless' 'trouble-makers,' and for three verses with discreetly varying choruses, attempts to do little more than awaken our sympathies for—by characterizing—its protagonists. The joys of the song come from the sheer inventiveness of its dancing on the spot and the infectious affection it bespeaks for its subjects.

Crucial to the song's awakening of our sympathy is its benign adulteration of the speaking perspective. We have seen something of this already, for example, in 'We'll Let You Know' and 'Vicar In A Tutu,' where the character's voice is laced with the irony of an exterior perspective. In 'Nobody Loves Us,' the singer expertly balances an ironizing of negative and uncaring attitudes towards the protagonists ('and we just can't stress / how more of a mess / and complete distress / won't make much difference to us') with a wonderful childlike envisioning of their interior perspective ('kiss our cheeks'; 'hug us hard'; 'make us our favourite jam'). The call on the listener's imaginative sympathy is reinforced by explicit injunction ('imagine this') and, more persuasively, by the singer's inclusion of himself within the 'us' of the unloved protagonists, not merely as a kind of holidaying consciousness ventriloquizing their perspective, but—if we recall his earlier 'Unloveable,' on *The World Won't Listen*—as actually comprising one of their number. We are also, finally, called upon to extend our sympathies to the song's protagonists by the subtle but salutary sting in its tail:

Useless and shiftless and jobless
But we're all yours.

The concluding 'yours' is double-edged, for whilst it draws a disarming innocent resonance from the childlike idiom with which it is continuous, it at the same time carries a more challenging claim of kinship—'we are of your kind'—that appeals in a different register to our sense of charity. (This last appeal is figuratively reflected and hence bolstered by the song's melody, which stops short of a return to its root of A major, which is anticipated but suspended by the final E seven that awaits resolution.)

'Nobody Loves Us' is especially effective in awakening the charitable affection it bespeaks towards its 'unloved' protagonists, but its procedures are characteristic of Morrissey's practice and exemplify the recurrent attempt throughout his writing to lure our sympathies into territories we may naturally shy away from.[82] In view, then, of the way in which he is oriented towards the divine by his 'infinite longing'—and it's clear from 'I Have Forgiven Jesus' and 'Dear God Please Help Me' that the crisis of desire in Morrissey's writing is presented as a theological problem—and in view of the 'agapeistic' tendencies in his imagining of the unlovable, it may be argued—reversing Blake's famous comment about Milton—that the singer is of God's party without apparently knowing it.

HOPEFUL DARKNESS

Hope against hope

In the last section, we compared the no-saying of Morrissey and Larkin on the subject of love. What this comparison between the two poets of deprivation surprisingly revealed is that, in spite of love's failure 'to solve, and satisfy,' in spite of its failure even to arrive, and in spite of the singer's inability to believe in it, there somehow remains in Morrissey's writing an element of hope—a residual, submerged or benighted hope; a hope perhaps that there may be hope; but nonetheless, an element of hope.[83] The singer's predicament puts one in mind of a story concerning Beckett's television play *Ghost Trio*, which involves the

---

82. Whilst I think it's possible to refute the unthinkingly recited accusations of racism by showing that the evidence doesn't support them, one might also more positively point towards a body of counterevidence—such as the singer's imaginative sympathy with the marginalized other, his corollary complaint that the president of America is never 'black, female or gay,' and the inclusive incitements to charity in his work—which brings to light his consistent defence of difference.

83. Larkin doesn't have a Tenebrae poem—a poem, that is, of darkness, outside of which is light; in fact he has the opposite: a nihilistic ironic Aubade—a poem of dawning light, outside of which is darkness.

famously baffling stage direction about a door which is 'imperceptibly ajar.' On finding the set designer agonizing over how to stage its
precise degree of openness, the author apparently remarked: 'If the
door is "imperceptibly ajar," it means it's shut.'[84] Morrissey's hope
would seem to be like Beckett's imperceptibly open door.

As we saw in 'I Know It's Over,' all hope is scrupulously taken
from the speaker by the cauterizing questioning of the self-tormenting
mind (as if to make doubly sure of the affair's nonexistence, we are
told 'it's over' *and* 'it never really began'); and yet the singer insists that
'love is Natural and Real.' As we discovered in 'Yes, I Am Blind,' the
singer is likewise wholly incapable of seeing 'the good things'; and yet
in saying so, he posits their existence outside the darkness in which he
stands. Such paradoxical hope that there may be hope is also played
out, to take one final example, in 'The Edges Are No Longer Parallel.'
In the first half of the song the singer resolutely maintains that 'there
is no law of averages here / if you feel down, then you're bound to stay
down,' and includes a verse in which he sings nothing but what sounds
like 'oh' and 'no.' (The lyrics, furthermore, allow a physical sense of
'bound' to emerge, so that if anything an *anti*law of averages appears
to operate, which recalls the sense of self-fuelling darkness in 'I Know
It's Over' and 'Last Night I Dreamt That Somebody Loved Me.') And
yet, in spite of this, the song breaks in the middle, and for the remaining two minutes Morrissey sings, over and over:

> My only mistake is I'm hoping
> I am hoping
> I keep hoping . . .

To be sure, the singer describes such hoping as a 'mistake.' But the
present continuous tense of the assertion ('I am hoping') pulls against
this judgement and shows that hope persists *in spite of* it.

Such benighted affirmations are a recurrent feature of Morrissey's
lyrics. What's more, these affirmations seem paradoxically to be
prompted by the very *extinction* of hope. This is the case in 'I Know
It's Over,' 'Yes, I Am Blind' and 'The Edges Are No Longer Parallel.'
It is even apparent in a song as tenaciously pessimistic as 'Life Is A
Pigsty'—which is *about* the endurance of the singer's pessimism—in

---

84. The story was related by the producer Tristram Powell in the programme *Shades*, broadcast
on April 17, 1977. I am grateful to Mark Nixon of the Beckett International Foundation for the
source of the anecdote.
85. There is an obvious analogy between Beckett's imperceptibly open door and the hopeful darkness of Tenebrae.

which we witness the emergence out of nowhere of an extraordinary final affirmation, like the overflow of something that hasn't first of all been full:

> I can't reach you anymore
> Can you please stop time?
> can you stop the pain?
> I feel too cold
> and now I feel too warm again
> can you stop this pain?
> even now, in the final hour of my life
> I'm falling in love again
> again
> again
> again . . .

Writing about the pessimism of Thomas Hardy, Philip Davis has eloquently observed that the author's no-saying is 'broken-heartedly loyal . . . to the human ideals and the religious needs it finds so utterly defeated.'[86] This is manifestly very close to Morrissey. But whilst hope, for Hardy, is a matter of anxiously calibrating ever-finer gradations of not quite giving up, for Morrissey hope is something that springs up almost miraculously—which is to say, unforeseen and 'excessively'—paradoxically after the loss of hope.[87]

No doubt, such a paradoxically 'hopeless' hope will seem hardly worth the name, and a long way from the vigorous hymn-singing hope traditionally associated with the religious. However, as John Caputo points out, 'Are not those bleak and hopeless times just when hope is required? Is not hope really hope only when things begin to look hopeless and it is mad to hope? Is that not when we need to brave the stormy waters of hope, undertake the risk of hope?'[88] Moreover, as Caputo goes on to argue, such 'hoping against hope' is precisely the nature of religious hope (the phrase in quotation marks is taken from Paul's letter to the Romans [4:18] and his description of the faith of Abraham):

---

86. Davis, *The Victorians*, p. 546.
87. This pattern of unforeseen and prodigal flourishing that comes about *after* all grounds for hope have gone corresponds to the 'hyperbolic' logic of the Bible's miracle narratives. One thinks, for example, of the wedding at Cana, the miraculous draught of fishes and the feeding of the five thousand (John 2; Luke 5; and Luke 9), where in each case what is given is radically in excess of what is needed.
88. Caputo, 'The Experience of God and the Axiology of the Impossible,' p. 134.

> Hope is only hope when one hopes against hope, only when the situation is hopeless. Hope has the full force of hope only when we have first been led to the point where it is impossible to hope—and then we hope against hope, even as faith is faith in the face of the incredible. Hope is only hope when all I can do is to try to keep hope alive even though there is no hope. There is no hope, I know that and I am convinced of that, but still I hope.[89]

Such hope resembles Morrissey's hope, which turns out like so many features of his art, in spite of its wholly secular cast, to correspond uncannily to a religious model.

If this is so, and there is in Morrissey's work a light or a hope, in spite of the darkness, 'that never goes out,' it suggests that a crucial qualification is necessary to any absolutizing of the singer's pessimism. For what these reflections require us to countenance is the possibility that no-saying may not be his final word. Indeed, they suggest, in the phraseology of Maurice Blanchot, a 'Yes in the No itself.'[90]

We find corroborating evidence of this possibility in the prodigal no-saying which is in fact a yes-saying in 'I Wont Share You':

> or is life just sick and cruel, instead?
> "Yes!"
> No—no—no—no—no—no—no—no—no—no—no—no.[91]

We might furthermore recall that this is the logic of the complaint which is also a love song that opens *You Are The Quarry* ('America Is Not The World'). Here again we have a song in which the singer has difficulties with the word 'love.' In this case, however, his resistance *precedes* the utterance and even appears to make it possible;[92] the point being that nowadays if you want to say 'I love you' to America—as Morrissey evidently does—you have to say a whole lot of other things first (such as 'You big fat pig' and 'you know where you can shove your hamburger').

What this last example reveals is that Morrissey's no-saying may be a prefatory form of hope—which is to say, a holding out for something more, something beyond the horizon of the present—and

89. Caputo, 'The Experience of God and the Axiology of the Impossible,' p. 134.
90. Blanchot, *The Infinite Conversation*, p. 179.
91. See pp. 186–9 for a discussion of 'Shakespeare's Sister' and another example of the singer's no-saying to his customary no-saying.
92. The song concludes with Morrissey singing 'I love you / I love you / I love you.'

may thus covertly be in league with, in keeping a space 'impercep-tibly' open for, yes-saying.[93] Similarly, what is revealed in the lyrics of benighted affirmation is a 'back-to-front' logic whereby hope is engendered by hopelessness and plenitude paradoxically succeeds exhaustion. The general conclusion to which all of these examples point is in one sense not surprising, since it confirms what the singer insistently claims in his iconic stance as the persecuted Man of Sor-rows—namely, that 'behind the hatred there lies / a murderous desire for love.'[94] Yet in another sense it represents what is perhaps the most surprising reversal in all his work—even for an artist whose peculiar forte is revealing the sanity of the upside-down. For whilst leaving intact his iconoclastic protest against pop music's conventional 'yeah yeah yeah,' and without in any way mitigating his unflinching and obstinate chronicling of darkness, it suggests in the words of Wallace Stevens that 'under every no / [lies] a passion for yes that [has] never been broken.'[95]

The light that never goes out

The darkness of which Morrissey characteristically sings is sundered by an enigmatic light. It appears out of nowhere; its existence is asserted in a single song; and we know next to nothing about it. Once again, it is not explicitly religious in character and it emerges out of a darkness it does not dispel. I am of course referring to the climactic refrain at the end of 'There Is A Light That Never Goes Out.' Yet appear it does; and its existence *is* asserted. And these qualifications are not sufficient to eliminate its religious resonances.[96]

Light, like love, is one of the most traditional ways of designat-ing the divine. And whilst all the singer asserts about this light is that it 'is' and will be, forevermore, this would seem to carry it decisively

---

93. Nietzsche is an unexpected ally in this connection, whose Zarathustra declares: 'I love the great despisers, for they are the great venerators and arrows of longing for the other bank' (*Thus Spoke Zarathustra*, p. 44).

94. Stevens, 'The Boy With The Thorn In His Side.'

95. 'Esthétique du Mal,' IX.

96. This is how the light 'that never goes out' is described at the start of the fourth Gospel: 'In the beginning was the Word, and the Word was with God, and the Word was God. The same was in the beginning with God. All things were made by him; and without him was not any thing made that was made. In him was life; and the life was the light of men. And the light shineth in dark-ness; and the darkness comprehended it not. There was a man sent from God, whose name was John. The same came for a witness, to bear witness of the Light, that all *men* through him might believe. He was not that Light, but *was sent* to bear witness of that Light. *That* was the true Light, which lighteth every man that cometh into the world' (John: 1–9).

in a religious direction (what other light never goes out?)—a reading which is supported by the singer's making the sign of the cross during the song's live performance. The apparently religious character of the utterance is further reinforced by the suggestion that it is a transcendent light—for it would seem unnecessary so emphatically to assert the existence of that which was immediately evident to the senses. It is clearly implied too by its occurrence at the end of a narrative which is concerned, however hyperbolically, with death—against which the eternity of the light's duration is held. To understand the emphatic affirmation fully, though, it's obviously necessary to consider its relationship to the preceding narrative.

According to Johnny Rogan, the song involves 'an incredible lust for life and intense need to escape the shackles of home, but no happy ending.'[97] Yet surely this undersells the conclusion and elides the drama of its emergence? For whilst it's obviously true that the final refrain doesn't represent a 'happily ever after' coda, it would be equally mistaken to speak as though it in *no* way diverged from the foregoing narrative. Indeed, the hardest thing to make sense of in 'There Is A Light That Never Goes Out' is the fact the final insistently affirmative claim—which was deemed significant enough to serve as the song's title—appears to come virtually out of nowhere and bear little relation to the melancholy character of the rest of the song.[98] Let us consider the two sections again.

> Take me out tonight
> where there's music and there's people
> and they're young and alive
> driving in your car
> I never never want to go home
> because I haven't got one
> anymore
> take me out tonight
> because I want to see *people* and I
> want to see *lights*
> driving in your car

---

97. Rogan, *Morrissey*, pp. 69–70.
98. Rogan is also wrong to suggest that 'the light that never goes out reiterates the light in the eyes referred to in "The Boy With The Thorn In His Side"' (ibid.). This isn't merely imprecise ('The Boy With The Thorn In His Side' makes no reference to light), it distorts by domesticating the *strangeness* of the later claim (what about its 'never'? How—if at all—does it manifest itself? Isn't the careful preservation of its placelessness even slightly intriguing?).

oh, please don't drop me home
because it's not *my* home, it's *their*
home, and I'm welcome no more . . .
take me out tonight
oh take me anywhere, *I don't care*
I don't care, I don't care
and in the darkened underpass
I thought *Oh God, my chance has come at last*
(but then a strange fear gripped me and I
just couldn't ask)
and if a double-decker bus
crashes into us
to die by your side
is such a heavenly way to die
and if a ten-ton truck
kills the both of us
to die by your side
well, the pleasure, the privilege is mine.
Oh, there is a light and it never goes out . . .

The first part of the song is uttered from an extraordinary 'nowhere' place—an exilic, 'intervallic' space of nonbelonging or of being in transit—in between an ahead which is out of reach and a behind which doesn't exist.[99] This existential sense of being in exile is obviously reflected by the speaker's physical vagrancy ('driving in your car'—a phrase which swallows its grammatical subject and dilates the experience into a condition of being in its timeless gerund). The sense of perpetual nonarrival or life deferred that is evoked in the verse also recalls the melancholy to-ing and fro-ing of desire and the paradox of a goal that recedes upon approach. In this case, to begin with, what the speaker desires is to be 'taken out'; and yet once this is achieved and he is driving in the addressee's car, a new goal emerges to take its place—'and in the darkened underpass / I thought *Oh God, my chance has come at last*.' Indeed, the closer he seems to get to the goal, the more the deferrals multiply. (The utterance 'I thought *Oh God, my chance has come at last*' is an apostrophe or a 'turning away'

---

99. Morrissey is fond of the 'double undoing' involved in the logic of the latter claim: 'I never never want to go home / because I haven't got one'; 'I know it's over / and it never really began'; 'I was praying for love / for love that never comes / from someone who does not exist' ('There Is A Light That Never Goes Out,' 'I Know It's Over,' 'That's How People Grow Up').

in speech, in this instance turning away to address God, which represents a miniature 'Hamletic' shift into contemplation—which displaces action—the moment an opportunity arrives. The speaker is then 'gripped' by a debilitating fear which is set over against the speaking self, as though it assailed from without and with an agency of its own.[100])

The strange 'nowhere' place of the verse, which figures a characteristic sense of wandering somehow outside of life, is carried over into the chorus, whose hypothetical imaginings open up a subjunctive space outside of that which 'is.'[101] Tonally as well, on account of its 'ironic' romanticism, the chorus lacks a determinate site—realizing the singer's avowed aim of operating simultaneously 'at opposite ends of the emotional scale.' (Irony, we might say, is the trope of exile, since it's a gesture that signifies a thing's nonbelonging to itself.) In fact, the chorus is a kind of urban parody of the *Liebestod* of Tristan and Isolde, which deliberately seeks out the least romantic causes of death (a double-decker bus and a ten-ton truck) as a way of uniting the would-be lovers. It is also of course a fate that would *replace* actual union, and thus—for Morrissey—a fittingly asexual consummation.[102] On the one hand, then, the chorus's hypothetical imaginings clearly have an ironic function in subverting the conventions of romantic narrative and in preserving the singer's customary alienation even in the moment of consummation. And yet, on the other hand, it is an *intensely* romantic lyric, whose unidyllic urban setting *adds* to the force of its extravagant gestures, as the value attached to tragic events signals the extremity of the singer's devotion.

All of this is characteristic of Morrissey: the perpetual state of homelessness, the sense of an existence 'outside' being, the self-estranging use of irony, the 'excessive' negation ('never never') and the

100. It is easy to overlook the oddity of Morrissey's earlier use of 'alive' ('where there's music and there's people / and they're young and alive'), which implies a familiar sense of 'famished ontology' and along with the obverse personification of fear constitutes a kind of uncanny chiasmus in its exchange of animism, as witnesses earlier in 'Shakespeare's Sister,' 'The Headmaster Ritual' and 'I Know It's Over.'

101. The subjunctive announces an imaginary or hypothetical space, as opposed to the realm of fact designated by the indicative. In the words of the anthropologist Victor Turner—who invokes the subjunctive as a way of defining an interval which is 'neither here nor there' or 'betwixt and between [known] positions'—the subjunctive represents 'a world of as if . . . it is "as if it were so" not "it is so"' (cited in Auslander, *Performing Glam Rock*, p. 150).

102. The singer's use of 'heavenly' in the first chorus—which wittily smuggles an 'afterwards' into the time before—suggests a further ironic parallel with *Tristan und Isolde*, in light-heartedly seeking to open an eternity within a transitional state. Thus, even the idealized 'goal'—dying in a 'heavenly way'—is presented as a place of nonarrival.

encompassing grasp of 'living darkness.' But here he takes another step; a step which *overturns* the dominion of such things, and recalls the 'peripeteia' of 'I Know It's Over' and other lyrics of benighted affirmation.[103] Having begun with an urgent plea to be removed from a darkness that is predatory on being, the song ends with an insistent affirmation of light that offers hope and succour for its own distress. The consolation offered by the conclusion isn't only unexpected though. It also brings forth *more than* what was hoped for, since the song begins with a desire for temporal light ('I want to see *people* and I / want to see *lights*') and ends up with an *eternal* light. The second section of the song thus speaks from a space beyond the 'nowhere' place of the earlier narrative, and moves from the worldly to the other-worldly and from what he wants to see to what he *sees*. How, then, are we to make sense of this radical overturning, which seems to come out of nowhere and exceed expectations?

According to Simon Goddard, 'The literal meaning of the song's title [and hence its concluding refrain] was clarified' by initial vocal takes where Morrissey sings 'there is a light in your eye and it never goes out.' This 'explanatory revelation,' as Goddard describes it, was 'oddly' omitted from the finished record, 'which procured greater ambiguity as a result.'[104] The obvious problem with this kind of argument is that it elevates that which was rejected by the author over what was chosen. It is of course interesting to see the steps that led Morrissey to what he ultimately wrote; however, surely we should base our reading on what the work actually says. And given that the singer evidently decided *against* the earlier version, we shouldn't assume it necessarily offers any clue as to how we should read the final version. He may simply have changed his mind or found only gradually what he wanted to say.

Based on what the text actually says, I want to propose an alternative reading, which doesn't seek to elide the lacuna or dramatic shift between the conclusion and the rest of the song, and instead suggests that this unexpected leap—this suddenly speaking from another space—is in fact the greatest clue the song gives us as to what the utterance means. For doesn't the assertion in this way stage the stepping across a gap which is the act of faith? In other words, isn't it precisely in preserving an irreducible interval which the assertion

---

103. 'Peripeteia' is Aristotle's term for a sudden reversal of fortune in drama.
104. Goddard, *The Smiths*, p. 162.

must traverse that the song reveals the utterance to be religious? The impression of speaking from the other side of an interval that can only be traversed by faith is underwritten by the singer's 'never'; for 'never' is a place from which we cannot speak, other than with faith, in our finite condition. Likewise, the 'is' of the assertion—which categorically affirms what cannot be seen—has what we might refer to as an 'eschatological' cast, since the reality to which it bears witness belongs, as it were, to the afterwards of the 'last things.'[105] And finally the 'excessive' character of the singer's claim, which recalls the prodigal and unheralded flourishing of his other lyrics of benighted affirmation, resembles the scriptural logic of the 'good catastrophe'—the sudden 'excessive' affirmative turn of the Psalms of new orientation and the overabundance with which need is answered in the miracle narratives (which prefigure the exorbitant beneficence of the other kingdom).[106] What we can see, then, in 'There Is A Light That Never Goes Out,' in spite of its avoidance of explicitly religious language, is a compelling illustration of the Tenebrae logic of hopeful darkness.[107] That is to say, without any diminution of the encompassing darkness, and with nothing to which he can point that warrants this step, the singer affirms *as a matter of faith* the existence of a light which cannot be seen but which lies beyond the reach of darkness.

Longing for a better country

Whilst Morrissey doesn't recur to the subject of the light that never goes out, he does evince something resembling a correlative belief in 'another world.' At the end of 'Asleep,' for example, he sings—

> There is another world
> There is a better world
> Well, there must be

—wistfully repeating 'Well, there must be.' Manifestly, there is an element of stand-up antiphonal comedy in this which weakens the

---

105. When Christ says, for example, in the sermon on the mount, 'Blessed are the poor in spirit, for theirs is the kingdom of heaven' (Matthew 5:3), the assertion involves an eschatological 'is,' for its copula points beyond the present to a reality which is as yet 'without' being, and which must in our present state be asserted *in the face of* contrary evidence.
106. The phrase a 'good catastrophe' is borrowed from Tolkien's essay 'On Fairy-Tales' (Tolkien, *Tree and Leaf*, p. 68).
107. Traditionally, during the Tenebrae service, the church's candles are put out one by one, until only a single lighted candle remains, which is hidden—but not extinguished—to signify the darkness of the 'long Saturday' that appears to, but does not in fact, obtain dominion over Christ.

assertion (at least the first time he sings 'there must be'), for the reason he offers in support of the claim that there is a better world is *that this one's so bad*. Yet the line's irony doesn't exhaust what is said, and the repetition of 'there must be'—which, like the rest of the song, wears its pathos on its sleeve—appears to bespeak a longing which is the ground of its own hope.[108]

One way of describing this kind of self-substantiating faith is to call it 'wishful thinking.' Which is perfectly correct, as long as we remember two things. Firstly, this doesn't amount to a disproof or even a critique: wishing or hoping that a thing may be so obviously doesn't make it so, but neither does it mean it *cannot* be so. And, secondly, disbelief is subject to the same objection: if I believe—and am comforted by the belief—that after death there is nothing and no one to whom I may be answerable, this too is an unsubstantiated faith and may be described as wishful thinking. What determines whether such hope is fallacious (the pejorative connotation the phrase usually carries) is what turns out to be the case on the other side of finitude— and the data are not yet in. Morrissey's assertion does not therefore necessarily collapse or lose its significance as an assertion, if it is discovered to be founded on nothing other than its own yearning.

There is another, more positive, way of looking at such 'longing for a better country.'[109] Morrissey's assertion may, it is true, have the weakness of a hope. However, hope may itself be a sort of 'evidence.'[110] Indeed, the reasoning of the claim at the end of 'Asleep' corresponds to the logic of what is sometimes called the 'conative' argument, or the argument from dissatisfaction, which recalls what was said earlier about the affective teleology of infinite desire. This argument proposes that if we are lured outside ourselves by our longing, and if this longing seems in some sense endless, since it insatiably exceeds its own satisfaction, then might not the cause and consummation of our longing lie beyond this world? Aidan Nichols explains the logic of this as follows: if 'we are striving for something

---

108. It's interesting to discover that the phrase 'Deep in the cell of my heart,' which occurs in 'Asleep,' alludes to *De Profundis* and a passage in which Wilde is discussing his belief in 'the city of God' (Wilde, *De Profundis and Other Writings*, pp. 162–3).

109. This is how faith is described in Hebrews (11:16).

110. Strictly, it is not possible to interpret such hope conclusively until the Last Day, for, if the ultimate reality is purely material or nothingness in flux, this hope will prove to have been sheer delusion. Yet if such hope finds corroboration in the eschaton, it will turn out to have been a sort of cosmic 'homing device' or sublime clue, which alerts us to—whilst leaving us free to refuse or accept—that which is beyond us (and yet also within our reach).

beyond this world, . . . it seems more reasonable to posit that something as the ground of our striving rather than to write off our striving as absurd.'[111]

If the longing at the end of 'Asleep' were the only allusion to 'something beyond this world,' the evidence in favour of anything resembling faith in this 'something' would plainly be rather thin. But the singer *recurrently* alludes to the subject;[112] often passingly, lightheartedly and enigmatically, to be sure, but with a frequency that countermands this apparent insouciance. Let us consider another example.

'I Will See You In Far-Off Places' is a stylistically characteristic Morrissey lyric, in that it alludes obliquely or elliptically to things without exactly being 'about' them. Its context, for example, appears to be the Iraq war; yet we are left to deduce this from its reference to the threat of U.S. bombing (which leaves a number of options open!) and its courting of what Armond White refers to as a 'deliberate orientalism,' melodically and in its outro sampling.[113] Nonetheless, the focus of its oblique reflections is the continuity of things after their end in 'far-off places.'

Two things in particular are of relevance to our discussion. Firstly, the song is concerned with what we know and do not know, as well as what we know about our knowing. For instance, the singer is emphatic in his assertions about the end not being the end and about the existence of such 'far-off places':

---

111. Nichols, *The Shape of Catholic Theology*, p. 58. C. S. Lewis offers an extended consideration of this issue in his chapter on the virtue of hope in *Mere Christianity*. According to Lewis, there are three responses to our 'excessive' longing: 'First, that of the Fool, who dismisses these simply as bad specimens, and goes on looking for better ones.' (This is the only option allowed by Žižek's reading of desire.) 'Second, that of the disillusioned Sensible Man, who recognizes that further searching will only result in repeated disappointment, and so concludes that it was a mistake to seek for better than the mundane.' (This is roughly Larkin's position.) 'Last is the response of the religious believer who argues . . . that natural desires are not in vain, and hence that the longing for deeper satisfaction than this existence can offer, points to another world within which fulfilment may be found' (Haldane, 'Philosophy, the Restless Heart and the Meaning of Theism,' p. 47). On the evidence of 'Asleep,' Morrissey seems to lie somewhere between 'the disillusioned Sensible Man' and the religious believer.

112. See, for example, 'A Rush And A Push And The Land Is Ours,' 'Death Of A Disco Dancer,' 'Ouija Board, Ouija Board,' 'There Is A Place In Hell For Me And My Friends' and 'Satan Rejected My Soul.'

113. 'The Politics of Morrissey,' on *Slate* (*http://www.slate.com/id/2140918*) posted May 2, 2006. These deductions have been confirmed by Morrissey in interview: 'Yes, I do feel very sad for the people of Iraq having been invaded by Bush and Blair—so many people have unnecessarily lost their lives and Bush and Blair don't care. But within the song I feel there's a spiritual sensation whereby, although we know that life will end, we all have a feeling that we will meet again. Now why should I have that feeling? If we realize that everything is temporary, why do we all have this innate feeling that we will be together in some place?' (cited in Rogan, *Morrissey*, p. 296).

yes, one day I
will close my eyes forever
but I will see you
in far-off places

. . .

Destiny for some
is to save lives
but destiny for some is to end lives
but there is no end
and I will see you in far-off places.

And yet he is equally emphatic in his assertions concerning our *lack*
of knowledge, and is baffled by what he does know (the third 'why'
in the following lines appears to hover between asking how he knows
and whether his knowing has a purpose):

Nobody knows what human life is
why we come, why we go
so why then do I know
that I will see you
in far-off places?

A possible, partial answer to this question is brought into view at
the start of the second verse, where he sings: 'The heart knows why
I grieve.' The idea of course isn't dwelt upon, and the knowledge he
mentions pertains to 'grieving,' but there may be an allusion in Morrissey's utterance to Pascal's celebrated remark that 'the heart has its
reasons of which reason knows nothing.'[114] In any case, the singer's
curious formulation—referring to 'the heart' as a quasi-independent
entity, capable of 'knowing' in a manner that is not available to the
self as such—clearly corresponds to Pascal's Old Testament conception of the heart as an organ of knowing.[115] It also accords with
Paul's famous account of the virtues in 1 Corinthians 13, in which
he maintains that the reach of love extends infinitely beyond the
reach of our other faculties.[116]

---

114. Pascal, *Pensées*, no. 423, p. 127.
115. As J. C. L. Gibson reminds us, 'The Hebrews thought with their "heart" . . . rather than their
heads' (Gibson, *Language and Imagery in the Old Testament*, p. 8).
116. Morrissey's lyrics are full of somewhat surreal references to the heart as an exposed or 'ecstatic'
entity ('with my heart on a string,' 'with my heart in my hands,' 'my heart it left with you') and
as a source of knowledge independent of the speaking self ('the heart knows why I grieve,' 'heart
pointing to the sky,' 'me and my heart we just knew').

The second thing of particular interest to us here concerns the singer's presentation of these 'far-off places.' In referring to the continuity of things after their finite end in this way, he reveals a characteristic disinclination to use orthodox religious language (the designation 'heavenly,' it will be recalled, is smuggled under the fence into finitude and preferred as a signifier of *this*-worldly bliss in 'There Is A Light That Never Goes Out'). In this case, however, Morrissey seems to be additionally concerned to employ a nondenominational designation which transcends differences between Christians and Muslims, whilst the reference to 'your God' preserves the distinctiveness of their traditions. More interesting still, though, is the song's final description of life in such 'far-off places':

> I believe I will see you
> somewhere—safe
> looking to the camera
> messing around and pulling faces.

The singer's envisioning of the next world as a kind of cinematic space in which mischievous behaviour continues to take place is of course characteristic of his *own* mischievous and playful imaginings. But it is at the same time a reflexive conceit—like the mirrors in seventeenth-century Dutch paintings—which draws attention to its own aesthetic staging and recalls the self-referential gestures or 'looking to the camera' in 'Such A Little Thing Makes Such A Big Difference' and 'Certain People I Know,' etc. Now this playful envisioning of life in the next world unquestionably evinces a familiar element of scepticism or irreverence. Yet, coming as it does in a song which is dominated by emphatic assertions, based on something other than reason, and given the singer's conspicuous avoidance of traditional conceptions of that which is asserted, the lyric's inclusion of a self-referential trope—that foregrounds its own representational strategies—may also incorporate a caveat concerning its attempt to depict a place of which we cannot speak.[117] If this is the case, and the lines problematize their own ability to refer, the singer's playful envisioning of the next world by way of a Laurel and Hardy vignette would turn out paradoxically to *endorse* the traditional conception

---

116. Technically, the lines constitute what's known as a 'mise en abyme,' since here we have a work of art, which alludes to a work of art which acknowledges its aesthetic status.

of such a place, even as the lines gently make fun of it, by covertly underscoring its ineffability.

There is one further aspect of the song worth mentioning here, which relates to the foregoing discussion of loving the 'unlovable.' According to Armond White, at the end of the song 'the tempo rises and soars towards resolution through powerful repetitive murmurs' as Morrissey 'affects the sound of a Middle Eastern muezzin' (a Muslim crier who leads the call to prayer).[118] In White's view, this 'lends shocking implications to the final lyric: "I will see you somewhere safe." Insurrectionists and suicide bombers—of all stripes—fondly embraced.'[119] White's final comment seems to me to overstate the case, as the song's unspecified and potentially plural 'you' may equally apply to unresisting victims as well as insurrectionists. Nevertheless, the conclusion he draws is astute and lucidly calls attention to something insufficiently regarded:

> Only pop's greatest malcontent would dare such extreme humanist-verging-on-seditious solidarity. Everyone else in the pop world lags far behind Morrissey's willingness to identify with the unpopular. We're used to pop music that brazens predictable positions on topical grievances ('They paved paradise, put up a parking lot,' 'Don't push me cuz I'm close to the edge'), but Morrissey has often dared to court disreputable figures (criminals, skinheads) as a way of pulling discontents back into the human fold. His method insists that we recognize the unmanageable part of ourselves in our aberrant, felonious, and forsaken brethren.[120]

What conclusions of our own can be drawn from the singer's allusions to 'a better world' and 'far-off places'? In a long range of songs, throughout his career, without espousing or subordinating his imagination to orthodox doctrine, and whilst at the same time making fun of and asking questions about the possibilities he entertains, Morrissey seems to be discreetly challenging us to do something quite shocking—something much more subversive than what John Lennon asked of his listeners; he seems to be asking us, that is, to imagine there *is* a heaven.

---

118. White, 'The Politics of Morrissey.'
119. Ibid.
120. Ibid.

SUBVERSIVE VIRTUE

What I have been pointing towards in this chapter are correspondences, suggestions, openings and convergences—inchoate or ambiguous orientations in Morrissey's writing that, without making him what we could in any comfortable sense call a religious writer, trouble any attempt to see him as a purely secular artist. In the process, I have tried to show that, far from a recent and unheralded anomaly, the religious has *always* been a recalcitrant, shadowy or antagonistic presence in Morrissey's writing, and even his critiques—whether vitriolic or playful—suggest that it remains for him not only a source of fascination and a deep-seated reference point but also an unsettled (and unsettling) question. We must be careful of course not to push this too far. Morrissey has a salutary aversion to systems and is a thorn in the side of organized religion. Yet he is as well a thorn in the side of a complacent secularism, and the unwittingly conservative world of popular music, for which the love 'that moves the sun and the other stars' has become the love 'that dare not speak its name.'[121]

Whilst it's perhaps inevitable for rebellious pop stars to lose their oddity over time and be tamed by the industry they once shook up, Morrissey has somehow managed to retain his eccentricity, in spite of his success, and can legitimately still refer to himself as 'ringleader of the tormentors.' To be truly subversive, what is required is a reflexive critique—which is prepared to transgress the convention of transgression. And this is precisely what pop music has traditionally lacked. Morrissey, however, has resisted the seductive domestications of the industry, and with a singularly obdurate sense of purpose has spoken out forcibly (and wittily) against the symbolic institutions of his culture—the government, the church and the state apparatus—but has equally poured scorn on and performatively made fun of the conventionalized gesture of such rebellion itself. In this way, he disturbed the coffee-table coziness of pop-star 'transgression' and brought about what John Saward has referred to as a 'revolution by tradition.'[122] It is for this reason that his not belonging to anyone or

---

121. 'The love that moves the sun and the other stars' ('L'amour che move il sole e l'altre stelle') is how Dante refers to God at the end of *Paradiso*; and the second phrase in quotation marks was coined by Lord Alfred Douglas in a poem entitled 'The Two Loves,' published in 1894 in *The Chameleon*.

122. Saward, *Perfect Fools*, p. 203.

anything—his not-fitting-in with things—is essential to his art and a 'subversive virtue.'[123]

At a time that witnesses, simultaneously, the exponential growth of religious fundamentalism and an ideologically sanctioned ecstasy of materialism, Morrissey's 'eccentric' engagement with theological concerns is especially vital—and vital because and not *in spite of* his eccentricity. This is because the singer's 'scandalous religious yearnings' are, like Wilde's, troubling both to religious orthodoxy and to the unthinking atheism of popular culture; for in this respect, too, he is a kind of alien in both realms, whose presence helps to keep the former from sinking into a genteel unawareness of the radical charity of its own teaching, and prompting the latter to ask itself if it might not be guilty of adding up too soon.[124]

And yet perhaps such a radically 'eccentric' figure is the most appropriate prophet in our epistemological situation.[125] And what's more, perhaps such eccentricity isn't so unorthodox after all. According to the author of Hebrews—who speaks of 'a longing for a better country'—to be faithful is to leave home without knowing where you are going; it is to be a refugee, an alien, a 'stranger on the earth.' It is to subsist in a permanent state of not belonging—'a beggar-man who nobody owns,' a 'traveller to the grave'—certain only of what's lacking, and 'foolishly' risking everything on the basis of a rumour. To be faithful obviously also

---

123. The phrase is borrowed from James A. Francis, *Subversive Virtue*. In interview, Morrissey has explicitly related this nonbelonging to his rebelliousness as an artist: 'It's actually very difficult to look or appear rebellious in a new way. Most people take the very traditional paths of leather jackets and just extremely loud music. But that's not my tactic. I tend to do it by default. I tend to do it by just simply being me, who I am, and that seems to distress certain people enough. . . . But it means simply that I'm entirely outside of what's happening and I feel that very strongly. I always felt it. Ultimately I didn't even belong within The Smiths—that ended' (*Cream*, April/May 1991).

124. I allude to Arthur Hugh Clough's formulation of the doubts to which doubt itself is subject:

> The faces, and the voices, and the whole mass
> O' the motley facts of existence flowing by.
> O perfect, if 'twere all. But it is not.
> Hints haunt me ever of a More beyond:
> I am rebuked by a sense of the incomplete,
> Of a completion over-soon assumed,
> Of adding up too soon.

(*Dipsychus*, Part 2, scene iv, 36–42).

125. Derrida made a similar point in the 1980s concerning deconstruction: 'It is possible to see deconstruction as being produced in a space where the prophets are not far away. . . . I am still looking for something . . . [in a] search without hope for hope. . . . Perhaps my search is a twentieth-century brand of prophecy?' (Kearney, *Dialogues with Contemporary Continental Thinkers*, p. 119).

involves hope—the 'arrows of longing for the other bank; though the insignia of this hope is an obstinate no-saying—concerning the ultimacy of finite satisfactions—which is fuelled by a haunting sense of something more: another world, a better world, an 'elsewhere' that answers our infinite longing. But above all, central to the 'eccentricity' of faith is love; a love that is 'ever seeking and never satisfied,'[126] which carries us ecstatically away from ourselves, and reaches unsqueamishly out to the fallen, the 'queer,' the outcast and the 'unlovable.'

No doubt, Morrissey would baulk at the thought of being described as virtuous (which would of course itself be a sign of virtue). And yet, in attesting the existence of a light that never goes out, in longing insatiably for another country, and in luring us into a love of the 'unlovable,' his work exhibits the theological virtues of faith, hope and charity. (If this seems to be crediting the singer with more belonging than he would want, it is worth remembering that Christianity has its own cautionary variant of Woody Allen's joke about not wanting to belong to a club that would have him as a member, in insisting that the only thing inimical to membership is the sense that one is *entitled* to it.)

It's important to recognize such deep connections in Morrissey's work, to counter the general neglect of the subject but also the trivializing attention paid to it in Mark Simpson's *Saint Morrissey*, which treats the religious as an analogy or a kind of costume jewellery. However, it's equally important to emphasize, in spite of his claim that 'everything' he's written is a result of his Catholic upbringing, that the religious remains to a large extent a conflictual and *submerged* presence in the singer's work. The following fable may help to convey this.

At the end of a 'searching examination' of Kantian ethics in *On the Basis of Morality* (1840), the notoriously pessimistic Schopenhauer offers us what he describes as a 'facetious' and 'frivolous' comparison: 'I should liken Kant to a man at a ball, who all evening has been carrying on a love affair with a masked beauty in the vain hope of making a conquest, when at last she throws off her mask and reveals herself as his wife.'[127] The 'masked beauty' in Schopenhauer's miniature allegory is Christianity.

---

126. The quotation is taken from Pope John Paul II's analysis of The Song of Songs in the General Audience of June 6, 1984, delivered in St Peter's Square.
127. Schopenhauer, *On the Basis of Morality*, p. 103.

To suggest that Morrissey, like Kant, is drawn to a religion to which he is already unwittingly wedded is undoubtedly to overstate the case. Though not by much. For one of the most surprising findings of this chapter is that we can see in the singer's radical eccentricity, in making himself weak to protest against the strong, in 'assuming the features of the mutilated human' and in becoming a fool in the eyes of the world, that his ultimate archetype turns out to be Christ—the exemplary 'fool':[128]

> Like the jester, Christ defies custom and scorns crowned heads. Like a wandering troubadour he has no place to lay his head. Like the clown in the circus parade, he satirizes existing authority by riding into town replete with regal pageantry when he has no earthly power. Like a minstrel he frequents dinners and parties. At the end he is costumed by his enemies in a mocking caricature of royal paraphernalia. He is crucified amidst sniggers and taunts with a sign over his head that lampoons his laughable claim. . . . Only now, in our secularized, postChristian era, is [the image of Christ the clown] able to emerge again. A weak, even ridiculous church, somehow peculiarly at odds with the ruling assumptions of its day, can once again appreciate the harlequinesque Christ. His pathos, his weakness, his irony—all begin to make a strange kind of sense again.[129]

What has emerged from this chapter's inquiry is a complex, evolving and equivocal comportment towards the divine; a comportment which involves both a movement towards and a keeping of distance—or a holding on within a letting go—since it tends to advance 'negatively' by means of complaint, irreverence or play; a comportment which is informed by a profound sense of grievance, injustice and lack, which is restless in suspecting itself and agile in its own overthrow, but which is, nonetheless, *a comportment towards*. It is a comportment, moreover, that is flooded with yearning and which bears witness to the rumour it can barely pronounce of a love that is said to be stronger than death and a light that shines in, without being comprehended by, the darkness.

---

128. Wilde of course came to a similar conclusion—concerning his identification with Christ —as he reflects upon his life in *De Profundis*.
129. Cox, *The Feast of Fools*, pp. 140–1.

EPILOGUE

A Ticklish Subject

I just wanted to be me, which is somewhere
between this world and the next world.

—Morrissey, *Melody Maker*, September 27, 1986

Henry James once made the following remarks about the works of Oscar Wilde: 'Everything Oscar does is a deliberate trap for the literalist, and to see the literalist walk straight up to it, look straight at it, and step straight into it, makes one freshly avert a discouraged gaze from this unspeakable animal.'[1] If we leave aside the peculiar swerve into distaste at the end and see the setting of such 'traps' as something positive, these comments could equally be applied to Morrissey and his critics. Having for the most part of the book focused attention on particular facets of the singer's work, it may be helpful, in conclusion, to pull some of these strands together and say something more summarily about this 'unspeakable' artist.

To claim at the end of a detailed study that there is something 'unspeakable' about its subject—in the sense of consistently eluding description—may seem to be stabbing oneself in the back. However, one of the primary aims of this book has been to problematize the enterprise of speaking about Morrissey and challenge the reign of his literalist commentators. To put this more positively, the book has sought to recover the *strangeness* of Morrissey's art and wrest it away from a kind of proprietorial blokeishness that impoverishes even as it claims to defend the significance of his work.

---

1. James, *Henry James, Letters*, p. 373.

I

SPECTRALITY

The study began with the difficulty of beginning, on account of the spectral nature of that ever escaping fox 'Morrissey.' The singer's persona, it was noted, is a ghostly effect or narrative projection—a 'quasi-transcendent' that operates within and beyond his lyrics—which informs and is informed by his every performance. His songs thus peculiarly have a history which is prior to their inception and bring with them a narrative 'outside' themselves, which is nowhere fully present but which crucially contributes to their meaning. (And since the 'I' that sings is continually in the process of being formed outside the songs, his lyrics are in a sense open to the future as well, which may retroactively affect their meaning.) This is why his lyrics are 'self-transcending' and not fully in control of their own meaning—which is one reason why they are a trap for the literalist.

The singer's persona isn't only what Stephen Dedalus refers to as 'a ghost by absence,'[2] which teases with its elusiveness. As we have seen, one of the most extraordinary features of Morrissey's recordings is a kind of beneficent ghostliness or a promise of presence, which underwrites an offering of communion in the space of the song ('See with your eyes / touch with your hands . . . / know in your soul'). In these moments of haunting intimacy, what we are confronted with is a *surplus* of presence and an 'ontological scandal,' as in spite of our temporal and spatial separation, the singer claims to give himself into our present in what he sings ('for haven't you me with me now?').[3] The singer thus claims to exceed his absence in the manner of a ghost and be with us, as it were, from 'beyond.' To use his own perfectly precise formulation, he is 'a living sign.'

A related aspect of Morrissey's work uncovered by the study is a deep-seated suspicion of essentialist thinking. It was noticed, for example, that camp—a style beloved of the singer—is an extravagant indwelling of the adjectival or adverbial, which seeks to sever 'doing' from 'being' and suggests that identity is less a fixed essence

---

2. Joyce, *Ulysses*, p. 155.
3. There is an ingenious pun to this effect in 'Rubber Ring,' where Morrissey sings: 'I'm here with the cause / I'm holding the torch / In the corner of your room / Can you hear me?' In claiming to be there with 'the cause,' the singer appears to be declaring his solidarity with the listener. Yet the utterance permits a stronger assertion of presence as well, for 'the cause' also obviously refers to that which produces an effect or gives rise to a phenomenon—in this case the song—so that the line allows a 'scandalous' assertion of presence in the recording.

and more a slippery, shadowy effect that nonchalantly floats across artificial categories. This view of identity is consonant with Morrissey's comments on sexual orientation and his notorious refusal of the conventional labels. It is also a logic that is brought into view by the singer's misgivings on the threshold of predication and his raising of the possibility of a 'does' without an 'is' in 'Sister I'm A Poet.' Identity, for Morrissey, would therefore seem to be a free-floating, protean, spectralized phenomenon—or what Judith Butler refers to as a phantasmatic effect—which disports like a perfume and 'is' its activity.[4]

The ghostly is a recurrent concern in Morrissey's writing in another strangely correlative sense. For his lyrics—as well as his comments in interviews—are flooded with a sense of being 'outside of' life; a sense, that is, of a life that has never quite come into being or has passed out of existence before coming to an end.[5] Such ghostly states, it was suggested, are a way of signifying a 'desert of loneliness' or a privation so great it eats away at the very fabric of one's being.[6] (The sense of loneliness as an *existential* crisis is impressionistically conveyed in 'The Boy With The Thorn In His Side,' where Morrissey sings of 'a murderous desire for love'; although as he does so, that ticklish word 'love'—which so often trips him up from within— seems to slide irresistibly into the word 'life,' as he rhymes it with 'side,' 'lies' and 'eyes.') At the same time, though, these recurrent allusions to spectral states point towards another underlying theme in Morrissey's work—namely, his nonbelonging.

It is of course well known that the singer doesn't belong 'to anyone' or 'anywhere' and that he feels like 'a foreigner on the earth.' (Morrissey once described 'The Smiths' as 'a stray kind of a name'[7]—which, one might add, appropriately described a 'stray' kind of thing.) But it has also emerged in the course of the study that such alienation is an even more fundamental condition that amounts to a sense of ontological nonbelonging. In other words, *being alive*, for Morrissey, is a matter of exile and alienation.[8] As one

4. In 'At Last I Am Born,' Morrissey refers to himself as a 'spectral hand'—a ghostly synecdoche that evokes a de-essentialized subject which is, as it were, a by-product of its activity.
5. Here, for example, is how the singer described himself in 1991: 'I think there are some people who hover at the edge of life and never quite jump in . . . and here I am. . . . Well, I'm teetering on the edge. [Laughs] I've got one foot in and one foot out' (*Cream*, April/May 1991).
6. The phrase in quotation marks comes from Samuel Beckett's *Proust*, p. 54.
7. Robertson, *Morrissey: In His Own Words*, p. 58.
8. There is an interesting parallel between the topos of spectrality in Morrissey's lyrics and the recurrence of space imagery and alien personae in the work of David Bowie ('Space Oddity,' 'Starman,' 'Life On Mars,' 'Ashes To Ashes,' *The Man Who, Fell to Earth,* etc.). According to Ken McLeod, Bowie's alien personae were 'emblematic of his bi-sexual alienation from the heterosexual

of Samuel Beckett's moribunds remarks: 'You're on earth, there's no cure for that!'[9]

If the singer's state of nonbelonging stems partly from a sense of 'famished ontology'—his sense, that is, of being 'half a person' or the ghost of someone who hasn't even died—it's equally a matter of internal estrangement or a 'disphasure' within *the self.*[10] This sense of alterity within the self prohibits a full involvement in things and entails a 'toxic' surplus of subjectivity, since some part of the self is always playing truant or vetoing its own activities. In 'There Is A Light That Never Goes Out,' for example—in which the singer laments his state of homelessness—when an opportunity for involvement presents itself, he claims 'a strange fear gripped me and I just couldn't ask,' as though that which impeded him were a kind of foreign body or an otherness within the self.[11]

Whilst this lack of self-coincidence is manifestly something that torments the singer, it is one of the underlying claims of the book that it is a *positive* feature of Morrissey's art—and one that relates it to deconstruction, which according to Derrida is inseparable from 'the logic of spectrality.'[12] This is because it is precisely a lack of self-coincidence that constitutes the 'oxymoronic self' and informs the singer's art of embarrassment. It is furthermore a preoccupation with

---

male-dominated world of rock music' ('Space Oddities,' p. 341). This is true enough and a valuable reminder for those who dismiss such pieces as 'novelty' songs. Yet Bowie's work—like Morrissey's—is filled with a more generalized, existential sense of alienation ('I'm living in a silent film'; 'the shrieking of nothing is killing me'; 'we should be on by now'), which his alien personae and songs about being lost in space also seem to reflect.

9. Beckett, *Endgame*, p. 44.

10. Morrissey's lyrics frequently advert to a state of self-alienation ('I don't get along with myself'; 'Irish blood, English heart / this I'm made of'; 'I am two people'). This sense of self-estrangement is complicated even further in 'Still Ill,' where the singer asks 'does the body rule the mind or does the mind rule the body?' Whichever it is, the two are, for Morrissey, at odds with each other, and the 'I' that doesn't know is different from both.

11. One of the oddest instances of this occurs in 'I Am Hated For Loving,' in which Morrissey sings 'I am haunted for wanting'; not, we should note, 'I am haunted *by* wanting,' which would spectralize and attribute independent agency to an interior condition, as he does elsewhere. Here, instead, the haunting is something that takes place *apart from* the wanting, as a supplementary torment, as though the self were reflexively adding to its own misery. Except that no 'thing' is doing the haunting, which is left strangely without agency. As a result, in a way that once again reminds one of Beckett, it is as if *awareness itself* somehow turns against him and, in the absence of otherness, engenders its own interior tormentor ('Devising figments to temper his nothingness,' as Beckett writes of the self-savaging consciousness in *Company*, p. 64); however, it is a splintering or multiplication of the self that paradoxically increases its isolation.

12. Derrida, *Spectres of Marx*, p. 225, n. 3. Jacques Derrida, whose profoundly unsettling works haunt this study, once described himself as a 'foreign body' in the institution of psychoanalysis ('Geopsychoanalysis—"and the Rest of the World,"' pp. 202–3). Morrissey, whose 'deconstructive' art seeks to save the tradition it brings to an end, may likewise be described as a foreign body in the institution of popular music.

the body 'that doesn't quite fit with itself' which helps to explain why camp—with its staged insynchronicity and self-alienating gestures— appeals so much to Morrissey.[13] Art of this kind, like deconstruction, which advertises a self out of joint, involves a sort of 'responsible anarchy,'[14] for it heralds 'a force of dislocation that spreads itself throughout the entire system'[15] and contaminates what it touches with the ticklishness that inspired it.

It is the nature of the ghostly to confuse the distinction between inside and outside, and Morrissey's lyrics are teeming with allegorical presences and animistic imaginings which do just that (the 'it' of 'Ammunition,' the stock characters he addresses in 'I Know It's Over,' the 'inbuilt guilt' in 'Will Never Marry').[16] This 'gothic' aspect of Morrissey's writing is rarely, if ever, touched upon in commentary on the singer. And yet, as we have seen, the darkness to which his writing bears witness is characteristically an uncanny entity—which is to say, an effect which suggestively exceeds its cause—whose 'excessive' presence is the counterpart of the singer's sense of sepulchral life. (It will be recalled that Morrissey's sense of 'death-in-life' is often involved in an uncanny chiastic exchange of animism, and as such is accompanied by a converse sense of 'life-in-death' in the realm of inanimate objects.[17]) Such darkness hovers on the verge of life and is disturbing precisely because it cannot be assigned to one or other realm. Instead, it appears as a quasi-animate Thing, which exists within but haunts from without; which appals and yet exerts an 'erotic' lure over the singer; which presents itself as a voice without a bearer; which is plural, amorphous, familiar yet unnameable; and which slowly undoes the buttons of one's being . . .

Spectrality in Morrissey's lyrics obviously isn't always a gothic phenomenon and as often as not it is a matter of farce (though one of

---

13. On account of its tendency simultaneously to disown the gestures it adopts, camp may be seen as a light-hearted strain of the uncanny (if one can say so without robbing camp of its disturbing character or the uncanny of its kinship with the absurd).

14. Derrida, 'Deconstruction and the Other,' pp. 120–1.

15. Derrida, *Writing and Difference*, p. 20.

16. Morrissey's songs are also haunted by more 'traditional' ghosts ('The Hand That Rocks The Cradle,' 'Suffer Little Children,' 'A Rush And A Push And The Land Is Ours,' 'Ouija Board, Ouija Board,' 'I'll Never Be Anybody's Hero Now,' 'At Last I Am Born'). Though we should of course take heed of Derrida's admonition: 'Let's not act as if we knew what a phantom or a phantasm was' (Derrida, 'The Rhetoric of Drugs,' p. 238).

17. There is a perfect illustration of the uncanny in 'The Hand That Rocks The Cradle' (in which the singer succeeds in haunting himself in seeking to comfort the child): 'Wavering shadows loom / a piano plays in an empty room / there'll be blood on the cleaver tonight.'

the things the ghostly does is blur the distinction between gothic and farce). The most prominent haunting of this kind concerns eros—a winged and elusive deity that is known through its invisible wounding. For the object of desire in Morrissey's lyrics is typically a haunting presence, which calls from an inaccessible place and evades the singer with cartoon dexterity ('I'm always there / It's always elsewhere'). Satisfaction, for the singer, thus appears to be a phantom that retreats upon arrival or preserves its distance in spite of his approach. It exists, we might say, in a 'now' which is always teasingly in the future.[18]

Whether we're talking, then, about the clutches of darkness or the Sisyphean whimsies of the object of desire, in common with the fugitive spectrality of his persona, the singer's torments are 'ticklish' too. If we add to these the contagiously disconcerting effects of the singer's 'deconstructive' art, which similarly involves what might be described as an aesthetics of tickling, what we find is that presiding over Morrissey's work—and celebrating the subversive virtues of awkwardness, embarrassment and eccentricity—is the gauche Muse.

II

IMPOSSIBILITY

There is a further, superordinate dimension to this pattern of elusiveness, in addition to the ticklishness of the singer's persona, and the haunting presences of which he sings, and that is the instability of the songs themselves. We have already noted that the meaning of the lyrics is affected from without by the quasi-transcendental narrative of the singer's persona. However, a number of other destabilizing devices have come to light in the course of the study which prime the trap for the literalist.

First of all, one might allude to Morrissey's flagrant playing with signifiers ('I'm a girl and you're a boy'; 'Leave me alone—I'm only singing'; 'Blah, blah, blah, blah'). In reflexively drawing attention to

---

18. This is the case if we accept Žižek's Lacanian reading of desire, but it also corresponds to a religious account of the elusive call of the divine. As Michel de Certeau writes: 'The God of my faith does not cease to mislead and to guide the desire which seeks to grasp him. He misleads it, because nothing of what I know is him. He guides it, because I do not expect him there where he comes. Encounters, events, mutations, protect him and reveal him. In the movement of so many different histories, he is only the Same in always appearing as the Other.' (*L'Étranger ou l'Union Dans le Différence*, p. 5 [translation by F. C. Bauerschmidt]).

the level of signification, the singer advertises the artifice of the songs and the metaphoricity of the speaking 'I.'[19] Similarly, the emergence of a 'cartoon universe' in Morrissey's lyrics ('he does the military two-step / down the nape of my neck'; 'he broke my spleen / he broke my knees / (and then he really laid into me)') clearly signals a movement away from realism and into a realm of aesthetic play, which deprivileges the mimetic function of language.[20] Such instability is likewise a feature of camp, which, as we have noted, is a *flirting* with meaning that obscures the difference between the serious and the nonserious and celebrates a kind of semiotic infidelity (which is to say, the fact that signs can mean 'more, less, or something other than' their author intended).

Additionally, one might point to the singer's habit of interruption and penchant for the fragmentary ('When in his charming car, this charming man . . .'). As we have seen, the act of excision is paradoxically creative and opens up a space that shimmers with suggestions. Yet these are a 'matter' of absence as well as presence, and no reduction or translation of their apparitional play is possible. The same holds true for his customary secrecy, which is teasingly presented as a kind of disclosure, for Morrissey often tells us a story about a story he isn't telling. Such 'tickling' is of course part of the pleasure. But it is a pleasure that is dependent upon a *withholding* of meaning.[21]

If the lack of information in Morrissey's lyrics is a trap for the literalist, so too is the *excess* of what's said, which raises important epistemological issues overlooked in existing commentary. In

19. If we take the singer's use of first-person pronouns literally, we are compelled, for instance, to believe that Morrissey is a 'working girl,' who has killed a nun and has a child ('Maladjusted,' 'Is It Really So Strange?' and 'The Hand That Rocks The Cradle'). Of course, no one's going to be blind to the metaphoricity of the speaking 'I' in the foregoing utterances. Yet, the destabilizing principle that such examples announce is impossible to arrest and mischievously haunts *all* first-person utterances—many of which *are* read literally and unreflectively ascribed to the singer. Such blindness to tropes has bedevilled commentary on Morrissey for too long.

20. This shift away from realist modes may of course be signalled in other ways too. The singer's comically proliferating lists, for example ('you can kick me / and you can butt me / and you can break my spine'; 'he stole from the rich and the poor / and the not-very-rich / and the very poor') suggest that Morrissey is not attempting to express 'his heart and soul' or refer to an extralyrical state of affairs, but is instead following an internal, aesthetic logic.

21. Such secrecy may even paradoxically be a constitutive feature of the singer's persona. As Slavoj Žižek explains: 'A Master Signifier is always virtual in the sense of involving some structural ambiguity. . . . The point is that the situation has to remain open, undecidable: if the gaps were to be filled in here, if we were to learn the true state of things, the entire symbolic universe . . . would disintegrate' (*The Plague of Fantasies*, p. 157). If the singer does in fact publish his autobiography and takes 'Steven Patrick' out of the box on top of his wardrobe, we might therefore expect 'Morrissey' to disappear.

particular, we should notice the singer's habit of altering his lyrics in live performances. Sometimes these are straightforward jokes (instead of 'lonely,' in 'The Queen Is Dead,' he has sung 'life is very long when you're a *bouncer*'); sometimes they court a kind of whimsical irrelevance (in 'Now My Heart Is Full,' instead of 'puny brothers,' he has sung 'just some rain-coated lovers *Everly* brothers'); and sometimes they are, conversely, a facetious gesture of relevance (on tour in America, instead of 'chemists,' for instance, he occasionally sang 'loafing oafs and all-night pharmacies').[22] These kinds of alterations are testimony to the singer's knockabout skills as a comedian and don't really threaten to subvert the lyrics. Yet there are other alterations which have a bearing on the songs' meaning and which make it difficult to speak about 'the lyrics' in such a monolithic way. Some of these introduce allusions to the singer's persona, which are consistent with the familiar picture but tangential to the recorded lyrics (in 'Our Frank,' for example, instead of 'only,' he has sung 'but look, I'm *practically* human,' and in 'In The Future When All's Well,' instead of 'all,' he has sung 'I thank you with *what's left* of my heart'—in both cases introducing a 'gothic' hue that is absent in the recordings). In other cases, they make explicit the singer's mobile subjectivity and the reflexive bearing of his second- and third-person utterances (in 'Reader Meet Author,' in place of 'you,' he has been known to sing '*I'd* be the first away because *I'm* that type,' and in 'November Spawned A Monster,' in place of 'her,' he has sung 'could you even bear to kiss *me* full on the mouth' and '*I'm so ugly*').[23] In some cases, though, the alterations participate in the songs' play of meanings in a way that undermines the apparent determinacy of the recorded lyrics. To illustrate this, it will be helpful to focus on a particular example.

In 'You've Got Everything Now,' as it is recorded on *The Smiths*, Morrissey sings 'I've never had a job / because I'm too shy.' Though in live performances he has on occasion sung: 'I've never had a job / because I'm too sensible'; 'because I'm too fey'; 'because I've never

---

22. The singer's comically proliferating lists also afford an irresistible opportunity for the free play of alterations. In 'Is It Really So Strange?' for example, he has sung 'Oh yes, you can *slice* me, and you can butt me, and you can *dislocate my shoulder*,' and 'you can *chin* me, and you can *shin* me, and later you can *skin* me.'

23. There is a lovely instance of an alteration that obliquely alludes to the practice of alteration, in live versions of 'Maladjusted,' where he subverts the focalized character perspective by singing '*I'm* never to be *trusted*.'

had an interview'; and 'because, frankly, I just don't want one.' Well, which is it?! Are all of these true? Is one of them true? Are none of them true? Of course in a sense it doesn't matter, as there is a delightful comedy in the singer's self-burlesquing inventiveness. However, it does matter that it *doesn't* matter, since this means that we have ceased to be concerned with 'truth' and are instead enjoying the ride and the singer's pulling rabbits out of hats. The other important consequence of such 'joyful excess' is what I have referred to as a usurpation of textual authority, for if 'truth' ceases to be a relevant consideration and all variants are equally valid, the 'original' text loses something of its sovereign status (and ceases in a sense to be an 'original' at all).[24]

This 'diachronic' deferral of authority has a lateral or 'synchronic' equivalent, since there is a *multiplicity* of discourses which contribute to what the songs mean (the recording, the cover art, the singer's comments in interviews), none of which is determinative or outside of the signifying chain. Consider, for example, the following slippery explanation, where the singer is asked by Shaun Phillips if he 'really' sang 'It was a good lay' at the end of 'Suedehead':

Morrissey: No. It was a bootleg. I mean, good heavens, in my vocabulary? Please . . .

Phillips: Honestly?

Morrissey: Well, have I ever been dishonest? [He laughs] Do people *think* it was 'a good lay'?

Phillips: I do.

Morrissey: And is that quite racy?

Phillips: Oh, yes.

Morrissey: Well, it was actually 'a good lay.'

Phillips: And was there one?

Morrissey: No, I just thought it might amuse someone living in Hartlepool.[25]

Conventionally, the interview is supposed to be the place of disclosure and authoritative comment (Phillips asks what he 'really' sings, if he's being 'honest' and whether the lyrics are literally true). However, not only does the singer avoid giving anything definitive away—on

24. The phrase 'joyful excess' is borrowed from Bernard Cerquiglini, *In Praise of the Variant*, chapter 3.
25. *Sounds*, June 18, 1988.

all three counts—he also reproduces the playfully evasive mobility of his lyrics in apparently establishing what they mean.[26]

Finally, it's important to take into account the singer's textual mobility and another kind of multiplicity which crucially complicates his voice. As we have seen, in his lyrics, Morrissey has a tendency to 'migrate' between disparate positions and subjectivities, without exclusively identifying with any of them ('Cemetry Gates,' 'Reader Meet Author,' 'You're Gonna Need Someone On Your Side'). We also observed passing apparitions of the singer's persona in the utterances of other characters, in songs where he is otherwise absent ('Will time never pass?'; 'To be finished would be a relief'). Relatedly, he frequently speaks with what Robert Browning refers to as the voices of 'imaginary persons, not mine'—either in his use of dramatic personae or, more locally, in his use of intertextuality ('rattle my bones all over the stones / I'm only a beggar-man whom nobody owns'[27]). Perhaps most subversive of all, though, are the hybrid or heterogeneous voices he conjures up; voices, that is, which flicker and swirl with internal differences and resemble the free indirect discourse favoured by the modernists.[28] A good illustration of this kind of voice is to be found in 'Sweet And Tender Hooligan':

> he was a sweet and tender hooligan
> and he swore that he'd never, never do it again

---

26. Morrissey's way of speaking in interviews—which is as shaped by aesthetic concerns as the lyrics themselves—is manifestly indebted to the dandyism of Wilde. As Norbert Kohl observes: 'Instead of communicating ideas by elucidating viewpoints, exchanging opinions or discussing problems, [Wilde's dandies] formulate for the sake of formulating. Their reluctance to be pinned down to content or to any sort of commitment is both result and evidence of their use of language as an intellectual game' (Kohl, *Oscar Wilde*, p. 227).

27. It's worth noting in passing that the lines quoted by Morrissey in 'The Hand That Rocks The Cradle,' which he claims 'fit [him] like a glove,' were originally addressed to a corpse, in Thomas Noel's funeral elegy 'The Pauper's Drive' (c. 1839). The lines are quoted—and again addressed to the deceased—in Joyce's *Ulysses* (in the Hades episode), and by Shelagh Delaney in *The Lion in Love*, where one of the characters imagines she's dead and applies the lines to herself in the third-person ('rattle her bones over the stones, she's only a beggar whom nobody owns,' p. 24). In keeping with the haunting imagery of the song, the singer thus renders *himself* uncanny in speaking, as it were, from the perspective of the dead. If this seems like a mere coincidence, we might also consider Morrissey's allusions to Louis MacNeice in 'Trouble Loves Me' ('console me'; 'O please fulfil me,' 'otherwise, kill me'), for the poem to which the singer alludes turns out to be 'Prayer Before Birth'—a poem that is spoken from an uncanny space which is outside of life and yet other than death.

28. As Claire Colebrook notes, in free indirect discourse, 'the text is neither in the first person— referred back to the expressing "I"—nor in an omniscient third person who could oversee and speak objectively about characters and the world' ('Deleuzean Criticism,' p. 227). Instead, the viewpoint above the subject or outside the narrative leaks into and merges with the viewpoint of characters within the narrative.

and of course he won't (not until the next time)
poor old man
he had an 'accident' with a three bar fire
but that's OK
because he wasn't very happy anyway.

The narrative voice, which is ostensibly identified with the advocate, is laced with the ironizing accents of an exterior perspective (the 'urr' that the singer interpolates between 'of course he won't' and not until the next time') comically marks the confluence of these inconsonant voices). We are thus presented with a flux of differences within a single 'schizophrenic' voice, which ceases to belong to its speaker and shatters the illusion of a unitary subject. In 'Deleuzean' terms, it is an assemblage of voices in which style is no longer a function of the subject and instead starts to speak itself. It's no wonder, then, that the song collapses into an abyssal 'et cetera.'

What we can see in these last examples of Morrissey's mobile and multiple utterances is a determined refusal of the univocal voice.[29] And what this refusal crucially means is that it is hard to extract 'opinions' or attitudes from the singer's lyrics and even more difficult, if not impossible, to attribute any of these to Morrissey.

In all sorts of ways, then, the singer's lyrics are a trap for the literalist. Either because he doesn't say or because he says something else as well or because he says 'the thing which is not' or because he speaks with the words of another or because it isn't him speaking or because the speaker is a multiplicity or because aesthetic speech has a special status, his lyrics elude determinate meaning. What's more, if we draw our conclusions together, the radical indeterminacy of his lyrics is mirrored by the elusive spectrality of his persona, which informs and further destabilizes the lyrics, which in turn unsettle even as they constitute his persona (which is why it is especially strange that 'every -ist and every -ism' should be thrown his way[30]). The disturbing consequence of all this is that we are faced with a ceaseless sliding of meaning, for the subject 'Morrissey' is reciprocally constituted and thus itself determined by a range of performances it circularly determines. Attempting to say something about this 'unspeakable' artist, one therefore feels rather like Alice in *Through the*

---

29. The singer started experimenting most intensively with the 'equivocal' voice on *Your Arsenal*, at the time when he seemed most keen to escape the caricature of his persona.
30. 'You Know I Couldn't Last.'

Looking-Glass, who sees all manner of things on the shelves around her, but when she tries to look at any particular shelf, it turns out to be empty, and the thing she is pursuing is always on the shelf above. Recognizing this elusiveness and radical indeterminacy doesn't bring interpretation of Morrissey to an end; on the contrary, I am arguing it is with this recognition that interpretation of this ticklish subject should *begin*.

SELECTED BIBLIOGRAPHY

Abrams, M. H. *A Glossary of Literary Terms*, 5th ed. (New York: Holt, Rinehart and Winston, 1988).

Altick, R. D. ' "A Grammarian's Funeral": Browning's Praise of Folly?' in *Studies in English Literature, 1500–1900* 3, no. 4 (Autumn 1963).

Alvarez, A. *Beckett* (London: Fontana, 1973).

André, Naomi. *Voicing Gender: Castrati, Travesti, and the Second Woman in Early Nineteenth-Century Italian Opera* (Bloomington: Indiana University Press, 2006).

Armstrong, Isobel. *Victorian Poetry, Poetics and Politics* (London: Routledge, 1993).

Arnold, Matthew. *The Poetry of Matthew Arnold*, ed. Kenneth Allot and Miriam Allot (London: Longman, 1979).

Augustine, Saint. *Confessions*, trans. Henry Chadwick (Oxford: Oxford University Press, 1991).

Austen, Jane. *Pride and Prejudice* (New York: Norton, 2001).

Bannister, Matthew. *White Boys, White Noise: Masculinities and 1980s Indie Guitar Rock* (Aldershot: Ashgate, 2006).

Bakhtin, Mikhail. *Rabelais and His World*, trans. Hélène Iswolsky (Bloomington: Indiana University Press, 1984).

Bartlett, Neil. *Who Was That Man? A Present for Mr Oscar Wilde* (London: Serpent's Tail, 1988).

Baudelaire, Charles. *The Flowers of Evil*, trans. James McGowan (Oxford: Oxford University Press, 1993).

———. 'On the Essence of Laughter,' in *The Mirror of Art*, trans. Jonathan Mayne (New York: Doubleday, 1956).

Bayley, John. 'Linguistic and Class Resource: Keats to Betjeman,' in *The Monstrous Debt: Modalities of Romantic Influence in Twentieth-Century Literature*, ed. Damian Walford Davies and Richard Marggraf Turley (Detroit: Wayne State University Press, 2006).

Beckett, Samuel. *All That Fall* (London: Faber and Faber, 1957).

———. *Collected shorter Prose 1945–1980* (London: John Calder, 1984).

———. *Company* (London: John Calder, 1980).

———. *Eh Joe and Other Writings* (London: Faber and Faber, 1967).

———. *Endgame* (London: Faber and Faber, 1964).

———. *More Pricks Than Kicks* (London: Calder and Boyars, 1934).

————. *Molloy, Malone Dies, The Unnamable* (London: Calder and Boyars, 1959).

————. *Proust; Three Dialogues* (London: Calder, 1965).

————. 'Three Dialogues,' in *Disjecta: Miscellaneous Writings and a Dramatic Fragment*, ed. Ruby Cohn (London: John Calder, 1983).

————. *Waiting for Godot* (London: Faber and Faber, 1956).

Behn, Aphra. *The Works of Aphra Behn*, ed. Janet Todd vol. 1 (London: William Pickering, 1992).

Berlin, Isaiah. 'The Hedgehog and the Fox,' in *Russian Thinkers* (London: Hogarth Press, 1978).

Betjeman, John. *Collected Poems* (London: John Murray, 1958).

Blake, William. *The Complete Poetry of William Blake*, ed. David V. Erdman (Berkeley: University of California Press, 1982).

Blanchot, Maurice. *The Infinite Conversation*, trans. Susan Hanson (Minneapolis: University of Minnesota Press, 1993).

Bracewell, Michael. *England Is Mine* (London: HarperCollins, 1997).

Bret, David. *Morrissey: Scandal and Passion* (London: Robson Books, 2004).

Brisman, Leslie. 'Back to the First of All: "By the Fire-side,"' in *Robert Browning: A Collection of Critical Essays*, ed. Harold Bloom and Adrienne Munich (New Jersey: Prentice-Hall, Inc., 1979).

Brophy, Brigid. *Prancing Novelist: A Defense of Fiction in the Form of Critical Biography in Praise of Ronald Firbank* (London: Macmillan, 1973).

Brown, Len. *Meetings with Morrissey* (London: Omnibus Press, 2008).

Browning, Robert. *Dramatic Lyrics*, 1842, in *The Poems of Robert Browning*, ed. John Woolford and Daniel Karlin, vol. 2 (London: Longman, 1991).

Brueggemann, Walter. *The Message of the Psalms: A Theological Commentary* (Minneapolis: Augsburg Publishing House, 1984).

Butler, Judith. *Gender Trouble: Feminism and the Subversion of Identity* (New York: Routledge, 1990).

Byron, George Gordon. *Byron's Letters and Journals*, ed. Leslie A. Marchand, vol. 6 (London: John Murray, 1976).

Calvino, Italo. *Six Memos for the Next Millennium*, trans. Patrick Creagh (Cambridge, MA: Harvard University Press, 1988).

Campbell, John. *Margaret Thatcher*, vol. 1 (London: HarperCollins, 1993).

Caputo, John D. 'The Experience of God and the Axiology of the Impossible,' in *Religion after Metaphysics*, ed. Mark A. Wrathall (Cambridge: Cambridge University Press, 2003).

Carman, Richard. *Johnny Marr: The Smiths and the Art of Gun-Slinging* (Shropshire: Independent Music Press, 2006).

Carroll, William. *Mystical Theology* (Oxford: Blackwell, 1998).

Celan, Paul. *Selected Poetry*, trans. Michael Hamburger (London: Penguin, 1996).

Cerquiglini, Bernard. *In Praise of the Variant: A Critical History of Philology*, trans. Betsy Wing (Baltimore: Johns Hopkins Press, 1999).

Certeau, Michael de. *L'Étranger ou l'Union Dans le Différence* (Paris: Desclée De Brouwer, 1969).

———. *The Practice of Everyday Life*, trans. Steven Rendall (Berkeley: University of California Press, 1984).

———. 'The Weakness of Believing,' in *The Certeau Reader*, ed. Graham Ward (Oxford: Blackwell, 2000).

Chauncey, George. *Gay New York: Gender, Urban Culture, and the Making of the Urban Gay World, 1890–1940* (New York: Basic, 1994).

Chesterton, G. K. *Orthodoxy* (San Francisco: Ignatius Press, 1995).

Cleto, Fabio, ed. *Camp: Queer Aesthetics and the Performing Subject* (Ann Arbor: University of Michigan Press, 1999).

Clough, Arthur Hugh. *Selected Poems*, ed. J. P. Phelan (London: Longman, 1995).

Clum, John. *Something for the Boys: Musical Theatre and Gay Culture* (New York: St Martin's, 1999).

Cohan, Steven. *Incongruous Entertainment: Camp, Cultural Value, and the MGM Musical* (Durham, NC: Duke University Press, 2005).

Colebrook, Claire. 'Deleuzean Criticism,' in *Introducing Criticism at the 21st Century*, ed. Julian Wolfreys (Edinburgh: Edinburgh University Press, 2002).

———. *Irony*, The New Critical Idiom (London: Routledge, 2003).

Core, Philip. *Camp: The Lie That Tells the Truth* (London: Plexus, 1984).

Cox, Harvey. *The Feast of Fools: A Theological Essay on Festivity and Fantasy* (New York: Harper & Row, 1969).

Dante, Alighieri. *The Divine Comedy*, vol. 3, *Paradise*, trans. Mark Musa (London: Penguin, 1986).

Darwin, Charles. *The Expression of the Emotions in Man and Animals* (New York: Appleton and Company, 1898).

Davis, Philip. *The Victorians* (Oxford: Oxford University Press, 2002).

Delaney, Shelagh. *The Lion in Love* (London: Methuen & Co., 1961).

Deleuze, Gilles, and Félix Guattari. *A Thousand Plateaus: Capitalism and Schizophrenia*, trans. Brian Massumi (New York: Continuum, 1988).

Derrida, Jacques. 'Deconstruction and the Other,' Interview with Richard Kearney, in Kearney, *Dialogues with Contemporary Continental Thinkers* (Manchester, Manchester University Press, 1984).

———. 'Living On: Border Lines,' trans. James Hulbert, in *Deconstruction and Criticism* Harold Bloom et al. (New York: Seaburg Press, 1979).

———. *Of Grammatology*, trans. Gayatri Spivak (Baltimore: Johns Hopkins University Press, 1976).

———. *Positions*, trans. Alan Bass (Chicago: Chicago University Press, 1981).

————. 'The Rhetoric of Drugs,' in *Points . . . Interviews, 1974–1994*, ed. Elisabeth Weber, trans. Peggy Kamuf, et al. (Stanford, CA: Stanford University Press, 1995).

————. *Mémoires: for Paul de Man*, trans. Cecile Lindsay, Jonathan Cutter and Edvardo Cadava (New York: Columbia Univerity Press, 1986).

————. 'Some Statements and Truisms about Neo-Logisms, Newisms, Postisms, Parasitisms, and Other Small Seismisms,' in *The States of 'Theory': History, Art, and Critical Discourse*, ed. David Carroll (New York: Columbia University Press, 1990).

————. 'Geopsychoanalysis—"and the Rest of the World,"' trans. Donald Nicholson-Smith, in *American Imago* 48, no. 2 (1991).

————. *Spectres of Marx: The State of the Debt, the Work of Mourning and the News International*, trans. Peggy Kamuf (London: Routledge, 1994).

————. *A Taste for the Secret*, trans. Giacomo Donis (Cambridge: Polity, 2001).

————. 'This Strange Institution Called Literature,' trans. Geoffrey Bennington and Rachel Bowlby, in *Acts of Literature*, ed. Derek Attridge (London: Routledge, 1992).

Donaldson, Ian. *The World Upside-Down: Comedy from Jonson to Fielding* (Oxford: Clarendon Press, 1970).

Drewal, Margaret Thompson. 'The Camp Trace in Corporate America: Liberace and the Rockettes at Radio City Music Hall,' in *The Politics and Poetics of Camp*, ed. Moe Meyer (London: Routledge, 1994).

Dyer, Richard. 'Judy Garland and Gay Men,' in *Heavenly Bodies: Film Stars and Societies* (London: Macmillan, 1986).

Eagleton, Terry. 'Introduction,' in *Oscar Wilde: Plays, Prose Writings and Poetry* (London: Everyman's Library, 1991).

————. *Sweet Violence: The Idea of the Tragic* (Oxford: Blackwell, 2003).

————. 'Introduction' *The Gospels* (London: Verso, 2007).

Eco, Umberto. *Reflections on* The Name of the Rose (London: Secker & Warburg, 1983).

Eliot, George. *The George Eliot Letters*, ed. Gordon S. Haight (New Haven: Yale University Press, 1954).

————. *Middlemarch* (London: Penguin, 1985).

————. 'The Natural History of German Life,' in *Selected Essays, Poems and Other Writings* (London: Penguin, 1990).

Eliot, T. S. *The Complete Poems and Plays of T. S. Eliot* (London: Faber, 1969).

————.*Selected Essays* (London: Faber and Faber, 1932).

Ellmann, Richard. *Oscar Wilde* (London: Hamish Hamilton, 1987).

Emerson, Ralph Waldo. *Essays and Lectures* (New York: Library of America, 1983).

Empson, William. *Seven Types of Ambiguity*, 2nd ed. (London: Peregrine Books, 1961).

Flinn, Caryl. 'The Deaths of Camp,' in *Camp: Queer Aesthetics and the Performing Subject, a Reader*, ed. Fabio Cleto (Ann Arbor: University of Michigan Press, 1999).

Fonarow, Wendy. *Empire of Dirt: The Aesthetics and Rituals of British Indie Music* (Middletown, CT: Wesleyan University Press, 2006).

Francis, James A. *Subversive Virtue: Asceticism and Authority in the Second-Century Pagan World* (State College: Pennsylvania State University Press, 1995).

François, Anne-Lise. 'Fakin' It/Makin' It: Falsetto's Bid for Transcendence in 1970s Disco Highs,' *Perspectives of New Music* 33, no. 1/2 (Winter/Summer, 1995).

Freud, Sigmund. *Jokes and Their Relation to the Unconscious*, trans. James Strachey (London: Penguin, 1976).

———. *The Uncanny*, trans. David McLintock (London: Penguin, 2003).

Frith, Simon. 'Art versus Technology: The Strange Case of Popular Music,' in *Media, Culture and Society: A Critical Reader*, ed. Richard Collins (London: Sage, 1986).

Gaerlick, Rhonda K. *Rising Star: Dandyism, Gender, and Performance in the Fin de Siècle* (Princeton, NJ: Princeton University Press, 1998).

Garber, Marjorie. *Vested Interests: Cross-Dressing and Cultural Anxiety* (New York: Routledge, 1992).

Gibson, J. C. L. *Language and Imagery in the Old Testament* (London: SPCK, 1988).

Gilbert, Jeremy, and Ewan Pearson. *Discographies: Dance Music, Culture and the Politics of Sound* (London: Routledge, 1999).

Gilbert, Sandra, and Susan Gubar. *The Madwoman in the Attic: The Woman Writer and the Nineteenth-Century Literary Imagination* (New Haven, CT: Yale University Press, 1979).

Goddard, Simon. *The Smiths: Songs That Saved Your Life*, 2nd ed. (London: Reynolds & Hearn, 2004).

Goethe, Johann Wolfgang. *Willhelm Meisters Wanderjahre*, in *Sämtliche Werke*, ed. Gonthier-Louis Fink, Gerhart Baumann and Johannes John (Munich: Carl Hanser Verlag, 1991).

Goffman, Erving. 'Embarrassment and Social Organisation,' *American Journal of Sociology* 62, no. 3 (1956).

Gregory of Nyssa. *From Glory to Glory*, trans. and ed. Herbert Musurillo, S. J. (New York: St. Vladimir's Seminary Press, 2001).

Grossberg, Lawrence. 'Is Anybody Listening? Does Anybody Care?: On Talking about the State of Rock,' in *Microphone Fiends: Youth Music and Youth Culture*, ed. Andrew Ross and Tricia Rose (London: Routledge, 1994).

———. 'The Media Economy of Rock Culture: Cinema, Postmodernity and Authenticity,' in *Sound and Vision*, ed. Simon Frith, Andrew Goodwin and Lawrence Grossberg (London: Routledge, 1993).

Guignon, Charles. *On Being Authentic* (London: Routledge, 2004).

Haldane, John. 'Philosophy, the Restless Heart and the Meaning of Theism,' in *The Meaning of Theism*, ed. John Cottingham (Oxford: Blackwell, 2007).

Hamilton, Ian. 'Four Conversations: Philip Larkin,' *London Magazine* 4, no. 8 (November 1964).

Haraway, Donna. 'A Game of Cat's Cradle: Science Studies, Feminist Theory, Cultural Studies,' *Configurations* 2, no. 1 (Winter 1994).

Hardy, Thomas. *The Complete Poems of Thomas Hardy*, ed. Samuel Hynes, vol. 1 (Oxford: Clarendon Press, 1982).

Harmon, Maurice, ed. *No Author Better Served: The Correspondence of Samuel Beckett and Alan Schneider* (Cambridge, MA: Harvard University Press, 1998).

Harrington, Joe S. *Sonic Cool: The Life and Death of Rock 'n' Roll* (Milwaukee: Hal Leonard, 2002).

Harris, John. *The Last Party: Britpop, Blair and the Demise of English Rock* (London: Harper Perennial, 2004).

Haughton, Hugh. 'Preface,' in Wilde, *The Decay of Lying* (London: Syrens, 1995).

Haupfuhrer, Fred. 'Roll Over Beethoven, and Tell Madonna the News: The Smiths' Morrissey Is Pop's Latest Messiah,' *People Weekly,* June 24, 1985.

Hawkins, Stan. *Settling the Pop Score: Pop Texts and Identity Politics* (Aldershot: Ashgate, 2002).

Hebdige, Dick. 'Style as Homology and Signifying Practice,' in *On Record: Rock and Pop, and the Written Word*, ed. Simon Frith and Andrew Goodwin (London: Routledge, 1990).

Heriot, Angus. *The Castrati in Opera* (London: Secker & Warburg, 1956).

Hofmannsthal, Hugo von. *The Lord Chandos Letter*, in *Selected Prose*, trans. Mary Hottinger and Tania and James Stern (London: Routledge, 1952).

Holland, Vyvyan. *Son of Oscar Wilde*, revised and updated by Merlin Holland (New York: Carroll and Graf, 1999).

Homberger, Eric. *The Art of the Real* (London: Dent, 1977).

Honour, Hugh. *Romanticism* (Harmondsworth: Penguin, 1981).

Horder, Mervyn, ed. *Ronald Firbank: Memoirs & Critiques* (London: Duckworth, 1977).

Howe, Julia Ward. 'Battle Hymn of the Republic,' in *The New Anthology of American Poetry*, vol. 1: *Traditions and Revolutions, Beginnings to 1900*, ed. Steven Gould Axelrod, Camille Roman and Thomas Travisano (New Brunswick: Rutgers University Press, 2003).

Hubbs, Nadine. 'Music of the "Fourth Gender": Morrissey and the Sexual Politics of Melodic Contour,' in *Bodies of Writing, Bodies in Performance*, ed. Thomas Foster, Carol Siegel and Ellen E. Berry (New York: New York University Press, 1996).

Huq, Rupa. *Beyond Subculture: Pop, Youth and Identity in a Postcolonial World* (London: Routledge, 2006).

Huysmans, Joris-Karl. *Against Nature*, trans. Margaret Mauldon (Oxford: Oxford University Press, 1998).

James, Henry. *Henry James, Letters*, ed. Leon Edel, vol. 3 (Cambridge, MA: Belknap Press of Harvard University Press, 1974–84).

Jenkins, Simon. *Thatcher and Sons: A Revolution in Three Acts* (London: Allen Lane, 2006).

Joyce, James. *Ulysses* (London: Penguin, 1986).

Juliet, Charles. 'Meeting Beckett,' *TriQuarterly* 77 (1989–90).

Kearney, Richard, ed. *Dialogues with Contemporary Continental Thinkers* (Manchester: Manchester University Press, 1984).

Keats, John. *The Complete Poems*, ed. John Barnard (London: Penguin, 1988).

———. *Letters of John Keats*, ed. Robert Gittings (Oxford: Oxford University Press, 1970).

Kern, Edith. *The Absolute Comic* (New York: Columbia University Press, 1980).

Killeen, Jarlath. *The Faiths of Oscar Wilde: Catholicism, Folklore and Ireland* (Basingstoke: Palgrave, 2005).

Knight, Mark, and Emma Mason, ed. *Nineteenth-Century Religion and Literature* (Oxford: Oxford University Press, 2006).

Knight, Philip. *Flower Poetry in Nineteenth-Century France* (Oxford: Clarendon Press, 1986).

Koestenbaum, Wayne. *The Queen's Throat: Opera, Homosexuality, and the Mystery of Desire* (New York: Da Capo Press, 1993).

Kohl, Norbert. *Oscar Wilde: The Works of a Conformist Rebel* (Cambridge: Cambridge University Press, 1989).

Lacoste, Jean-Yves. 'Liturgy and Kenosis,' from *Expérience et Absolu*, in *The Postmodern God*, ed. Graham Ward (Oxford: Blackwell, 1997).

Langbaum, Robert, *The Poetry of Experience: The Dramatic Monologue in Literary Tradition* (New York: Random House, 1957).

Larkin, Philip. *Collected Poems*, ed. Anthony Thwaite (London: Faber and Faber, 1988).

———. *Required Writing: Miscellaneous Pieces 1955–1982* (London: Faber and Faber, 1983).

Lecercle, Jean-Jacques. *Philosophy through the Looking-Glass* (Illinois: Open Court, 1985).

MacNeice, Louis. *Selected Poems*, ed. Michael Longley (London: Faber and Faber, 1988).

Marquand, David. 'The Paradoxes of Thatcherism,' in *Thatcherism*, ed. Robert Skidelsky (London: Chatto & Windus, 1988).

McCormack, Jerusha, ed. *Wilde the Irishman* (New Haven, CT: Yale University Press, 1998).

McHale, Brian. *Constructing Postmodernism* (London: Routledge, 1992).

McLeod, Ken. 'Space Oddities: Aliens, Futurism and Meaning in Popular Music,' *Popular Music* 22, no. 3 (October 2003).

McMahon, Gary. *Camp in Literature* (London: McFarland, 2006).

Medhurst, Andy. 'Batman, Deviance and Camp,' in *The Many Lives of the Batman: Critical Approaches to a Superhero and His Media*, ed. Roberta Pearson and William Uricchio (New York: Routledge, 1991).

Middles, Mick. *The Smiths: The Complete Story* (London: Omnibus, 1988).

Miller, Henry. *Tropic of Cancer* (London: Panther Books, 1965).

Milton, John. *Paradise Lost*, ed. Scott Elledge, 2nd ed. (New York: Norton, 1993).

Morrissey. 'Foreword, in Toni Visconti, *Bowie, Bolan and the Brooklyn Boy* (London: HarperCollins, 2007).

———. *James Dean Is Not Dead* (Manchester: Babylon Books, 1983).

———. *New York Dolls* (Manchester: Babylon Books, 1981).

Napier-Bell, Simon. *Black Vinyl White Powder* (London: Ebury Press, 2002).

Nattiez, Jean-Jacques. *Music and Discourse: Toward a Semiology of Music*, trans. Carolyn Abbate (Princeton, NJ: Princeton University Press, 1990).

Newton, Esther. *Mother Camp: Female Impersonators in America* (Englewood Cliffs, NJ: Prentice Hall, 1972).

Nichols, Aidan. *The Shape of Catholic Theology* (Collegeville, MN: Liturgical Press, 1991).

Nietzsche, Friedrich. *Beyond Good and Evil*, trans. R. J. Hollingdale (London: Penguin, 1973).

———. *Thus Spoke Zarathustra*, trans. R. J. Hollingdale (London: Penguin, 1969).

Noel, Thomas. 'The Pauper's Drive,' in *Victorian Parlour Poetry: An Annotated Anthology*, ed. Michael R. Turner (New York: Dover Publications, 1992).

O'Malley, Patrick R. 'Religion,' in *Palgrave Advances in Oscar Wilde Studies*, ed. Frederick S. Roden (London: Palgrave Macmillan, 2004).

Pascal, Blaise. *Pensées*, trans. A. J. Krailsheimer (London: Penguin, 1995).

Philips, Adam. *On Flirtation* (London: Faber and Faber, 1994).

Redfern, Walter. *Puns* (Oxford: Blackwell, 1984).

Reid, Pat. *Morrissey* (Bath: Absolute Press, 2004).

Reynolds, Simon. 'Against Health and Efficiency: Independent Music in the 1980s,' in *Zoot Suits and Second-Hand Dresses: An Anthology of Fashion and Music*, ed. Angela McRobbie (Hampshire: Macmillan, 1989).

———. *Bring the Noise: 20 years of Writing about Hip Rock and Hip Hop* (London: Faber and Faber, 2007).

————. *Rip It Up and Start Again: Postpunk, 1978–1984* (London: Faber and Faber, 2005).

Ricks, Christopher. *Dylan's Visions of Sin* (London: Viking, 2003).

————. *Keats and Embarrassment* (Oxford: Oxford University Press, 1976).

Robertson, John, ed. *Morrissey: In His Own Words* (London: Omnibus Press, 1988).

Rogan, Johnny. *Morrissey: The Albums* (London: Calidore, 2006).

————. *Morrissey and Marr: The Severed Alliance* (London: Omnibus Press, 1992).

Roland, Barthes. *A Lover's Discourse: Fragments*, trans. Richard Howard (London: Penguin, 1990).

Rossetti, Christina. *Christina Rossetti: The Complete Poems* (London: Penguin, 2001).

Royle, Nicholas, ed. *Deconstructions: A User's Guide* (Hampshire: Palgrave, 2000).

————. *Jacques Derrida* (London: Routledge, 2003).

Said, Edward. *On Late Style: Music and Literature against the Grain* (London: Bloomsbury, 2006).

Saward, John. *Perfect Fools: Folly for Christ's Sake in Catholic and Orthodox Spirituality* (Oxford: Oxford University Press, 1980).

Schaffer, Talia. 'Fashioning Aestheticism by Aestheticizing Fashion: Wilde, Beerbohm, and the Male Aesthetes' Sartorial Codes,' *Victorian Literature and Culture*, 28 (2000).

Schlegel, Friedrich. *Philosophical Fragments*, trans. Peter Firchow (Minneapolis: University of Minnesota Press, 1991).

Schopenhauer, Arthur. *On the Basis of Morality*, trans. E. F. J. Payne (Indianapolis: Hackett Publishing, 1998).

Shakespeare, William. *Hamlet*, ed. G.R. Hibbard (Oxford: Clarendon Press, 1987).

————. *Richard III*, ed. Peter Ure (London: Methuen, 1961).

————. *Shakespeare's Sonnets*, ed. Katherine Duncan-Jones (London: Thomas Nelson and Sons, 1997).

Shaw, George Bernard. *Our Theatres in the Nineties*, vol. 1 (London: Constable & Company, 1932).

Shelley, Mary. *Frankenstein*, in *The Novels and Selected Works of Mary Shelley*, ed. Nora Cook, vol. 1 (London: William Pickering, 1996).

Simpson, Mark. *Saint Morrissey* (London: SAF, 2004).

Slee, Jo. *Peepholism: Into the Art of Morrissey* (London: Sidgwick and Jackson, 1994).

Smith, Stan. 'Auden's Light and Serio-Comic Verse,' in *The Cambridge Companion to W. H. Auden* (Cambridge: Cambridge University Press, 2005).

Sontag, Susan. 'Notes on Camp,' in *A Susan Sontag Reader* (London: Penguin, 1983).

Stein, Gertrude. *Gertrude Stein, Writings 1903–1932* (New York: Library of America, 1998).

Steiner, George. *Real Presences* (London: Faber and Faber, 1989).

Sterling, Linder. *Works 1976* (Zurich: JRP/Ringier, 2006).

Stevens, Wallace. *Collected Poems* (London: Faber and Faber, 1984).

Stringer, Julian. 'The Smiths: Repressed (But Remarkably Dressed),' *Popular Music* 11, no. 1 (January 1992).

Swift, Jonathan. *Battle of the Books,* in *The Tale of the Tub and Other Works* (Oxford: Oxford University Press, 1986).

Thompson, Juliet S., and Wayne C. Thompson. *Margaret Thatcher: Prime Minister Indomitable* (Oxford: Westview Press, 1994).

Tolkien, J. R. R. *Tree and Leaf* (London: HarperCollins, 2001).

Vidal, Gore. 'Sex Is Politics,' in *United States: Essays: 1952–1992* (New York: Random House, 1993).

Ward, John Powell. *The English Line: Poetry of the Unpoetic from Wordsworth to Larkin* (Hampshire: Macmillan, 1991).

White, Armond. *The Resistance: Ten Years of Pop Culture That Shook the World* (New York: Overlook Press, 1995).

White, Armond. 'Anglocentric: Morrissey,' *Village Voice,* September 1, 1992.

Wilde, Oscar. *Complete Shorter Fiction*, ed. Ian Small (London: Penguin, 2003).

———. *Complete Writings of Oscar Wilde: Miscellanies* (New York: The Nottingham Society, 1909).

———. *De Profundis and Other Writings* (London: Penguin, 1986).

———. *Essays and Lectures,* in *The First Collected Edition of the Works of Oscar Wilde* (London: Methuen & Co., 1908).

———. *Oscar Wilde: The Major Works*, ed. Isobel Murray (Oxford: Oxford University Press, 1989).

———. *The Picture of Dorian Gray* (New York: Norton & Co., 1988).

———. *The Soul of Man under Socialism and Selected Critical Prose*, ed. Linda Dowling (London: Penguin, 2001).

Woolf, Virginia. *Collected Essays*, vol. 4 (London: Hogarth Press, 1967).

———. *A Room of One's Own* (London: Hogarth Press, 1929).

Wordsworth, William. *The Poetical Works of William Wordsworth*, ed. E. de Selincourt vol. 1 (Oxford: The Clarendon Press, 1946).

———. and Samuel Taylor Coleridge. *Lyrical Ballads*, 2nd ed. Derek Roper (London: MacDonald and Evans, 1976).

Žižek, Slavoj, *Looking Awry* (Cambridge, MA: MIT Press, 1991).

———. *The Parallax View* (Cambridge, MA: MIT Press, 2006).

———. *The Plague of Fantasies* (London: Verso, 1997).

———. *The Sublime Object of Ideology* (London: Verso, 1989).

Zuberi, Nabeel. *Sounds English: Transnational Popular Music* (Chicago: University of Illinois Press, 2001).